RAMPAGE NATION

LOUIS KLAREVAS

RAMPAGE NATION

SECURING AMERICA FROM MASS SHOOTINGS

Prometheus Books

59 John Glenn Drive
Amherst, New York 14228

Published 2016 by Prometheus Books

Inquiries should be addressed to
Prometheus Books
59 John Glenn Drive
Amherst, New York 14228
VOICE: 716–691–0133
FAX: 716–691–0137
WWW.PROMETHEUSBOOKS.COM

20 19 18 17 16   5 4 3 2 1

Library of Congress Cataloging-in-Publication Data

Names: Klarevas, Louis, author.
Title: Rampage nation : securing America from mass shootings / by Louis Klarevas.
Description: Amherst, New York : Prometheus Books, 2016. |
    Includes bibliographical references and index.
Identifiers: LCCN 2016011430 (print) | LCCN 2016018097 (ebook) |
    ISBN 9781633880665 (hardcover) | ISBN 9781633880672 (ebook)
Subjects: LCSH: Gun control—United States. | Firearms ownership—United
    States. | Violent crimes—United States—Prevention. | Mass murder—United
    States—Prevention.
Classification: LCC HV7436 .K53 2016 (print) | LCC HV7436 (ebook) |
    DDC 364.4/0450973—dc23
LC record available at https://lccn.loc.gov/2016011430

Printed in the United States of America

For Rada

CONTENTS

PREFACE

In 2003, a lone gunman tried to shoot me, my cousin, and four of our friends as we were sitting at a *taverna* on the Greek island of Ikaria. The violent events of that evening were set in motion several hours earlier. After an entire day of binge drinking, a local fisherman drove his car through the narrow public square where we were enjoying dinner, bumping several chairs and tables. While no one was hurt, his recklessness drew the ire of numerous patrons. Following a few exchanges of boisterous threats, he departed for his house. An hour later, driving a pickup truck this time, he raced through the same space, forcing the dozen or so of us who were still at the *taverna* to jump from our seats and take cover as he smashed through several chairs en route to the nearby marina. Within minutes, we heard the distinct *putt-putt-putt-putt* of his caique's diesel motor as he sailed away. We knew that he had inherited a second house from his late father, which was located about twenty minutes away by boat; so we presumed he was heading there to sleep it off.

We were wrong. After about an hour, he was back.

Driving his pickup at a high rate of speed, he pulled up on the one group that was still left at the *taverna*—my group. Jamming his brakes right in front of us, he grabbed a vintage shotgun that was resting on the passenger seat. My friend, seeing the gunman maneuvering to get the weapon around the steering wheel and out the driver's side window, lunged toward the truck, allowing him to grab the barrel just as it was positioned to shoot.

Standing about fifteen to twenty feet behind the truck, I saw a flash of bright light and heard a thunder reminiscent of cannon fire as my friend pushed the barrel upward and to the side at the precise moment the gunman pulled the trigger, causing the blast to go off-target. My friend yanked the shotgun from the shooter's hands and began to smash it on the pavement.

It was then that, through the rear cab window, I saw the driver reach for something behind his seat. I was frozen in disbelief; the next few seconds felt like time moving in slow motion.

"He's got another weapon! He's got another weapon!" Yelling at the top of my lungs, I bolted toward the truck.

My cousin, who was watching our friend take his frustration out on the first gun, turned around just in time to grab the second gun before the driver could point it out of the cab. As my cousin tried to wrestle the weapon away from the shooter, I opened the passenger-side door and reached in to grab a hold of him. Wrapping my hands around his neck, I was able to dig my fingers into his throat. Overwhelmed, he released the shotgun—which my cousin pulled out through the driver's side window—and punched the accelerator, forcing me to let go.

It was over. The gunman had fled and no one was seriously injured.

Afterward, as we were trying to make sense of what had just happened while waiting for the police to arrive, one of my friends suggested, "We had a guardian angel looking out for us."

Did we really?

For years, the incident haunted me. Why did this person go on a rampage? What did we do to warrant being the target of his rage? And most important of all, how was it that not a single one of us was seriously wounded?

The more I played out the incident in my head, the more I relayed it to others, and the more I analyzed it, the more I realized that our good fortune that evening had nothing to do with any sort of divine intervention.

The gunman was ultimately convicted of attempted murder and received a stiff sentence by Greek standards: seven years in prison. The judge's decision not to show much leniency was partly related to the shooter's violent past. As I learned after the shooting, the perpetrator had a history of physical altercations and at one point even tried to cut out his girlfriend's tongue with a knife. The amateur psychologist in me concluded that this guy had the hallmarks of a sociopath.

Of course, while some sociopaths occasionally engage in violence—even mass violence—that didn't fully explain why he chose to come after us that evening. I always suspected that catching hell from his fellow villagers as he recklessly drove through the pedestrian path provoked him. But even that still left one question unanswered for me: Why did this guy, who had no history of gun violence, take up arms that night? In particular, it struck me as odd that he went to the trouble of traveling to his late father's place by boat to grab his firearms so that he could shoot us. If he wanted to harm us, why not just run us over with his pickup truck? He certainly had an opportunity to do so when he burst through the public square en route to his caique. Even though many of us jumped out of the way, he easily could have hit several people by driving down one of the sides of the path, rather than through the middle. Something no doubt primed him to think *guns.* As it turned out, he didn't have a history of gun violence because he never owned firearms—until he inherited his father's shotguns a few years earlier. He finally resorted to gun violence because he could.

Why us, though? What did we do to him that he wanted us dead? The simple answer: Nothing. We were just in the wrong place at the wrong time. His assault was more than just an act of violence. It was a statement. Hours earlier, he felt besieged by the village—and he was returning to the same spot to exact his revenge. Sitting there, we became targets by association.

We were six sitting ducks in the sights of an unstable, angry, armed man who wanted to send a message to the entire village. So how was it that we escaped without serious injury that night? His choice of firearm. Long shotguns are conspicuous and difficult to maneuver. I have no doubt, had the shooter been carrying a concealed, lightweight, high-capacity, semiautomatic weapon, the outcome would've been drastically different. For starters, we likely wouldn't have seen the attack coming, thereby depriving us of the crucial seconds we needed to react. And even if we had time to jump the gunman, grabbing a firearm that's ergonomically designed to shoot a dozen rounds in just a few seconds would've been much more difficult than grabbing a shotgun. Picture yourself trying to fire upon a group of people with an easy-to-wield 9mm handgun or an AR-15 assault rifle. Now imagine trying to shoot those same individuals with a much longer and heavier shotgun. If your goal is to cut down a crowd of people by riddling their bodies with bullets, and time—even a few seconds—is of the essence, the choice of firearm is a no-brainer.

My personal experience illustrates the difference that the weapon makes.

We were lucky that night in Greece. Only one of us was hit by the gunfire—my friend who was superficially grazed by a shotgun pellet. Back home in the United States—where there are millions of mentally ill and emotionally disturbed people, with easier access to far deadlier firearms, in what is arguably the most open society in the world—those who find themselves on the other end of the gun barrel are generally not so fortunate. Drawing on this three-pronged calculus of unstable *perpetrators*, vulnerable *targets*, lethal *weapons*—what I call *the trinity of violence*—I examine how and why the United States has evolved into a rampage nation.

ACKNOWLEDGMENTS

On April 18, 2007, I was scheduled to cover the topic of balancing civil liberties and national security in my graduate seminar on terrorism at NYU. But two days earlier, a disturbed gunman went on a shooting spree that claimed the lives of thirty-two people at Virginia Tech in Blacksburg, Virginia. When I got to class, my students were still in shock and wanted to discuss the rampage. So I scrapped my lesson plan and devoted the entire three-hour session to what was, at the time, the deadliest act of violence on American soil since 9/11. That night I had a realization: mass shootings are just as much of a threat to the American public as are terrorist attacks.

Over the years, I have been fortunate to benefit from interactions with my students that have helped refine my thoughts on this topic. As such, I owe my first debt of gratitude to my students. Three of my students—Terri Garneau, Kelly McDermott, and especially Simran Maker—also assisted me with research on this project.

At various stages, I have benefited from the encouragement and input of numerous colleagues and friends. In particular, special thanks go to Deb Azrael, Sarah Caldwell, Kristin Finklea, Bill Hartung, David Hemenway, Brian Kamoie, Vesna Markovic, Howard Schiffman, Dan Snodderly, and Steve Stratakos.

Dominic Tierney suggested that I write a book on our nation's growing mass shooting problem, addressing it from a homeland-security perspective. Along the way, he read every page of the manuscript and offered invaluable advice regarding the manuscript as well as the publishing process.

My agent, Don Fehr, immediately recognized the importance of this topic and went the extra mile to make sure my ideas would one day appear in print.

I am also grateful to Steven L. Mitchell and the entire staff at Prometheus Books. While many people were involved in the production and publication of my book—too many to identify here—there are two individuals who have earned my sincerest thanks: Hanna Etu went above and beyond the call of duty in fielding my (sometimes-pestering) questions and requests; and Jade Zora Scibilia worked tirelessly to edit and improve my manuscript, proving she is one of the best at her trade.

Writing a book is no easy feat, often requiring a support system to keep you on track and in good spirits. To this end, my family has been amazing. My parents, James and Frideriki; my brother, Steve; and my son, James, have been there for me every step of the way. My cousin Christina Plakas Katsifas deserves special acknowledgment. She served as my sounding board—reading every page of the manuscript, offering excellent suggestions, and keeping me sane (which is vital when you're steeped in the tragedies that often result from shooting rampages).

This book would not have been possible were it not for my partner in life, Rada. I doubt even she knows how many times she read the manuscript and offered comments and suggestions. She has been my crutch these last couple of years, propping me up whenever I needed it. Quite simply, without her, there is no me.

PART 1

PROBLEM

CHAPTER ONE

SANDY HOOK

America is a rampage nation, where mass shootings now pose the greatest credible threat to public safety, surpassing even terrorism. On December 14, 2012, we were reminded of this in the most heart-wrenching manner. That morning in Newtown, Connecticut, twenty-year-old Adam Lanza went on a shooting spree that claimed the lives of twenty-seven innocent people—twenty of them young children between the ages of six and seven. Like many gun massacres, it was premeditated and it began at home.

The night before, Nancy Lanza, mother of Adam Lanza, returned from New Hampshire, where she had been on a four-day escape from her life as the full-time caretaker of her emotionally volatile son. After slipping into her pajamas, she plopped into bed and drifted off to sleep. Maybe she should've seen the writing on the wall: that her child had a predisposition for violence and that her life was in jeopardy. But she didn't. She never saw her son's rampage coming. It was this false sense of security that allowed him unfettered access to her firearms.[1]

Grabbing a .22-caliber rifle, Adam Lanza crept up on his mother shortly after 8:00 a.m. as she was still fast asleep in her bed.[2] Without disturbing her from her slumber, he aimed the barrel directly at her face and pulled the trigger four times, all head shots. According to Adam's estranged father, Peter, each bullet likely represented a member of their broken nuclear family: Adam, Nancy, Peter, and brother Ryan—a trait of many gun rampages, employing violence in a symbolic fashion.[3]

✳ ✳ ✳

With the task of killing his mother behind him, Adam Lanza geared up for slaughter: four firearms, twenty-four magazines (twenty-two of them extended-capacity magazines capable of holding more than ten rounds), and nearly 530 rounds of ammunition.[4] Dressed almost entirely in black but for an olive-green vest worn to hold magazines, and armed with more firepower than an American soldier on combat foot patrol, he jumped into his mother's Honda Civic for the ten-minute drive to Sandy Hook Elementary School. He did little to avoid drawing attention to himself, pulling right up to the main entrance of the school and blocking the fire lane.

After Lanza readied his arsenal, he approached the school's front doors, only to find them locked.[5] To his right was a video call box that dialed the main office. Lanza must have known he wouldn't get buzzed in, so he improvised another form of entry. Moving to his right, he aimed his assault rifle at the plate glass and popped off eight rounds. The glass was no match for his 5.56mm bullets. With the window shattered, Lanza walked right through the gaping oval-shaped hole and into the lobby. He was in with practically zero resistance.

Sandy Hook Elementary School was rectangular in shape, opening to an interior courtyard in the middle.[6] As Lanza navigated around the mass-produced furniture in the lobby that was typical of a hospital waiting room, clumsily knocking over a potted plant, he came upon two hallways. Straight ahead was the western corridor that led toward the gym, and to his left was the northern corridor that led toward the main office. His decision about which way to head was solidified a few seconds later when three staff members emerged in the northern corridor.

Two doors down from the main office, in Room 9, Principal Dawn Hochsprung was chairing a meeting involving six other staff members and a parent. The meeting was interrupted by what many described as the sound of loud pipe-banging. Hochsprung stood up to investigate. As she reached for the door, she admonished the rest of the meeting participants to remain in the conference room. School psychologist Mary Sherlach was already on Hochsprung's heels, though. The two women exited, and head teacher Natalie Hammond decided to follow them out. It would be a fateful, split-second decision.[7]

At the far end of the northern corridor, in Room 1, kindergarten teacher Deborah Pisani also heard the strange noise and decided to step out into the hallway to see what was happening.

Barbara Halstead was managing the main office by herself that morning. When she heard the sound of the lobby window being shot out, she looked up to see Lanza holding his assault rifle at shoulder height, aiming down the northern corridor. Unbeknownst to Halstead, Lanza had Hochsprung, Sherlach, and Hammond in his sights. He opened fire, spraying the hallway with seventeen shots. All three went down in an instant. As soon as Halstead saw Lanza pull the trigger, she dropped to the floor and yelled, "Sally!" Hearing the panic-stricken voice, school nurse Sally Cox looked over from the adjoining infirmary to see Halstead hiding underneath her work station. Cox followed Halstead's cue and hit the deck. A moment later, Lanza walked into the main office, hunting for more people to shoot.

In Room 1, Deborah Pisani's colleague heard "Oh my God!" as she looked toward the main classroom door just in time to see "black pieces of things hitting the wall." Pisani had managed to shut the door behind her and alert her colleagues that "someone is in the building." It registered immediately: *active shooter*. Instantly, the kindergarten class went into lockdown mode and the children were rushed into a back corner, where they were instructed to lay flat on the carpet, shielded behind a bookcase. As Pisani was crossing the classroom, she noticed that her left foot felt "squishy." When she looked down and saw blood on her shoe, she suddenly knew why something was off with her step. She had been shot.

Not far from the main office, Hochsprung and Sherlach lay dying. Hammond, who was fifteen feet behind them, was also down—playing dead. When Lanza entered the main office, it was the break Hammond needed. Unable to stand as a result of two separate gunshot wounds to her left arm and left foot, she crawled back to the conference room. Extending her right arm and opening the door, she dragged herself back into the room.

"I've been shot twice," Hammond cried out as she closed the conference room door, holding it tightly shut with her uninjured arm. The participants of the meeting had already sheltered in place, scampering for cover when a bullet ripped through the open, solid-wood door that Hammond had exited through moments earlier. Upon seeing Hammond, one of her colleagues grabbed the conference room telephone to call 911. Instead of dialing authorities, she fumbled with the keypad, tripping the school-wide "all-call" feature, which started broadcasting the commotion to every classroom in the building. It allowed every child in the school to eavesdrop on the horror, but it also alerted every teacher that something was terribly wrong at Sandy Hook and that they needed to go into lockdown immediately.

Back in the main office, Lanza approached Halstead's work station, where he hovered briefly before continuing on to the nurse's office. Through a tiny hole in the back of her desk, Cox could see Lanza's legs. He stood facing her desk for approximately five seconds, before turning around and leaving. Halstead, still under her desk and trying desperately to avoid making even the slightest sound, heard Lanza's footsteps approaching. This time he didn't stop. Seconds later, he had exited. Scurrying under their desks was a decision that saved their lives.

Although we can't be exactly sure what Lanza did next, most likely he walked out of the main office, turned right, and came upon Room 12, which housed Kaitlin Roig's first-grade class. When Roig heard the initial sounds of Lanza shooting out the adjacent main-entrance glass, her hypervigilance kicked in. She turned the lights off and began ushering everyone in her room into the tiny bathroom located in the corner of her classroom. Cramming fifteen children into a bathroom that is only sixteen square feet is no easy feat. It took some quick maneuvering—perching one child on the toilet-paper dispenser, five more on the toilet, two behind the bathroom door. Roig pulled it off, though. She got everyone in and locked the door—all in under sixty seconds. That was the easy part. Next, she had to keep her pupils quiet. She explained, "There are bad guys out there now. We need to wait for the good guys." Most children remained calm, and the few that started to fret were met with calls from Roig to show their smiles. Roig did her best to reassure her kids that everything is "going to be okay," telling them, "I need you to know that I love you all very much." Following Roig's direction, the students kept their cool. One student even offered to guide them to safety, telling Roig, "I know karate. It's okay. I'll lead the way out."[8]

Lanza likely approached the door to Roig's classroom to look through the porthole window, only to find it covered with construction paper. By sheer luck, Roig had forgotten to take down the paper from a previous lockdown drill. It's not known if Lanza opened the door to peek inside. If he did, he found an empty, dark, and quiet room. Regardless, he moved on to adjacent Room 10—Victoria Soto's first-grade classroom.

The first call to 911 came in at 9:35. Dispatcher Robert Nute answered. "Newtown 911. What's the location of your emergency?"

"Sandy Hook School. I think there's somebody shooting in here, in Sandy Hook School." The panicked caller was Barbara Halstead.

For emergency-service operators in peaceful Newtown, the report of a shooting was out of the ordinary. Caught a bit off guard by the nature of the call, Nute pressed for some sort of confirmation. "Okay, what makes you think that?"

"Because somebody's got a gun. I got a glimpse of somebody running down the hallway," Halstead replied, her voice shaking. "They're still running. They're still shooting." As she made a plea for help—"Sandy Hook School, please!"—the sound of gunfire filled the background, Lanza's semiautomatic rifle firing three rounds per second. Right before she hung up, Halstead let out one last, desperate utterance of fright: "Ooohhh!"

The shots heard during Halstead's call were most likely the sounds of Lanza assaulting Victoria Soto's first-grade class. The teacher had just finishing shepherding her students away from the main door and was standing near the windows when Lanza burst into the classroom. It was an eerie moment, as no one spoke. Lanza just stood in the room, pointing his AR-15 at the first-graders in an almost eeny-meeny-miny-moe fashion. He had a few rounds still left in his magazine and, after staring down the children, he turned toward Soto and opened fire. The twenty-seven-year-old teacher never stood a chance. She was cut down instantly as bullets riddled her body and shattered the glass behind her—with several fragments finally coming to rest in vehicles parked in the outside lot.

No sooner had Lanza started shooting, than he was out of ammunition, which forced him to switch magazines. Having duct-taped two thirty-cartridge magazines together in a tactical configuration, Lanza needed only a few seconds to flip the magazines and reload.

Six-year-old Jesse Lewis knew what was coming. In an act of heroism beyond his years, he yelled "Run!" urging his classmates to make a break for it. Unfortunately, Jesse's bravery also turned him into an instant target. Rearmed, Lanza pointed his rifle at the charging little boy and squeezed off a single round right to Jesse's head, killing him instantly.[9] Lanza then tried to shoot some of the others stampeding toward the door. He managed to kill one more child attempting to get away.

Some of the fleeing students physically bumped Lanza aside as they passed him; one even stumbled near the door. But the children made it into the hallway, where they darted past the two dead women who were on the ground, and out the front entrance. Before Lanza could shift his body to block their exit, they were gone. Those few precious seconds that Lanza needed to swap out magazines had proved enough.

Heeding Jesse's advice, nine students got away, following a very familiar escape path—the fire-evacuation route that had been seared into their memories several times earlier in the school year. The fire drill wasn't designed for an active-shooter scenario, but it saved the first-graders' lives nonetheless.

Lanza turned to those left in the room and continued his offensive. On the floor behind some desks, he spotted special-education teacher Anne Marie Murphy, holding six-year-old Dylan Hockley in her arms. Kaitlin Roig, who was hiding in the adjacent room, heard someone in Victoria Soto's classroom imploring Lanza to spare their lives: "Oh please no! Please no!" It was likely Murphy. The pleas did little to curb the ruthlessness of Lanza, who emptied the second magazine into those remaining in the classroom, before leaving in search of his next victims.[10]

Two rooms down from Victoria Soto's classroom, where Lanza had just killed two adults and five children, special-education teachers Laura Esposito and Kerri Sommer and one of their students were waiting for four other students to arrive before beginning the day's lesson plan. Hearing the shooting, the two teachers rushed the little girl into the bathroom and locked the door. While in hiding, they heard bursts of gunfire mixed with the screams of children. After a pause, the sounds of horror were repeated, this time in Room 8—the classroom adjacent to their room.[11]

When the rampage began, Amy Taylor, a second-grade teacher in Room 5, ran to her classroom door to shut it. Looking through the porthole window, she locked eyes with substitute teacher Lauren Rousseau, directly across the hallway in Room 8. Taylor remembers the look of fear on Rousseau's face. Terrified and perhaps unfamiliar with the full lockdown repertoire, Rousseau never covered her door window. With the help of special-education teacher Rachel D'Avino, Rousseau gathered her students near the bathroom. Both women tried frantically to get all sixteen children into the tiny space, but unlike Kaitlin Roig, Rousseau and D'Avino struggled. A police report filed several days after the tragedy captured the chaos this way:

> The children that were sitting on the floor of the bathroom were packed in like sardines. . . . As the pile got higher it appeared that there was a mad scramble to get into the bathroom, with people stepping on one another and climbing on top of each other. The teachers would not have been able to get into the room even if they wanted to.

To further complicate matters, the door, which swung inward, couldn't be shut. Everyone was exposed, and the teachers knew it. Unfortunately, before the children could be repositioned, Lanza appeared.

With a fresh extended-capacity magazine loaded into his semi-automatic rifle, Lanza stormed into Room 8. The two teachers were caught in the act of hiding their first-graders in the corner lavatory. One of the teachers tried to stand in the way and shield her vulnerable students from harm. It was a valiant effort, but her body afforded little protection against Lanza's assault weapon.

When the disturbed gunman paused mid-shooting to switch magazines, the people hiding in Room 6 suddenly heard the cries of the first-graders who, on the other side of the thin wall that separated the adjacent classrooms, had survived the first thirty-round barrage. "I don't want to be here!" called out one child.[12]

"Well, you're here!" Lanza retorted.

"Help me!" pleaded another.

"Shut the fuck up!" Lanza yelled back, before continuing his onslaught.

With his execution of the children complete, Lanza turned his sights to the second teacher, who was standing just off to the side of the bathroom. He was livid, perhaps from the teacher's attempt to hide the children. Calling her an "asshole," he demanded that she examine the carnage. "Come over here! Look at them!" Petrified by fear, she couldn't move. Lanza inserted a new magazine and shouted "Look at me!" just prior to unleashing his fury on her. She was killed instantly.

The massacre in Room 8 was over. Unbeknownst to Lanza, one little girl at the bottom of the pile of students in the bathroom had miraculously survived, unscathed. But the others would not be so lucky.

Armed with an AR-15 and numerous thirty-round magazines, it had only taken Lanza one minute to take the lives of seventeen victims—eighty bullets in a single minute!

The first report of actual casualties came at 9:38 when Deborah Pisani phoned 911 and informed authorities that she had been shot. "I'm bleeding. My foot's bleeding." As she was about to provide a callback number, the gunfire resumed. "Oh gosh, I still hear him shooting." Lanza was firing off one to two rounds per second in the background.

Less than a minute after Pisani's initial call to 911, the parent trapped in the conference room also made contact with a different dispatcher at a Connecticut State Police call center. "Sandy Hook School. Oh my God. . . . I have five adults and one's been shot twice. This is crazy."

For 911 operator Karen LaPrade, the experience must have bordered on the bizarre. Just moments before receiving the call from Sandy Hook, LaPrade was chatting away with a retired state trooper who was seeking her help in locating information on an accident investigation. As if jinxing herself, she complained about "country dispatchers that are not accustomed to how busy it is" where she was stationed. She had no idea how true her statement was about to ring.

The parent in Room 9 informed LaPrade that the gunman was "right outside the door." LaPrade repeated this, seeking confirmation from the caller that she was indeed that close to the shooter. "God, he's shot a hundred shots. He must have some big artillery," the caller reported.

LaPrade told the parent that she would patch her through to Newtown 911. As she attempted to transfer the call, Lanza again went on the offensive, firing over a dozen rounds. Hearing the gunshots in the background, LaPrade knew something bad was happening on the other end. She decided that it was best to stay on the line with the clearly frightened caller, rather than transfer her to another call center. Softening her tone, LaPrade asked, "What's going on? Talk to me."

Whispering now, the parent replied, "He's stalking us right outside the door."

LaPrade pulled herself away from the call just long enough to dispatch an alert to all state police units in her zone: "Code 3. All units be advised, we're working on an active shooting in Newtown right now. We are working on an active shooting at a school in Newtown right now." It was 9:40, and within seconds, troopers had begun radioing in that they were responding to the area. LaPrade relayed the information that the police were en route to the caller.

"Please hurry, please hurry, please hurry," the parent begged.

By this time—five minutes into his shooting spree—Adam Lanza must have grown tired. His lanky frame and awkward gait were not cut out for arduous physical activity. And most certainly the thirty pounds of weaponry he was toting had to be taking a toll on his 112-pound body.[13] Just picture yourself lugging over a quarter of your body weight. It's not an easy task for well-conditioned police officers and soldiers, let alone those lacking any sort of athletic prowess, like Lanza.

Fatigue was probably not the only thing slowing down Lanza. Boredom was likely setting in as well. During the massacre at Columbine High School in 1999, the shooters also gave up mid-rampage. In that incident, Eric Harris and Dylan Klebold killed thirteen people in the initial seventeen minutes of the attack. They then spent the next thirty-two minutes wandering around the school aimlessly, never once shooting at any of the several dozen students they encountered. As one observer familiar with the footage from the school's surveillance cameras characterized the two teenagers after their initial murder spree: "The excitement had drained out of them; the bravado was gone."[14]

The not-so-distant gunfire that LaPrade heard in the background at 9:39, while on the phone with the parent trapped in Room 9, was coming from just across the hallway. The forensic evidence suggests that when Lanza exited Lauren Rousseau's classroom, he swapped out his magazine for a fresh one in the hallway and returned to Victoria Soto's classroom. In Room 10, he resumed his shooting, firing several more rounds into the victims who were already sprawled out on the floor. Lanza could've gone to other rooms to seek out more people to murder. He was certainly surrounded by classrooms filled with students. Instead, he came back to a place where he had already wreaked havoc, and he discharged several additional rounds.[15] It seemed less purposeful; more impulsive. But it was hardly an unprecedented behavior for a rampage gunman. The Columbine killers also by-passed rooms where they knew students were sheltering in place, only to enter empty rooms and fire their weapons at inanimate objects—another example of the weariness felt by mass murderers during a shooting spree.[16] Lanza seems to have not been much different. His assault was winding down. One final burst of gunfire stood between him and death.

At exactly 9:39:59 and then again at 9:40:05, the 911 calls from both Deborah Pisani and the parent in the conference room recorded two distinct gunshots in the background. The first shot was Lanza test-firing his 10mm Glock handgun. It was working. Seconds later, he raised the handgun to the right side of his head, placed the barrel up against the black boonie-style hat he was wearing, and fired his 160th and final bullet of the day.

Adam Lanza's rampage was over. It had lasted a mere six minutes.[17]

THE TRINITY OF VIOLENCE

Who could do such a thing? Why did the shooter go after innocent children at an elementary school? How was the gunman able to pull off a massacre of such magnitude in so little time? Answering these questions will not only help us make sense of what at first glance seems senseless but also provide vital insights for reducing the carnage of mass shootings in the future. I propose that we start by viewing the rampage in Newtown through a framework that will help us understand all mass shootings—a framework that I call the *trinity of violence.*

All acts of violence involve a combination of ill intentions, vulnerable victims, and harmful capabilities. You can possess instruments of death and have potential victims in your sights, but without any desire to employ your weapons for violent purposes, the only threat is an accidental use of force. Think about it. Billions of people have access to gasoline and matches. But almost every single one of them avoids setting other people on fire. By the same token, you can be angry and armed, but if you can't get to those you would like to harm, you'll encounter frustration in launching an assault. Hardened government facilities offer good examples. There's a reason why most insurgents attack combat soldiers in the field as opposed to on the grounds of fortified military compounds. It also holds that you can have evil intentions and unobstructed marks, but without the means to pull off your scheme, you'll be limited in the damage you can cause. Case in point: policy analysts have long speculated that al Qaeda desires to direct a nuclear attack against the American homeland. However, because it's basically impossible to obtain a viable nuclear weapon, such a strike is just not in the cards for the terrorist organization. The only feasible danger results when those driven to attack reach their potential victims with destructive capabilities in hand.

As long as we can prevent people from contemplating acts of physical aggression, exploiting vulnerabilities to hurt others, *or* possessing instruments of deadly force, we can keep society safe. This three-prong strategic calculus speaks to the trinity of violence (see figure 1.1). Pursuant to the trinity model, every act of violence requires three components: a perpetrator, a target, and a weapon.

Fig. 1.1. The Trinity of Violence.

Every intentional attack is carried out by someone with some purpose in mind. It seeks to victimize someone or something located within a particular environment. And it always involves some sort of instrument of brute force employed in a manner that either threatens or causes harm. Without all three elements, you can't have an act of violence. This rule holds for armed robberies, physical assaults, arsons, terrorist bombings, and military invasions. Massacres involving guns are no exception. Every mass shooting involves a perpetrator, a weapon, and a target.

Breaking down the study of multiple-victim shootings into distinct examinations of each of the trinity's three components offers some fascinating insights into several important questions:

- Perpetrators: Who tends to commit mass shootings? Why do gunmen go on such rampages?
- Targets: Which targets do mass shooters usually assault? Where are these attack sites typically located?
- Weapons: What type of firearms do rampage gunmen use? How do they utilize their weapons?

Understanding how the trinity of violence applies to mass shootings allows us to come up with effective ways of breaking the trinity. If all three components of the trinity are required in order to stage an attack, then all we need to do is take away one element from the equation and an attack will be either foiled or mitigated. In essence, each prong of the trinity offers a unique strategy: prevention, protection, and preclusion. Applied to each of these three elements, the model suggests we can make America safer by dissuading perpetrators, defending targets, and denying weapons.

Rampage Nation provides an in-depth analysis of America's mass shooting problem. The core thesis of the book is that gun massacres aren't just criminal justice offenses and public health scourges. They're bona fide homeland security threats that deserve the resources and urgency that government devotes to protecting the United States from terrorists and pandemics. My objective is to reframe our understanding of this disturbing phenomenon, which strikes on an almost daily basis and claims far more lives than domestic terrorism does. To kick-start a national dialogue on how to best secure our society from mass shootings, I have structured my book into three distinct segments: an overview of the problem, a probe of its roots, and a prescription for reducing its occurrence.

Beginning with this chapter, part 1 introduces the problem of rampage violence. Chapter 2 discusses the nature of mass shootings, including the controversy over how to define these unique acts of gun violence. Chapter 3 establishes that shooting sprees pose the most troubling individual violent threat to American society in the current era—a threat that, in contrast to nearly all other forms of deadly violence, is growing.

Part 2 probes the roots of rampage violence by applying my original framework—the trinity of violence—to explain such acts of brutal aggression. Each element of the trinity points to a corresponding set of explanations. Chapter 4 addresses perpetrators, wrestling with who goes on rampages and why they do it. Chapter 5 discusses targets, identifying which sites are usually victimized and where those targets are usually located. Chapter 6 focuses on weapons, uncovering what types of firearms rampage gunmen prefer and how they employ those weapons.

Part 3 proposes a prescription for reducing the carnage of mass shootings. The trinity of violence doesn't just offer a framework for understanding rampage violence, it also suggests three strategies for arresting the problem: dissuasion, defense, and denial. Chapter 7 argues that, while all three strategies are valuable, one in particular—denial of weapons to dangerous people through heightened regulation of firearms—offers the most effective approach. Chapter 8 presents a set of eight specific policy proposals that, if enacted and enforced, will drastically reduce the bloodshed. Chapter 9 concludes with a final thought on how mass shootings have become routine, a trait indicative of a rampage nation.

CHAPTER TWO

THE BEGINNING OF WISDOM

You would think that with everything Ka'Nard Allen has been through in his short life—including surviving not one, but two mass shootings—he would be one of the most recognized children in America. Yet few people have ever heard of him. Here's why.

When Tynia Allen told her son Ka'Nard that they were going to the 2013 New Orleans Second-Line Mother's Day Parade, he likely reacted the way most children would: jubilation. After all, who doesn't love a parade?

The ten-year-old was due for some cheer in his life. It had been a rough year for the little boy. In May of 2012, Ka'Nard's great-grand-mother hosted a party to mark his tenth birthday. Because her house was located on Simon Bolivar Avenue, near the boundary between the gang-plagued Second and Third Wards of New Orleans, the Allens had certainly seen their fair share of turf battles play out in neighbor-hood. But with little children celebrating and playing out in front of the home, in broad daylight, no one envisaged violence erupting.

The festive mood was shattered when four gang members, driving by, spotted some rival gang members who were at the party, standing out on the street median, just across from the Allen resi-dence. After parking their vehicle around the corner, three of the men drew their weapons and approached the area, hoping to settle an old score. Catching their intended targets by complete surprise, the trio of shooters opened fire on the crowd, killing two people and leaving another three wounded.[1]

When the gunfire erupted, Ka'Nard's five-year-old cousin Briana Allen cried out, "Grandma, something's wrong."

Her grandmother's memory of that moment will always remain vivid: "When I looked down it was like her little stomach was blown out and her intestines was all over the floor."[2] Briana had been cut down by a single AK-47 round to the abdomen. First responders rushed her to the hospital, but she never stood a chance.

The blasts fired from the assault rifle were so powerful that they also claimed the life of a thirty-three-year-old mother of three who happened to be driving through the area at that precise moment. Even though Shawanna Pierce was three entire city blocks away from the location of the attack, the stray round traveled down the street and easily penetrated her windshield, striking her in the head and causing her vehicle to crash into a utility pole. She too never stood a chance.

One of the three gunshot victims who survived that day, in what has become known locally as the Simon Bolivar shooting, was Ka'Nard Allen, who was hit twice; once in the neck and once in the leg.

Ka'Nard has been left with two permanent scars—reminders of that horrible day when he watched his little cousin bleed to death. But, a few months later, just as he was starting to heal—physically and psychologically—Ka'Nard suffered through another trauma: his father was stabbed to death by the boy's stepmother during a domestic altercation. Ka'Nard was left devastated, telling his mother at one point, "I wish my daddy was still living. I'd have everything I want."[3]

After two personal tragedies in such a short period of time, Tynia Allen knew her son needed a pick-me-up. What better way to lift the spirits of a child than a parade? What could possibly go wrong?

★ ★ ★

The annual Second-Line Mother's Day Parade in the Seventh Ward of New Orleans typically draws several hundred spectators. In 2013, one of those in attendance was Leonard Epps. According to authorities, Epps was affiliated with a Ninth Ward gang known as the Deslonde Boys. When two brothers, Akein and Shawn Scott, members of the rival Frenchmen and Derbigny gang, noticed Epps in the crowd, they took positions on opposite sides of the street and began shooting. With no regard for innocent bystanders, the brothers sprayed the parade-goers with bullets, striking Epps and eighteen others. One witness described the barrage as if the gunmen were "hunting ducks in the sky."[4]

Some onlookers heard the gunshots. Others felt the burn of being grazed by a projectile. When people broke into a mad scramble—pushing each other out of the way and, in some instances, trampling on those in their path of escape—everyone realized that something was wrong. Within minutes, the ten police officers guarding the parade route had all descended on the intersection where the shooting occurred to discover that there was at least one person bleeding at each of the four corners. As authorities raced to attend to the injured, they called in what they were seeing. The two-way radio transmissions captured the chaos:

"There may be multiple victims."

"We have a male shot over here."

"A lady was shot over here."

"Two more victims over here."[5]

Miraculously, no one died, although Epps and several others sustained life-threatening injuries. Among the gunshot victims were two children, an unidentified girl who suffered a wound to the side of her abdomen and a boy who was hit in the cheek. When first responders reached the boy, they radioed it in: "We have a ten-year-old shot."[6] Police later identified the ten-year-old as none other than Ka'Nard Allen.

Not even in her wildest dreams—make that nightmares—could Tynia Allen have imagined that the Mother's Day Parade would be transformed into a bloody crime scene; and, worse, that her son would become a gunshot victim for the second time in less than a year. As she exclaimed, "It was Mother's Day! No one expected that!"[7]

★ ★ ★

Ka'Nard Allen survived not one but two multiple-casualty shootings.[8] Yet odds are that unless you're a resident of New Orleans, you probably have never heard of Ka'Nard Allen, let alone what he's endured. He remains, quite simply, another relatively overlooked victim of gun violence. If you have access to a news-archive database like Lexis-Nexis, you can easily see this for yourself. Just search for Ka'Nard Allen in *New York Times* articles.[9] When I did it, I found no entries. Now to put the national coverage of his personal tragedies in perspective, try a couple of different searches. Look for *New York Times* stories mentioning Christina-Taylor Green, the nine-year-old girl who was killed during Jared Loughner's gun rampage at a Tucson political event organized by Congresswoman Gabrielle Giffords. In stark contrast, I found thirty-seven news items. One more search: try six-year-old Sandy Hook victim Jesse Lewis. While I only found eleven entries—far fewer than those mentioning Christina-Taylor Green—the coverage Jesse Lewis received is still greater than that devoted to Ka'Nard Allen. This little test holds for other national media outlets as well. For instance, *USA Today* ran twenty-nine articles on Christina-Taylor Green and three on Jesse Lewis. Ka'Nard Allen, however, never made the paper—not even once. The same with CNN: ninety-three broadcast segments discussed Christina-Taylor and forty discussed Jesse, yet none mentioned Ka'Nard.[10]

The coverage of these shootings fits a similar pattern. To take CNN as an example, it devoted just a few segments to the Mother's Day Parade shooting, even though the melee produced one of the highest casualty tolls in recent history (*casualty* defined as including both lethal and nonlethal injuries). The only time an actual CNN correspondent reported live from the scene was during the morning show the day after Mother's Day. As for the Simon Bolivar attack, it didn't even warrant a single mention on the channel.

It's not that mass shootings don't draw national attention. Quite the opposite. The gun attacks that the media consider to be of such magnitude that they warrant the label "mass shooting" almost always receive extensive coverage. Take the rampages in Tucson and Newtown as examples. Within a day of the former and within hours of the latter, television correspondents from every major network descended on each location to report live from the scene. For days, each incident dominated the news. To date, CNN has discussed each of these two rampages in over two thousand broadcast segments. That's an astronomical difference in comparison to the Mother's Day Parade shooting. In fact, the tragedies in Tucson and Newtown were so disturbing that President Obama visited both sites to lead memorial services and try to help each community begin the healing process.

How the nation reacted to the attacks in Arizona and Connecticut was grossly different from how it reacted to the shooting of nineteen people in Louisiana. What's particularly mind-boggling is that the parade gunmen fled the scene, resulting in a large-scale manhunt. Yet none of the news networks flocked to the Crescent City to bring the American public nonstop coverage of the search for the fugitives.[11] Instead, as authorities were on the hunt for the Scott brothers, CNN was leading its news coverage with updates on Angelina Jolie's double mastectomy. Now, compare this to the Boston Marathon bombing. When two other brothers staged a violent attack against a crowd of spectators, the ensuing manhunt dominated the national news for days. Why the disparity? Weren't both attacks mass crimes that greatly endangered public safety?

When you think about it, Ka'Nard Allen's relative anonymity makes sense in a way. After all, if you haven't heard of the Simon Bolivar and Mother's Day Parade shootings because they received minimal national attention, then you're not going to know much about Ka'Nard Allen. But why is it that most Americans are familiar with attacks like Tucson and Newtown, but unfamiliar with those that brought Ka'Nard Allen close to death on two separate occasions?[12]

Many multiple-victim shootings often go unnoticed outside of their local news markets because they lack certain elements that propel them to the level of a so-called mass shooting. Those incidents are instead seen as the typical shootings that plague America on an hourly basis. "Run-of-the-mill" was how one *Washington Post* journalist characterized them.[13] Or, as two noted gun-violence researchers put it, "the more mundane attacks."[14] This raises another, related question: Why do some shootings captivate our collective consciousness while others, like the two attacks that left Ka'Nard Allen scarred for life, get relegated to the realm of banality?

To answer this question, let's begin with a concession: shootings that result in fatalities are more disturbing than those that don't; the higher the death toll, the more troubling the attack. As such, the more lethal an act of gun violence is, the more it warrants coverage and examination, especially for purposes of understanding and prevention. This belief might explain—and even justify—why the Simon Bolivar and Mother's Day Parade attacks have been largely overlooked by public officials, scholars, and journalists. After all, the Tucson rampage left six dead and the Newtown shooting left twenty-seven dead. In contrast, the Simon Bolivar onslaught resulted in far fewer fatalities and, more on point, no one was killed in the Mother's Day Parade shooting. But if it were the case that high death tolls resulting from heinous acts are responsible for elevating particular acts of gun violence to the level of *mass* shootings, then why have people generally paid no mind to the massacre that took place in Copley Township, Ohio?

"THERE'S NO MAGICAL DOOR"

Copley Township is a quaint little suburb located about seven miles west of Akron, Ohio. Many people move to the area because of its picturesque landscapes, bustling economy, and low crime rate. In 2007, *Akron Life* magazine identified the community as one of the five safest residential areas in the Akron region.[15] But what happened on August 7, 2011, has called that perception into question.[16]

That morning, local residents noticed an unfamiliar woman running through the neighborhood, screaming frantically. "My husband has a hole in his head! I'm a widow!"[17] As one couple came to the aid of the distressed woman, she pointed down the street and shouted, "Somebody get my son!"[18]

Her child was sprinting for his life. Moments earlier, her husband, Craig Dieter, had been executed—and now the killer was on the trail of her eleven-year-old, Scott. Beth Dieter, clearly in shock, was making a desperate plea for someone to save her little boy.

✶ ✶ ✶

The Dieters had driven up from Kentucky to visit Craig's sister, Becky Dieter, and her boyfriend, Michael Hance. Two years earlier, following the death of Becky's parents, the couple had moved into the Dieter family home on Goodenough Avenue in Copley. But shortly after that, Hance began exhibiting signs of depression, perhaps exacerbated by his inability to secure employment. Becky was worried about Hance's deteriorating mental state, and had sought the counsel of her siblings.

The Johnson family, longtime friends and next-door neighbors of Becky's late parents, were also concerned about Hance. They were sick and tired of what they felt was Hance's disregard for community standards. From constantly leaving broken-down automobiles strewn across the property to dressing inappropriately in skimpy clothing, Hance was a menace to the neighborhood, the Johnsons felt. Generally, they lodged their complaints with Becky; but in the early part of the summer, Gerdie Johnson finally went directly to Hance, asking him to remove a vehicle, which was up on blocks, from visibility, and to clean up the house's exterior.

Hance had had an equal fill of the Johnsons. The previous summer, Hance caught the Johnsons' grandson shooting at squirrels on his property. Hance grabbed the child and dragged him back to his father's house—located just behind the elder Johnsons' residence. Instead of getting some sort of resolution, Hance caught an earful from the boy's father, Michael Johnson, for what he saw as Hance's improper physical accosting of the child. Hance left further infuriated, warning Michael Johnson, "You just wait, I'm going to finish it!"—a reference to the escalating feud between him and the Johnsons.[19] By the time Gerdie approached Hance to complain about the home's appearance, he wanted nothing to do with her or her kin, telling her, "Get off my property and don't come back!"[20]

Everything finally came to a head during Craig's visit. The Dieters were passing through town en route to a family gathering in Pennsylvania. The plan was to drive to the reunion in two cars—Craig's family in one vehicle and Hance and Becky in another. All morning, Hance had been packing Becky's car. But at the last minute, while outside loading up, Craig threw a wrench in Hance's plan when he informed Hance that everyone would drive up in Craig's vehicle. Hance nodded his acknowledgment and went inside the house.

As Craig and his family were in the driveway, bidding farewell to the Johnsons, Hance reappeared, armed with two handguns—a .357 revolver and a .45-caliber pistol. Ambushing both families, he killed Craig, Gerdie, and her husband, Russell, with three direct headshots. At the sight of her husband collapsing, Beth raced from the scene. One of the Johnsons' grandchildren and her high-school friend were nearby and tried to hide in a minivan parked in the driveway, but Hance walked up and executed both teens.

Becky, hearing all the commotion, grabbed a phone and went outside to see what was happening. Hance shot her once in the back as she was communicating with 911. The bullet pierced her lung and shattered her shoulder, but she was alive. She closed her eyes and played dead—a tactic that saved her life.

Gerdie's sons, Michael and Bryan, also came out to investigate. As the two brothers approached the driveway, they spotted bodies on the ground and saw Hance reloading. Sensing danger, the men ran for their lives. Bryan made it about five hundred yards before Hance closed in and cut him down. Hance then reversed course, setting his sights on Michael, who was fleeing in a different direction. But Hance was soon distracted by the appearance of eleven-year-old Scott Dieter, who was on the heels of Michael.

Michael ran into the nearby Bagley residence. Scott, desperate, followed him in. Despite the gallant efforts of the neighbors, Hance forced his way into the house and found Scott hiding in the base-ment boiler room. Hance shot him with a single round to the head. The home's occupant, Melonie Bagley, tried her best to shield Scott along with three of her children, but they were cornered and her options were limited. As she recalled, when you're trapped during a shooting, "there's no magical door" through which to escape.[21]

Hance's rampage came to an end when he exited the Bagley residence and was killed by a Copley Township police officer. The murder spree lasted about ten minutes. Scott was the final victim.[22]

★ ★ ★

The attack on the Dieter and Johnson families claimed the lives of seven people, including three minors, and it left an eighth person in critical condition. Like the New Orleans Mother's Day Parade shooting, the Copley massacre was largely ignored by prominent news organizations. CNN mentioned it in passing on the day it occurred, just as the late evening news anchor was signing off. Two days later, the network provided a brief recount of the event. But at no time did any of its correspondents report live from Copley. *USA Today* also covered the incident only twice—once in a news-at-a-glance section and the other as a relay of an Associated Press news wire article that was fewer than five hundred words. As for the *New York Times*, it opted not to report on the shooting.

Why haven't most people heard of this brutal attack that devastated the once serene and peaceful suburban community of Copley? Why didn't the national media pick up on this story? Why didn't the victims of this shooting earn more compassion and outpouring from society? Why, like the Simon Bolivar and Mother's Day Parade shootings in New Orleans, does the shooting spree in Copley remain largely overlooked? Doesn't this tragedy deserve the scrutiny that other high-fatality tragedies have received? Just look at how it compares to the ambush, in 2011, of a political meet and greet featuring Congresswoman Gabrielle Giffords in Tucson, Arizona, or the so-called virgin killings that, in 2014, targeted University of California–Santa Barbara students in Isla Vista, California. Six people were murdered in both attacks—fewer fatalities than in the Copley massacre. Yet these rampages—perpetrated, respectively, by Jared Loughner and Elliot Rodger—have been treated far differently than the rampage committed by Michael Hance. If high death tolls aren't enough to elevate shootings into mass shootings, what more does it take? What is it that distinguishes mass shootings from "mundane," "run-of-the-mill" acts of gun violence?

DEFYING CONSENSUS

When I began researching rampage violence, I was surprised to learn that how shootings are classified is a point of bitter contention. To date, there's no agreed-upon definition of *mass shooting*. Moreover, the definitions that are often cited tend to be of limited value.

Criminologist Gary Kleck was one of the first people to recognize mass shootings as a unique form of gun violence. Following the two high-profile rampages that spurred the passage of the 1994 federal Assault Weapons Ban (AWB)—the 1993 California Street and Long Island Rail Road attacks—Kleck undertook a study that defined mass shootings as "incident[s] in which six or more victims were shot dead with a gun, or twelve or more total were wounded."[23] Applying this definition, which sets a relatively high casualty threshold, he identified fifteen incidents that had occurred in the decade extending from 1984 to 1993, the decade immediately prior to the enactment of the AWB.

Despite the efforts of Kleck and a few others, analysis of mass shootings remained largely dormant until 2012, when the Aurora and Newtown massacres revived interest in the topic.[24] Suddenly, it seemed as if every major media outlet was undertaking some sort of examination of this unique form of gun violence in the aftermath of these attacks. Two news organizations in particular published systematic studies of rampage violence. But, as their respective working definitions illustrate, there's still significant disagreement over what constitutes a mass shooting. The debate—which continues to play out in government hearings, academic conferences, news programs, and blogs—numbs the mind at times. It's worth taking a quick detour to review these competing perspectives, treating them as stepping-stones toward building an accurate and useful definition of this pressing phenomenon.

Just a month prior to the Newtown attack, *Mother Jones* published what has arguably become the most well-known examination of mass shootings in the United States.[25] To guide its research—which is periodically updated—the magazine adopted three criteria to identify mass shootings. First, the attack had to be a single, isolated incident that occurred in a public space. Second, at least four people had to have been murdered by a *lone* gunman. Third, the motive had to be indiscriminate, which excludes incidents of gang strife, armed robbery, and domestic violence at home. Applying its criteria, *Mother Jones* has identified eighty mass shootings over a nearly thirty-five-year period (January 1, 1982–February 29, 2016).[26]

Following Adam Lanza's murder spree, *USA Today* also began tracking mass shootings in America. Compared to the *Mother Jones* definition, which contains numerous disqualifying criteria, *USA Today* adopted a far less restrictive conceptualization, counting *any* firearm incident "where four or more people are killed." This broader approach has yielded 211 incidents over a nine-and-a-half-year period (January 1, 2006–June 30, 2015).[27] By including mass murders committed by more than one gunman, occurring in a private setting, or involving additional criminal motives, *USA Today* has identified almost three times as many mass shootings as *Mother Jones* has identified—and that's over a time period that's less than one-third of that examined by *Mother Jones*. To put it in slightly different terms, *USA Today* found that the average number of mass shootings is twenty-two per year, whereas *Mother Jones* found that the average is two such shootings per year. That's an eleven-fold discrepancy. As this snap comparison makes abundantly clear, different definitions lead to starkly different conclusions.

And it's not just the news media. Even the federal government—which is responsible for maintaining accurate statistics on crime—has failed to embrace a uniform definition of mass shootings. For example, in the legislative branch, the Congressional Research Service (CRS)—an agency that provides research and analysis at the request of Congress and its committees—defines a mass shooting as "a multiple homicide incident in which four or more victims are murdered with firearms—not including the offender(s)—within one event, and in one or more locations in close geographical proximity."[28] Meanwhile, in the executive branch, the Office of Community Oriented Policing Services (COPS) at the US Department of Justice eschews the four-fatality minimum, instead defining multiple-victim shootings as "pre-planned multiple casualty violent events within the United States, excluding terrorist acts, killings in conjunction with the commission of other crimes, and domestic violence incidents in which only family members are killed."[29] The adoption of two distinct perspectives reflects the inconsistency with which the federal government views mass shootings.[30]

✷ ✷ ✷

A comparison of the various definitions indicates that there are basically four key factors that the experts emphasize when making a determination as to what constitutes a mass shooting:

1. Number of Casualties: Must people die for an act of gun violence to be a mass shooting? If so, how many victims must die as a result of gunshot wounds? If not, what's the minimum number of nonlethal casualties that must be incurred for an attack to rise to the level of a mass shooting?
2. Number of Shooters: Is a mass shooting limited to being the undertaking of a lone gunman, or can it be perpetrated by more than one shooter?
3. Location: Is a mass shooting limited to a public space or can it also occur in a private setting?
4. Motivation: Can the use of a gun attack in furtherance of a criminal activity—terrorism, gang warfare, robbery, or domestic violence—constitute a mass shooting?

Given the room for variance, it's easy to see how many shootings—even high-fatality shootings like the Copley Township massacre—might slip through the cracks.

While we are far from consensus on how to define mass shootings, the experts are generally of the view that the three shootings we reviewed earlier—the Simon Bolivar, Mother's Day Parade, and Copley Township assaults—are of a lesser magnitude, that somehow they don't warrant the special attention reserved for acts of violence like the Columbine, Aurora, and Newtown attacks. For starters, every single authority discussed above feels that neither of the New Orleans attacks rises to the level of a mass shooting.[31] Both involved the use of firearms in furtherance of criminal activities beyond the shootings themselves, namely, gang warfare. Moreover, both attacks were perpetrated by more than one gunman. In addition, the Mother's Day Parade attack did not result in any fatalities. The Copley Township massacre—which on the other hand involved a lone perpetrator murdering numerous individuals—is also largely overlooked by most media and academic experts because it was largely a domestic dispute.[32]

In both New Orleans attacks, people attending celebrations were shot by sociopaths who had it out for their rivals. These acts of public endangerment deserve national attention and study, but they continue to be dismissed because they were perpetrated by multiple gunmen engaged in gang-related criminal activities. In the suburban Akron shooting, a group of people just going about their morning routines were cut down by a mentally disturbed acquaintance. This tragedy also deserves national attention and study, yet it too has been discounted as just another one of those "more mundane attacks" because it was prompted by a family quarrel.

By coming up with largely subjective reasons for excluding certain multiple-victim acts of gun violence from consideration, we are doing a disservice to the investigation of mass shootings. It's time to change that.

ENDING THE CONTROVERSY

Years ago, the noted American theologian Tryon Edwards quipped, "Most controversies would soon be ended, if those engaged in them would first accurately define their terms, and then adhere to their definitions."[33] By allowing for the exclusion of relevant cases for a variety of arbitrary reasons, we are further compounding the problem of better understanding mass shootings. The reality is that the more criteria we utilize, the higher the risk of subjective and flawed examination. This rings especially true when reporters and analysts capriciously apply the criteria of their own established definitions. Case in point: *Mother Jones* magazine.

I suspect that every one of you considers the Newtown massacre to be a mass shooting. *Mother Jones* certainly does, and that makes perfect sense to me, except for one problem: applying the magazine's criteria should result in exclusion. The Newtown rampage was neither limited to one location nor was it completely perpetrated in a public space. It began at the Lanza residence—a private space—where the gunman murdered his mother, and then it continued at Sandy Hook Elementary School after a brief pause. Domestic violence was clearly a factor. Adhering to the strict criteria established by *Mother Jones*—excluding any attack that involved more than one location, more than one gunman, or any sort of precursor criminal activity—should result in a rejection of the attack as a mass shooting. Of course, when the team at *Mother Jones* realized that massacres like Sandy Hook and, for that matter, Virginia Tech didn't mesh neatly with its criteria because those rampages involved multiple locations—some of which were residential settings—it amended its study to include killings that were perpetrated in more than one place (even private dwellings), so long as they "primarily" occurred in public and "over a short period of time."[34] Basically, in order to include the Newtown and Virginia Tech incidents in its data set, the magazine had to bend its own rules.

Even more egregious, *Mother Jones* identifies the assaults on Columbine High School and Westside Middle School as mass shootings, even though it insists only attacks perpetrated by a lone gunman qualify as mass shootings.[35] So how did Columbine and Westside— which both involved shooter teams—make the list? Simple. *Mother Jones* essentially made a decision to ignore its own criterion and add these two attacks. Good thing, because dismissing Columbine and Westside on such an arbitrary ground is about as silly as insisting that the 9/11 attack wasn't technically an act of terrorism because it was executed by multiple perpetrators as opposed to one.

The magazine's goal was to approach the topic in a manner that made "some sense intuitively."[36] Instead, it led to a perverse oversight of many important cases.[37] When *Mother Jones* saw the errors of its way, it sacrificed rigor for common sense.[38]

Why are these incidents counted when they clearly don't meet the working definitions established for the purpose of analysis? Because common sense tells us that all of these attacks are mass shootings.

Let's try a little exercise. Imagine that there's an attack in your community that leaves lots of people wounded. If there are multiple gunmen, will that make you less concerned or upset? How about the method of attack? Will it really make a difference to you if the shooting occurred in just one spot as opposed to, say, an attack where the perpetrator was firing from his car and, thus, constantly moving?

Even if the attack is stationary, will you see it as less tragic because the victims were in a house as opposed to an office? And what about the motive? Do you think it matters to the victims whether the bullets lodged inside their bodies are there because the gunman is mad at his employer as opposed to being mad at the government?

It's the *mass* violence itself that matters most. Not the number of shooters. Not the precise location or setting. Not the motive. Variables beyond the number of victims and the nature of their injuries are indisputably arbitrary. While they're useful for categorizing acts of violence for purposes of uncovering patterns, they shouldn't necessarily be employed to exclude shootings from analysis. Yet this is exactly what many media reports and policy studies have done—resulting at times in odd outcomes. To avoid this, I propose viewing shootings from the victims' perspective. I suspect Ka'Nard Allen and Becky Dieter would agree.

A mass shooting is just that; a shooting. It's not necessarily a mass murder. Conflating mass shootings and mass murders leads to a discounting of the vast majority of multiple-casualty gun attacks; attacks like the Simon Bolivar and Mother's Day Parade shootings. Similarly, insisting that mass shootings are only perpetrated by a lone gunman, occur only in public, or involve only instances when force is not a means to another nefarious end is dubious. Yet this is exactly what many definitions dictate.

If mass shootings are limited to acts undertaken by only one shooter, then that would exclude some of the most high-profile incidents, including the massacres at Columbine High School and the San Bernardino Inland Regional Center. If rampages must take place entirely in a public setting in order to qualify as mass shootings, then that would exclude three of the deadliest killing sprees in American history: Virginia Tech, Sandy Hook, and University of Texas–Austin. If, as one government study maintains, mass shootings don't involve using violence as "a means to an end" . . . let me stop right there.[39] Every single criminal shooting involves some sort of objective—even those perpetrated by delusional gunmen.

If the process of distinguishing mass shootings from other acts of violence leaves you scratching your head, don't worry, it initially had the same impact on me. A major part of the problem is that analysts and commentators are trying too hard to find exclusionary criteria.

The easiest way to assure that such arbitrary practices are avoided—to end the controversy as Tryon Edwards proposed—is to streamline the concept of mass shooting. In this vein, I propose we adopt a simpler, more useful definition that, as of late, has started to come into favor with some of the nation's leading media outlets: *a mass shooting is any violent attack that results in four or more individuals incurring gunshot wounds.*[40] It doesn't matter if there's one gunman or several gunmen. It doesn't need to occur in public. And it can be for any reason whatsoever. It only needs to result in multiple casualties. This approach is commonsensical and fair. As long as four or more people are struck by gunfire, it's a mass shooting.[41]

In addition, to avoid further confusion that often results from terminological nuances, I will use the terms *mass shooting, multiple-casualty shooting, shooting spree,* and *rampage* interchangeably throughout this book. Some commentators try to reserve certain words for particular types of violence. For instance, *Mother Jones* considers mass shootings as generally distinct from shooting sprees because, in its view, the former occur in one place whereas the latter occur in different locations. Again, common usage dictates otherwise. Not to make light of gun attacks by comparing them to consumer purchasing activities, but when someone goes to a single department store and buys several items, it's no less of a shopping spree than when they make such purchases across different retail establishments. Why should the word *spree* have a unique connotation when characterizing acts of violence? Similarly, a rampage—which generally refers to a sudden act of destruction—can be synonymous with a mass shooting. While some might prefer to limit the use of the term to incidents where people snap and resort to violence for the sake of violence itself (as opposed to using force in support of another criminal activity), this again would lead to flawed study of the phenomenon at hand. After all, how is a gang member spotting a foe and then suddenly striking with a barrage of gunfire—harming numerous bystanders in the process—any less of a rampage than a student taking his frustration with a particular teacher out on fellow classmates caught in the line of fire? To avoid skewed analysis—and an unnecessary semantic debate—I will employ a variety of terms in a manner consistent with their common usage in the English language.

Returning for a moment to the earlier example of terrorism, even though it would be foolish to discount attacks like 9/11 strictly because they involved multiple assailants, that doesn't mean that we can't categorize incidents based on the number of perpetrators. In fact, in security studies, acts of violent political extremism undertaken by single individuals are referred to as "lone wolf" terrorism. Such analytical breakdowns can—and should—be applied to the study of mass shootings as well. This would allow us to discern differences between "lone wolf" and "wolf pack" rampages, for example, without dismissing one or the other type of event. The same holds for every other factor that is frequently employed to classify mass shootings: victims, motive, location, time frame, and weapon(s), just to name a few.

One factor, in particular, is extremely valuable in assessing the level of damage *mass* shootings inflict in America: casualties. To better comprehend the scale of rampage violence, I propose three categories of mass shooting: nonfatal, fatal, and massacre (see table 2.1). Working off the premise advanced earlier that the more lethal an attack is, the more troubling it is, I posit that gun massacres—high-fatality mass shootings resulting in six or more deaths, not including the perpetrator(s)—are the worst kind, making them the most dangerous and threatening to American public safety. As such, I will often focus my attention and discussion on gun massacres, incorporating insights and lessons from the other two categories where appropriate.[42]

Table 2.1. The Concept of a Mass Shooting.

Definition of a Mass Shooting:

Any violent attack that results in four or more individuals incurring gunshot wounds.

Categories of Mass Shooting:

1. *Nonfatal*
   Mass shootings in which no one dies.

2. *Fatal*
   Mass shootings in which at least one victim dies.

3. *High-Fatality / Gun Massacre*
   Mass shootings in which six or more victims die.

It's easy to dismiss conceptual discussions and debates as exercises in Ivory Tower intellectualism. But how we identify and think about mass shootings impacts which attacks capture national attention and which are disregarded—something which has far-reaching policy consequences. Thus, coming up with the best possible definition and conceptualization is a vital first step toward explaining and preventing rampage violence. As the Socratic adage reminds us, "The beginning of wisdom is the definition of terms."[43]

CHAPTER THREE

A GROWING THREAT

Bill Iffrig was having a great race. Nothing like the seventy-eight-year-old's performance the previous year, when he survived the sweltering heat to complete the 26.2 mile Boston Marathon in a disappointing seven and a half hours. In 2013, he was back to prove to himself that the year before he had caught a rotten break. Four hours and 26 miles into his third Boston Marathon, he turned onto Boylston Street and the finish line came into sight. He had two-tenths of a mile to go—the home stretch. *You got this*, he must've thought. *No problem. You got this.*

A few yards before the finish line, Iffrig's legs turned into "spaghetti" and gave out from underneath him. He had been blown to the pavement by an explosion that came from just feet away to his immediate left. As he lay on the ground, he tried to make sense of what had happened. He remembered the "really loud" boom. Then there were "tin-can-like things" flying by him. Looking up, he saw a plume of white smoke rising into the air and immediately knew: *Bomb!*[1]

Seconds later, a second blast detonated two hundred yards farther back on Boylston Street. It was 3:00 p.m. on April 15, 2013—Patriots' Day in Massachusetts, the state holiday that commemorates the opening salvo of the Revolutionary War. Immediately, the news media began fueling speculation that this might be a right-wing militia terrorist attack.[2] Those claims would later turn out to be half-accurate. The double explosions at the Boston Marathon were indeed part of a coordinated terrorist attack. But the perpetrators weren't right-wing extremists. They were violent jihadists.

★ ★ ★

Disgruntled with the economic opportunities available following the collapse of the Soviet Union and fearful of the growing Russian criminal underworld, Anzor Tsarnaev and his wife, Zubeidat, wanted a fresh start for their family. In 2002, they immigrated to the United States in search of a better life for their four children. Settling into a third-floor walk-up in Cambridge, Massachusetts, the family looked forward to experiencing the American Dream.[3]

It never materialized.

Anzor eked out a living doing automobile body work—a far cry from the more promising tobacco trade that he engaged in back in Russia. Zubeidat got off to a better start, providing home health-care. But when that work dried up, she was forced to turn to cosmetology as a means to supplement Anzor's income. Things quickly turned sour for the children as well. Both daughters married young, becoming mothers and divorcees while still teenagers—and saddling Anzor and Zubeidat with two additional children to feed. The two sons didn't fare much better, either, turning to alcohol and drugs as coping mechanisms for their difficulties assimilating with American culture.

The Tsarnaevs were lost in a foreign land. To help, Zubeidat turned to Islam for direction. In short time, her eldest son, Tamerlan, followed suit.

Tamerlan Tsarnaev struggled with school. It wasn't his calling. Boxing was, and on this front he had a lot going for him. In 2009, he won the New England regional Golden Gloves tournament and traveled to Salt Lake City, Utah, to fight in the national championships—and perhaps earn a coveted spot on the US boxing team. While he lost a close first-round bout, his trainers knew that the following year he would be back, tougher and smarter. But there would be no next year, as his once-promising fighting career ran into a dead end after the tournament rules were changed in 2010 to prohibit non-US citizens from competing for the national title. Devastated and suddenly adrift, Tamerlan filled the newfound void in his life with religion.[4]

Tamerlan married in 2010 and, several months later, welcomed a daughter into the world.[5] To make ends meet, Tamerlan's wife found work, while he stayed home and served as their child's caretaker.[6] Whenever Tamerlan needed a break from home life, he would visit the local mosque. He spent long periods of time at the Islamic Society of Boston, where he developed far-out views on faith and politics. Many of his conspiracy theories were buttressed by his mother, who believed among other things that 9/11 was really a plot to get Americans to hate Muslims. Surrounded by people who encouraged such thinking, Tamerlan soon developed a strong distaste for American policies.[7]

In 2012, Tamerlan returned to his former homeland of Dagestan in search of spiritual growth. While in the southern Russian republic, he immersed himself in a community that displayed a much more fervent devotion to Islam than most Muslims in America do. In particular, he began praying at a mosque that promoted an extreme, Salafist interpretation of Islam—a house of worship that, according to Russian authorities, also served as a gathering place for supporters of the jihadist insurgency in the Caucasus.[8]

The time Tamerlan Tsarnaev spent overseas transformed him. He returned highly suspect of the United States, and he took to jihadist websites to profess and reinforce his anti-American views. Among his new beliefs: devout Muslims in the United States should refrain from celebrating secular American holidays; the military campaigns in Afghanistan and Iraq were really masked wars against Islam; and jihad—violent jihad if necessary—was an obligation against those who mistreated Muslims and disrespected their faith.[9]

Tamerlan's younger brother, Dzhokhar, was also an accomplished athlete who found himself adrift when his tenure in sports came to an end. All during high school, the youngest Tsarnaev had wrestling as his anchor. No matter what problems there were at home, the wrestling captain always had the support and admiration of his teammates. After graduating from high school, he abruptly found himself without a social safety net.[10]

At first, the plan was to start anew as a freshman at the University of Massachusetts at Dartmouth. But his new environment proved more conducive to partying and drug-dealing than to studying—which quickly landed him on academic probation.[11]

Upon Dzhokhar's return to Cambridge in the summer between his freshman and sophomore years of college, he found a drastically different home from the one he had left a year earlier: a broken home. His parents were now divorced, with his father back in Dagestan, and his mother about to return as well. Even his sisters were gone, now living in New Jersey. The only family left was Tamerlan, who by the end of that summer had emerged as the head of the Tsarnaev family.

Sensing that Dzhokhar was in need of new direction, Tamerlan offered his little brother some simple advice: embrace Islam.[12]

With his grades continuing their nosedive in his sophomore year, perhaps Dzhokhar realized that his time at university was about to come to an end. Or perhaps he was just burned-out by life in Dartmouth, Massachusetts. Whatever the reason, he started spending less time on campus following the winter break. Instead, he found himself frequently back home, where he and his more radicalized older brother started exchanging ideas far different than those imparted by his professors in the UMass system.[13]

The new curriculum contained criticisms of American foreign policy, highlighting alleged atrocities committed against Muslims abroad and even here in the United States; extremist interpretations of Islam that justified the use of violence against infidels, including the preachings of the radical cleric Anwar al-Awlaki, an American citizen who moved to Yemen and took on the role of an informal spiritual advisor to al Qaeda in the Arabian Peninsula (AQAP); and weapons training.[14]

Tamerlan Tsarnaev's time in Dagestan radicalized his views on religion. As Dzhokhar spent more time with his brother, he underwent a similar transformation. The more they discussed the relationship between Islam and the West, the more irate they became. In short time, both began contemplating violent jihad.

* * *

After Tamerlan Tsarnaev and his younger brother, Dzhokhar, devised designs for a strike against the American homeland, the siblings

scoured the Internet for instructions on how to construct an improvised explosive device (IED). It didn't take much searching. *Inspire*,
an online magazine affiliated with al Qaeda, had published an article
titled, "How to Make a Bomb in the Kitchen of Your Mom"—a step-by-
step guide for designing a crude IED from readily-available materials.[15]

The Tsarnaev brothers decided to strike on July 4, 2013.[16] They
knew that the symbolism of hitting the United States on its most
revered national holiday would not be lost on Americans. But the
brothers were surprised at how simple and quick it was to put together
fully functional, crude IEDs. Ready to go months in advance, they
opted to attack sooner. They concluded that the Boston Marathon
provided the perfect opportunity.

Carrying backpacks loaded with homemade pressure-cooker
bombs, the Tsarnaev brothers walked nonchalantly among the spectators cheering marathon runners. On Boylston Street, the two men
separated and proceeded to locations that were roughly a block
apart. Unslinging their backpacks and resting them on the sidewalk,
they stood around briefly, observing the race, before inconspicu-
ously departing—leaving their remotely detonated bombs behind.

Despite sustaining injuries from the attack, Bill Iffrig stood up and
completed the race. Many others on Boylston Street were not so fortunate. Tamerlan's bomb—the initial blast that knocked Iffrig to the
ground—killed a woman who was awaiting her boyfriend to cross
the finish line. Seconds later, Dzhokhar's device claimed the lives of
two other spectators—a graduate student from China and an eight-
year-old boy. In addition to leaving three dead, the two IEDs seriously injured approximately sixty others, several of whom required
amputations.[17]

Security cameras captured the Tsarnaevs in the act, prompting
an intense search for the fugitives. In the early hours of April 19, the
siblings exchanged gunfire with police in nearby Watertown.[18] After
watching Tamerlan get shot in the skirmish, Dzhokhar hopped into a
stolen car and fled the scene, inadvertently striking his dying brother
with the getaway vehicle.[19] Later that evening, authorities located

the injured Dzhokhar hiding in a boat parked in a Watertown resident's backyard. After a tense standoff, he surrendered, bringing the manhunt to an end. An examination of the boat uncovered a note left behind by Dzhokhar explaining why the brothers perpetrated the attack:

> He who Allah guides no one can misguide. A[llah Ak]bar!
>   The U.S. Government is killing our innocent civilians but most of you already know that. . . . I can't stand to see such evil go unpunished, we Muslims are one body, you hurt one you hurt us all. . . .
>   Stop killing our innocent people and we will stop.[20]

For purposes of tracking attacks, the National Counter-Terrorism Center (NCTC) defines terrorism as "premeditated, politically motivated violence perpetrated against noncombatant targets by subnational groups or clandestine agents."[21] As Dzhokhar Tsarnaev's writings confirmed, the attack on the Boston Marathon was indisputably an act of terrorism.

The news media ran with the story, calling it "the worst terrorist attack" and "the deadliest terrorist attack" on American soil since 9/11.[22] One problem with this though: Both characterizations are wrong. A far worse and deadlier terrorist attack had occurred four years earlier at Fort Hood, Texas.

SOLDIER OF ALLAH

Right around lunchtime on Thursday, November 5, 2009, Maj. Nidal Malik Hasan, a US Army psychiatrist, entered the Soldier Readiness Processing Center at Fort Hood and reminded us that, while we often associate terrorism with bombs, guns in the hands of violent extremists can often be deadlier. Locating an empty table, he sat down and bowed his head in what seemed like a moment of prayer. A short time later, he stood up and drew a handgun from his military-issue cargo pants. Shouting "Allahu Akbar!" Hasan opened fire on nearby GIs, who were awaiting predeployment medical exams.[23]

Caught in the chaos of what many initially thought was a training exercise, the soldiers trapped in the large room had mere seconds to act. Reactions varied: sprinting for an exit; hitting the deck and crawling to a nearby table or cubicle for cover; playing dead. Many prayed. A few rushed the shooter, throwing furniture at him; heroic maneuvers that, sadly, resulted in every single one of those brave individuals getting shot.

Sgt. First Class Maria Guerra, the noncommissioned officer in charge of the medical department at the processing center, was in her office when she heard Hasan yell "God is great!" in Arabic. Her first thought was, "Who is yelling in my building?" The question became moot a second later, when she heard the distinct sound of gunfire. Instinct kicked in, and she ran toward the commotion. "Soldiers and civilians were running, running and screaming . . . and all I could hear was rapid fire," she testified at a court-martial hearing.[24] From the doorway where she took cover, she witnessed the initial barrage. She watched Hasan reload three times. He was "very efficiently dropping his magazine and coming up with another magazine—I mean, it was seconds. Down came the magazine, up came another one . . . he was firing at anyone who was moving and anyone who was trying to get out of the building." When Hasan turned toward her direction, Guerra retreated back into her office.[25]

As many witnesses testified, Hasan intentionally passed over civilians, targeting only men and women in uniform. One survivor, civilian immunization specialist Theodore Coukoulis, recollected how the gunman crossed the room, methodically searching for wounded and immobile soldiers to finish off. There were so many spent cartridges on the ground that Hasan couldn't avoid stepping on them. After a while, several shell casings lodged into the treads of Hasan's boots, telegraphing his comings and goings with a distinct "clack, clack, clack" sound.[26]

Eventually, Hasan exited the building to hunt for additional GIs. Outside, he was confronted by Fort Hood police. The first officer on scene was Kimberly Munley. Darting out of her patrol car, she sprinted toward to the processing center while trying to line up a shot at Hasan. The gunman was in front of her, but so too were several individuals attempting to flee the onslaught. Hasan shot at her. When she had a clean shot, she returned fire. The two exchanged rounds, but suddenly her gun jammed. Hasan hit her twice in the leg. The second bullet shattered her femur into 120 pieces, sending her toppling to the ground. She was a sitting duck as the gunman approached. Desperate, she tried to fix her handgun but couldn't. When Hasan got right up to her, Munley locked eyes with him: "He had a determined look on his face. Solemn. No expression."

Hasan kicked the weapon out of her hands and raised his gun, only to notice that it too was malfunctioning. Unlike Munley, he was able to unjam it, by which time he had spotted another police officer on scene, which forced Hasan to move toward cover.[27] Seconds later, Munley's colleague Sgt. Mark Todd ordered Hasan to drop his gun. Hasan turned and opened fire on Todd. From his position of cover, Todd got off five shots. It was enough. Four of Todd's rounds struck Hasan, with one hitting his spine and instantly paralyzing him. The rampage was over.[28]

When Hasan moved his shooting spree outside, Sgt. Guerra sprang into action, racing toward the main entrance and securing the double doors shut with her belt so the gunman couldn't reenter the building.

"Nurses and medics get the fuck out here now! We have soldiers bleeding!" She was barking orders at the top of her lungs. "Triage! Triage everyone! Let's go!"

Hasan had fired his gun so many times that the smoke had clouded the otherwise-bright room, making it dark inside. To further complicate rescue efforts, the overwhelming smell of gunpowder was sickening and the pools of blood on the floor made conditions slippery. But the medical team grabbed supplies and ran to the injured. Guerra took it upon herself to do the unenviable task of separating the dead from the wounded by checking for vitals and marking the deceased with a blue letter "D" on their foreheads.

"If they are dead, you've got to move on!" she ordered.[29]

By the time the scene was finally cleared, the tragedy's toll had reached forty-five gunshot casualties, thirteen of them fatal.[30] Investigators eventually determined that the carnage was produced by a single semiautomatic handgun—an FN Herstal 5.7 equipped with two trajectory-guiding lasers for accuracy. The US Army's Criminal Investigative Division (CID) recovered 214 spent shell casings—146 inside and 68 outside. CID agents also found six empty magazines inside the processing center. Another seven loaded magazines, containing a total of 172 bullets, were seized from Hasan's person after Sgt. Todd placed him under arrest.[31]

With the how understood, authorities turned to the why. What was Hasan's motive? Why did he go on a rampage that targeted his fellow soldiers? In particular, was this an act of terrorism? In the years immediately following the shooting, Hasan remained largely silent. But investigators combing through records uncovered that Hasan had grown increasingly radicalized following the onset of the Iraq War. Piecing the bits of evidence together, law enforcement started to see a bigger picture.

As a psychiatrist, Hasan often treated soldiers returning from battle. Hearing the horrors of combat seemed to tax him greatly. His secondary trauma left him disillusioned with the wars in Afghanistan and Iraq. In particular, he became incensed by the abuses that his patients admitted to perpetrating in the field.[32] In 2007, Hasan delivered a presentation suggesting that America's military campaigns were wars on Islam.[33] He also e-mailed the radical Muslim cleric Anwar al-Awlaki—the same person whom the Tsarnaev brothers would later turn to for religious guidance—to inquire into whether a Muslim serviceman killing his fellow soldiers would be considered a martyr and whether "indiscriminately killing civilians" was permissible under Islam. None of these red flags, however, caught the attention of the appropriate authorities.[34]

According to relatives, Hasan wanted to leave the army—even offering to pay back the money he received for his medical education—but his request for an early discharge was denied. In 2009, Hasan's worst fears materialized when he learned that he was being deployed to Afghanistan—a decision that left him "mortified."[35] As part of the transition, he was sent to Fort Hood for predeployment processing. While there, he experienced harassment for his religious views. In one incident, a fellow soldier living in the same apartment complex vandalized Hasan's car, causing extensive damage to the vehicle. The offender, who had just returned from Iraq, told authorities that he objected to Hasan's beliefs and was especially irked with the "Allah is Love" bumper sticker on Hasan's car.[36]

For Hasan, encountering servicemen holding negative opinions of Muslims was hardly new. Many of the soldiers under his care had expressed such sentiments. In fact, after arriving at Fort Hood, Hasan met with legal advisors and requested that some of his patients be investigated for prosecution, alleging that their actions in battle constituted war crimes. His requests were never pursued, however, reportedly because the evidence he offered to provide would be disclosed in violation of doctor-patient confidentiality.[37]

On August 1, 2009, with his disenchantment with the military continuing to mount, Hasan walked into Guns Galore in Killeen, Texas, to purchase a handgun. His only requirement, according to a fellow soldier in the store at the time: "the most technologically advanced handgun on the market" capable of receiving large-capacity magazines. After easily clearing a background check, Hasan walked out with his FN Herstal 5.7—the same weapon he used to kill thirteen and wound another thirty-two at Fort Hood.[38]

Nidal Hasan finally confirmed his terrorist motives when, during his court-martial, he admitted to perpetrating the attack in order to protect the Taliban from imminent danger.[39] Acting as his own attorney, Hasan insisted that killing American soldiers awaiting deployment to Afghanistan was justifiable under the legal doctrine of "defense of others," which permits the use of lethal force to save the lives of innocent people in harm's way.[40] In documents sent to Fox News shortly thereafter, he implied his actions were further driven by his anger with America's war on Islam—"the illegal and immoral aggression against Muslims, their religion and their lands." In several places, he signed his statements with the abbreviation "SoA"—Soldier of Allah.[41]

In August 2013, a jury of Hasan's military peers found him guilty of thirteen counts of murder and thirty-two counts of attempted murder. He was subsequently sentenced to death for his act of terror.[42]

From his jail cell at Fort Leavenworth, Kansas, where he awaits the exhaustion of his appeals, Hasan continues to espouse hatred and political violence, most recently declaring his allegiance to the Islamic State in Iraq and Syria (ISIS) and, in a separate letter sent to Pope Francis, warning the Vatican of a coming jihad against non-Muslims.[43]

Nidal Hasan perpetrated a far deadlier terrorist attack than the Boston Marathon bombing. To put the damage Hasan caused in perspective, armed with a single handgun, he killed over four times the number of people the two Tsarnaev brothers were able to slay with two separate bombs. Hasan's rampage is a prime example of how, in the current era, no single act of violence produces more fatalities on American soil than the mass shooting—and the assault on Fort Hood isn't even the deadliest terrorist attack in the United States since 9/11.

IN A UNIQUE CLASS

As exemplified by the Fort Hood and San Bernardino massacres, mass shootings pose a unique and troubling threat to American public safety. But are they presently the worst form of violence? To answer this, let's take a look at the deadliest acts of intentional violence from the past decade. As table 3.1 displays, all of the incidents on the list are mass shootings.[44]

What's missing in table 3.1 is as equally illuminating as what's included. For instance, conspicuously absent is the ever-frightening—but practically impossible—detonation of a nuclear device. So too is the release of a fatal biological agent. Even the explosion of a bomb didn't make the list. In the past decade, no other willful violent assault surpasses the mass shooting in terms of lethality, putting this vicious form of gun violence in a unique class.

Table 3.1, of course, only reflects the past decade. The Virginia Tech massacre that claimed thirty-two lives is far from the deadliest act of criminal violence in American history. That distinction belongs to the 9/11 attack. Critics might dismiss my concern about mass shootings as the opinion of someone who lacks perspective. After all, nearly three thousand dead is astronomically greater—and therefore graver—than thirty-two dead. But doesn't arguing this without acknowledging that the United States instituted drastic policy changes after 9/11—for all practical purposes preventing anyone from pulling off a hijacking of such magnitude—display a more fundamental lack of perspective? If you've flown in a commercial airliner since 9/11, then you know that pirating passenger planes in American airspace—let alone turning them into flying missiles—is a thing of the past. Mass shootings, on the other hand, remain an ever-present danger.

Table 3.1. The Deadliest Acts of Violence in the United States, 2006–2015.

Deaths	Incident Type	Date	Perpetrator(s)	City	State
32	Mass Shooting	4/16/2007	Seung Hui Cho	Blacksburg	VA
27	Mass Shooting	12/14/2014	Adam Lanza	Newtown	CT
14	Mass Shooting	12/2/2015	Syed Rizwan Farook and Tashfeen Malik	San Bernardino	CA
13	Mass Shooting	4/3/2009	Jiverly Wong	Binghamton	NY
13	Mass Shooting	11/5/2009	Nidal Hasan	Fort Hood	TX
12	Mass Shooting	7/20/2012	James Holmes	Aurora	CO
12	Mass Shooting	9/16/2013	Aaron Alexis	Washington	DC
10	Mass Shooting	3/10/2009	Michael McLendon	Kinston, Samson, and Geneva	AL
9	Mass Shooting	5/17/2015	Undetermined	Waco	TX
9	Mass Shooting	6/17/2015	Dylann Roof	Charleston	SC
9	Mass Shooting	10/1/2015	Christopher Harper-Mercer	Roseburg	OR
8	Mass Shooting	12/24/2008	Bruce Pardo	Covina	CA
8	Mass Shooting	12/5/2007	Robert Hawkins	Omaha	NE
8	Mass Shooting	3/29/2009	Robert Stewart	Carthage	NC
8	Mass Shooting	1/19/2010	Christopher Speight	Appomattox	VA
8	Mass Shooting	8/3/2010	Omar Thornton	Manchester	CT
8	Mass Shooting	10/12/2011	Scott Dekraai	Seal Beach	CA
8	Mass Shooting	8/8/2015	David Conley	Houston	TX

The other criticism that might follow is that the carnage caused by mass shootings is a small subset of the damage inflicted by gun violence. Shouldn't I be more focused on overall gun homicides? Over eleven thousand Americans are murdered annually by someone with a firearm—a death toll that's the equivalent of nearly four 9/11s.[45] Mass shootings are, by contrast, "rare events." At least that's what pundits tell us. Gun-rights advocate Emily Miller, for instance, decried over-reaction to such acts of "great rarity," which only "account for an average of 18 lives a year in this country."[46] Conservative columnist John Fund also tried to minimize public concern, asserting that "the chances of being killed in a mass shooting are about what they are for being struck by lightning."[47]

There are two problems with this line of reasoning. First, downplaying the need to address mass shootings because they purportedly occur infrequently is like insisting that there was no need, back in 2001, to get worked up about 9/11—a far more uncommon occurrence. Think back to how you felt in the immediate aftermath of 9/11. Did you demand policy adjustments to make us safer following al Qaeda's strike against our nation? Or did you dismiss the threat of terrorism on the grounds that you were more likely to be struck by lightning? Can you imagine the administration of George W. Bush reacting by telling the public that there was no need to implement significant changes, because such deadly acts of terrorism on American soil are rare?

Discounting a danger based simply on its rate of incidence displays a fundamental misunderstanding about how the American political system operates. In the United States, government usually doesn't implement major changes in response to frequent, common events. Policy—especially security policy—is instead largely driven by rare events, which tend to be of greater salience and consequence than routine occurrences.

As humans, our minds operate according to what psychologists call the availability heuristic—a process by which our judgments are heavily biased by salient and dramatic incidents. Nobel laureate Daniel Kahneman explained the phenomenon this way:

> [Media] coverage is itself biased toward novelty and poignancy. The
> media do not just shape what the public is interested in, but also

are shaped by it. Editors cannot ignore the public's demands that certain topics and viewpoints receive extensive coverage. Unusual events (such as botulism) attract disproportionate attention and are consequently perceived as less unusual than they really are.[48]

Availability biases lead us to naturally focus on extreme events, especially when those events involve risk, as public-safety threats necessarily do. These extreme incidents capture media attention and, in turn, provoke society and political leaders. Let's not forget, elected officials watch the same news broadcasts that the general public watches. As a result, rare events that monopolize media coverage usually serve as the most influential catalysts for policy change.

When it comes to gun violence, therefore, the American people don't learn of most shootings, whereas many mass shootings are often front-page items, sometimes dominating media coverage for weeks.[49] The same holds for other types of extreme events. Most storms are not memorable to the population as a whole. But when a hurricane results in tragedy, it resonates. Similarly, over one thousand aviation accidents occur annually, yet the majority of people likely can't identify them. But I suspect they can readily recall mishaps like the crash of TWA Flight 800 and Malaysian Airlines Flight 370. Even terrorist strikes on American soil tend to go unnoticed unless they involve some sort of sensational element. How many terrorist attacks can you name that have occurred in the United States since 9/11? The Fort Hood, Boston Marathon, and San Bernardino attacks for sure. Perhaps a few others. But I'm fairly confident you didn't list over one hundred incidents. And yet there have been that many attacks.[50]

While we're on the subject, it's not just the general public. Elected officials are also unaware of many of these incidents. If people can't identify all of these individual dangers, how can they be expected to press for political adjustments to reduce such risks? Simple. They react to the most memorable ones, the standouts. Given that availability bias frequently sways thinking, it's only natural that policy responds to outliers.

After all, can you recall a radical shift in counter-terrorism strategy occurring in response to the routine and frequent attacks orchestrated by animal-rights extremists against scientific facilities to protest the inhumane treatment of their laboratory subjects? How about a complete overhaul of emergency management procedures resulting from everyday heavy storms that typically produce little more than minor damage to properties in their paths? Now, compare how society reacts to typical occurrences with how it reacts to infrequent events of great magnitude. The entire national-security posture of the United States changed after 9/11. Similarly, emergency management was reconstituted as a homeland security matter following Hurricane Katrina. Yet, to build on John Fund's comparison, lightning strikes Americans with greater frequency than 9/11-like terrorist attacks or Katrina-like superstorms.

Extreme single events like 9/11 and Hurricane Katrina are outliers, and in politics, outliers matter most.

There's a good reason why the United States devotes a huge pool of resources defending against an isolated nuclear attack, despite the fact that there are no terrorists in the world capable of striking the American homeland with such weaponry of mass destruction.[51] Would you want the government to chance it even though the odds of such an attack are as close to zero as any act of violence can get? Or would you prefer the government maintain its vigilance against such an extremely unlikely incident, given the magnitude of damage it would inflict?

What holds for nuclear terrorism holds for mass shootings. It's precisely because both are uniquely disturbing forms of violence that they're worthy of attention and action. It's the *outlier effect*, and in the public sector—especially in the area of homeland security—it's one of the most powerful factors at play in driving policy.

The second problem with dismissing concern over mass shootings as nothing more than alarmist over-reaction to incidents of "great rarity" is that the rarity of such gun attacks is not as great as some commentators would have us believe.

One of the most hotly contested points pertaining to mass shootings involves their numbers. Particularly, how often are these extreme acts of gun violence committed in the United States; how many lives do they tend to claim; and are they increasing or decreasing in frequency and lethality? Because the experts can't agree on a definition, it's near impossible to agree on the frequency, lethality, and trajectory of mass shootings. When disagreement exists, it's an open invitation to politicize a controversy. And this is exactly what has happened with regard to mass shootings. The two different sides of the political spectrum have embraced the studies that help advance their political agendas, while attacking the ones that lend support to what they oppose.[52]

People who lean left politically are more likely to see gun rampages as occurring enough times and hurting enough people to warrant drastic policy changes. The most disturbing finding of all, according to liberals, is that mass shootings are on the rise. Some even insist that this tragic form of gun violence has reached epidemic status in the past decade. In support of these conclusions, they highlight two recent reports: one from a progressive news outlet and the other from a gun-control organization.

The study of mass shootings published by *Mother Jones* following the cinema massacre in Aurora has been instrumental in bringing new attention to rampage violence. The magazine has identified eighty mass shootings, claiming a total of 621 lives, since 1982. Over half of these incidents have occurred since 2006.[53] When a team of Harvard researchers took the data compiled by *Mother Jones* and analyzed it for frequency, they found that between 1982 and 2011, mass shootings occurred at an average rate of one every two hundred days. Since then, they have been occurring at an average rate of one every sixty-four days, which is triple the rate.[54]

As I noted in chapter 2, *Mother Jones* arbitrarily excludes many incidents. Employing a less restrictive definition of any shooting in which "at least four people were murdered with a gun," Everytown for Gun Safety, the gun-control organization established by former New York City mayor Michael Bloomberg, documented 133 mass shootings that killed a combined 673 individuals in a six-and-a-half-year period (January 2009–July 2015).[55] Interestingly, despite identifying almost twice as many multiple-victim gun attacks as *Mother Jones*, in one-sixth the time no less, both analyses agree that mass shootings of late have been occurring at the fairly rapid rate of one every two months.

Of course, not everyone agrees with the conclusions of *Mother*

Jones and Everytown. In particular, conservatives who align themselves with gun-rights organizations have been quick to level criticism
against studies that support increased gun control. Those who lean
right often argue that multiple-victim gun attacks are rare events that
result in a miniscule number of deaths annually. They've crunched
their own numbers—and what their data show is that, like most other
forms of homicide, gun massacres are on the wane. The commentators in this camp suggest that if mass shootings are claiming few lives
and occurring with less frequency, then our attention and resources
should be devoted to more pressing societal problems.

One of the more prominent voices in this debate is conservative
media personality Glenn Beck:

> Gun massacres are not becoming more common. There is a per-
> ception that we have a sudden crisis . . . but perception does not
> equal reality. . . .
>
> The massacres that most of us hear about and react to—the
> Columbines, Virginia Techs, Auroras, and Newtowns of the world—
> are extremely uncommon events. . . .
>
> [People] who claim that mass killings are on the rise never
> bother to look into the facts. Instead they rely on reports like the
> one done by *Mother Jones* . . . without questioning their method-
> ology. But that's a big mistake, because the *Mother Jones* report does
> not stand up to any kind of scrutiny, let alone academic standards.[56]

Beck's correct. Given the stakes at hand, studies addressing mass
shootings—including mine—should survive the test of scrutiny. And
he's also right about the *Mother Jones* analysis. It's flawed because, as
I demonstrated in the previous chapter, it employs rather arbitrary
selection criteria. As Beck concurs, *Mother Jones* fails to "look at the
data far more broadly and take into account all gun-related mass killings."[57] He points us instead to the findings of two researchers: James
Fox and John Lott.[58] One problem for Beck, though: while he was
willing to hold *Mother Jones* to a high standard, he seems to have given
Fox and Lott a free pass.

For instance, Fox, one the country's foremost academic authorities
on mass murder, maintains that "mass shootings have not increased in

number or in overall body count, at least not over the past several decades."[59] The problem with Fox's conclusion is that it's based on a data set that, like the *Mother Jones* data set, is flawed. Rather than compile a data set by sifting through countless media reports from the last four to five decades (which I admit is extremely time-consuming), Fox instead took a shortcut and based his analysis on readily available Supplementary Homicide Reports (SHRs).[60] Every year, numerous state and local law enforcement agencies voluntarily submit SHRs to the FBI. These SHRs contain data such as the date and location of murders, the types of weapons employed, and the demographic backgrounds of the perpetrators and the victims. This information is coded and then made available to the public for analysis. In theory, it's a wonderful resource. In practice, it's of limited value.

When I first started studying mass shootings, I turned to SHRs for data. What better resource than an official government data set? It was all right there, in one place and in an easy-to-analyze format. Except it wasn't. It turns out that many murders, let alone fatal mass shootings, never make the FBI's books. Some jurisdictions like Florida and the federal government, for instance, don't participate in the SHR system.[61] That's correct: many federal law enforcement agencies don't contribute to it even though it's their data bank. Others, while encouraging their police departments to submit SHRs, don't require it—leading to numerous omissions, including the high-profile Sandy Hook massacre.[62] And, as if leaving out cases isn't enough, many of the reports that are on file are riddled with errors, including a few crimes listed as homicides, although they were actually attempted homicides where no one actually died. In fact, when I ran the actual number of gun massacres against the SHR entries for shootings that resulted in six or more deaths for the time period 1976–2011, I found an error rate of 40 percent—an exorbitantly high score.[63] Because Fox relies on unreliable data, his conclusions about mass shootings warrant a heavy degree of skepticism.[64]

So too do the conclusions of John Lott, who employs arbitrary criteria in a manner akin to *Mother Jones* in order to exclude certain mass shootings from his analyses.

Why does Beck dismiss the work of *Mother Jones* and yet embrace that of Lott, even though both, in Beck's words, fail to "take into account all gun-related mass killings"? The answer is simple: politics. Lott's assessments bolster Beck's ideologically driven arguments regarding guns in America.

As I discuss in great detail in chapter 5, Lott is a favorite "scholar" of many pro-gun conservatives.[65] Now a Fox News commentator and president of the Crime Prevention Research Center (CPRC)—a euphemistically named gun-rights advocacy organization—he has devoted decades to promoting increased ownership of firearms as a way to lower crime.[66] In 2014, the CPRC issued its first report, an analysis of mass shootings authored by Lott that was largely a point-by-point attack of Everytown's report. The primary gripe: Everytown "greatly exaggerated their number [of incidents] by including gang killings and shootings as part of some other crime (robberies etc.) as well as residential killings involving families."[67] When Lott applied his more restrictive definition, he found that during the same time period, there were only twenty-five mass shootings, resulting in 180 cumulative fatalities.[68] By changing parameters, Lott recalculated the overall number of multiple-victim shootings between January 2009 and July 2014 to be 77 percent less and the number of total deaths to be 68 percent less than Everytown's tallies. Lott drew on this drastic difference to conclude, "shootings, where the shooter intends to commit mass murder in a public place, has [sic] not 'exploded' over the last few years, as frequently claimed in the media."[69]

Of course, redefining the problem is a bit disingenuous on Lott's part. As I argued in chapter 2, mass shootings are best viewed in broad terms. The fewer arbitrary exclusions we apply, the more accurate our understanding will be. If there's a criticism to be leveled at the Everytown report, it's that its time frame is too short to allow for long-term trend analysis. It's hard to say that mass shootings are on the rise or decline based on just a few years of data. Yet, instead of raising this issue, Lott fell into the same trap by applying the identical time frame.[70]

So who's right and who's wrong? If only there was a way to subject these studies to intense scrutiny so that we could weed out the mistakes, exaggerations, and outright falsehoods, in order to come up with accurate data and trends.

Fortunately, there is.

THE REAL NUMBERS

It's easy to be dismissive of pundits and partisans, even ones with *PhD* after their names like John Lott. After all, they often take to the airwaves, the print media, and the blogosphere to impart a variety of assertions about rampage violence, usually with little consequence for being erroneous, biased, or intentionally deceptive. But there's one place where claims don't get a free pass: the courts. Under oath and subject to cross-examination, "experts" aren't afforded an escape from scrutiny during litigation. Case in point: the legal battle over the constitutionality of Colorado's recent ban on large-capacity magazines.

After a mentally disturbed man wielding an assault weapon armed with a 100-round magazine killed twelve and wounded an additional fifty-eight cinema patrons in Aurora, Colorado, the state legislature enacted tight restrictions on the sale, possession, and transfer of any magazines that held more than fifteen rounds of ammunition. The objective of the statute was to reduce the carnage of shooting sprees by limiting the number of bullets a semiautomatic weapon can fire in a single feed. In 2013, this law came under attack when a group of thirty plaintiffs—a combination of gun-rights organizations, firearms dealers, and individual gun owners—asked a federal court to strike it down, arguing that it violated the Second Amendment. At the crux of their case, the plaintiffs asserted that mass shootings are rare to begin with, so magazine restrictions are likely to have little to no positive impact on the casualty tolls of gun attacks. Believing that the ban would have a negligible impact on gun violence, they insisted that it unnecessarily infringed on their rights to lawfully own large-capacity magazines.[71]

To help establish their claim, the plaintiffs in *Colorado Outfitters Association et al. v. Hickenlooper* put criminologist Gary Kleck on the stand to make a key point: "Mass shootings are extremely rare."[72] Perhaps you'll recall the name from the previous chapter. Kleck was the first scholar to define and study mass shootings as a unique subset of gun violence. In the past decade, he has become one of the go-to scholars for the gun-rights movement, earning $350 an hour as an expert witness who testifies against certain gun-control measures.[73]

When Kleck conducted his initial study of mass shootings in 1997, he defined them as "incident[s] in which six or more victims were shot dead with a gun, or twelve or more total were wounded."[74] He has since broadened his definition to "shooting[s] in which more than six people were shot, fatally or nonfatally, in a single incident."[75] While Kleck's conceptualization still maintains a fairly high casualty threshold—remember the emerging consensus is that mass shootings are acts of violence where four or more people are shot—he testified that in the nearly two decades between January 1994 and July 2013, there were only fifty-seven mass shootings in the United States. With fewer than three mass shootings per year, on average, Kleck concluded that any such attack was a "rare event."[76]

On cross-examination, Assistant Attorney General for Colorado Matthew Grove began with a simple question: "So if you missed a quarter of the data, that might be a problem, right?"[77] Kleck admitted it would. When the time came to discuss Kleck's analysis, Grove asked: "You testified earlier that you considered *all* mass shooting incidents that met your criteria of seven or more killed or wounded, correct?" Again, Kleck confirmed Grove's leading question, acknowledging that there were only fifty-seven such attacks in the twenty-year period he examined.[78] Grove then turned to the data set. Handing Kleck a binder full of exhibits, Grove had Kleck read through each document. Here's a sampling from the transcripts of how this played out:

Q. Please take a moment to read Exhibit 101. . . . This article is entitled, "Tech worker charged in seven deaths at Massachusetts firm." Correct?

A. That's correct.

Q. And in the second paragraph, it says, "Prosecutors accuse McDermott of acting with premeditation and without mercy when colleagues were shot repeatedly with a 12-gauge shotgun and an assault rifle fed with a 60-round magazine," correct?

A. Yes.

Q. And the next paragraph says, "The seven Edgewater Technology employees were shot a combined 30 times," correct?

A. Correct.

Q. This meets your criteria for inclusion in your report, correct?

A. It does.

Q. And it was not included in [your expert report], right?

A. Correct. . . .

Q. Let's turn to Exhibit 102. . . . Title of this is, "Factory feud is cited in shooting in Indiana." Do you need a moment to read this?

A. Yes, please. Okay.

Q. So the very first sentence of this says, "The factory worker who killed a co-owner of the factory and wounded six others before fatally shooting himself was apparently angered over a dispute." So that's one dead, six wounded, correct?

A. That's correct.

Q. That meets your criteria?

A. Yes, it does.

Q. And you didn't include this in your report, did you?

A. No.[79]

This painful cross-examination continued for approximately forty-five minutes; each time, Kleck confirmed that he had omitted the specific mass shooting from his inquiry.[80] When Grove was finished, he had successfully pointed out that, even under Kleck's high casualty threshold, there were at least twenty-nine mass shootings that the plaintiff's expert failed to report. As Kleck admitted on the stand, "Yes, it's about 50 percent of the ones I analyzed."[81] Earlier, Kleck had testified that investigations that overlooked a quarter of the cases were problematic. Grove had just established that Kleck's analysis—which disregarded at least a third of the data (twenty-nine out of eighty-six cases)—was flawed by his own standards.

Grove followed up by reminding Kleck that, in his official expert report submitted to the court, he asserted "all [mass] shooting incidents were examined."

Kleck backtracked on his claim: "Yes, I did say all. Had I been more precise, I would have said, all that I knew of, or all that I could discover, or words to that effect."

"'All' would suggest every one, though, right?"

"Well, to me, it suggested all that I knew about," Kleck replied in one final attempt to salvage his testimony. But it was too late.[82]

On June 26, 2014, the judge in the case issued a fifty-page ruling upholding Colorado's restrictions on large-capacity magazines. Kleck's name, let alone his claims, never appeared in the decision. Not even in passing. Meanwhile, the court expressly stated that it accepted the views of the state's expert witness, Jeffrey Zax, who offered testimony that at times directly contradicted Kleck. It was a signal. Like the pro-gun-rights lawsuit itself, the argument that mass shootings occur too infrequently to merit legislative action was dismissed.[83]

Testifying under oath, Gary Kleck was forced to acknowledge that mass shootings occur with greater frequency than his research confirmed. In fact, they take place more often than most Americans probably realize—at a higher rate of incidence than even many in the gun-control camp claim. The real numbers are actually quite disturbing.

When I started conducted research for this book, I decided to collect information on every known gun massacre that took place in the United States over the past fifty years. While it was a labor-intensive process that required a full year of searching through a variety of data sets and news banks, I came up with 111 attacks that resulted in six or more people—not including the perpetrator(s)—*dying* as a result of gunshot wounds (see table 3.2).[84] As these are the deadliest gun attacks of the past five decades, they are the most disconcerting, deserving special attention.

The statistics paint a troubling picture. Since 1966, gun massacres have claimed 904 lives (see figure 3.1). What's most alarming about these extreme acts of violence is that they're taking place with greater frequency, with the sharpest increase in deaths occurring in the past decade (see figure 3.2).[85] Specifically, over one-third (39 out of 111) of gun massacres during the past fifty years occurred in the past decade (2006–2015). That's a 160 percent increase from the previous decade, which only experienced fifteen high-fatality mass shootings (see figure 3.3). Equally disturbing, the total number of people killed in gun massacres in the past decade (349 out of 904) accounts for nearly 40 percent of all murders in such acts of violence during the same fifty-year span (see figure 3.4). This is a massive increase from the previous decade, when only 111 people died in such shootings. The past decade has clearly been the worst, exceeding the second worst (1976–1985) by way more than a third in terms of number of incidents and by more than double in terms of total deaths.[86] It's also the only decade to average roughly nine deaths per attack (see table 3.3).

Table 3.2. Gun Massacres in the United States, 1966–2015.

	Date	City	State	Perpetrator(s)	Deaths
1	8/1/1966	Austin	TX	Charles Whitman	14
2	8/26/1966	New Haven	CT	Arthur Davis	6
3	10/23/1967	Lock Haven	PA	Leo Held	6
4	3/16/1968	Ironwood	MI	Eric Pearson	7
5	6/25/1968	Good Hart	MI	Undetermined	6
6	12/19/1968	Napa	CA	Charles Bray	6
7	9/3/1971	Phoenix	AZ	John Freeman	7
8	6/21/1972	Cherry Hill	NJ	Edwin Grace	6
9	1/7/1973	New Orleans	LA	Mark Essex	7
10	6/21/1973	Palos Hills	IL	William Workman	7
11	4/22/1973	Los Angeles	CA	William Bonner	7
12	6/9/1973	Boston	MA	George O'Leary	6
13	11/4/1973	Cleveland	OH	Cyril Rovansek	7
14	2/18/1974	Fayette	MS	Frankie Lias	7
15	11/13/1974	Amityville	NY	Ronald DeFeo	6
16	3/30/1975	Hamilton	OH	James Ruppert	11
17	10/19/1975	Sutherland	NE	Erwin Simants	6
18	3/12/1976	Trevose	PA	George Geschwendt	6
19	7/12/1976	Fullerton	CA	Edward Allaway	7
20	7/23/1977	Klamath Falls	OR	DeWitt Henry	6
21	8/26/1977	Hackettstown	NJ	Emile Benoist	6
22	7/16/1978	Oklahoma City	OK	Harold Stafford, Roger Stafford, and Verna Stafford	6
23	1/3/1981	Delmar	IA	Gene Gilbert	6
24	1/7/1981	Richmond	VA	Artie Ray Cherry, Michael Finazzo, and Tyler Frndak	6
25	5/2/1981	Clinton	MD	Ronald Ellis	6
26	8/21/1981	Indianapolis	IN	King Bell	6
27	2/17/1982	Farwell	MI	Robert Haggart	7
28	8/9/1982	Grand Prairie	TX	John Parish	6
29	8/20/1982	Miami	FL	Carl Brown	8
30	9/7/1982	Craig	AK	Undetermined	8
31	9/25/1982	Wilkes-Barre	PA	George Banks	13
32	2/18/1983	Seattle	WA	Kwan Fai Mak and Benjamin Ng	13
33	3/3/1983	McCarthy	AK	Louis Hastings	6
34	10/11/1983	College Station and Hempstead	TX	Eliseo Moreno	6
35	4/15/1984	Brooklyn	NY	Christopher Thomas	10
36	5/19/1984	Manley Hot Springs	AK	Michael Silka	8
37	6/29/1984	Dallas	TX	Abdelkrim Belachheb	6
38	7/18/1984	San Ysidro	CA	James Huberty	21
39	10/18/1984	Evansville	IN	James Day	6
40	8/20/1986	Edmond	OK	Patrick Sherrill	14
41	12/8/1986	Oakland	CA	Rita Lewis and David Welch	6
42	2/5/1987	Flint	MI	Terry Morris	6
43	4/23/1987	Palm Bay	FL	William Cruse	6
44	7/12/1987	Tacoma	WA	Daniel Lynam	7
45	9/25/1987	Elkland	MO	James Schnick	7
46	12/30/1987	Algona	IA	Robert Dreesman	6
47	2/16/1988	Sunnyvale	CA	Richard Farley	7
48	9/14/1989	Louisville	KY	Joseph Wesbecker	8
49	6/18/1990	Jacksonville	FL	James Pough	9
50	1/26/1991	Chimayo	NM	Ricky Abeyta	7
51	8/9/1991	Waddell	AZ	Jonathan Doody and Alessandro Garcia	9
52	10/16/1991	Killeen	TX	George Hennard	23
53	11/7/1992	Morro Bay and Paso Robles	CA	Lynwood Drake	6
54	1/8/1993	Palatine	IL	James Degorski and Juan Luna	7

55	5/16/1993	Fresno	CA	Allen Heflin and Johnnie Malarkey	7
56	7/1/1993	San Francisco	CA	Gian Luigi Ferri	8
57	12/7/1993	Garden City	NY	Colin Ferguson	6
58	4/20/1999	Littleton	CO	Eric Harris and Dylan Klebold	13
59	7/12/1999	Atlanta	GA	Cyrano Marks	6
60	7/29/1999	Atlanta	GA	Mark Barton	9
61	9/15/1999	Fort Worth	TX	Larry Ashbrook	7
62	11/2/1999	Honolulu	HI	Byran Koji Uyesugi	7
63	12/26/2000	Wakefield	MA	Michael McDermott	7
64	12/28/2000	Philadelphia	PA	Shihean Black, Dawud Faruqi, Khalid Faruqi, and Bruce Veney	7
65	8/26/2002	Rutlegde	AL	Westley Harris	6
66	1/15/2003	Edinburg	TX	Humberto Garza, Robert Garza, Rodolfo Medrano, and Juan Ramirez	6
67	7/8/2003	Meridian	MS	Douglas Williams	6
68	8/27/2003	Chicago	IL	Salvador Tapia	6
69	3/12/2004	Fresno	CA	Marcus Wesson and Sebhrenah Wesson	9
70	11/21/2004	Birchwood	WI	Chai Soua Vang	6
71	3/12/2005	Brookfield	WI	Terry Ratzmann	7
72	3/21/2005	Red Lake	MN	Jeffrey Weise	9
73	1/30/2006	Goleta	CA	Jennifer San Marco	7
74	3/25/2006	Seattle	WA	Kyle Huff	6
75	6/1/2006	Indianapolis	IN	James Stewart and Desmond Turner	7
76	12/16/2006	Kansas City	KS	Hersel Isadore	6
77	4/16/2007	Blacksburg	VA	Seung Hui Cho	32
78	10/7/2007	Crandon	WI	Tyler Peterson	6
79	12/5/2007	Omaha	NE	Robert Hawkins	8
80	12/24/2007	Carnation	WA	Michele Anderson and Joseph McEnroe	6
81	2/7/2008	Kirkwood	MO	Charles Lee Thornton	6
82	9/2/2008	Alger	WA	Isaac Zamora	6
83	12/24/2008	Covina	CA	Bruce Pardo	8
84	1/27/2009	Los Angeles	CA	Ervin Lupoe	6
85	3/10/2009	Kinston, Samson, and Geneva	AL	Michael McLendon	10
86	3/29/2009	Carthage	NC	Robert Stewart	8
87	4/3/2009	Binghamton	NY	Jiverly Wong	13
00	11/5/2009	Fort Hood	TX	Nidal Hasan	13
89	1/19/2010	Appomattox	VA	Christopher Speight	8
90	8/3/2010	Manchester	CT	Omar Thornton	8
91	1/8/2011	Tucson	AZ	Jared Loughner	6
92	7/7/2011	Grand Rapids	MI	Rodrick Dantzler	7
93	8/7/2011	Copley Township	OH	Michael Hance	7
94	10/12/2011	Seal Beach	CA	Scott Dekraai	8
95	12/25/2011	Grapevine	TX	Aziz Yazdanpanah	6
96	4/2/2012	Oakland	CA	One Goh	7
97	7/20/2012	Aurora	CO	James Holmes	12
98	8/5/2012	Oak Creek	WI	Wade Page	6
99	9/27/2012	Minneapolis	MN	Andrew Engeldinger	6
100	12/14/2012	Newtown	CT	Adam Lanza	27
101	7/26/2013	Hialeah	FL	Pedro Vargas	6
102	9/16/2013	Washington	DC	Aaron Alexis	12
103	7/9/2014	Spring	TX	Ronald Lee Haskell	6
104	9/18/2014	Bell	FL	Don Spirit	7
105	2/26/2015	Tyrone	MO	Joseph Jesse Aldridge	7
106	5/17/2015	Waco	TX	Undetermined	9
107	6/17/2015	Charleston	SC	Dylann Roof	9
108	8/8/2015	Houston	TX	David Conley	8
109	10/1/2015	Roseburg	OR	Christopher Harper-Mercer	9
110	11/15/2015	Palestine	TX	William Hudson	6
111	12/2/2015	San Bernardino	CA	Syed Rizwan Farook and Tashfeen Malik	14

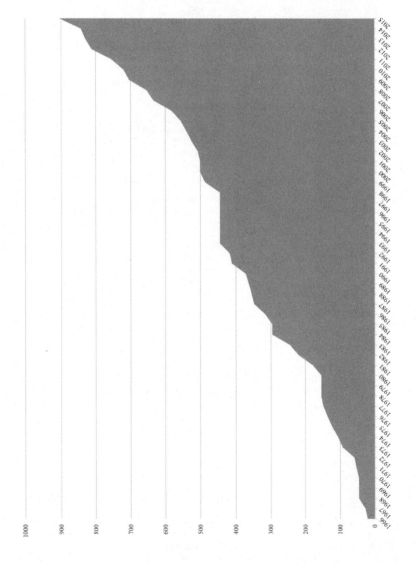

Fig. 3.1. Cumulative Death Toll of Gun Massacres in the United States, 1966–2015. Source: Table 3.2.

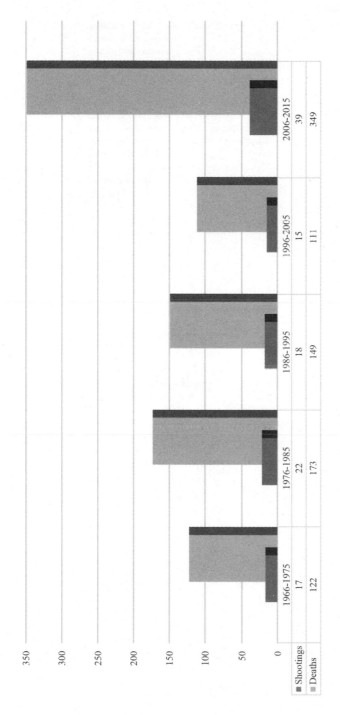

	1966-1975	1976-1985	1986-1995	1996-2005	2006-2015
Shootings	17	22	18	15	39
Deaths	122	173	149	111	349

Fig. 3.2. Gun Massacres in the United States by Decade, 1966–2015. Source: Table 3.2.

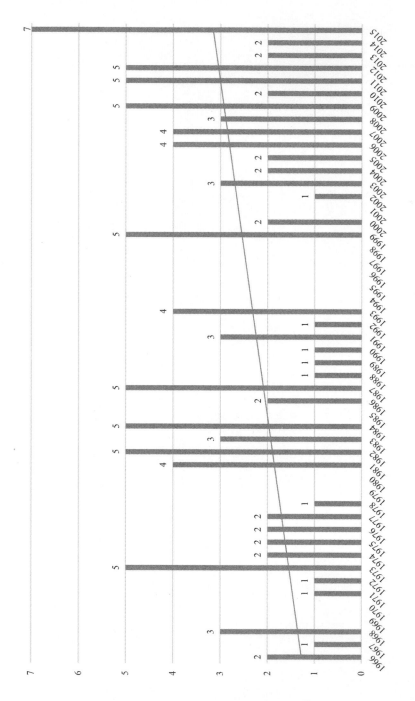

Fig. 3.3. Annual Number of Gun Massacres in the United States, 1966–2015. Source: Table 3.2.

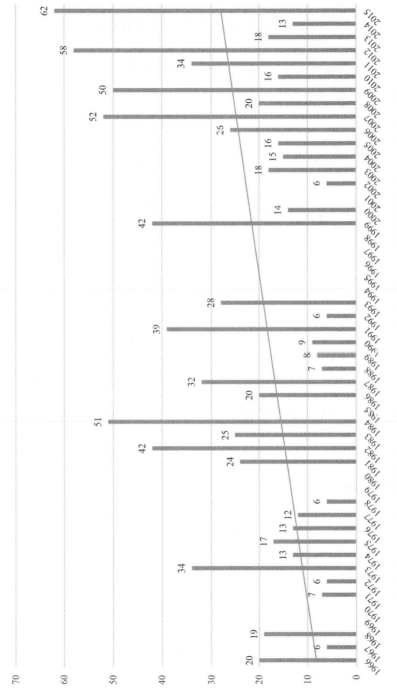

Fig. 3.4. Annual Death Toll of Gun Massacres in the United States, 1966–2015. Source: Table 3.2.

Table 3.3. Average Death Tolls of Gun Massacres in the United States by Ten-Year Period, 1966–2015.

Ten-Year Period	Average Death Toll Per Gun Massacre
1966–1975	7.2
1976–1985	7.9
1986–1995	8.3
1996–2005	7.4
2006–2015	8.9

A breakdown of the data shows how this disturbing pattern came to be. Until 2015, there has never been a year with more than five gun massacres. In 2015, there were seven gun massacres. Moreover, the past decade has experienced more "five-plus-shooting-years"[87] than any other decade (see figure 3.3). It's also the only decade with consecutive five-plus-shooting-years (2011 and 2012). When expanded to track four-plus-shooting-years, the past decade qualifies as the most disturbing ten-year-period, surpassing the next closest ten-year-period (1976–1985) by three additional years of four-plus gun massacres.

The past decade is also the only decade not to have had a year without a gun massacre. Every other decade under study had at least two years of reprieve from such heinous acts of gun violence—and the five-year period from 1994 to 1998 experienced no such shootings at all. In terms of lethality, the past decade again stands apart from the others. For instance, while there have been only five years that experienced fifty or more deaths as a result of gun massacres, four of those years were in the past decade (see figure 3.4). Indeed, 2015 is the deadliest year on record for murders resulting from gun massacres, with sixty-two combined fatalities. Furthermore, a comparison of the last two decades reveals an eight-fold increase in the number of double-digit fatality shootings (see table 3.4).

Between 1966 and 2015, the population of the United States has increased nearly 65 percent, from approximately 195 million people to over 320 million people. Yet even this demographic shift has failed to reverse the troubling trend in rampage violence, as evidenced by incidence rates, which assess the occurrence of attacks and fatalities relative to the population in a given time. Over the past ten years, gun massacres have taken place at an unprecedented rate of one for roughly every eight million residents and deaths have been incurred at a rate that exceeds one fatality for every one million residents (see table 3.5). Even when accounting for population growth, the past decade still stands out as the worst ten-year period of the last fifty years, marked by a rising trajectory that doesn't bode well for the coming decade (see figure 3.5).

Table 3.4. The Deadliest Mass Shootings in the United States, 1966–2015.

Death Toll	Date	Perpetrator(s)	City	State
32	4/16/2007	Seung Hui Cho	Blacksburg	VA
27	12/14/2014	Adam Lanza	Newtown	CT
23	10/16/1991	George Hennard	Killeen	TX
21	7/18/1984	James Huberty	San Ysidro	CA
14	8/1/1966	Charles Whitman	Austin	TX
14	8/20/1986	Patrick Sherrill	Edmond	OK
14	12/2/2015	Syed Rizwan Farook and Tashfeen Malik	San Bernardino	CA
13	9/25/1982	George Banks	Wilkes-Barre	PA
13	2/18/1983	Kwan Fai Mak and Benjamin Ng	Seattle	WA
13	4/20/1999	Eric Harris and Dylan Klebold	Littleton	CO
13	4/3/2009	Jiverly Wong	Binghamton	NY
13	11/5/2009	Nidal Hasan	Fort Hood	TX
12	7/20/2012	James Holmes	Aurora	CO
12	9/16/2013	Aaron Alexis	Washington	DC
11	3/30/1975	James Ruppert	Hamilton	OH
10	4/15/1984	Christopher Thomas	Brooklyn	NY
10	3/10/2009	Michael McLendon	Kinston, Samson, and Geneva	AL

At a time when modern emergency medicine can save the lives of most gunshot victims if they reach the hospital alive within the "golden hour," the death rate of mass casualty gun attacks should've gone down significantly in the past decade.[88] That this hasn't happened speaks to the danger mass shootings pose.

Table 3.5. Ten-Year Incidence Rates for Gun-Massacre Attacks and Deaths, 1966–2015.

Decade	Attack Rate	Death Rate
1966–1975	0.08	0.59
1976–1985	0.10	0.76
1986–1995	0.07	0.59
1996–2005	0.05	0.39
2006–2015	0.13	1.12

Note: Rates are calculated using the mean population estimates for the United States (in millions) over the applicable ten-year periods.

Source: Attack and death tolls are drawn from table 3.2. Population data are drawn from United States Census Bureau, "Population Estimates," www.census.gov/popest/index.html (accessed May 3, 2016).

Above, I argued that high-fatality mass shootings are now in a distinct class. This becomes abundantly clear when gun massacres are compared to other common forms of homicide. The most recent decade of available data illustrates that, while most forms of homicide continue to decline, gun-massacre deaths are heading in the opposite trajectory (see figure 3.6). This presents a troubling mystery: Why are such deadly shooting sprees on the rise when most other homicides are on the wane? Equally baffling, this increase is occurring despite a steady decrease in gun-ownership rates (see figures 3.7 and 3.8).[89] Even if we allow for the fact that the absolute number of households with firearms has consistently held at around forty million over the last forty years, it still fails to correlate with the upsurge in gun massacres.[90]

My data set, while unique, is limited by the exclusion of mass shootings that didn't result in at least six victims being murdered. Indications are that if the bar is lowered below a minimum of six deaths, the rate of occurrence is even more disturbing. Unfortunately, due in part to a funding prohibition enacted by Congress—at the urging of the National Rifle Association (NRA)—government agencies eschew research that would compile such data.[91] Frustrated by these restrictions, a group of social-media-savvy individuals launched a crowdsourcing experiment on Reddit to track every gun assault in the United States that resulted in four or more people being shot.[92]

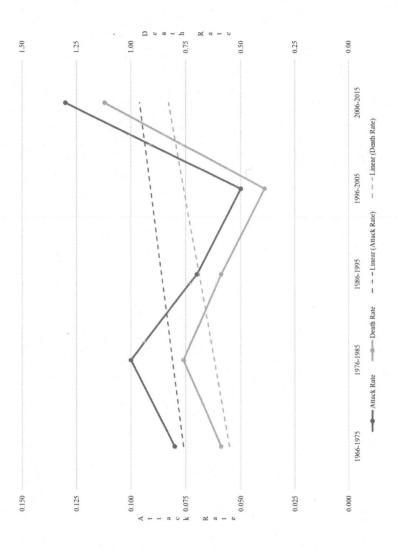

Fig. 3.5. Ten-Year Incidence Rates for Gun-Massacre Attacks and Deaths, 1956–2015. Source: Table 3.5.

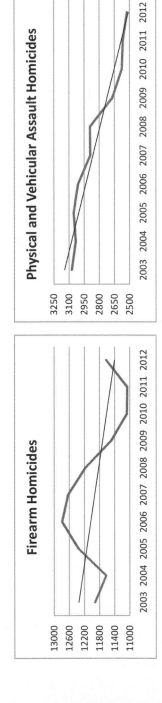

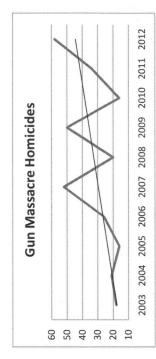

Fig. 3.6. Trends in Common Forms of Homicide, 2003–2012.

Note: The data represent the most recent decade of available data and indicate the cumulative number of such homicides per year. All data except for gun-massacre homicides are drawn from the Center for Disease Control WONDER Database (available at wonder.cdc.gov). Gun-massacre homicides are drawn from table 3.2.

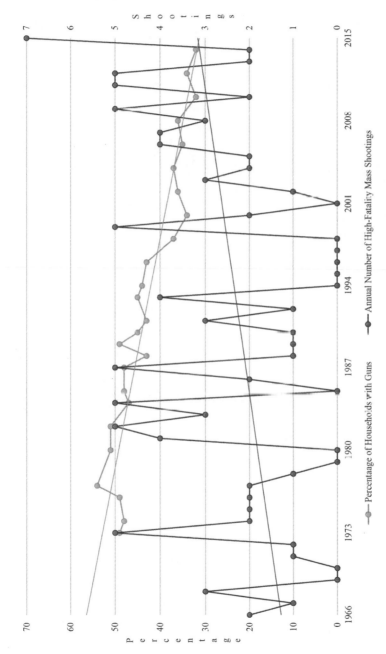

Fig. 3.7. Comparison of Trends in Gun Massacres and Gun-Ownership Rates, 1966–2015.
Source: Table 3.2 and General Social Survey Data (1973–2014).

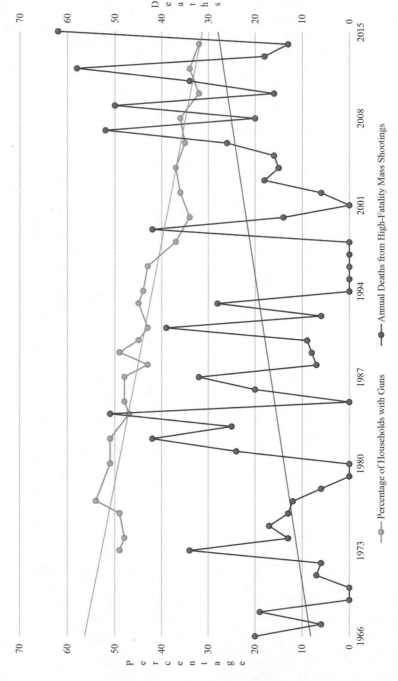

Fig. 3.8. Comparison of Trends in Gun-Massacre Deaths and Gun-Ownership Rates, 1966–2015.
Source: Table 3.2 and General Social Survey Data (1973–2014).

Table 3.6. Mass Shootings in the United States, 2013–2015.

Number of Mass Shootings Resulting in	2013	2014	2015	Combined
0 Deaths	130	145	159	434
1 Death	93	95	108	296
2 Deaths	47	30	38	115
3 Deaths	22	26	26	74
4 Deaths	34	19	26	79
5 Deaths	8	7	5	20
6 Deaths	3	2	3	8
7 Deaths	1	0	0	1
8 Deaths	0	1	2	3
9 Deaths	0	0	2	2
10 Deaths	0	0	1	1
...	...	...	...	...
13 Deaths	1	0	0	1
...	...	...	...	...
16 Deaths	0	0	1	1
Total Shootings	339	325	371	1,035
Total Deaths	467	364	469	1,300

Note: The Mass Shooting Tracker defines mass shootings as any gun attack where four or more people, including the shooter(s), are shot. As a result, the death tolls in this table include gunmen, if they died during the perpetration of their crimes.

Source: www.massshootingtracker.org.

In its first year (2013), the Mass Shooting Tracker logged a total of 339 multiple-victim shootings (see table 3.6). This dropped by fourteen, to 325 incidents, the following year. By 2015, however, the total number of mass shootings had jumped to 371, surpassing the rate of one per day. A review of the three-year period indicates that 1,300 people lost their lives during the commission of these 1,035 gun attacks. That's an annual average of 433 fatalities—a far cry from the "18 lives a year" gun-rights activist Emily Miller tells us die on average in mass shootings in the United States. What's arguably most alarming is that, in all three years, the number of lethal incidents in the Mass Shooting Tracker's data set exceeds the number of nonlethal incidents. Indeed, on an annual average, six in ten mass shootings result in at least one death, and three in ten result in multiple deaths.˙

Remember John Fund? He's the conservative columnist who claimed that, for Americans, the odds of dying in a mass shooting are equal to those of being struck by lightning. Well, not so. According to the National Weather Service, an average of 267 people are struck by lightning in the United States every year.[93] That's far less than the 433 individuals who lose their lives annually in a mass shooting. In fact, in any given year, the odds of being struck by lightning are about one in 1.2 million, whereas the odds of dying in a multiple-victim gun attack are about one in 700,000. And those are the chances of dying in a mass shooting. If we expand this calculation to the number of people who are shot in a mass shooting every year—so as to make a true apples-to-apples comparison—the odds increase significantly.

Since we're putting mass shootings in a proper perspective, let's add one final comparison to what most Americans consider to be the gravest threat to their security: terrorism.[94] Certainly, given the way politicians in Washington are always carrying on about groups like al Qaeda and ISIS, you might think that you're more likely to be killed by a terrorist than by a rampage gunman. But the opposite is true. In the ten years immediately following 9/11, terrorists killed twenty-seven individuals in the United States.[95] That's the same number of people Adam Lanza killed in Newtown. In other words, what terrorists took a decade to accomplish, a single, well-armed individual on a gun rampage pulled off in one morning.[96]

The bottom line is that, no matter how you crunch the numbers, the outcome is consistently the same: in the past decade, no single incident of violence has killed more people in the United States than the mass shooting. Quite simply, the most credible violent threat to American society currently comes out of the barrel of a gun—and, unfortunately, the threat is growing.

PART 2

PROBE

CHAPTER FOUR

UNSTABLE, ANGRY, ARMED MEN

Senior year in college is usually a stressful time. Most seniors take advanced courses in their final year. It's also a time of capstone projects, theses, and applications for graduate school and full-time employment.

In 2007, Seung Hui Cho was one of those seniors struggling with school. But if the twenty-three-year-old Virginia Tech student hung in there, he was going to graduate with a Bachelor's degree in English, and the turmoil of his time at college would be behind him. He just needed to tough it out for a little bit longer.

He couldn't do it.

Seung Hui Cho never made it up to the commencement stage. Neither did thirty-two of his fellow students and professors.

The truth is that Cho had long struggled in school.[1] As early as the third grade, his teachers in Fairfax County, Virginia, a suburb of the Washington, DC, metropolitan area, detected unusual speech patterns and an abnormal degree of shyness. Cho and his family had immigrated to the United States from South Korea when he was eight years old. It made sense at first to suspect that his difficulties stemmed from the typical English-as-a-second-language hurdles that children sometimes encounter when they're suddenly immersed into a foreign culture. But his elementary school teachers and counselors sensed that something far more serious was adversely affecting Cho.

In the summer prior to the seventh grade, Cho's parents heeded the advice of the school district and took him for a mental-health assessment. The initial evaluation determined that he had severe social anxiety disorder "rooted in acculturation challenges—not fitting in and difficulty with friends."[2] As a result, his social maturity level and verbal skills were representative of someone younger in age. Cho nevertheless had an above average IQ—and his performance in school reflected this.

Good student or not, immediately following the massacre at Columbine High School in April 1999, Cho wrote a paper for his English class that reflected similar homicidal-suicidal thoughts. Fearing that Cho "wanted to repeat Columbine," according to someone familiar with the incident, the school again pressed his family to have him evaluated by a psychiatrist.[3] That summer, he was diagnosed as suffering from major depression and selective mutism (which results in a reluctance to speak and painful shyness). He was put on anti-depression medication for a year. Initially, the pills worked, but in high school, his introversion returned. Realizing that their son was clearly not cured of his ailments, Cho's parents arranged for him to receive recurring counseling at a local mental-health clinic.

At first, Cho complied with his parents' wishes. After a while, though, the sessions began grating on him. His parents remember him asking, "Why do I have to go?" Just prior to his eighteenth birthday, he stopped going to therapy, insisting, "There is nothing wrong with me."[4]

But there was something wrong with him—and without regular mental-health treatment in his life, things only got worse.

* * *

In 2003, Cho graduated from high school and commenced his studies at Virginia Tech. He soon developed a passion for writing and would often spend countless hours in front of his computer, tapping away at the keyboard. He thought his work was brilliant. His professors thought otherwise, finding it unsettling due to its baleful and gruesome nature. Several faculty members complained that Cho was making people uncomfortable. It's not hard to understand why some students stopped attending classes when they were forced to sit through readings that turned into tirades: "I don't know which uncouth, low-life planet you come from but you disgust me. In fact, you all disgust me."[5] It might have been ignored as the overwrought words of an immature writer. But Cho made it personal, going as far as to identify specific classmates by name.

In the fall of 2006, Cho foreshadowed the tragedy that was to come in a macabre story written for Professor Robert Hicok's fiction workshop. The tale centered around a main character named Bud, "who gets out of bed unusually early . . . puts on his black jeans, a strappy black vest with many pockets, a black hat, a large dark [pair of] sunglasses, and a flimsy jacket," and heads to school. There, Bud watches "students strut inside smiling, laughing, embracing each other."[6]

Psychologists have coined a term—*leakage*—to capture the hints prospective mass killers often drop. Channeling his own visceral anger through his protagonist, Cho was leaking an impending school shooting: "A few eyes glance at Bud but without the glint of recognition. I hate this! I hate all these frauds! I hate my life. . . . This is it. . . . This is when you damn people die with me."[7]

Bud's fictional rampage was just one of many red flags that, in hindsight, were clearly missed.

Cho's actions inside the classroom were the tip of the iceberg. Outside the classroom, he was displaying even more disturbing behavior. His suitemates were the first to notice that something was wrong when, during his junior year, Cho took a knife and began stabbing the carpet in a female student's room where they were hanging out. A few months later, Cho showed up in disguise to another female student's dorm room, startling her. Given that Cho had also pestered her with e-mail and text messages, her resident advisor (RA) alerted the campus police. Officers met with Cho and admonished him to avoid contact with the student, but because she declined to press charges, Cho was not arrested. In the ensuing two weeks, Cho stalked two more female students, resulting in another visit from the Virginia Tech police. After the officers left, Cho told one of his suitemates, "I might as well kill myself."[8] Worried that Cho would go through with his threat, the suitemate contacted the authorities. When campus police officers returned, they decided to take Cho for a behavioral-health screening.

The next morning, following two assessments, a Virginia judge ruled that Cho "presents an imminent danger to himself as a result of mental illness."[9] Cho was ordered to pursue outpatient treatment. That afternoon, he visited the on-campus counseling center. After a brief session, Cho left—and never returned. Because it was the policy of the Virginia Tech counseling center to allow its patients to schedule subsequent appointments at their convenience, the clinic never followed up with Cho. For all practical purposes, he was lost within the mental-health system.

Although he continued to worry his professors, Cho managed to avoid any extreme form of harassing behavior that would have caught the attention of law enforcement. It was the calm before the storm.

Just a few weeks into what should have been his last semester, Cho bought a Walther P22 semiautomatic handgun. When he entered the licensed firearms store located just across the street from the Virginia Tech campus to pick up his purchase, he was handed two forms to fill out—one for a federal background check and the other for a state background check. Pursuant to federal law, a person "adjudicated as a mental defective or who has been committed to any mental institution" is prohibited from procuring a firearm.[10] Cho's psychiatric history, including being ordered into outpatient treatment by a court, was enough to disqualify him from taking possession of the weapon. After running Cho's name and Social Security number, the gun dealer should have received a notification that the completion of the sale was barred. Yet, on February 9, 2007, Cho passed the background check and walked out of J-N-D Pawnbrokers as the owner of a P22. A month later, he purchased a Glock 19 semiautomatic handgun from a licensed dealer in Roanoke, Virginia, again clearing the background check with ease. In the ensuing weeks, he bought over a dozen magazines, several of them extended-capacity, and hundreds of rounds of ammunition. Never once did his purchases raise any suspicions—even though they were prohibited by law.

Cho should have been flagged as someone barred from owning a gun. But because the state of Virginia misinterpreted the federal statutes prohibiting firearms purchases by the mentally ill as applying only to individuals ordered into *inpatient* treatment, the FBI (which maintains the nationwide background-check database) was never informed of Cho's disqualifying grounds. Once again, the system failed, this time with fatal consequences.

On the morning of April 16, 2007, Seung Hui Cho snuck into the West Ambler Johnston residence hall. At roughly the same time, freshman Emily Hilscher was returning to her room after having spent the weekend off-campus with her boyfriend. Somehow, she and Cho crossed paths and he ended up in her room, where he shot and killed her, along with the floor's RA, Ryan Christopher Clark. While investigators have never been able to uncover a direct connection between Cho and Hilscher, she happened to live on the same floor as the first female student Cho stalked back in November 2005, and it was Clark's RA predecessor on that floor who initially reported Cho to the police, initiating his series of run-ins with the law. As rampage shootings often involve symbolic targets, it's possible that Cho was striking at the students who represented the start of his legal troubles: the residents of West Ambler Johnston's fourth floor.

Based on information provided by Hilscher's friend, the police initially felt that the shooting was an act of domestic violence. While investigators at the residence hall began securing the crime scene, law enforcement officers in the region were put on the lookout for the boyfriend's pickup truck. Informed that authorities had a suspect and that he was off-campus, university officials decided not to cancel classes.

Meanwhile, a bloodstained Cho made his way back to his dormitory without being noticed by anyone. Once inside his room, he changed clothing, deleted his entire e-mail account, removed his computer's hard drive for disposal, and packed all of his weapons into a backpack. Unbeknownst to authorities who were preoccupied with hunting down Hilscher's boyfriend, her real killer was two buildings away, undertaking the next steps in his mass-murder scheme. He just had one more thing to do before continuing his shooting spree: visit the post office to mail a DVD containing a twenty-five-minute collection of video clips and forty-three photos, along with a twenty-three-page manifesto explaining his actions, to NBC News in New York.

Just a little over two hours after the murders in the West Ambler Johnston residence hall, a Montgomery County deputy sheriff spotted Hilscher's boyfriend driving his pickup truck. The law enforcement officer pulled over the vehicle and requested backup. For a fleeting moment, the police thought they had their man.

At nearly the exact same time as the police were converging on Hilscher's boyfriend, Cho—dressed just like his fictional protagonist Bud—casually walked across campus and entered Norris Hall, where he began chaining shut the building's three double-door entrances, to prevent those inside from exiting and those outside from entering. Armed with two semiautomatic handguns, nineteen magazines (many of them extended-capacity), and close to four hundred rounds of ammunition, he proceeded upstairs to the second floor. Five classes were meeting on the second floor that morning. Cho popped his head into the various classrooms, perhaps looking for someone in particular or maybe just to get a lay of the land.

At 9:40 a.m., Cho entered Professor G. V. Loganathan's advanced hydrology engineering class and shot him dead. Without uttering a word, Cho then turned to the thirteen students present that morning and opened fire, striking eleven of them. Next, he crossed the hallway to the German class, where he again first took out the professor and then went after the students, this time walking up and down the classroom aisles in order to shoot anyone who was not immediately killed in the initial barrage.

As gunshots rang out, faculty and students in Norris Hall began barricading themselves in their rooms. From the German class, Cho walked over to the French class, where he forced his way past the makeshift desk-blockade and repeated the attack pattern he had employed in the previous classroom. Afterward, Cho proceeded to the scientific computing class. Using their bodies as a counterweight, several students were able to prevent Cho from opening the door. Even though he fired shots through the door, Cho was never able to breach this classroom. Their quick thinking and determination spared them from Cho's wrath.

When Cho set his sights on Professor Liviu Librescu's solid mechanics class, the seventy-six-year-old Holocaust survivor urged students to jump out the window. Using his body to block access to the room, Librescu valiantly held off Cho long enough for ten of his students to escape. Eventually, Cho gave up on trying to push past Librescu and just shot him through the door. By the time he accessed the classroom, only six students were left (and two of them were in the process of trying to jump from the window). Cho squeezed off several quick bursts of gunfire, striking four of them.

Despite having attacked four of the five classes in session on the second floor, Cho was not done. He returned to some of the classrooms to finish off any survivors. The commission impaneled by the governor to review the events of that day described how students were basically trapped with only three defensive options available to them: jump out the window, barricade the door shut, or play dead.[11] As the final report noted:

> Cho returned to most of the classrooms more than once to continue shooting. He methodically fired from inside the doorways of the classrooms, and sometimes he walked around inside them. It was very close-range. Students had little place to hide other than behind the desks. By taking a few paces inside, he could shoot almost anyone in the classroom who was not behind a piece of overturned furniture.

The attack came to an abrupt end after about ten minutes. Despite still having over two hundred live rounds on his person, Cho—perhaps experiencing rampage weariness akin to that experienced by the perpetrators of the Columbine and Sandy Hook massacres—turned one of his handguns on himself and committed suicide. But the damage had been done. Cho had fired 174 rounds in Norris Hall, killing thirty

people and wounding another seventeen.[12] Every single person murdered in the classroom building was hit by at least three bullets, and
thirty of the thirty-two killed that day incurred a head wound. It was—
and remains—one of the deadliest mass shootings in history.

INSIDE THE MIND OF A KILLER

Cho's parcel was delivered to NBC News two days after the shooting.
Following deliberations, network executives decided to air some of
the contents of the enclosed DVD. Seeing a mass murderer lay out
his motives on national television was something most Americans
had never experienced before—and it was disturbing to watch:

> You had everything you wanted. Your Mercedes wasn't enough, you
> brats. Your golden necklaces weren't enough, you snobs. Your trust
> fund wasn't enough. Your vodka and cognac weren't enough. All
> your debaucheries weren't enough. Those weren't enough to fulfill
> your hedonistic needs. You had everything.[13]

Often invoking religious references, Cho insisted that he had no
choice but to kill:

> You had a hundred billion chances and ways to have avoided today,
> but you decided to spill my blood. You forced me into a corner and
> gave me only one option. The decision was yours. Now you have
> blood on your hands that will never wash off, you Apostles of Sin.[14]

Cho's manifesto clearly established that his goal was to incite
others to replicate his actions—in much the same way that he felt he
was following in the steps of the Columbine shooters:

> We have no sympathy in killing humans who have no respect for
> other people's lives. . . .
>   I say we take up the cross, Children of Ishmael, take up our
> guns and knives and any sharp objects, and take no prisoners and
> spare no lives until our last breath and last ounce of energy. . . .

Generation after generation, we martyrs, like Eric and Dylan, will sacrifice our lives to fuck you thousand folds for what you Apostles of Sin have done to us. . . .

Let the revolution begin!

Die you Descendants of Satan! Fuck you, and die now!

I am Ax Ishmael. I am the Anti-Terrorist of America.[15]

To the general public, these were the strange rants of an extremely disturbed young man. To his former professors, however, the anger and the violent imagery were eerily familiar. What NBC News was broadcasting to the world had already been projected in Cho's earlier writing assignments. And like the tale of Bud he had submitted to Professor Hicok a year earlier, his final essay plotted a similar storyline: "All the shit you've given me, right back at you with hollow points."[16]

The decision by NBC News to air portions of Cho's video rants was met with an onslaught of criticism. But network executives felt that the news value outweighed the nation's need for sensitivity in this matter. As NBC News president Steve Capus explained: "Ever since we heard the first reports about what had happened on that campus, we all wanted to know why. And I'm not sure that we'll ever fully understand why this happened, but I do think that this is as close as we may ever come to having a glimpse inside the mind of a killer."[17]

During the initial airing of the material, the staff of *NBC Nightly News* was very restrained and neutral in its assessment of Cho, referring to him only as "the gunman" and "a very troubled young man."[18] The closest the network came to offering any sort of insight into "the mind of a killer" came when the network's law enforcement expert, former FBI profiler Clint van Zandt, suggested that, while Cho's troubles had been plaguing him for quite a while, something likely caused him to snap: "What was the final catalyst? What finally broke that camel's back and moved him on?" Whatever the answer, van Zandt felt that the material mailed to NBC News was Cho's way of "further victimizing all of us by reaching out from the grave and grabbing us and getting our attention and making us listen to his last rambling words and pictures."

By the next day, the caution started to give way. Anchor Brian Williams described Cho as "mentally ill."[19] A former judge appearing as a legal expert referred to the shooter as "deranged." And van Zandt called him "pathetic." In an interview, one Virginia Tech student came to the conclusion that only a "psycho" could commit such a horrible act of violence.

Trying to make sense of what NBC News had broadcast, members of the press donned their amateur criminologist hats and attempted to answer the question that NBC News president Steve Capus correctly noted was on nearly everyone's mind: What drove Seung Hui Cho to commit such an atrocity?

The early assessments were—to put it mildly—unscientific. News anchors and correspondents referred to Cho as a "crazy," a "wacko," a "loser," a "barbarian," and a "monster."[20] Such visceral characterizations are understandable to an extent. The United States had just experienced the worst mass shooting in its history, and Americans—including those who report the news—were upset and incensed.

But it wasn't just the media. Experts offered similar characterizations. Former secretary of education Bill Bennett labeled the Virginia Tech gunman a "lunatic."[21] Clinical psychologist N. G. Berrill deemed him to have been "nuts."[22] And Phil McGraw—better known as "Dr. Phil"—diagnosed him as a "madman."[23]

The perception that developed in the first few days following the tragedy was one of a deranged young man who lost it and went on a killing spree. But why exactly? What provoked him? Mental illness seemed like an obvious factor. Yet, just as *New York Times* columnist David Brooks predicted would happen in response to such a tragedy, almost instantly the fingers began pointing at larger societal factors:

> Responsibility shifts outward from the individual to wider forces. People interviewed on TV tend to direct their anger at the gun, the university administration, society and so on. If they talk about the young killer at all, the socially acceptable word seems to be "troubled." He's more acted upon than acting.[24]

Many risked the wrath of the gun-rights movement and highlighted the nation's lax firearms laws as the root of the problem.

Others singled out the school's failure to cancel classes after the first shooting in the dormitory. Some blamed law enforcement officials as well for their role in that decision. All of these, no doubt, represent blown opportunities—failures—to prevent the massacre. But they still didn't get to the attack's impetus.

Why did Seung Hui Cho do it?

In the rush to identify what brought about the massacre, the talking heads quickly gravitated to two particular explanations often cited as the forces behind the killing spree at Columbine—and several subsequent school shootings: bullying and violent entertainment.[25]

Every single network speculated that Cho was the victim of bullying, and that his act of violence was the reaction of someone who had had enough. This perception was fueled, in part, by an Associated Press story that was reproduced in countless newspapers throughout the country. While researching Cho's background, Associated Press correspondents came across one of Cho's former high school classmates who was also attending Virginia Tech. Here's what the reporters took away from that interview:

> Classmates in Virginia, where Cho grew up, said he was teased and picked on, apparently because of shyness and his strange, mumbly way of speaking. Once, in English class . . . Cho began reading in a strange, deep voice that sounded "like he had something in his mouth. . . . The whole class started laughing and pointing and saying, 'Go back to China.'"[26]

Leaving aside that the words of one classmate somehow became the view of "classmates" in the plural, what this newswire story did was transform an incident from years back into a possible explanation for the massacre at Virginia Tech. Mocking a student and telling him to "go back to China" is certainly a painful and humiliating experience. But people usually don't go on killing sprees because of something that happened years ago in secondary school.

It's not that Cho wasn't given a hard time growing up. Other former classmates eventually confirmed that Cho was teased by his fellow students in high school. But in its urge to uncover some sensational link to the mass shooting at Virginia Tech, the news media made logical leaps and outrageous assertions. One of the wildest claims was that Cho maintained a list of high school students he planned to kill. This was first reported by the *New York Post* in an article titled "Bullied Cho's 'HS Death List.'" But for those who read beyond the attention-grabbing headlines that have become a trademark of New York City's largest tabloid paper, they would have learned that Cho was only "thought to have had a 'hit list' of students he wanted to kill." As one classmate elaborated, "We don't know for certain. We never saw it, nobody ever said for sure. . . . Everybody just took it as a joke."[27]

Based on a slew of news reports that Cho was a down-on-himself victim of harassment, an explanation rooted in bullying began to emerge. By the end of the week, the experts had taken their cue from the media and were running with it. One of those who tried to shed some insight into the horror that occurred in Blacksburg was Virginia Tech psychology professor E. Scott Geller. Speaking at an event at East Tennessee State University that drew national media, Geller told the audience, "[Cho] had no friends. He had no social structure and no sense of belonging. . . . When people do things like this, their self-esteem is low [and] their sense of belonging is low."[28] Many others concurred. As the Associated Press noted:

> As experts analyzed the disturbing materials [mailed to NBC News], it became increasingly clear that Cho was almost a classic case of a school shooter: a painfully awkward, picked-on young man who lashed out with methodical fury at a world he believed was out to get him. . . .
>
> When criminologists and psychologists look at mass murders, Cho fits the themes they see repeatedly: a friendless figure, someone who has been bullied, someone who blames others and is bent on revenge, a careful planner, a male.[29]

While a great deal of attention was devoted to bullying as a root cause of the Virginia Tech massacre, American culture—particularly its obsession with violent entertainment—received its share of the blame too. Video-game critic Jack Thompson appeared on Fox News within hours of the shooting and, without even knowing the gunman's identity, attributed the murders to violent video games like Grand Theft Auto and Doom.[30] The experts pounced on this cue, with Dr. Phil leading the charge:

> The problem is we are programming these people as a society. You cannot tell me—common sense tells you that if these kids are playing video games, where they're on a mass killing spree in a video game, it's glamorized on the big screen, it's become part of the fiber of our society. . . . We're going to have to start addressing those issues and recognizing that the mass murderers of tomorrow are the children of today that are being programmed with this massive violence overdose.[31]

His colleagues in pundit psychology followed suit. And it didn't stop with video games. Film was implicated as well.

This is perhaps a good time to step back and explain how news items go viral. In the United States, there are certain media organizations that serve as primary information disseminators. In particular, articles in the *New York Times* and the *Washington Post* and wire stories from the Associated Press tend to get picked up by other outlets, driving the typical news cycle. If it runs in one of the above sources, there's a good chance it could become a national news story.

Within two hours of NBC News airing images of Cho, one photo in particular—Cho posing with a hammer—caught the eye of Virginia Tech film professor Paul Harrill. He immediately contacted the *New York Times*, and minutes later the "paper of record" had a post on its website noting that the photo mimics a scene from the Korean film *Oldboy*.[32] Reporters at the Associated Press and the *Washington Post* took notice and further flushed out the connection.[33] From there, the explanation spread like wildfire, appearing in newspapers nationwide and becoming a point of discussion on the cable-news networks.

What was the link? Perhaps it's best to let Stephen Hunter, the author of the *Washington Post* article, answer this question:

Oldboy must feature prominently in the discussion, even if no one has yet confirmed that Cho saw it. On the surface, it seems a natural fit, at least in the way it can be presumed that Cho's hyper-fervid brain worked. It's a Korean story—he would have passed on the subtitles and listened to it in his native language—of unjust persecution and bloody revenge. A narcissist with a persecution complex would identify with its plot.

Among Cho's photos were close-ups of himself clenching a hammer in a pose that recalled the pose of the persecuted man in *Oldboy*.[34]

Our thirst for explanation in the immediate aftermath of mass shootings is so strong that we are willing to grasp at nearly any theory that has a chance of plausibility, even if remote. That Hunter—as well as the AP, the *New York Times*, and Professor Harrill—had no evidence that Cho actually saw *Oldboy* didn't matter. The filmmaker was Korean, and Cho was of Korean descent. To Hunter, Cho had to have seen it.

Of course, Cho used a gun, not a hammer, which led Hunter to an even more far-fetched culprit: John Woo movies. Given Woo's proclivity to feature gun violence, Hunter sensed that films like *Face/Off* and *The Killer* "clearly" played some role in the massacre:

> It is not certain that Cho saw Woo's films, though any kid taken by violent popular culture in the past 15 or 20 years almost certainly would have, on DVD, alone in the dark, in his bedroom or downstairs after the family's gone to bed. They're not family fare; they're dreamy, angry adolescent fare. They were gun-crazed ballets, full of whirling imagery, grace, masculine power and a strange but perhaps not irrelevant religiosity. They were close to outlaw works of art: They celebrated violence even as they aesthetized [*sic*] it, streamlined it and made it seem fabulous fun. Their possible influence on Cho can be *clearly* seen in 11 of the photos that feature handguns.
>
> Cho's activities so closely reflect the Woo *oeuvre* that it seems somewhat fair to conclude that in his last moments, before he blew his brains out, he was shooting a John Woo movie in his head.[35]

Again, the absence of a concrete connection didn't stop the speculation.

★ ★ ★

The truth is that the theories that are initially offered up in an attempt to make sense of a horrific act of violence are usually amiss. Certainly that was the case in the Virginia Tech rampage. Bullying and violent media are, of course, straightforward and convenient explanations. But, in most gun massacres, there's something a bit more complex at work. Understanding why people are willing to go on rampages begins with the recognition that certain individuals are predisposed to committing acts of mass violence. The answer to the question "why?" begins with another question: "who?"

A MODEL FOR MASS VIOLENCE

On March 24, 2015, Germanwings Flight 9525 en route from Barcelona, Spain, to Dusseldorf, Germany, slammed into the French Alps, killing all 150 people on board. Aviation accidents are rare to begin with, but analysts were particularly troubled that the plane crashed without any sort of distress call. What could have gone wrong? What brought down a passenger airliner that just one day earlier had passed a brief check-over inspection?[36] Within forty-eight hours, investigators had their first answers—and they couldn't believe what they were learning.

The voice recorders recovered from the impact site captured the sounds of the captain desperately attempting to regain entry into the cockpit. Joined by at least one other member of the flight crew, the pilot can be heard bashing the door while pleading with the copilot to let him in. As the chaotic scene played out in the background, the copilot could be heard breathing calmly and methodically.[37] It was the first clue of many that indicated the plane was not brought down by mechanical failure or human error. This was mass murder.

In the weeks that followed, more evidence hinting of foul play came to the attention of authorities. The copilot, twenty-seven-year-old Andreas Lubitz, had a history of mental illness, including a psychosomatic condition that caused deterioration in his eyesight. At one point, Lubitz's psychiatric problems were so debilitating that he was forced to take medical leave from pilot training. In the months leading up to the crash, his health had begun worsening. He was becoming increasingly paranoid about his well-being and job security, leading doctors to put him on a regimen of antipsychotic medication. He had also researched suicide and cockpit doors. And, on the previous leg of the flight, he practiced an early descent.[38]

Every time we fly, we put our fates into the hands of the flight crew. We do so on the assumption that safeguarding the passengers is the top concern of the pilots. And in nearly every instance, it is. Nearly.

Turns out, Lubitz isn't the first pilot to deliberately bring down a passenger plane.

As Japan Airlines Flight 350 was making its final approach to Tokyo's Haneda Airport on February 8, 1982, the flight's captain, Seiji Katagiri, abruptly sent the aircraft into a nose-dive. The copilot tried to reverse the maneuver as the flight engineer physically restrained the captain. While the quick reflexes of both men certainly saved the lives of most of the 174 people on board, it wasn't enough to fully correct the trajectory. The plane slammed into the water short of the runway, killing twenty-four passengers.[39]

When the police finally interviewed Katagiri—who had discarded his uniform jacket and fled the aircraft, getting onto the first rescue boat to arrive on scene—he claimed that he blacked out and thus had no memory of the accident.[40]

The investigation quickly began focusing on the pilot—and what authorities uncovered was disturbing. Somewhat like Lubitz, Katagiri reportedly attempted a similar high-risk maneuver the day before, as the same crew was flying to Fukuoka. Katagiri's cockpit colleagues dismissed it as error and decided not to report the incident. But it was enough to raise concern and to leave them vigilant for the next day's return flight.[41]

Further probing uncovered that Katagiri had a history of bizarre behavior consistent with psychosis, including a deep paranoia about being monitored by people out to get him and psychosomatic intestinal issues (similar to Lubitz's alleged psychosomatic vision problems)—conditions which led him to take a leave of absence from work (akin to Lubitz's break from flight training for medical reasons). Authorities also found that just prior to the crash, Katagiri's marriage had begun falling apart and that he was on the police radar after they received calls about him behaving strangely.[42]

As one contemporaneous account put it, "The airline was on the point of grounding him again, this time for good, but Katagiri seems to have beaten them to it."[43]

The downing of Japan Airlines Flight 350, while tragic, is not the worst episode of pilot mass murder. That distinction belongs to Egypt Air Flight 990, en route from New York to Cairo in 1999. About twenty minutes after takeoff from JFK, relief crew First Officer Gamil al-Batouti entered the cockpit and offered to take over for the active duty first officer, several hours before the planned switch. Moments later, when the captain got up to visit the lavatory, Batouti—repeatedly saying "I rely on God" in Egyptian Arabic—plunged the plane into the Atlantic Ocean, approximately sixty miles south of Nantucket Island, killing all 217 people on board.[44]

Even though Egyptian authorities continue to insist that mechanical failure was the cause of the crash, an independent investigation by the US National Transportation Safety Board (NTSB), supplemented by a probe conducted by the FBI, determined that Batouti was responsible for the carnage. While his motive was withheld from the NTSB's final report, information leaked to the press indicated that Batouti had been seething for quite some time prior to the incident.[45]

In particular, Batouti had long resented the airline's refusal to promote him to captain, despite his years of distinguished service in the Egyptian Air Force and as the head instructor at the Egypt Air Institute, where he trained many of the pilots who would later fly alongside him, as his superiors. His agony was compounded by the fact that his daughter ailed from lupus, which taxed his family financially. He made up some of the monetary shortfall by flying long trans-Atlantic flights, which paid extra. But the evening prior to the downing of Flight 990, Batouti reportedly had an altercation with his superior. Batouti allegedly had been engaging in bizarre sexual misconduct during overnight stays in the United States—likely a by-product of his growing mental anguish. Following a heated exchange regarding his inappropriate behavior, the head of the 767 pilot group stripped Batouti of his American routes.[46]

Afterward, Batouti approached a fellow pilot who was assigned to a different flight. Eerily, he handed his colleague money and asked him to give it to his son, should anything happen to him. Hours later, sitting near his supervisor in first class, Batouti excused himself and entered the cockpit to exact his revenge.[47]

While the in-flight rampages of Katagiri and Batouti might be the most infamous of such incidents, there have been others. Former Connellan Airways pilot Colin Forman crashed a plane into the offices of the airline in 1977, killing four people, including his former boss, whom he blamed for derailing his career;[48] Younes Khayati allegedly brought down Royal Air Maroc Flight 630 in 1994, killing forty-four, to punish his female copilot for terminating their romantic relationship;[49] and Tsu Way Ming reportedly crashed Silk Air Flight 185 in 1997, claiming the lives of all 104 on board, in retaliation for being withdrawn from a flight instructor's program and as payback against his copilot, who had lodged a formal complaint against him.[50]

✳ ✳ ✳

Like Seung Hui Cho, history will remember Andreas Lubitz, Seiji Katagiri, and Gamil al-Batouti as cold-blooded killers. They took the lives of innocent victims, many of whom they did not know, in an act of mass murder. And they left the rest of the world wondering how someone could commit such a heinous crime.

Taking a step back and comparing all four killers leads to several important observations. First, all four men—the sex of the perpetrator is not immaterial here—exhibited signs of mental instability prior to their rampages. Second, all four held themselves in high regard and took offense to being mistreated. Third, employing a weapon that was readily available to them, all four undertook a calculated, retaliatory attack. Each of these three elements represents a different stage in the process of mass violence. For starters, those who are willing to endanger the lives of many share a *predisposition* that clouds their judgment and leaves them susceptible to reprehensible conduct. After they experience what they perceive to be a severely humiliating or threatening *provocation*, dangerous thoughts of retribution are set in motion. And it's the possession of weapons that fuels their rage, *priming* their deadly act of premeditated violence.

Predisposition, provocation, and priming. These are the three *P*s of mass violence. And just like they create a model for mass murder, they also help explain why most mass shootings occur.

Predisposition: Who?

Did you know that just as the presence of the *BRCA1* and *BRCA2* genes significantly increases a woman's chance of developing breast cancer, there is a genetic factor that, when present, increases the likelihood of a person becoming a perpetrator of mass violence? It's true. It's the Y chromosome.

Of the 111 gun massacres that comprise my data set, only one—one!—was perpetrated exclusively by a woman.[51] That was former postal worker Jennifer San Marco's 2006 shooting spree in Goleta, California, which left seven people dead. Besides her rampage, women have played a role in another five gun massacres, acting alongside at least one male co-conspirator (with whom they were romantically involved, in each case). Ninety-five percent of gun massacres were perpetrated exclusively by men (see table 4.1). There are no two ways about it. The indisputable answer to the question of who goes on deadly shooting rampages is men.[52]

My data set allows us to identify two other important demographic characteristics about high-fatality mass shooters: age and race. The age of those who have taken six or more lives in a shooting ranged from sixteen to fifty-nine (see table 4.1). Despite the common perception that many of these killers are disaffected youth, only five of the 128 known gunmen in my data set were minors. The remaining 123 offenders were eighteen years of age or older. Indeed, in the past decade—the deadliest decade to date—not a single minor has perpetrated a gun massacre. Crunching the numbers generates a mean as well as median age of thirty-three. Still, most gunmen were in their twenties. None of this data should be read as ruling out minors and senior citizens as mass shooters. They obviously attempt such crimes.[53] But, since 1966, few teenagers and no persons over the age of fifty-nine have killed six or more people in an individual act of gun violence in the United States.[54]

Table 4.1. Demographic Characteristics of Gun-Massacre Perpetrators.

Sex	
Male Perpetrators	122
Female Perpetrators	6
Gun Massacres Involving Female Perpetrators	6
Gun Massacres Perpetrated Exclusively by Females	1

Age	
Age Range	16–59
Mean Age	33
Median Age	33
Mode Age	28
Minors (Under 18)	5
Senior Citizens (Over 64)	0
Teens (16–19)	9
20s	48
30s	33
40s	29
50s	9

Race	Number of Gun-Massacre Perpetrators (by Race)	Percentage of Gun Massacres Involving Perpetrators (by Race)	Percentage of US Population (2015 Est.) (by Race)
Whites	74	58	68
Blacks	32	25	12
Asians	10	8	3
Hispanics	11	9	12
Native Americans	1	1	1

Note: Based on the 128 known perpetrators of gun massacres in the United States between 1966 and 2015.

Source: Table 3.2

The other common belief about massacre gunmen is that they are almost always white people.[55] And, as my data confirm, there is some truth to this, at least in absolute terms. A total of seventy-four whites perpetrated high-fatality mass shootings in the past fifty years, outnumbering the next closest group—blacks—by more than double (see table 4.1).[56] Eleven Hispanics, ten Asians, and one Native American also committed gun massacres.[57] However, when compared to the racial composition of the United States, we see that whites, Asians, and Native Americans roughly reflect their group's national population (in terms of percentages). On the other hand, blacks are overrepresented, and Hispanics are underrepresented. Given such broad distributions, trying to identify potential mass shooters based on race is likely to be of little, if any, utility.

Assessing these demographic factors together leads to a rather broad profile of a high-fatality mass shooter: adult men of working age. To put that in a slightly different perspective, about three in ten Americans comprise the demographic group that is likely to commit a gun massacre. That means that, in a country of approximately 320 million people, 96 million, myself included, are potential mass killers—no doubt a sizeable segment. But there's another factor that further delimits this group: mental illness.

In the late spring of 2015, another group of innocent Americans was executed by a coldblooded killer armed with a handgun. This time the victims were black church parishioners attending a Bible study and prayer group at Emanuel African Methodist Episcopal (AME) Church in Charleston, South Carolina. At some point during their evening meeting, twenty-one-year-old Dylann Roof entered the church and joined the worshipers, spending approximately one hour with them. Suddenly, and without warning, Roof pulled out a Glock .45-caliber semiautomatic pistol and began shooting. Reportedly shouting, "Y'all want something to pray about? I'll give you something to pray about," he unleashed a barrage of gunfire that left nine people mortally wounded.[58] Right before executing one of his victims, he allegedly stated his motive: "You rape our women and you're taking over our country. And you have to go."[59]

Some who took to the Internet and the airwaves to explain this gun massacre tried to draw parallels with other such atrocities, including playing up the idea that Dylann Roof must have been suffering from some form of mental illness. *Newsweek*'s Matthew Lysiak, for instance, noted that the gunman was "reportedly taking a drug that has been linked with sudden outbursts of violence."[60] Based on this, Lysiak suggested that "the shooter most likely has a history of severe mental health issues that have either gone untreated or undiagnosed." It was a sentiment echoed by psychologist Keith Ablow, who opined from first impressions that Roof had "showed all the signs of severe and worsening mental illness."[61]

But this line of thinking was quickly met with a fierce backlash. As far as the critics could tell, mental disorder had little to do with this particular attack, and to suggest as much is, in the words of *Salon* contributor Arthur Chu, "a goddamn cop-out."[62] As Chu and a few other commentators noted, there was no official record that, prior to his rampage, Roof had ever been diagnosed with a psychiatric condition.[63] Instead, he held a warped view of African Americans, and it was this demented ideology that fueled his heinous act of mass murder. This was a racist-driven hate crime, and, as one headline emphasized, "racism is not a mental illness."[64]

When medical professionals are queried about the culpability of mental illness in mass shootings, they are quick to remind us that most mentally ill Americans pose no violent threat to society.[65] Indeed, only about 4 percent of all violent crimes and 5 percent of all homicides are committed by persons who had been diagnosed with a serious psychiatric disorder beforehand.[66] If anything, those suffering from mental-health problems are eleven times more likely to be the victims, as opposed to the perpetrators, of violent crime.[67] As one popular study notes, "persons with mental illness might well have more to fear from 'us' than we do from 'them.'"[68] And from what we know from academic research, all of these claims are accurate. They're also misleading.

Few would dispute the claim that the mentally ill, in general, commit only a tiny fraction of all violent crimes. But that is neither here nor there when it comes to rampage violence. Shooting sprees are unique offenses. Conflating them with other forms of crime, including most homicides, creates a logical fallacy known as a "red herring." The real question is, To what extent are most mass shootings perpetrated by individuals afflicted with psychiatric problems?

Till now, a systematic answer to this question has largely eluded us. At best, we were able to draw on several high-profile cases like the Columbine and Virginia Tech attacks to generalize that mental illness must play some contributing role in rampage violence.[69] My data set of all gun massacres from the past five decades allows us to shine additional light on this nexus. A detailed examination reveals that four out of five of these incidents involved a gunman who had been observed by family members, close friends, colleagues, or health professionals as displaying some form of behavioral instability. To be more precise, perpetrators of eighty-six gun massacres (80 percent) exhibited signs indicative of mental illness, with at least thirty-two of these eighty-six incidents involving shooters who at some point in their lives received a formal diagnosis of a mental disorder from a psychiatric professional.[70]

Out of the remaining twenty-two incidents, the gunmen in eleven of those incidents either committed suicide or died as a result of a gunfire exchange with police—also known as "suicide by cop"— which offers *prime facie* evidence of psychiatric instability.[71] Furthermore, five additional gun massacres were perpetrated by individuals with histories of alcohol and substance abuse.[72] In other words, only six of the incidents in my data set were committed by gunmen who did not display any reported signs of mental disorder. The remaining gun massacres (94 percent) from the past fifty years were perpetrated by at least one gunman who had exhibited behavior consistent with some form of mental illness.[73]

The list of mentally disturbed mass shooters includes many of the individuals we have already discussed in detail, such as Shawn and Akein Scott, who both exhibited degrees of depravity that some have linked to antisocial personality disorder;[74] Michael Hance, who—in a delusional manner—often sat in a kayak on his lawn, pretending to be floating;[75] and Nidal Hasan, who was distressed about being deployed to a war zone, an anxiety brought on by "secondary trauma" from attending to combat veterans with post-traumatic stress disorder (PTSD).[76] The same holds for Boston Marathon bomber Tamerlan Tsarnaev, who heard voices in his head, likely the result of schizophrenia, as well as Japan Airlines pilot Seiji Katagiri, who suffered from deep paranoia and felt that he was under constant surveillance.[77] It turns out that even Dylann Roof—who at first glance might seem mentally sound—exhibited behavioral characteristics consistent with a diagnosis of psychopathy.[78]

The desire to distance mental illness from crime is understandable. We don't want to further stigmatize the mentally ill. Moreover, we don't want to discourage them from seeking the medical attention they might need. At the same time, there is another factor we shouldn't brush aside: evidence suggests that the vast majority of deadly mass shooters likely suffered from mental disorders. Again, it bears repeating that in many instances, the disturbing behaviors are noted by lay persons (usually family members, friends, and colleagues). Yet, because many people with mental-health problems tend to avoid seeking professional care, a formal diagnosis is often unavailable, and as such our understanding is limited to the evidence at hand.

There is one more point that deserves emphasis: mental illness does *not* cause rampage violence. An estimated 25 percent of the adult population—approximately sixty-two million Americans—experiences some form of mental illness in any given year.[79] According to recent survey figures, 4.2 percent of the adult population struggles with serious mental illness such as major depression, bipolar disorder, schizophrenia, paranoia, and psychosis.[80] By some estimates, nearly half of all adult Americans will develop at least one mental illness.[81] The odds are one in two that Americans reading this book will experience a psychiatric problem at some point in their life. It doesn't mean that they—or any of their fellow citizens—are necessarily going to take up arms and go on a rampage. If it did, there would be millions of mass shootings in the United States every year.

When it comes to mass shootings—or at least to high-fatality mass shootings—mental illness should be considered a gateway, not a cause. That is, mental illness affects the judgment of those who decide to go on shooting sprees; but on its own, it does not bring about the massacre of innocents.[82] As with the presence of a Y chromosome, it merely predisposes adults of working age to such behavior. But there is more to rampage violence than just biology. There's an intricate psychology at play as well.

Provocation: Why?

In the mid-1970s, psychologist Leonard Berkowitz set out to find if the brutal beatings perpetrated by criminals were a by-product of a culture of violence. As Berkowitz phrased his research question, "Was their violence instrumental to the attainment of their peers' approval or at least to the avoidance of disapproval for violating their group's expectation?"[83] To answer this, Berkowitz interviewed sixty-five white, British males who had been convicted of inflicting bodily harm on another male in the course of an attack unrelated to robbery. What he found was that social norms were not a powerful influencing factor. Violent criminals certainly had reasons for hurting others, but impressing their friends and peers was generally not one of those reasons. Instead, the primary motive behind most physical assaults was hostile aggression: "The aggressor's major aim in this instance, usually when he is angry, is to harm or perhaps even destroy his victim."[84] Criminal violence was, quite simply, driven by a fundamental desire to inflict pain and suffering.

In a sense, there's nothing shocking about this finding. Anyone who has ever lashed out at someone else can probably relate to such an instinct. But it's another theme that ran through the interviews of British convicts that has elevated Berkowitz's study to the level of seminal. Many of the offenders reported that much of their anger arose from threats to their self-esteem. "Their egos were fragile indeed," Berkowitz noted.[85] He explained the dynamic this way:

> The men readily developed situations in which they thought their pride was at stake. They were quick to see themselves as challenged and frequently interpreted someone else's remarks as belittling them, even if . . . the other person was only boasting or insisting on his own viewpoint in an argument. They felt called upon to prove themselves again and again, to others and to themselves.[86]

And how did these convicts usually "prove" themselves? Through the exercise of physical force. The violent criminals "struck out at their antagonist in rage, wanting more than anything else to hurt him."[87]

Berkowitz's study of British prisoners is important because it suggested that violence might be related to favorable evaluations of oneself, which in turn led to a lot of theorizing that people who resort to violence as a form of lashing out are really just people with self-esteem issues—low self-esteem to be exact. As the theory holds, people who see themselves as inadequate attempt to compensate for their feelings of inferiority by faulting other external forces, particularly other people. This often produces situations in which insecure individuals will try to elevate their self-esteem through aggression and brute force aimed at those whom they blame for their shortcomings. Resorting to violence, in other words, makes people with low self-esteem feel better about themselves, while at the same time punishing those whom they hold responsible for their problems.

In the literature on psychology and criminology, low self-esteem has long been held as a primary factor behind many egregious acts of violence. Dozens of studies have suggested that low self-esteem is a driving force in domestic violence, adolescent violence, gang warfare, armed robbery, and even terrorism.[88] Thus, when Seung Hui Cho went on his bloody rampage at Virginia Tech, it was hardly surprising to find commentators insisting that he must have been suffering from low self-esteem. After all, for decades, this has been one of the more powerful hypotheses in the field. By raging against his fellow classmates, whom he loathed for putting him down, Cho was improving his self-image and enjoying the satisfaction that comes from hurting those whom he felt were to blame. Or so the theory goes.

In recent years, psychologists have begun challenging this paradigm. As one group of scholars noted, "the motivation to seek self-enhancement has been shown to be characteristic of people high (rather than low) in self-esteem, and in fact it appears to be weak or absent among people with low self-esteem. Indeed, people with low self-esteem appear to be ambivalent about rising in esteem, and they often avoid circumstances that might raise their self-esteem."[89]

Intuitively, the people most likely to seek out confrontations, especially high-risk, violent ones, are those with the ego and confidence to undertake such aggressive actions. The new theory that follows is that it's the people with high self-esteem—not low self-esteem—who are most likely to commit acts of criminal violence.[90]

You're probably wondering: aren't people with high self-esteem secure enough in their perceptions of themselves to be immune from criticism and personal attack? Wouldn't these people be the least likely to resort to violence as a form of compensation? Coming into this study, that was certainly my understanding of individuals with high self-esteem. But it turns out that self-esteem doesn't vary on only one spectrum, between low and high. There are also people with stable and unstable self-esteem. Research has begun to establish that this distinction is crucial to explaining violent outbursts.[91] In one study, individuals were given beepers and instructed to fill out a brief questionnaire every time their beeper buzzed, resulting in several daily measures of self-esteem. The subjects were subsequently assessed using four traditional measures of anger and aggression. The researchers made two significant discoveries. First, there are certain individuals who, despite having a positive view of themselves, also have a fragile view of themselves, leaving them highly sensitive to criticism or ridicule. Second, this subset of people—those with unstable high self-esteem—is generally the most likely group to resort to violence.

When your view of self-worth is high but sensitive, you tend to be vulnerable to negative evaluations. In the vernacular of psychology, these appraisals are known as "ego threats."[92] On its own, unstable high self-esteem doesn't cause violence. It's the addition of an ego threat that sends someone over the edge. The dynamic works this way:

> When favorable views about oneself are questioned, contradicted, impugned, mocked, challenged, or otherwise put in jeopardy, people may aggress. In particular, they will aggress against the source of the threat.
>
> In this view, then, aggression emerges from a particular discrepancy between two views of self: a favorable self-appraisal and an external appraisal that is much less favorable. That is, people turn aggressive when they receive feedback that contradicts their favorable views of themselves and implies that they should adopt

less favorable views. More to the point, it is mainly the people who refuse to lower their self-appraisals who become violent.[93]

To test this theory, psychologists came up with one of those wild experiments reminiscent of Bill Murray's laboratory tests in *Ghostbusters*. A group a students was tasked with writing an essay. Afterward, by a flip of a coin, half of the subjects received positive feedback, including the comment: "No suggestions, great essay!" The other half received negative feedback—an artificially generated ego threat—on a variety of factors such as composition, originality, and persuasiveness. At the end of these essays, experimenters wrote, "This is one of the worst essays I have read!" After receiving their marked-up essays, the subjects were then placed in a competition against another person who, they were told, was the evaluator of their essay. (In actuality, the competitor was a computer.) The object of the interaction was to press a button quicker than your opponent when prompted (try to picture the initial matchup in *Family Feud*). Whoever won got to blast the loser with white noise, selecting a level ranging from 60 dB to 105 dB. Moreover, the winner also got to select the duration of the noise blast.[94] "In effect, each participant controlled a weapon that could be used to blast the other person if the participant won the competition to react faster," the researchers wrote.[95] Exactly as they hypothesized, in instances where there was an ego threat (i.e., a negative evaluation), those with the highest levels of self-esteem (and high narcissism scores as well) were the most likely to punish the other person. In instances where there was either a positive evaluation or a negative evaluation received by someone with low self-esteem, the punishment was less severe.[96]

The picture that emerges from all these studies is that there is a particular psychological dynamic behind significant acts of mass violence.[97] The violence begins with perpetrators who hold themselves in high regard. Nonetheless, they're extremely sensitive to challenge and slight. When their fragile egos are threatened, they're provoked into lashing out in a manner that will hurt others, particularly those whom they associate with the threat.[98]

Priming: Why and Who?

After people go on shooting sprees, commentators often wonder what made them "snap." Nevertheless, with the exception of a handful of shootings in my data set, gun massacres are premeditated acts of violence. Rarely does one just snap. In the vast majority of instances, the gunmen have been scheming up their actions well in advance of their attacks. Evidence of preparation often includes the acquisition of a weapon, practice using that weapon, and in some instances research of the target. A few mass murderers even leave behind communiqués explaining their actions, such as in the case of Cho.

Nevertheless, even when notes and videos are not left behind by those who commit murder-suicide, investigators often uncover that the attacks were a reaction to some sort of ego threat. Of course, what sets off one mass shooter is not the same as what sets off another. For instance, Michael Hance was driven by intrafamily motives. Nidal Hasan was driven by political motives. And Dylann Roof was driven by racial motives. But whatever the differences between rampage gunmen, most of them share a desire related to righting a perceived wrong. No mass shooting is without purpose in a perpetrator's mind, sound or not.[99]

Just as well, no mass shooting is without a firearm. That's obviously a tautological observation. Nevertheless, beyond the superficiality of this statement is another important dynamic that drives rampage violence: the weapons-priming effect.

Let's begin with a few simple questions: Why is it that perpetrators of mass violence carry their hostility for days, weeks, and in some instances months? Why doesn't their ire dissipate? Why does it instead remain enflamed for sustained periods of time, allowing for preparation of premeditated acts of brutality? Again, through psychological research, we know that the possession of weapons primes violence.[100] When people have access to instruments that can inflict harm—knives, guns, explosives, cars, even airplanes—*and they perceive them as such*, their aggression spikes, especially when they physically come into contact with those weapons. In other words, the possession of weapons often changes the manner in which a person channels his aggression. In particular, it promotes thoughts of how to employ that weapon, resulting in use of that weapon when provoked. The mere presence of a weapon can be enough to push someone over the edge—from fantasy into execution—especially when faced with a severe ego threat.

Guns are remarkably powerful violence-priming forces.[101] As a recent study conducted by a team of Harvard researchers uncovered, gun availability fuels gun violence. According to the study's authors, "states with greater levels of private firearm ownership experienced greater rates of firearm-related violent crimes," including armed robbery, armed assault, and firearm homicide.[102] Or, to capture this dynamic using the words of those who have devoted years to researching the priming effect of weapons, "the gun helps pull the trigger."[103]

A few years ago, a team of psychologists set out to capture the roots of this phenomenon. Like their colleagues who examined the relationship between negative evaluations and hostility, they devised a two-step experiment to assess how guns impact aggression. First, a group of young men had their saliva swabbed so that their testosterone levels could be measured. They were then led into a room with a table and a chair. On top of the table, the subjects found either a pellet gun resembling a Desert Eagle handgun or the children's game Mouse Trap, as well as a piece of paper. The men were told to examine the object and then to take notes on it. After spending fifteen minutes handling the object, their testosterone levels were again measured. The researchers found that those subjects who handled the gun had significantly higher levels of testosterone than those who handled the game.[104]

The next phase of the experiment involved an assistant entering the room with a cup of water that had been laced with a single drop of hot sauce. The subject was told that the drink had been prepared by the previous subject. He was then asked to drink it and rate its taste. Afterward, the subject was given a cup of water and a bottle of hot sauce, and asked to prepare a drink for the next participant. The subject was told that he could add as much hot sauce as he desired, and that his identity would remain anonymous. The assistant then left the room temporarily while the subject prepared the next drink. When the assistant returned, the subject was thanked for his participation and the cup was taken to another room to measure how much hot sauce had been added.[105]

Those who handled the weapon and, therefore, had much higher levels of testosterone running through their bodies dumped more hot sauce into the test cup than did those who handled the game.[106] It might seem almost childish—and a bit sadistic—but this simple experiment provides proof that the mere possession of guns makes people more aggressive, in part by spiking testosterone levels. And this brings us full circle to offering a partial explanation for why men are more likely to go on shooting sprees than women are. Elevated testosterone, which is a hormone that is far more abundant in men than in women, partly increases aggression. When this aggression is the result of a severe ego threat, and guns are readily available for settling the score, the hostility can be perpetuated.

At their core, weapons prime violence, including premeditated mass violence. Every time someone who is overwhelmed by feelings of contempt or suffering interacts with a weapon, it can fuel his aggression and prompt elaborate visions of taking his anger out on those deemed responsible. This pattern is then repeated over and over until those fancies finally materialize—often with deadly results.

The case of Aurora theater gunman James Holmes offers an instructive real-world example of the priming phenomenon at work. During his trial for the murder of twelve cinema patrons, Holmes was ordered to undergo a mental-health evaluation as a condition of being allowed to put forward an insanity defense. In one of his video-taped sessions, Holmes told the court-appointed psychiatrist that he had initially purchased his Glock .40-caliber semiautomatic handgun for "self-defense." But the more time he spent with the weapon, the more he started to scheme up a "mission," as he called it.[107]

Holmes had a deep disdain for humanity. He decided that his mission was to kill as many individuals as possible. Somehow by eliminating people from the planet, Holmes felt that it would "save" his life. With time, he told the psychiatrist, "My planning got more deliberate. I got committed to the mission."[108]

Holmes acknowledged that his gun altered his thoughts, and that his thoughts provided a newfound purpose for his gun. It was a vicious cycle, the gun inciting violent thoughts and the violent thoughts fueling a desire to employ his firearm. "It just kept escalating," he said. He was "going from compulsion to compulsion." As he stated during one of his sessions, after constantly interacting with his handgun—taking it apart and then reassembling it "over and over"—it started going "towards other purposes." Driven by his inner impulses, he decided to buy additional firearms. Holmes noted that his mission "got real" after purchasing his shotgun. That was when he "started having 'realistic' thoughts about a group of people getting killed instead of mankind getting killed."[109]

The dynamic Holmes was describing to his court-appointed psychiatrist was the weapons priming effect.[110]

THE VIRGINIA TECH GUNMAN

There is one important caveat that needs to be stated about the predisposition-provocation-priming (3P) framework: its application to mass shootings is merely theoretical. For instance, none of the perpetrators of the gun massacres that comprise my data set were given pagers in advance and prompted to note their self-esteem levels in the days before they went on their murder sprees. Nor did any gunmen submit saliva swabs while in the midst of their rampages, so that we could measure their testosterone levels at the height of their aggression. At present, analysis is limited to applying the model inductively. And even then, the best we can do is collect evidence and work backward to see, were the mass shooters in question men of working age with some sense of high self-esteem who become enraged and planned an attack using readily available weapons when their fragile egos were threatened?[111]

Seung Hui Cho perpetrated one of the worst mass shootings in history and one of the deadliest acts of violence on American soil since 9/11. His actions shocked the nation and left us puzzled as to what would possess someone to undertake such a despicable action. Applying the 3P model offers some insights as to why Cho did it.

Predisposition. All but one of the 111 gun massacres that have occurred in the United States in the past fifty years have involved male perpetrators, and the massacre at Virginia Tech was no exception. Indeed, Seung Hui Cho fit the demographic profile of a deadly rampage gunman—an adult male of working age (18–59), most often in his twenties—to a tee.[112]

Cho also shared another trait with the typical firearm-wielding mass murderer: he suffered from mental illness. The precise nature of Cho's disorder remains a topic of dispute. Early in his life, he was diagnosed with severe social anxiety disorder, and then he was subsequently diagnosed with major depression and selective mutism. Other experts in the field have pored over Cho's behavioral background and have assessed him as additionally suffering from paranoia, psychosis, and schizophrenia.[113] Whatever Cho's particular disorder—or perhaps disorders in the plural—that he was mentally unstable is not in dispute. In this regard, he met the initial criteria of a mass shooter, leaving him predisposed to rampage violence.

Provocation. As with nearly every other perpetrator of a gun massacre, Cho was fuming inside and lashed out against victims whom he blamed—directly or indirectly—for his woes. The precise provocation seems to have been related to his passion: writing. As part of the official review of the Virginia Tech shooting ordered by the governor, Dr. Roger Depue took on the assignment of putting together a behavioral profile of Cho that offered a theory of the crime. Because of the value of this workup, it's worth quoting from it at length (the full profile is reprinted in the appendix):

> It was in his second and third year of college that he began to find what he thought would be his niche, his special talent that would set him apart from the sea of other students at the university. He would become a great writer. He changed his major from computer technology to English. He began to write in earnest banging out composition after composition on his computer keyboard. He began seriously to believe that his original material and unique style were very good. He sent a book proposal to a publisher with great expectations. When it was returned stamped "rejected" he probably was devastated.

He internalized this rejection for months. His sister tried to console him and offered to edit his work, but he would not let her even see the document. He tried to impress his English professors with his writing assignments but only one or two saw any particular talent. In fact many of his professors as well as his fellow students reacted negatively to his stories that were often laden with horror and violence. Cho's dream was slipping away because of people—people who could not see and appreciate his desperate need to be recognized as somebody of importance. Once again he could not function successfully in the real world of people and normal expectations. These rejections were devastating to him and he fantasized about getting revenge from a world he perceived as rejecting him, people who had not satisfied so many of his powerful needs. He felt this way despite the fact that many of his teachers, counselors, and family members had extended themselves to him out of a desire to help him succeed and be happy. . . .

Meanwhile he was constantly aware of his classmates taking from their affluent parents and squandering their money on luxuries and alcohol. He perceived that these students had no appreciation for hard work and sacrifice. He saw them as spoiled and wasteful. They drove their BMW's [sic], dressed in stylish clothes and consumed the best food and drink. They had parties where sex and alcohol were plentiful. These students whom he once secretly wished to join were now considered evil and his peers were conspicuously privileged. They were engaging in "debauchery" and they needed to be taught a lesson. . . .

Gradually, he realized he could extract a measure of revenge against the evil all around him. . . . He would plan a killing that would go down in history as the greatest school massacre ever. He would be remembered as the savior of the oppressed, the downtrodden, the poor, and the rejected. . . .

By this time Cho may have become submerged (immersed) into a state of self-pity and paranoia, and could not distinguish between constructive planning for the future and the need for destructive vengeance and retaliation. His thought processes were so distorted that he began arguing to himself that his evil plan was actually doing good. His destructive fantasy was now becoming an obsession. He had become a person driven by a need for vengeance and would now strike out against "injustice" and rejection. He would become the source of punishment, the avenger, against those he perceived as the insensitive hypocrites and cruel oppressors. He didn't need specific targets. His mission was to destroy them all. In his distorted fantasy world, he himself had actually become that which he seemed to despise most. He had become the instrument for the destruction of human dignity and precious potential.[114]

Seung Hui Cho didn't take well to criticisms of his work. In his mind, he was a great writer. But publishers, professors, and classmates thought otherwise. So he exacted a form of brutal revenge on those whom he felt unjustly denied him his due, particularly other Virginia Tech students who, in his words, "fuck[ed] the living shit out of me."[115] As Depue forcefully lays out, the ego threat was clear and present. But as the 3P framework also suggests, an ego threat on its own might not be enough to provoke mass violence.

It's a unique type of person who attempts to kill in reaction to a perceived injustice or injury: someone with high, but unstable, self-esteem. Here too, Cho fits the bill. In his mind, he was clearly a better person than those he loathed. He was an epic savior, perceiving himself as akin to "Moses" and "Jesus Christ," as his manifesto declares.[116] A review of the materials Cho sent to NBC News leaves little doubt that he held himself in extremely high regard. Nevertheless, he was sensitive to attacks on his self-esteem, as he himself conceded when he wrote, "You have vandalized my heart, raped my soul and torched my conscious [sic] again and again."[117] His wounded pride jumps off the pages he penned. And in Cho's warped reality, violence was the only remaining corrective measure to the provocation he was forced to endure: "You decided to spill my blood. You forced me into a corner and gave me only one option. Now you have blood on your hands that will never wash off. . . . "[118]

Priming. Cho bought two semiautomatic handguns and went on one of the worst rampages in modern history. But there's still one loose end that needs to be wrapped up. Why go on a shooting spree? Why not undertake some other type of "fix"? After all, it's not as if by killing his classmates he would suddenly become a better writer or even a more respected writer. So why did Cho take up arms? The answer is twofold.

First, mass shootings are communicative acts. Their purpose isn't just to hurt. They also send a message. Violence in such a context is a form of symbolic dominance. It "affirms one's esteem to the extent of being superior to the victim[s]."[119] As such, it adheres to the tenets of what is known as *self-affirmation theory*, which holds that "people who feel their esteem threatened in one sphere often respond by asserting their positive qualities in another sphere."[120] According to self-affirmation theory, when presented with a chance to right a perceived wrong and to send a powerful message to the others—maybe even to the whole world—perpetrators opt for measures that play to their strengths.

The easiest way to explain this rather-common human behavior is to give you a personal example and take you back to my young-adult years. My high school in northeastern Pennsylvania was, during my time there, a football powerhouse. We were not, however, always so fortunate when it came to other sports. When, for instance, basketball games would start winding down and it was clear that we were going to lose, as spectators we often broke out into a cheer—much to the chagrin of the head coach, I'm sure—that highlighted our "positive qualities in another sphere": "Let's play football!" It was a pattern that I contributed to in college as well, except that my alma mater wasn't really that competitive in any Division I sport beyond the Ivy League (to which it belonged). We were Ivy Leaguers and, when frustrated by an impending loss, we didn't hesitate to remind our opponents of our elitism: "That's alright! That's okay! You're gonna work for us someday!" In hindsight, such behavior seems juvenile. But immature or not, it did affirm our esteem by playing to our strengths—and reminding others of those strengths.

Returning to the topic at hand, second, Cho, like nearly every other rampage gunman, played to his strengths: firearms. Just like Andreas Lubitz took advantage of his unique access to the helm of an airplane, turning it into a lethal weapon, so too did Cho seize on the weapons readily available to him. Each action he took in his preparation for the attack fueled his ire and reinforced his commitment to go through with his scheme. What began as a fictional story turned into a realistic plan. But the tipping point came when Cho purchased his first handgun. That was in all probability when his fantasy turned into a self-fulfilling prophecy. Holding the gun. Posing with it. Loading it. Accessorizing it. Firing it. Buying a second pistol. Each action likely elevated his testosterone levels and compounded his aggression, further priming Cho to kill.

What about those preliminary assertions that Cho's rampage was sparked by bullying as well as by violent films and video games? As a general rule, those who have high self-esteem are more likely to be bullies than they are to be bullied. This ultimately turned out to be the case in the exemplar of school shootings: the massacre at Columbine High School. Despite initial news-media reports that the gunmen, Eric Harris and Dylan Klebold, were victims of repeated bullying, an in-depth investigation found that the two teens were often the ones doing the taunting.[121] Not that they weren't picked on once in a while. No student seems to be immune from occasional harassment. Even members of the in-groups like star athletes and affluent kids get teased. But the Columbine shooters, particularly Harris, had a knack for picking on his classmates.

The preponderance of evidence suggests that Cho was not that much different. The review board impaneled by the governor undertook an exhaustive investigation into the initial news accounts that Cho had been the victim of bullying. All it could find was that he, along with his sister, were subjected to harassment when they first arrived in the United States, but that "it was neither particularly threatening nor ongoing."[122] As for Cho being the victim of any sort of bullying at Virginia Tech, the panel was unable to confirm any of the reports and the rumors. On the other hand, the final report of the review panel documents that Cho harassed his fellow students and professors. Whether in the form of intimidating statements and gestures or stalking behavior, Cho made many people uncomfortable. In one particular instance, Cho's poetry professor Nikki Giovanni reported Cho to her department chair, accusing him of "trying to bully her."[123] These findings are consistent with what we would expect from someone with an artificially inflated sense of self-worth. Like most mass shooters, Cho was more the bully than the bullied.

Just to be clear, it's not that mass shooters don't at times feel mistreated. They might indeed. That seems to have been the case, for instance, with Omar Thornton, who went on a rampage in 2010 that left eight people dead at his former place of employment in Manchester, Connecticut, after becoming fed up with what he perceived as racially motivated abuse. As he told a 911 dispatcher shortly before taking his own life: "Uh, you probably want to know the reason why I shot this place up. This place here is a racist place. . . . They treat me bad over here, and they treat all the other black employees bad over here too, so I just take it into my own hands and I handled the problem—I wish I coulda got more of the people."[124] As this example demonstrates, *perceived* discrimination and harassment can be a catalyst for such violence. But the important point to emphasize is that it's the blow to the fragile ego itself—regardless of the form in which it is delivered—that drives mass violence. Blaming the practice of bullying misses the bigger picture. Few high-fatality mass shooters are really the victims of bullying. But nearly all see themselves as being the victims of an insufferable injustice.[125]

Like bullying, violent entertainment is another prevalent, yet largely unsupported, explanation for mass shootings. When reporters swarmed to Columbine in the aftermath of the rampage, they uncovered that Harris and Klebold were fans of Oliver Stone's *Natural Born Killers* as well as Quentin Tarantino's *Reservoir Dogs* and that they enjoyed playing Doom and Quake.[126] Again, in a rush to judgment, violent movies and video games became culprits for the massacre. Did the Columbine killers watch and reference violent movies? Yes. But in their communications they also mentioned *The Lion King* and *Ace Ventura: Pet Detective.*[127] Hardly what comes to mind when you think of violence on the big screen. Did they play and reference violent video games? Again, yes. But they also talked about playing Need for Speed and Ignition—automobile-racing games.[128] Critics of violent entertainment cherry-picked their evidence in an effort to promote a causal connection between violent media and mass murder.

Ever since the Columbine massacre, there has been a loud chorus of critics blaming violent entertainment for gun violence, especially mass shootings.[129] In the post–Sandy Hook era, the mantle has been taken up by conservative media personality and commentator Glenn Beck. In his bestselling book on guns and violence in America, *Control*, Beck insists:

> The video game generation gave us Sandy Hook in elementary school, Jonesboro in middle school, Columbine in high school, and Virginia Tech in college. And, considering how rudimentary these video games are compared with what's to come, it will only get worse.
>
> Those who've grown up being exposed to violence since the day they were born will eventually perpetuate massacres at our hospitals, our day-care centers, our Little League games, our churches, our school sporting events, and our school buses. There is no sacred place.
>
> How do I know this? Because there's no other choice; this is the way we are raising them.[130]

Let's start with a simple truth: most Americans enjoy violent films and television programs. In fact, they're pretty hard to escape. Yet most Americans don't go on shooting rampages, and, of those that do, rarely do investigators uncover any link between the gunmen and violent media. A review of the 111 cases in my data set turned up just a few shootings where there was even any mention of violent movies or television shows—and in these cases there was no concrete causal connection.[131]

The nexus between violent video games and mass shootings is even more tenuous. That's because most Americans don't sit around playing violent video games during their free time. Yes, teens in particular have a penchant for gaming. But as we have already seen, the gunmen who tend to go on shooting sprees are adults. Have they played video games in their lives? For those who have gone on rampages in the past two decades, most likely they have. However, looking back at fifty years of gun massacres in the United States reveals that most murderers from the 1960s through the 1980s weren't inspired by violent video games for a very simple reason: there really weren't any. Violent video games are recent phenomena. Mass shootings are not.

If violent entertainment does indeed fuel violence, especially youth violence, we should expect to see increases in all forms of violent crime as society becomes more saturated with gory movies and video games.[132] Yet the exact opposite has happened: violent crime is on the decline. Even violent offenses committed by young adults are continuing on a downward trajectory.[133] After examining these trends, a team of scholars recently concluded, "video games play no causal role in violent behavior."[134] What a lot of commentators like Glenn Beck take to be "common sense"—that violent-media consumption causes violent attacks—actually turns out to be largely nonsense.[135]

Nowhere is this more evident than in the case of mass shooter Seung Hui Cho. The Virginia Tech Review Panel uncovered that Cho was a fan of action movies. "My favorite movie is *X-Men*," he once wrote. This can certainly be interpreted as a moderately violent film, although one would be hard-pressed to argue that this PG-13 film is anywhere near the extreme end of the entertainment spectrum. He also played video games as a young child, although no one in his family can ever recall him playing violent games. The one that Cho seemed to enjoy the most growing up was Sonic the Hedgehog— hardly a brutal or bloody console game. But in college, it seemed that his interest in such activity all but vanished. According to the review panel's final report, Cho's suitemate "never saw him play a video game, which he thought strange since he and most other students play them."[136] As these findings make clear, violent media and entertainment did not cause the massacre at Virginia Tech.

The trinity of violence (perpetrator, target, and weapon) reminds us that in order to have an act of mass violence, first and foremost, there has to be a perpetrator—someone motivated to hurt and, most likely, kill. What an examination of the gun massacres from the past fifty years uncovers is that most perpetrators of these heinous crimes seem to fit within a general framework. They were males of working age, susceptible to repeated testosterone spikes; suffering from some form of mental illness that warped their responses to perceived ego threats; which, in turn, were the by-product of their high, albeit unstable, self-esteem being severely challenged; resulting in premeditated acts of violence that were primed by the possession of firearms.

Seung Hui Cho may have killed more people than any other mass shooter in American history, but in another sense, he's no different than most other mass murderers in that he seems to have fit this pattern perfectly. His rampage was the result of predisposition, provocation, and priming. It's this model—the 3P framework—that illuminates who goes on shooting sprees and why they do it.

In the past fifty years, the population of the United States has grown by over 60 percent—meaning there are significantly more mentally ill Americans who are dangerously vulnerable to perceived personal attacks. At the same time, the number of guns readily available has also increased drastically. That there has been a rise in the number of mass shootings is, therefore, hardly surprising. The simple math suggests it was to be expected.

The trinity of violence framework helps explain why people like Seung Hui Cho perpetrate mass shootings. But is there something in particular about university campuses that makes them more susceptible to attack? To better understand where gun massacres tend to take place and whom they usually victimize, we need to shift our focus to the second prong of the trinity: the targets.

CHAPTER FIVE

NO PLACE IS SAFE

Mike Ridgell must have been pretty upbeat when he woke up on the morning of Monday, September 16, 2013. The day before, his beloved Baltimore Ravens had come from behind to defeat the Cleveland Browns. As a season ticket holder, Ridgell didn't miss a home game. And seeing his football team down at the half, he must not have been 100 percent confident until the clock started winding down at the end of the fourth quarter. But for a die-hard fan like Ridgell, a win is a win. Regardless of whether it's pretty or not, it's always welcomed.

The other pro football team that plays in Maryland—the Washington Redskins—didn't fare as well as the Ravens did. Playing the Green Bay Packers away in Wisconsin, they lost by eighteen points. For supporters of the Redskins, returning to work the next day was not likely as pleasant. And at the Washington Navy Yard where Ridgell was a security guard, there were lots of Skins fans.

Bernard Proctor was one of those Redskins fans who reported to work at the navy yard likely a little bummed by his team's performance the previous day. But the civilian utilities foreman put the loss behind him and went to work in the boiler plant. At least the Redskins had a good shot at beating the Detroit Lions the following Sunday. It was something to look forward to.[1]

In the intrastate rivalry, Ridgell's team had certainly earned him bragging rights for Monday morning. Ridgell, however, was by all accounts a nice guy who didn't behave that way. Instead, he took up his post on the first floor of Building 197 and settled in for what he imagined would be another uneventful day.[2] Shortly after 8:00 a.m., that expectation was shattered when a mentally disturbed navy yard employee started shooting his colleagues, in what would be the deadliest rampage in Washington, DC. Among the twelve people killed that day were Ridgell and Proctor—the final two people to die.

★ ★ ★

The Washington Navy Yard in the southeast quadrant of the District of Columbia is the oldest naval shore facility in the United States. Established in 1799 to serve as the navy's primary shipbuilding and ship-fitting yard, it has since expanded to a massive forty-one-acre base that houses the office of the chief of naval operations as well as the Naval Sea Systems Command (NAVSEA). NAVSEA is the command tasked with designing, building, and supporting the navy's fleet of ships and submarines. Nearly three thousand of the navy yard's fourteen thousand employees work at NAVSEA, which is located in Building 197. The largest office complex on the compound, Building 197 rises five stories tall and consists of over six hundred thousand square feet of interior space. With thousands of cubicles and offices arranged in a dense and asymmetrical fashion, traversing the space can feel like navigating a maze (see figure 5.1).[3]

Aaron Alexis was one of the nearly three thousand people who worked in Building 197. The thirty-four-year-old civilian contractor provided information-technology support. On the morning of September 16, 2013, he parked his blue Toyota Prius in the garage located just across the street from Building 197. Grabbing a backpack from his car, he slung it over his shoulder and crossed over to NAVSEA headquarters. Scanning his identification at the security turnstile, he entered the building and made his way upstairs to the fourth floor, where he entered the men's restroom.

Inside the bathroom, Alexis removed a sawed-down 12-gauge Remington 870 Express Tactical shotgun from his backpack and loaded it with ammunition.[4] After exiting the men's room, he walked over to a section of cubicles near the building's atrium. At 8:16 a.m., he raised his weapon and opened fire on four employees, killing three of them. The shotgun blasts, which one witness described as sounding like a "large safe being dropped," echoed across the floor, leading many people to barricade their offices and hide under desks.

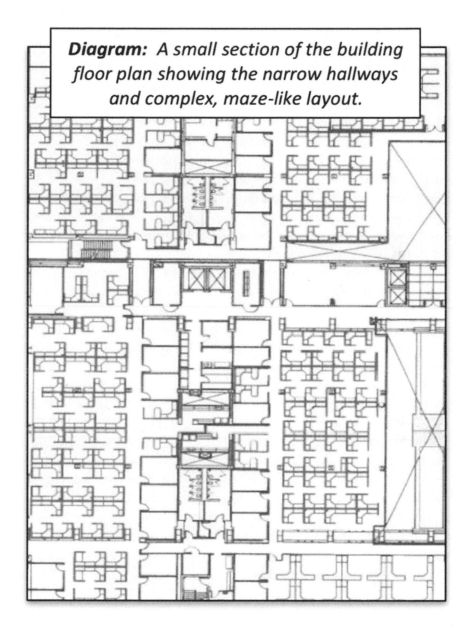

Diagram: *A small section of the building floor plan showing the narrow hallways and complex, maze-like layout.*

Fig. 5.1. Sample Layout of Office Space at Building 197 of Washington Navy Yard.

Source: Reproduced from District of Columbia Metropolitan Police Department, *After Action Report: Washington Navy Yard, September 16, 2013* (Washington, DC: Metropolitan Police Department, July 2014), p. 32.

Approximately ninety seconds after the initial shots were fired, the DC Metropolitan Police Department (MPD) received its first 911 call. Officers were immediately dispatched to the scene. Simultaneously, the base police force also started receiving phone calls over its four-digit internal-emergency number. Its officers were already on the premises, and they raced toward Building 197.

After ambushing his first victims, Alexis went on the prowl for more people to kill. Within minutes, the number of dead on the fourth floor had reached eight. He then proceeded downstairs to the third floor, where he surprised more employees, killing two of them. By 8:22, just six minutes into the rampage, Alexis had already murdered ten people—a death toll that would have been even higher had Alexis used an extended-capacity semiautomatic firearm.[5]

For one thing, shotguns are less effective than handguns and rifles against targets at far distances. Alexis was unable to hit many of the individuals he spotted and fired at down long corridors or in stairwells.[6] In addition, the shotgun that Alexis used had a capacity of seven shells. As a result, he periodically ran out of ammunition, which required him to pause his attack to reload.

After killing two victims and firing upon numerous others on the third floor, Alexis spotted a woman hiding next to a filing cabinet. He walked right up to her, aimed the shotgun at her, and pulled the trigger. Nothing happened. Alexis tried again, and for a second time the shotgun failed to fire. It was empty. Realizing that he needed to reload, Alexis took off down the hallway, away from the woman, so that he could insert fresh rounds into his weapon. The woman, who has never been publicly identified, crawled around the corner, took up a new hiding place, and waited for police officers to come and rescue her. Had Alexis's shotgun had a higher ammunition capacity, she likely would not have survived.

The procedure for handling an active shooter situation at the navy yard was to lock down the base and alert employees to shelter in place. For MPD officers arriving on scene, this presented a unique challenge. When the first officers got to the main entrance at 8:23

(approximately seven minutes after Alexis first pulled the trigger on his shotgun), they found the gate shut—a procedure designed to prevent outsiders from entering the base while guards leave their posts to respond to an emergency. After navigating their way around the exterior of the navy yard, they eventually located an open access point, allowing them to enter the facility.

In the meantime, a Navy MP, a Naval Criminal Investigative Services (NCIS) agent, two base police officers, and an armed guard had congregated in the lobby of Building 197. Weapons drawn, the five individuals split into two teams and began searching for the gunman, who by this time had made his way down to the first floor. At roughly the same time, the commanding officer of the base police and his deputy entered the building through a separate entrance, where they rendezvoused with Mike Ridgell. Over the blare of the fire alarm, which someone had pulled in an attempt to warn the building's occupants of the looming danger, the men started to assess the situation when suddenly they heard gunshots. Thinking that the sounds were emanating from the second floor—a deceiving echo effect created by the building's unique atrium layout—the two base police commanders decided to head upstairs to search for the shooter. As they started to depart, one of the commanders instructed Ridgell to stay behind and hold his position so as to prevent the gunman from leaving the premises.

Washington Navy Yard security guard Mike Ridgell had received extensive training in firearms use during his seventeen years of service as a Maryland state trooper. Sadly, given the bedlam of active-shooter situations, all the training in the world can't guarantee one's safety. Something can always go tragically wrong. And for Ridgell, it did. With gunshots echoing from all sides of Building 197, the fire alarm bellowing nonstop, the alarm system's strobe light flashing rhythmically, and police officers coming and going, the distractions that Ridgell had to overcome during the attack at the navy yard were many. Add to this that Ridgell had to secure an entire lobby area by himself and that the gunman could have approached from any direction—creating the near-impossible task of covering an entire 360-degree radius—Ridgell was clearly in harm's way.

As often happens in rampages, the gunman exploited the element of surprise. Sneaking up on Ridgell, Alexis ambushed him. Despite being armed, Ridgell never had time to react. He fell to a shotgun blast almost instantly.

At this point, nothing stood in the way between Alexis and the exit. He could have easily dropped his weapon and walked out of Building 197 as just another employee fleeing the violence. Instead, he chose to stay and seek more victims. However, Alexis must have sensed that he was running out of ammunition because he bent down and took Ridgell's Beretta 9mm semiautomatic handgun before returning back into the building.

He quickly ran into Ridgell's fellow security guard and the Navy MP. Alexis shot at them with his shotgun but missed. The security guard returned fire, but he too missed, as Alexis ducked into a corridor. As he was fleeing, Alexis encountered the other ad hoc active-shooter team. He opened fire on the three men, who exchanged rounds with Alexis, but no one was hit. Again, Alexis scattered into the mazelike hallways, allowing him to evade authorities.

As word began spreading throughout the navy yard that there was an active shooter at NAVSEA, employees in nearby buildings began making their way across the base in an effort to get away. Bernard Proctor was in the boiler plant located just across from Building 197. Sometime around 8:35, Proctor made his way to the alley that separated the two structures. There, he encountered US Navy Commander Tim Jirus, who had just descended from the fourth floor of Building 197. Standing in the alley just a few feet apart, the two tried to figure out what was happening. Proctor mentioned that he heard someone was shooting a gun inside the office building, but Jirus said he couldn't confirm that.

While wandering around the first floor, Alexis had entered a stairwell and opened the exit door. Spotting Proctor and Jirus alongside the building's exterior, Alexis raised his shotgun and pulled the trigger. It didn't discharge. The rampage should have ended right there when Alexis's shotgun was rendered inoperable. But Alexis had Ridgell's sidearm, which he aimed at the two men and fired.

As Proctor and Jirus were talking, two shots rang out. Jirus looked over and saw Proctor laying on the ground.[7] The sight of the utilities foreman mortally wounded by a gunshot to the head sent Jirus into a mad sprint for his life. Meanwhile, behind him, Alexis nonchalantly shut the door and resumed his hunt for more people to kill inside Building 197.

In the cruelest twist of fate, Proctor was killed with a firearm that was meant to protect him.

Moments before Alexis killed Proctor, the first MPD officers to arrive at the navy yard finally reached Building 197. Hearing the sounds of gunfire inside the stairwell, the police were again tricked by the acoustics into believing the shooter was upstairs. The officers assembled into active-shooter teams and made their way to the second floor, leaving a smaller contingent behind on the first floor. As police searched upper floors for Alexis, he spent the next fifteen minutes wandering around the first floor undetected.

At 8:55, Alexis decided to head to the second floor. When he climbed the flight of stairs, he found the door wide open. Alexis cautiously poked his head into the hallway. Peering first to his left, then to his right, he spotted the MPD officers who were looking for him. A review of footage from the navy yard's security camera system showed that twenty seconds before Alexis reached the second floor, the MPD officers had checked and cleared the stairwell where Alexis was now standing.

After spotting the active-shooter team, Alexis retreated into the stairwell and ascended to the third floor. He didn't notice any police activity, so he entered the floor and roamed around for a while. Eventually, he made his way to a large cluster of cubicles, where he took refuge under a desk, waiting for the right time to strike against law enforcement.

At 9:15, a team of four policemen began approaching the area where Alexis was hiding (see figure 5.2). They knew danger could be around any corner, but they didn't know that Alexis was just feet away, lying in wait. Suddenly, a call came over one of the officers' walkie-talkies. Upon hearing the police closing in, Alexis emerged and started shooting. MPD officer Scott Williams, who was on point, found himself directly in the line of fire. Struck in both legs, Williams

Diagram I: (1) Alexis has concealed himself in a bank of cubicles. (A)(D) MPD officers, along with (B)(C) two NCIS agents, make their way through the cubicle area. Alexis fires at the officers, striking the first MPD officer in both legs. *Location and positions are approximate.*

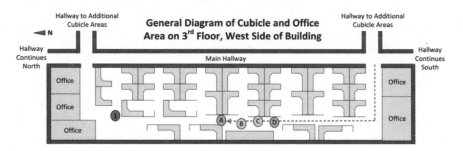

Diagram II: (1) Alexis remains concealed in a bank of cubicles. An (E) MPD officer and (F) U.S. Park Police officer enter the cubicle area to continue searching for the shooter after the injured MPD officer has been evacuated from the area. (G) Another U.S. Park Police officer remains at the intersecting hallways to provide cover. As the MPD officer rounds the partition to the last bank of cubicles, Alexis springs out from under a desk and fires at the officer, who returns fire, killing Alexis. *Location and positions are approximate.*

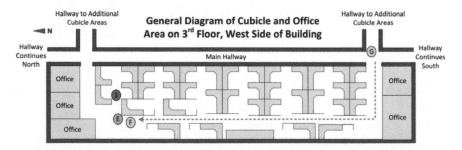

Fig. 5.2. Diagrams of Final Shootout on Third Floor of Building 197
at Washington Navy Yard.
Source: Reproduced from District of Columbia Metropolitan Police
Department, *After Action Report: Washington Navy Yard, September 16, 2013*
(Washington, DC: Metropolitan Police Department, July 2014), pp. 20–21.

went down, forcing the other officers to drag him to the safety of the main hallway.[8]

Hearing the "Officer down!" call, US Park Police officers Carl Hiott and Andrew Wong came to the assistance of the active-shooter team. When they reached their fellow officers, they were briefed on Alexis's approximate location. "We finally knew where he was," Hiott recalled.[9]

Just as the wounded MPD officer was being extricated to the first floor for medical attention, MPD tactical officer Dorian DeSantis arrived on scene. DeSantis turned to his Park Police colleagues—who normally protect national monuments and parks—and asked if they had active-shooter training. They both nodded yes. DeSantis replied, "Let's go." The three men had never before worked together as a team. The difference between them was physically obvious, with DeSantis dressed in typical SWAT gear right down to the protective helmet, whereas the Park Police officers were in their light-blue, short-sleeve patrol shirts. But they were all wearing protective vests, armed with assault rifles, and trained for this type of scenario. Forming an ad hoc active-shooter team, they went after Alexis.[10]

With Wong posting in the main hallway in case Alexis tried to flee the cubicle space from another access point, DeSantis and Hiott proceeded down the same corridor where their colleagues took gunfire just minutes earlier (see figure 5.2). Together, they took turns leaning around the six-foot-high partitions to look under desks. Row by row, they cleared the cubicles. At 9:25, they reached the end of the corridor. There was one last set of cubicles left to inspect. Alexis, who was under the last desk in this last row, jumped out and confronted the officers the moment they rounded the corner. Hiott remembered, "He came up and started firing." DeSantis, who was merely five feet away from the gunman, was hit in the chest but spared by his vest. Both officers returned fire, striking Alexis seventeen times and killing him almost instantly.[11]

"One shooter down!" Hiott radioed. After sixty-nine minutes, the rampage at the Washington Navy Yard was finally over.[12]

GUN-FREE ZONES

As often happens following high-profile rampages, experts took to the airwaves to make sense of the attack on the navy yard. Some echoed the concerns raised following the Virginia Tech massacre that America's broken mental-health system failed to identify and treat Alexis, who was no doubt "deranged." Others mistakenly claimed that this was another murder spree perpetrated with an AR-15 just like the one used in Aurora—indicting America's lax gun laws for allowing people to obtain weapons of war. (It took a few days for information to surface that the crime was not committed with an assault rifle). Alongside these traditional explanations of rampage violence, a relatively new culprit emerged: gun-free zones.

During the broadcast of CNN's *Piers Morgan Live* on the evening of the navy yard shooting, Morgan, a vocal proponent of strict gun control, engaged in a heated exchange with gun-rights advocate John Lott. Morgan insisted that the heart of the problem was America's "failure to do anything to even clot down on AR-15s."[13] Lott dismissed such claims by shifting culpability: "When you go and ban guns from certain areas, when you don't allow our soldiers or naval officers to be able to go and carry guns, you actually create a magnet for these types of attacks to occur." Lott added, "The problem here is . . . gun-free zones."[14] His point was that certain places prohibit civilians—and, in the case of the navy yard, some soldiers—from carrying personal firearms for self-protection. The argument goes, if only the people Alexis fired upon had been armed, they would have been able to shoot back and kill the perpetrator, preventing additional casualties.

In the back-and-forth, Morgan singled out the lethality of recent mass shootings that involved assault rifles, and Lott countered each example by drawing attention to the restrictions on carrying personal firearms at the locations the show's host mentioned:

> MORGAN: Aurora was the biggest single shooting in America by one shooter in terms of . . . people that he hit, 70 people.
> LOTT: It's a gun-free zone.
> MORGAN: Sandy Hook[,] it came a few months later[,] was the worst school shooting in American history.

LOTT: Gun-free zone.

MORGAN: We've now seen the second worst military base shooting in modern American history.

LOTT: Gun-free zone.[15]

In the days that followed, the gun-free-zone thesis was repeatedly advanced in the news and on social media, especially by supporters of expanded gun rights. Noted Second Amendment litigant Dick Heller, for instance, characterized the navy yard as "a perfect example of a gun-free, mass-murder-empowerment zone."[16] Gun Owners of America spokesman Erich Pratt declared, "We need to end gun-free zones at schools and military bases that make people sitting ducks."[17] Rock musician and NRA board member Ted Nugent tweeted, "America has lost her soul when we turn US Military bases into gunfree slaughterzones [sic] Shame on us."[18]

Conservative commentators followed suit, setting the right-wing blogosphere abuzz over how, yet again, a gun-free zone had facilitated a massacre. On *Reason* magazine's website, military regulations were branded as "sufficiently byzantine" on grounds that they "keep most (law-abiding) people largely disarmed."[19] At *Breitbart*, one blogger insisted that these rules allowed rampage gunmen to "shoot with impunity because our service men and women have no means of self-defense."[20] This point was echoed with a heavy dose of sarcasm at *The Daily Caller*: "Gun-free zones are the safest places around. For mass-murderers. They don't have to worry about anybody shooting back."[21] And the conspiracy-driven *Infowars* opined, "Any deranged shooter looking for defenseless victims need only look to a gun free zone, knowing that it will be populated by defenseless victims that provide no resistance."[22] Fox News anchor Martha MacCallum went so far as to suggest that Aaron Alexis might have purposely selected the navy yard because it was a gun-free zone, noting, "on a military base you're not allowed to carry weapons, at least military who have been issued weapons are not allowed to carry them on a base, and someone working or familiar with the area probably would know that."[23]

It might be tempting to dismiss these claims as the talking points of people with a larger political agenda. That would be a mistake. As an October 2015 Gallup survey revealed, 56 percent of those polled would feel safer if more civilians were armed with concealed weapons.[24] Findings such as this indicate that the issue of gun-free zones has now become a mainstream concern.

★ ★ ★

While gun-free zones have gained in prominence in the past few years as a casual factor contributing to rampage violence, the argument dates back to at least 1998, when John Lott published the first edition of his controversial book *More Guns, Less Crime.* As the title implies, Lott's primary thesis is that places where laws facilitate gun ownership experience lower crime rates. In particular, Lott maintains, "Allowing citizens to carry concealed handguns reduces violent crimes, and the reductions coincide very closely with the number of concealed-handgun permits issued."[25]

Examining multiple-victim shootings since 1977, Lott discerned a fascinating pattern in gun-rampage violence as well. When states adopted nondiscretionary, concealed-carry laws—also known as "shall-issue" right-to-carry laws—they at first experienced a "slight" increase in mass shooting deaths and injuries, followed by a dramatic reduction in such casualties.[26] The drops were so remarkable that, within five years, the rate of gun-rampage casualties in these right-to-carry locations bottomed out at zero.[27] In other words, Lott found that jurisdictions that encouraged their citizens to carry concealed handguns eliminated death and injury resulting from mass shootings.[28]

In 1990, Congress enacted the Gun-Free School Zones Act, which made it a crime to knowingly possess or discharge a firearm within 1,000 feet of school grounds.[29] The act—which applies to all elementary and secondary schools, regardless of whether they are public, private, or parochial—was partly a reaction to a mass shooting at Cleveland Elementary School in Stockton, California, that left five children dead and another thirty-two people wounded.[30] Lott drew on his findings to urge a significant exception to this law: "These results raise serious concerns over state and federal laws banning *all* guns from schools and the surrounding areas. At least permitting school employees access to guns would seem to make schools less vulnerable to mass shootings."[31] It was one of the first times that someone advocated for a policy that would allow teachers and/or administrators to carry personal firearms on school property.

In 2000, Lott published the second edition of his book. As it hit the shelves on the heels of the Columbine massacre, Lott naturally placed a great deal of emphasis on school shootings in those sections of his book discussing mass shootings. Offering support to his earlier thesis, he noted that in the time period since he had written the first edition of his book, there had been eight school shootings, two of which "were stopped only when citizens with guns interceded."[32] It was, of course, an anecdotal remedy. But he also reported that an extension of his data set to cover "all" mass shootings in the United States from 1977 to 1997 again found three important trends pertaining to mass shootings resulting from the adoption of right-to-carry laws: (1) the number of such attacks declined by 67 percent; (2) the number of deaths declined by 75 percent; and (3) the number of nonlethal injuries declined by 81 percent.[33] According to Lott, the only locations where mass shootings continued to occur in right-to-carry jurisdictions were places where civilians were prohibited from carrying concealed handguns—places like schools. For Lott, the lesson was undeniable: mass shootings could be deterred, and the best way to do this was to enact laws that empowered civilians to carry concealed firearms.[34] "Unfortunately," he wrote, "without concealed carry, ordinary citizens are sitting ducks, waiting to be victimized."[35]

By the time his book was reissued in its third edition in 2010, Lott was introducing us to a new concept that characterized places "where private citizens are not allowed to carry guns": gun-free zones.[36] In a forceful argument, he maintained that in right-to-carry states, where someone in a crowd of "dozens or even hundreds" is bound to be armed, rampage gunmen will be thwarted.[37] For this reason, Lott insisted that mass shooters—knowing they'll face far less resistance in places where their potential victims are unarmed—consciously seek out and target gun-free zones. He concluded his study with a warning that he would later repeat on Piers Morgan's show: "Gun-free zones are a magnet for deadly attacks."[38]

★ ★ ★

In addition to running the Crime Prevention Research Center, which he founded, John Lott is also a Fox News columnist. After practically every high-profile shooting rampage, you're likely to find Lott taking to the news channel's website to document how the latest assault in question took place in a gun-free zone. In fact, since 2010, when the third edition of his book was released, he has authored dozens of op-ed pieces pleading for the abolishment of gun-free zones. Given how influential his arguments have become, it's important to review some of Lott's more prominent viewpoints on mass shootings.

The United States has "an uncountable number of targets," Lott reminds us, and there is no better way to deter mass shootings in our communities than to allow Americans to bear arms practically everywhere—right down to government and military facilities like the Washington Navy Yard, where top-secret work is occurring.[39] Although a good start, law enforcement and armed guards are insufficient for the task of preventing rampage violence. "When police and the military can't be everywhere," he argues, "the last line of defense is having more citizens carry guns."[40]

The idea is that rampage gunmen are extremely rational when it comes to target selection. According to Lott, "they keep picking the few gun-free zones to do virtually all of their attacks."[41] As evidence, he cites the so-called virgin killings perpetrated by Elliot Rodger against University of California–Santa Barbara (UCSB) students and the Aurora theater massacre. According to Lott, Rodger ruled out his initial idea of attacking a popular spring break party called "Deltopia" because, in Rodger's words, "there were way too many cops walking around."[42] Regarding the Aurora shooting, Lott notes that James Holmes could have attacked a movie theater closer to his residence, or even one with a larger auditorium than the Century 16 Cineplex. "Instead, out of all the movie theaters within 20 minutes of his apartment showing the new Batman movie that night," Lott observed, "it was the only one where guns were banned." Lott goes so far as to hold the theater partly responsible for Holmes's killing spree on the grounds that it prohibited patrons from carrying their firearms into the complex.[43] The reasoning behind this indictment is that, in Colorado, over 4 percent of the adult population has licenses to carry concealed handguns. This translates into an "extremely high probability" that there would have been at least one armed individual who might have stopped Holmes before he could get around to shooting seventy people.[44]

As the above hypothetical suggests, if armed individuals fail to deter a mass shooting, they are at the very least well positioned to interrupt the attack and limit the bloodshed. One of Lott's contributions to the debate is that he has devoted considerable effort to assembling an anecdotal compilation of twenty-eight shootings that involved armed civilians intervening and halting rampage gunmen from completing their objective of killing as many people as possible.[45] Others have seized on his initiative, and the list of incidents now numbers thirty-six.[46]

Lott's contributions to the gun-violence debate have also been instrumental in allaying some of the concerns advanced by gun-control advocates. In particular, he assures us that a civilian armed with a concealed handgun has never accidentally shot an innocent bystander, and police officers have never shot an armed citizen mistaken for an attacker. The fears of innocent people getting shot and killed when armed civilians draw their weapons and attempt to stop a mass shooting are unfounded, according to Lott.[47]

All of the above claims, when considered individually certainly provide reason to give pause. When viewed in their totality, however, they present an extremely compelling case against gun-free zones. That said, the most powerful defense of Lott's thesis might just be to let his numbers speak for themselves: "With just two exceptions, from at least 1950, all the mass public shootings have occurred in these gun-free zones."[48]

John Lott has devoted a great deal of his career trying to raise public awareness of the dangers inherent in gun-free zones. In 2015, his thesis finally catapulted into the mainstream following four high-profile mass shootings, each one compounding the need for Americans to revisit the issue of how best to reduce the carnage of rampage violence. The first incident was the racially motivated attack on parishioners of the Emanuel AME Church in Charleston, South Carolina, that took place in June (discussed in chapter 4). After a twenty-one-year-old white male opened fire on a gathering of black worshippers, killing nine people, Lott penned a piece for Fox News suggesting that the gun massacre "possibly could have been avoided" had AME not been a gun-free zone.[49] Others ranging from pundits to law enforcement officials made similar claims on national television news networks.[50] NRA board member Charles Cotton went so far as to lay some of the blame on the church's pastor Clementa Pinckney, who was killed in the shooting. Cotton pointed out that Pinckney, who also served as a South Carolina state legislator, had been an opponent of concealed-carry and had, in the past, voted against right-to-carry legislation. Cotton's view was that Pinckney's actions contributed to the high death toll: "Eight of his church members who might be alive if he had expressly allowed members to carry handguns in church are dead. Innocent people died because of his position on a political issue."[51]

As the nation was beginning to heal from what had happened in Charleston, Muhammad Youssef Abdulazeez, a twenty-four-year-old man, with jihadist motives, opened fire on soldiers at a military recruiting office and a US Navy Reserve center in July, killing five servicemen.[52] As expected, Lott once again led the rally against gun-free zones, noting that—like the Fort Hood and Washington Navy Yard rampages—military facilities had come under attack because they were soft targets that prohibited soldiers and civilian employees from being armed while at work.[53] Other political commentators quickly echoed Lott's views.[54] But this time a new category of critics chimed in: presidential candidates.

No less than ten Republican presidential candidates questioned why the Obama administration was still prohibiting America's men and women in uniform from carrying firearms while on post. The first GOP hopeful to weigh in was Donald Trump, who within hours of the shooting spree, tweeted: "Get rid of gun free zones. The four great marines who were just shot never had a chance. They were highly trained but helpless without guns."[55] Seizing on Trump's cue, Jeb Bush, Chris Christie, Ted Cruz, Carly Fiorina, Mike Huckabee, Bobby Jindal, Rand Paul, Rick Perry, and Scott Walker quickly followed suit.[56]

When Christopher Harper-Mercer, a twenty-six-year-old mentally disturbed gun fanatic, went on a rampage in October that claimed nine lives at Umpqua Community College in Roseburg, Oregon, Lott's thesis was once again front and center. The Republican presidential candidates again raised concerns that civilians aren't able to defend themselves adequately during mass shootings.[57] This time nearly all of the GOP contenders were on board, forming a unified platform: gun-free zones are getting Americans killed.[58] By November 2015, when terrorists stormed Paris and killed 130 people—the vast majority of victims murdered by men wielding Kalashnikov assault rifles—the gun-free zone explanation had undeniably become a mainstream political position. A solution for curbing the carnage of mass shootings had emerged, reflected in the views of Trump. Speaking at a campaign rally a few days after the Paris attacks, the businessman-turned-politician observed: "Now, if you had 25 people in there that had guns, okay? It would have been a totally different story, folks. There would have been the shootout at the O.K. Corral."[59]

The implication is crystal clear: if the United States wants to reduce the bloodshed of rampage violence, it needs to revise its gun laws to make it easier for Americans to defend themselves in a mass shooting. In simple terms, we need to get rid of gun-free zones.

A LOTT OF QUESTIONABLE RESEARCH

John Lott's research on gun violence was revolutionary. His ideas were counterintuitive. His findings suggested that the way to reduce gun violence—including gun-rampage violence—was not to impose stricter gun-control laws, but instead to ease firearms laws. The solution wasn't less guns. It was more guns. As the title of his book stated, "more guns, less crime." And, by extension, more guns, less mass shootings. If only that was the case.

These days, with so much information at our fingertips, we often take to the Internet and research matters that could have a profound impact on our lives. Applying to college. Buying a house. Selecting a physician. Medical decisions, in particular, are of great importance because of their life-and-death consequences. So, imagine that you find your-self diagnosed with cancer and you need to find an oncologist. Odds are that there are dozens, if not hundreds, of oncologists within a one-hundred-mile radius of where you reside. Nowadays, it's easy to find information about medical professionals, allowing us to pick the one best suited to our needs. Google searches can instantly provide infor-mation on a doctor's education, training, residency, research, publica-tions, hospital affiliations, accreditations, and accolades. A new gener-ation of websites even allow potential patients to see how other people rate a specific doctor, and to learn if the doctor has ever committed medical malpractice or engaged in unethical conduct.

Of course, even with all the resources available to us, selecting an oncologist still tends to begin with a referral from a primary-care physician or a suggestion from an acquaintance. Now, imagine that a quick Internet search uncovers that your recommended oncolo-gist has a pretty impressive pedigree. He attended the best schools, completed his residency at a major research hospital, and published articles in top-tier medical journals. But as you keep digging, you dis-cover that his research methodologies and findings have been called into question by the leading experts in the field; that he has been accused of fabricating some of his research results; and that, after being criticized on online rating websites, he created a fake sock-puppet account to enter false reviews and artificially inflate his scores in an effort to salvage his reputation. Would you still be willing to trust that oncologist?

The truth is that most doctors and researchers adhere to a code of professional conduct that reinforces honesty and integrity. Pur-poseful violations are extremely rare. But they do happen every once in a while.

Accused of dubious practices and unethical behavior, John Lott is a prominent example of a researcher who has been plagued by such controversy. As a result, his findings, as well as the policy rec-ommendations based on those findings, have been called into ques-tion—kind of like fruit from the poisoned tree. This includes his thesis on gun-free zones.

***

John Lott looks impressive on paper. He holds a doctorate in economics from UCLA. Prior to taking the helm at the Crime Prevention Research Center, he worked at some of the best universities in world, including Rice University, Texas A&M University, Stanford University, Yale University, Cornell University, the University of Pennsylvania, and the University of Chicago. In the late 1980s, he served as the chief economist to the United States Sentencing Commission.[60] He has authored or coauthored eight books, one of which—*More Guns, Less Crime*—has sold over one hundred thousand copies.[61] He has also written hundreds of op-ed pieces, and, as mentioned above, he is now a Fox News columnist.[62]

Often academics are chided for conducting research that isn't "translational," meaning it doesn't really provide much value to everyday life. Lott is undoubtedly not such a researcher. Not only is he widely read and cited, his ideas have actually served as the foundation for numerous changes in gun laws. In particular, his thesis that right-to-carry laws significantly reduce crime has spurred the adoption of such laws in close to a dozen states.[63] More recently, his views have served as the intellectual backbone for what has become known as "campus-carry" legislation—which mandates that colleges and universities allow private guns on campus.[64]

Lott has been instrumental in promoting other pro-gun ideas as well. Guns, he claims, are used more frequently for self-defense purposes than for criminal activities.[65] Guns make women and the elderly safer.[66] Stand-your-ground gun laws reduce violent crime.[67] And, of course, eliminating gun-free zones reduces the carnage of mass shootings. In the words of one analysis, "John Lott is, without exception, the most prolific and influential writer on the topic of gun violence and gun control."[68]

It's no wonder that John Lott has been the leading go-to guy for "scientific" evidence to support the political advocacy of gun-rights associations like the NRA and Gun Owners of America. Not only do these organizations frequently reference Lott, they even occasionally promote his books and speaking engagements.[69] Furthermore, the relationship seems to be well entwined. NRA board member Grover Norquist, for instance, has coauthored a book with Lott on the flaws of the Obama administration's economic policies.[70] And NRA board member Ted Nugent—who refers to Lott as his "academic hero"—also serves on the board of directors of Lott's Crime Prevention Research Center.[71]

Inevitably, when a scholar weighs in on a controversial and politically charged topic like the debate between gun-control and gun-rights proponents, their work will come under attack from a firmly entrenched ideologue who is displeased by the message. But in the case of Lott's work, the taint extends beyond the partisan divide. This is particularly so in terms of his research practices and his attempts to defend those practices.

John Lott's research often feels like the body of scholarship that launched a thousand criticisms. It's difficult to find some seminal finding from his work on gun violence that has not faced challenge. This is especially true for *More Guns, Less Crime*. Criticisms of the book include charges that Lott created a model based on assumptions that were speculative; he cherry-picked his data; and he reached conclusions that seemed to be contradicted by actual outcomes.[72] As only a small portion of Lott's book addresses mass shootings, it's not vital that all the criticisms be reviewed here. In fact, because of the important policy implications of Lott's "more guns, less crime" thesis, a panel of sixteen experts at the National Research Council assessed the book. In a public report, all but one member of the panel held that, at best, there was no conclusive evidence that the adoption of right-to-carry laws resulted in a significant reduction in violent crime.[73] While there continue to be some academics who side with Lott on how guns impact crime, the majority of scholars who have weighed in—at least fifty to date according to one review—have expressed some degree of skepticism regarding his conclusions.[74]

Questions surrounding Lott's research methodology and practices are, in and of themselves, enough to warrant thorough inspection of his conclusions regarding mass shootings. But Lott's actions in defending himself have raised even more troubling concerns—furthering the need for analysts and policymakers to subject his work to scrutiny. Two examples establish why this is so.

In the first edition of *More Guns, Less Crime*, Lott asserted that national opinion surveys found that merely brandishing a firearm accounted for 98 percent of the instances involving a defensive gun use—implying that usually all it takes to prevent crime is to have a firearm in your possession.[75] By the time the second edition of his book came out, Lott claimed that the 98 percent figure was derived not from an aggregation of national polling data, but rather from a single survey that he had conducted.[76] It's a significant difference for sure. But, truth be told, when drafting a large manuscript, it's not unheard of to have an occasional oversight or mistake. Fortunately, when querying over 2,400 individuals, as Lott stated his survey did, there will be a record of poll results. Except there wasn't. As Lott noted: "My survey was conducted over 3 months during 1997. I had planned on including a discussion of it in my book, but did not do so because an unfortunate computer crash lost my hard disk right before the final draft of the book had to be turned in."[77]

With the veracity of his work in question, James Lindgren, a professor at Northwestern University's School of Law, stepped in to serve as an academic arbiter of sorts. Lindgren pressed Lott for evidence—any evidence—that this survey was actually performed. How about receipts confirming that the survey was conducted? It turned out the survey was not funded by any outside organization. All the costs were paid for by Lott personally, out of his own pocket. How about employment records for the students hired to place the phone calls? None of those existed. All the survey calls were supposedly conducted by undergraduate volunteers. How about phone records of the calls made to survey respondents? The calls were allegedly placed by the student assistants from their personal phones and all the costs were covered directly by Lott, with no paper record of reimbursements. How about identifying at least one—just one—student assistant by name so that he or she could confirm the survey? Lott couldn't recall any of them by name. How about the tally sheets on which the student assistants recorded survey responses? Lott couldn't find them. He thinks he likely threw them out during a move.[78]

Lindgren asked Lott to supply close to a dozen different items, any one of which could verify that the survey was performed. Lott was unable to provide any of the sought-after evidence. Although

Lindgren ultimately withheld judgment, he concluded his investigation with a plea for anyone who was involved in the survey to come
forward and confirm that it was indeed conducted.[79] Over ten years
later, not a single student assistant has surfaced.[80]

Lott has tried to quiet the storm by suggesting the survey is insignificant to the larger *More Guns, Less Crime* project. In his words, "The reference to the survey involves one number in one sentence in my book."[81]
But as two of his biggest critics point out, "One wonders why someone
who ostensibly went through such a herculean effort to conduct a huge
survey with his own money in three months' time would then turn
around and diminish his own work by insisting that it's *only* 'one number
in one sentence' in one book. That's a lot of work and a lot of excuses
for one sentence."[82] Others, like history professor Jon Wiener, have been
harsher in their assessment: "The conclusion seemed obvious: Lott had
never done the national survey. He was lying."[83]

At roughly the same time that Lott was coming under fire
regarding the survey, a student of his did come forward to speak in
his defense. Mary Rosh, who studied with Lott at the University of
Pennsylvania's Wharton School of Business in the early 1990s, had
nothing but high praise for her former instructor.[84] "The best professor that I ever had," she announced. Lauding Lott's book and
encouraging people to download his papers, Rosh went to bizarre
lengths to stick up for her mentor. Rosh posted hundreds of messages
online, often making extremely meticulous arguments pertaining to
Lott's work. It's not unusual for alumni to feel loyalty or affection for
their former professors and mentors, but this degree of effort and
passion was truly exceptional. Who was Mary Rosh, and why was she
so vested in protecting Lott's scholarship and reputation?[85]

On a hunch, a journalist at *Reason* magazine decided to compare
the Internet Protocol address of one of Rosh's posts with that of an
e-mail Lott had sent him. They were identical. Mary Rosh was not
Lott's student. She—or rather he—was John Lott himself.[86] When confronted with the evidence, Lott confessed, "The MaRyRoSh pen name
account was created years ago for an account for my children, using
the first two letters of the names of my four sons. . . . I shouldn't have
used it, but I didn't want to get directly involved with my real name
because I could not commit large blocks of time to discussions."[87] In

follow-up correspondence in *Science* magazine, Lott explained that he used a sock puppet in online forums because past postings under his real name had "elicited threatening and obnoxious telephone calls."[88] It was a justification that the editor-in-chief of *Science* found unconvincing. In his view, constructing and employing a "false identity" to defend one's work and attack one's critics "goes down as fraud."[89]

With his research and integrity in question, it seems irresponsible to accept Lott's assertions regarding gun-free zones without first subjecting his claims to intense scrutiny. So let's take a closer look.

As mentioned earlier, the concept of a gun-free zone actually traces its roots back to the Gun-Free School Zones Act of 1990.[90] Building on the idea of a gun-free school zone, commentators like John Lott proposed a much broader concept that came to be known as the gun-free zone—an area where anyone other than a police officer or authorized security guard is prohibited from possessing a firearm.[91] Unfortunately, the concept has never been properly defined, allowing for misuse of the term in a politically expedient manner that generally promotes the expansion of gun rights. Take John Lott's own use of the term.

In *More Guns, Less Crime*, Lott described gun-free zones as locales "where private citizens are not allowed to carry guns."[92] As an example, Lott cited properties where "owners ban guns provided they post clear signs." As time went on, however, Lott began embracing a looser conceptualization that deemed entire cities and counties to be gun-free zones if they were extremely restrictive in issuing concealed-carry permits. This was the case in his characterization of Santa Barbara County following Elliot Rodger's 2014 rampage.[93] But this is a bit disingenuous, as California residents aren't prohibited outright from possessing firearms, meaning these zones are not free of guns. Those with permits as well as those owning private property (like the Isla Vista Deli Mart that Rodger shot up) could have returned fire during the rampage against UCSB students had they been armed. There's no way that Rodger could have known if anyone on the streets or in the business establishments was carrying a weapon.[94]

Another problem with the term "gun-free zones" relates to how gun-rights advocates employ it only for private citizens. Even if there are law enforcement officers and armed security guards on the premises, many still insist that the property is a gun-free zone if civilians are prohibited from carrying their personal firearms on site. Case in point: Lott's characterization of military installations like Fort Hood and the Washington Navy Yard.[95] There's an obvious logical problem with such a conceptualization. How can a place be a gun-free zone if guns are present? The implication is that rampage shooters are only deterred by armed civilians, not by armed guards and cops. But that's an absurd suggestion. Certainly, a bullet fired out of a police officer's firearm has stopping power as well. If it's "more guns, less crime," as Lott proclaims, then it's the gun itself that prevents criminal violence—including rampage violence. The distinction between civilian and law enforcement guns shouldn't matter.

To avoid further confusion, I suggest we employ a commonsensical definition: gun-free zones are places where there are never armed personnel stationed on the property *and* private citizens are prohibited from being armed with personal firearms by law or appropriate notice.[96] Using the term in its literal sense not only provides clarity, it also frees us to generate an alternative concept that better captures the dynamic Lott conflates with true gun-free zones. In this vein, I propose utilizing the term "gun-restricting zones" for places where private citizens are barred from carrying personal firearms by law or appropriate notice, yet armed security is routinely present. This best describes locations like military facilities and college campuses, where armed guards and police are on regular patrol, but civilians are prohibited from bearing arms. To round out the possibilities, I suggest that we employ the term "gun-allowing zones" to represent those places where private civilians are not legally prohibited from carrying personal firearms.

Sharpening our definitions alleviates the ambiguities and inconsistencies surrounding gun-free zones and their impact on mass shootings.

The other major problem is that many of those who study this relationship often have a clear agenda and seem to go to great lengths to make the data fit the theory. Lott again stands out in this regard. Among other things, he has maintained:

1. States that enact right-to-carry laws see an elimination of mass shootings within five years;[97]
2. There have been only two mass shootings in the past sixty-five years that have occurred in a location where civilians were allowed to carry firearms;[98] and
3. More than two dozen mass shootings have been stopped by armed citizens.[99]

These are powerful statements. If Lott's findings are correct, then the clear conclusion is, as he put it in one of his Fox News commentaries, "gun-free zones are killing us."[100] This suggests that lawmakers concerned with protecting the American public from mass shootings should make the elimination of gun-free and gun-restricting zones a legislative priority. But before government goes down this path, it's important to ask, Do Lott's claims survive the test of scrutiny?

In 2002, a team of scholars lead by Grant Duwe tried to replicate Lott's finding that right-to-carry laws drastically reduced the occurrence and carnage of mass shootings—zeroing out such attacks within five years. Examining incidents from roughly the same time frame, the researchers concluded that permitting private citizens to carry concealed handguns had "no effect on mass public shootings at all."[101] As with other findings reported in *More Guns, Less Crime*, the pattern in multiple-victim shootings couldn't be replicated.

How does Lott's theory hold up when assessed using my data set of 111 gun massacres? There are currently forty-one states that have "shall-issue" right-to-carry laws. California, Connecticut, Delaware, Hawaii, Maryland, Massachusetts, New Jersey, New York, Rhode Island, and the District of Columbia are the only jurisdictions (outside of United States territories) that have not enacted such laws. They are instead guided by a discretionary system of "may-issue" laws, which generally requires prior authorization for many forms of firearm ownership. Three states—Vermont, New Hampshire, and Washington—had right-to-carry laws in effect prior to the starting date of my data set (1966). The other thirty-eight states adopted laws facilitating the carrying of concealed handguns subsequent to my start date, beginning with Indiana in 1980.[102] This presents an excellent opportunity to test Lott's thesis.[103]

The forty-one states that are currently shall-issue right-to-carry states experienced a combined forty-three gun massacres prior to adopting such laws. Under right-to-carry conditions, the total number of such high-fatality mass shootings dropped to thirty-eight, a 12 percent decrease (see table 5.1). It's not an insignificant drop,

Table 5.1. Gun Massacres Preceding and Following the Enactment of Right-to-Carry Laws.

Current Shall-Issue Right-to-Carry Jurisdictions (N = 41 States)

Number of Gun Massacres Pre-Enactment of Right-to-Carry Laws	43
Number of Gun Massacres Post-Enactment of Right-to-Carry Laws	38
Number of Gun Massacres 5+ Years after Enactment of Right-to-Carry Laws	31
Cumulative Gun-Massacre Deaths Pre-Enactment of Right-to-Carry Laws	323
Cumulative Gun-Massacre Deaths Post-Enactment of Right-to-Carry Laws	321
Cumulative Gun-Massacre Deaths 5+ Years after Enactment of Right-to-Carry Laws	257
Average Death Toll Per Incident Pre-Enactment of Right-to-Carry Laws	7.5
Average Death Toll Per Incident Post-Enactment of Right-to-Carry Laws	8.4
Average Death Toll Per Incident 5+ Years after Enactment of Right-to-Carry Laws	8.3

Current May-Issue Jurisdictions (N = 9 States Plus the District of Columbia)

Number of Gun Massacres	30
Cumulative Gun-Massacre Deaths	260
Average Death Toll Per Incident	8.7

All Jurisdictions, 1966–2015 (N = 50 States Plus the District of Columbia)

Number of Gun Massacres Not Occurring under Right-to-Carry Conditions	73
Number of Gun Massacres Occurring under Right-to-Carry Conditions	38
Cumulative Gun-Massacre Deaths Not Occurring under Right-to-Carry Conditions	583
Cumulative Gun-Massacre Deaths Occurring under Right-to-Carry Conditions	321
Average Death Toll Per Incident Not Occurring under Right-to-Carry Conditions	8.0
Average Death Toll Per Incident Occurring under Right-to-Carry Conditions	8.4

but it's hardly the decrease that Lott's model predicts. Also worthy of mention, thirty-one of those thirty-eight gun massacres occurred five or more years *after* the enactment of right-to-carry laws, indicating that such laws don't zero out deadly rampages within a five-year period. If anything, massacres in shall-issue right-to-carry states seem to increase as time passes.

In terms of fatalities, Lott also maintains that states will see less carnage after the passage of right-to-carry laws. But my data set establishes the opposite trend. In the forty-one shall-issue states, the cumulative death toll across the forty-three pre-enactment massacres since 1966 was 323, for an average of 7.5 deaths per incident. The combined death toll across the thirty-eight post-enactment massacres was 321, for an average of 8.4 deaths per incident. When the thirty massacres that took place in the remaining ten jurisdictions (resulting in a combined 260 deaths) are incorporated into the calculations, the results are even more damning for Lott's thesis. In areas where right-to-carry laws were not in effect at the time of a gun massacre, there have been seventy-three incidents, resulting in 583 total fatalities, for an average of 8.0 deaths per incident—a rate less than the 8.4 average that results after right-to-carry laws are in effect.

When assessing the data in a manner that accounts for population shifts, the incidence rates of gun-massacre attacks and fatalities also fail to support Lott's thesis (see table 5.2). When the incidence rates are mapped, it becomes obvious that the occurrence of high-fatality mass shootings and the carnage that results from such incidents both follow similar trend lines (see figures 5.3 and 5.4). If Lott's model was accurate, we should see a drastically different pattern: the incidence rates in right-to-carry states should be dropping precipitously, nearing zero as times passes. Instead, when it comes to incidents as well as deaths, the rates continue to rise in shall-issue states, just as they do in may-issue states.

No matter how you crunch the numbers, the conclusion is the same when it comes to gun massacres: the enactment of right-to-carry laws fails to eliminate gun massacres, and, arguably more disconcerting, correlates with an increase in deaths per incident.

Table 5.2. Five-Year Incidence Rates for Gun-Massacre Attacks and Deaths in Shall-Issue and May-Issue States, 1966–2015.

Five-Year Period	Shall-Issue Attack Rate	May-Issue Attack Rate	Shall-Issue Death Rate	May-Issue Death Rate
1966–1970	0	0.03	0	0.23
1971–1975	0	0.05	0	0.37
1976–1980	0	0.02	0	0.14
1981–1985	0.27	0.06	2.22	0.53
1986–1990	0.08	0.03	0.61	0.21
1991–1995	0	0.04	0	0.36
1996–2000	0.03	0.02	0.23	0.18
2001–2005	0.02	0.04	0.13	0.26
2006–2010	0.05	0.07	0.52	0.58
2011–2015	0.07	0.05	0.54	0.69

Note: Rates are calculated using the mean population estimates (in millions) of shall-issue and may-issue states over the applicable five-year periods.

Source: Attack and death tolls are drawn from table 3.2. Population data are drawn from United States Census Bureau, "Population Estimates," www.census.gov/popest/index.html (accessed May 3, 2016).

In all fairness to Lott, when he conducted his study, he employed a definition of mass shootings that was different from the ones used by Duwe's team and myself.[104] For Lott, mass shootings were those gun attacks that resulted in two or more victims being shot—either killed or wounded—in a public place. Moreover, he disqualified all shooting incidents that were part of a broader crime: "gang activity; drug dealing; a holdup or a robbery; drive-by shootings that explicitly or implicitly involved gang activity; organized crime, or professional hits; and serial killings, or killings that took place over the span of more than one day."[105] What he was left with were 563 gun attacks that occurred over a twenty-one-year period.[106] Lott insists that he compiled data on "all" mass shootings meeting his definition from 1977 to 1997.[107] It's hard to believe that in our country, where there are now easily over three hundred shootings a year that leave four or more people either dead or wounded, the number of shootings where two or more people were killed or wounded averaged

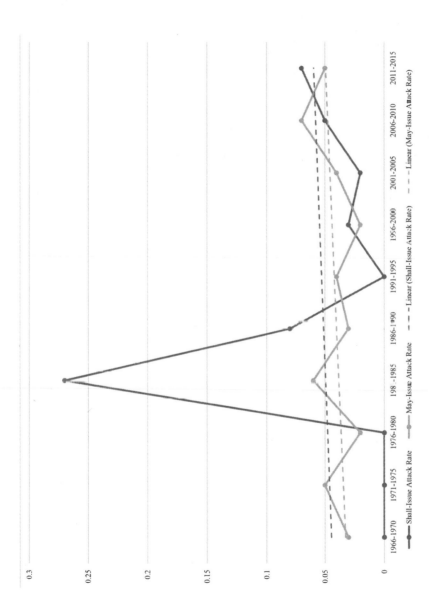

Fig. 5.3. Comparison of Incidence Rates for Gun-Massacre Attacks in Shall-Issue and May-Issue States. Source: Table 5.2.

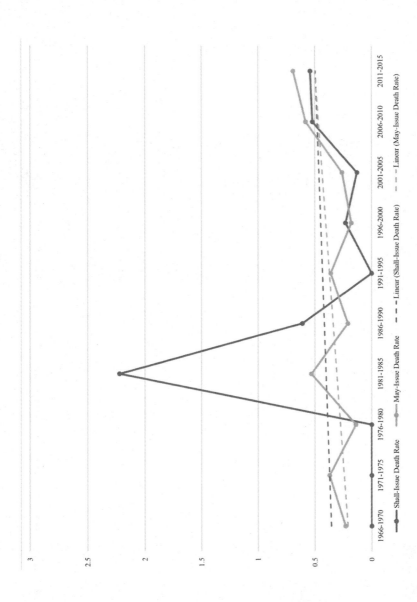

Fig. 5.4. Comparison of Incidence Rates for Gun-Massacre Deaths in Shall-Issue and May-Issue States. Source: Table 5.2.

only twenty-seven incidents per year. More likely, he didn't capture "all" the mass public shootings from his period of study.[108]

By 2015, Lott seemed to narrow his analysis of mass public shootings to those resulting in four or more deaths. In a Crime Prevention Research Center report, he claimed that, since 1950, there have been only two known instances of a mass public shooting that occurred in a location that permitted private citizens to carry their personal firearms.[109] Again, this is a bold assertion that can easily be examined using my data set (at least for the last fifty years).

A review of the 111 gun massacres that have occurred since 1966 indicates that only eighteen have taken place, in whole or in part, outside of a gun-allowing zone. (Three of these eighteen incidents occurred, in part, in gun-allowing zones.) Of these eighteen high-fatality mass shootings, thirteen took place in bona fide gun-free zones, where armed security or police were not on routine patrol. The remaining five incidents occurred in gun-restricting zones (see table 5.3.). Quite the contrary to what Lott argues, 84 percent of all gun massacres occurred in a location where there is no evidence that private guns were prohibited, and nearly 90 percent occurred outside true gun-free zones. Without question, gun-allowing zones do *not* deter gun massacres.

Opponents of gun-free zones, nevertheless, don't just argue that concealed- and open-carry laws usually prevent mass shootings from occurring in the first place.[110] They also maintain that, should deterrence fail, armed people will help reduce the bloodshed by neutralizing perpetrators before they can complete their rampages. In theory, this sounds logical. And my data offer some support for this position. In particular, the average death toll per incident across the massacres that occurred outside gun-free zones (as defined above) was 7.8, whereas inside gun-free zones the average was 11.0. This is a significant difference.

However, when gun-restricting and gun-free zone fatality counts are compared, a surprising pattern emerges. The average death toll for the five incidents that occurred in gun-restricting zones surpasses the average death toll for the thirteen incidents in strictly gun-free zones (15.2 compared to 11.0). It's surprising because, in four of those five incidents in gun-restricting zones, the perpetrators actually took gunfire

Table 5.3. Gun Massacres in Gun-Free, Gun-Restricting, and Gun-Allowing Zones, 1966–2015.

Gun Massacres in Gun-Free Zones

	Date	City	State	Perpetrator(s)	Deaths
1	8/20/1986	Edmond	OK	Patrick Sherrill	14
2	10/16/1991	Killeen	TX	George Hennard	23
3	11/2/1999	Honolulu	HI	Byran Koji Uyesugi	7
4	7/8/2003	Meridian	MS	Douglas Williams	6
5	8/27/2003	Chicago	IL	Salvador Tapia	6
6	3/21/2005	Red Lake	MN	Jeffrey Weise	9
7	1/30/2006	Goleta	CA	Jennifer San Marco	7
8	12/5/2007	Omaha	NE	Robert Hawkins	8
9	3/29/2009	Carthage	NC	Robert Stewart	8
10	4/2/2012	Oakland	CA	One Goh	7
11	7/20/2012	Aurora	CO	James Holmes	12
12	12/14/2012	Newtown	CT	Adam Lanza	27
13	6/17/2015	Charleston	SC	Dylann Roof	9

Gun Massacres in Gun-Restricting Zones

	Date	City	State	Perpetrator(s)	Deaths
1	4/20/1999	Littleton	CO	Eric Harris and Dylan Klebold	13
2	4/16/2007	Blacksburg	VA	Seung Hui Cho	32
3	2/7/2008	Kirkwood	MO	Charles Lee Thornton	6
4	11/5/2009	Fort Hood	TX	Nidal Hasan	13
5	9/16/2013	Washington	DC	Aaron Alexis	12

Gun Massacres in Gun-Allowing Zones

	Date	City	State	Perpetrator(s)	Deaths
1	8/1/1966	Austin	TX	Charles Whitman	14
2	8/26/1966	New Haven	CT	Arthur Davis	6
3	10/23/1967	Lock Haven	PA	Leo Held	6
4	3/16/1968	Ironwood	MI	Eric Pearson	7
5	6/25/1968	Good Hart	MI	Undetermined	6
6	12/19/1968	Napa	CA	Charles Bray	6
7	9/3/1971	Phoenix	AZ	John Freeman	7
8	6/21/1972	Cherry Hill	NJ	Edwin Grace	6
9	1/7/1973	New Orleans	LA	Mark Essex	7
10	6/21/1973	Palos Hills	IL	William Workman	7
11	4/22/1973	Los Angeles	CA	William Bonner	7
12	6/9/1973	Boston	MA	George O'Leary	6
13	11/4/1973	Cleveland	OH	Cyril Rovansek	7

14	2/18/1974	Fayette	MS	Frankie Lias	7
15	11/13/1974	Amityville	NY	Ronald DeFeo	6
16	3/30/1975	Hamilton	OH	James Ruppert	11
17	10/19/1975	Sutherland	NE	Erwin Simants	6
18	3/12/1976	Trevose	PA	George Geschwendt	6
19	7/12/1976	Fullerton	CA	Edward Allaway	7
20	7/23/1977	Klamath Falls	OR	DeWitt Henry	6
21	8/26/1977	Hackettstown	NJ	Emile Benoist	6
22	7/16/1978	Oklahoma City	OK	Harold Stafford, Roger Stafford, and Verna Stafford	6
23	1/3/1981	Delmar	IA	Gene Gilbert	6
24	1/7/1981	Richmond	VA	Artie Ray Cherry, Michael Finazzo, and Tyler Frndak	6
25	5/2/1981	Clinton	MD	Ronald Ellis	6
26	8/21/1981	Indianapolis	IN	King Bell	6
27	2/17/1982	Farwell	MI	Robert Haggart	7
28	8/9/1982	Grand Prairie	TX	John Parish	6
29	8/20/1982	Miami	FL	Carl Brown	8
30	9/7/1982	Craig	AK	Undetermined	8
31	9/25/1982	Wilkes-Barre	PA	George Banks	13
32	2/18/1983	Seattle	WA	Kwan Fai Mak and Benjamin Ng	13
33	3/3/1983	McCarthy	AK	Louis Hastings	6
34	10/11/1983	College Station and Hempstead	TX	Eliseo Moreno	6
35	4/15/1984	Brooklyn	NY	Christopher Thomas	10
36	5/19/1984	Manley Hot Springs	AK	Michael Silka	8
37	6/29/1984	Dallas	TX	Abdelkrim Belachheb	6
38	7/18/1984	San Ysidro	CA	James Huberty	21
39	10/18/1984	Evansville	IN	James Day	6
40	12/8/1986	Oakland	CA	Rita Lewis and David Welch	6
41	2/5/1987	Flint	MI	Terry Morris	6
42	4/23/1987	Palm Bay	FL	William Cruse	6
43	7/12/1987	Tacoma	WA	Daniel Lynam	7
44	9/25/1987	Elkland	MO	James Schnick	7
45	12/30/1987	Algona	IA	Robert Dreesman	6
46	2/16/1988	Sunnyvale	CA	Richard Farley	7
47	9/14/1989	Louisville	KY	Joseph Wesbecker	8
48	6/18/1990	Jacksonville	FL	James Pough	9
49	1/26/1991	Chimayo	NM	Ricky Abeyta	7
50	8/9/1991	Waddell	AZ	Jonathan Doody and Alessandro Garcia	9
51	11/7/1992	Morro Bay and Paso Robles	CA	Lynwood Drake	6
52	1/8/1993	Palatine	IL	James Degorski and Juan Luna	7
53	5/16/1993	Fresno	CA	Allen Heflin and Johnnie Malarkey	7
54	7/1/1993	San Francisco	CA	Gian Luigi Ferri	8
55	12/7/1993	Garden City	NY	Colin Ferguson	6

56	7/12/1999	Atlanta	GA	Cyrano Marks	6
57	7/29/1999	Atlanta	GA	Mark Barton	9
58	9/15/1999	Fort Worth	TX	Larry Ashbrook	7
59	12/26/2000	Wakefield	MA	Michael McDermott	7
60	12/28/2000	Philadelphia	PA	Shihean Black, Dawud Faruqi, Khalid Faruqi, and Bruce Veney	7
61	8/26/2002	Rutlegde	AL	Westley Harris	6
62	1/15/2003	Edinburg	TX	Humberto Garza, Robert Garza, Rodolfo Medrano, and Juan Ramirez	6
63	3/12/2004	Fresno	CA	Marcus Wesson and Sebhrenah Wesson	9
64	11/21/2004	Birchwood	WI	Chai Soua Vang	6
65	3/12/2005	Brookfield	WI	Terry Ratzmann	7
66	3/25/2006	Seattle	WA	Kyle Huff	6
67	6/1/2006	Indianapolis	IN	James Stewart and Desmond Turner	7
68	12/16/2006	Kansas City	KS	Hersel Isadore	6
69	10/7/2007	Crandon	WI	Tyler Peterson	6
70	12/24/2007	Carnation	WA	Michele Anderson and Joseph McEnroe	6
71	9/2/2008	Alger	WA	Isaac Zamora	6
72	12/24/2008	Covina	CA	Bruce Pardo	8
73	1/27/2009	Los Angeles	CA	Ervin Lupoe	6
74	3/10/2009	Kinston, Samson, and Geneva	AL	Michael McLendon	10
75	4/3/2009	Binghamton	NY	Jiverly Wong	13
76	1/19/2010	Appomattox	VA	Christopher Speight	8
77	8/3/2010	Manchester	CT	Omar Thornton	8
78	1/8/2011	Tucson	AZ	Jared Loughner	6
79	7/7/2011	Grand Rapids	MI	Rodrick Dantzler	7
80	8/7/2011	Copley Township	OH	Michael Hance	7
81	10/12/2011	Seal Beach	CA	Scott Dekraai	8
82	12/25/2011	Grapevine	TX	Aziz Yazdanpanah	6
83	8/5/2012	Oak Creek	WI	Wade Page	6
84	9/27/2012	Minneapolis	MN	Andrew Engeldinger	6
85	7/26//2013	Hialeah	FL	Pedro Vargas	6
86	7/9/2014	Spring	TX	Ronald Lee Haskell	6
87	9/18/2014	Bell	FL	Don Spirit	7
88	2/26/2015	Tyrone	MO	Joseph Jesse Aldridge	7
89	5/17/2015	Waco	TX	Undetermined	9
90	8/8/2015	Houston	TX	David Conley	8
91	10/1/2015	Roseburg	OR	Christopher Harper-Mercer	9
92	11/15/2015	Palestine	TX	William Hudson	6
93	12/2/2015	San Bernardino	CA	Syed Rizwan Farook and Tashfeen Malik	14

from the armed personnel on patrol at the attack site. Despite being engaged in shootouts, the gunmen in these cases still managed to kill more people, on average, than those who struck in gun-free zones, where no armed resistance was initially present. This raises an important question that merits further study: Does the presence of armed guards and police at the outbreak of rampage violence reduce casualties?[111]

Lott and other critics of gun-free zones would likely object to my findings on the grounds that I included a wide variety of gun attacks, including those that were related to broader criminal activities or domestic disputes. As explained in chapter 2, we do an injustice to the study of mass shootings when we use arbitrary criteria to exclude incidents that meet a commonsense understanding of the phenomenon. In this instance, it's even more inappropriate to exclude shootings that occurred in private or were undertaken in conjunction with the commission of some other crime. Wouldn't an armed person be able to prevent—or stop—a mass shooting in those scenarios Lott excludes? Is there some magic spell that keeps armed citizens from drawing their weapons and firing if someone goes on a rampage inside a private residence? How about inside a business establishment that's being robbed? Or how about during a gang turf battle?

Guns can be fired anywhere. The notion that we shouldn't judge the impact of gun-free and gun-restricting zones unless, to quote Lott, a mass shooting takes place "in a church, business, bar, street, government buildings, schools, public transit, place of employment, park, health care facility, mall or restaurant" fails the logic test.[112] But to placate potential critics, just in 2015 alone, there have been three mass public shootings (as defined by Lott) that occurred in gun-allowing zones: Christopher Harper-Mercer's shooting spree that claimed nine lives at Umpqua Community College in Roseburg, Oregon; William Hudson's rampage that claimed six lives at the Tennessee Colony campsite near Palestine, Texas; and Syed Rizwan Farook and Tashfeen Malik's attack that claimed fourteen lives at a holiday party being held at the Inland Regional Center in San Bernardino, California. At two of the three locations (Umpqua and Inland)—and possibly even at the third location—there were armed civilians present at the time of the shootings.[113]

John Lott's claim that only two mass public shootings since 1950 have occurred outside a gun-free zone is blatantly false. Of course, this doesn't mean that private citizens carrying personal firearms have never intervened to stop gun rampages. Gun-rights advocates cite thirty-six anecdotal examples of armed civilians drawing their weapons and stepping in to halt the carnage of mass shootings (see table 5.4).

But there is one substantial problem with this list. When we delve beyond the surface of these numerous instances where armed civilians purportedly intervened to end a mass shooting in progress, we find that, in reality, rarely do private citizens with personal guns stop rampages (see table 5.5). Of the thirty-six incidents, only four turn out to have been actual rampages in progress terminated by the actions of

Table 5.4. Purported Successful Civilian Defensive Gun Uses in Mass Shootings.

	Date	Location		Date	Location
1	12/91	Anniston, AL	19	8/10	Blountville, TN
2	8/95	Muskegon, MI	20	3/12	Spartanburg, SC
3	10/97	Pearl, MS	21	4/12	Aurora, CO
4	4/98	Edinboro, PA	22	4/12	Salt Lake City, UT
5	7/99	Santa Clara, CA	23	8/12	Early, TX
6	1/02	Grundy, VA	24	9/12	Plymouth, PA
7	2/05	Tyler, TX	25	12/12	Portland, OR
8	11/05	Tacoma, WA	26	12/12	San Antonio, TX
9	7/06	Memphis, TN	27	1/14	Portland, OR
10	2/07	Salt Lake City, UT	28	4/14	Austin, TX
11	3/07	Memphis, TN	29	5/14	North Logan, UT
12	4/07	Manchester, NH	30	7/14	Darby, PA
13	12/07	Colorado Springs, CO	31	7/14	Chicago, IL
14	5/08	Winnemucca, NV	32	3/15	Philadelphia, PA
15	5/09	College Park, GA	33	4/15	Chicago, IL
16	7/09	Richmond, VA	34	5/15	Conyers, GA
17	12/09	Oklahoma City, OK	35	5/15	New Holland, SC
18	5/10	New York Mills, NY	36	7/15	Winton, OH

Source: Material cited in endnotes 45 and 46 of this chapter.

Table 5.5. Assessment of Purported Successful Civilian Defensive Gun Uses in Mass Shootings.

Not a Mass-Shooting Situation

	Date	Location		Date	Location
1	12/91	Anniston, AL	12	4/12	Salt Lake City, UT
2	8/95	Muskegon, MI	13	8/12	Early, TX
3	7/99	Santa Clara, CA	14	1/14	Portland, OR
4	7/06	Memphis, TN	15	4/14	Austin, TX
5	3/07	Memphis, TN	16	5/14	North Logan, UT
6	4/07	Manchester, NH	17	7/14	Darby, PA
7	5/09	College Park, GA	18	7/14	Chicago, IL
8	7/09	Richmond, VA	19	3/15	Philadelphia, PA
9	12/09	Oklahoma City, OK	20	4/15	Chicago, IL
10	8/10	Blountville, TN	21	5/15	New Holland, SC
11	3/12	Spartanburg, SC			

Mass-Shooting Situation (DGU by Law Enforcement)

	Date	Location		Date	Location
1	1/02	Grundy, VA	4	4/12	Aurora, CO
2	2/07	Salt Lake City, UT	5	12/12	San Antonio, TX
3	5/10	New York Mills, NY			

Mass-Shooting Situation (DGU Occurred Post-Attack)

	Date	Location		Date	Location
1	10/97	Pearl, MS	2	4/98	Edinboro, PA

Mass-Shooting Situation (DGU Did Not End the Attack)

	Date	Location		Date	Location
1	2/05	Tyler, TX[1]	3	12/12	Portland, OR
2	11/05	Tacoma, WA[2]	4	5/15	Conyers, GA

Mass-Shooting Situation (Successful DGU)

	Date	Location		Date	Location
1	12/07	Colorado Springs, CO[3]	3	9/12	Plymouth, PA
2	5/08	Winnemucca, NV[4]	4	7/15	Winton, OH

1. Defender was shot and killed.
2. Defender was shot but survived.
3. Defender was a retired police officer serving as an armed security guard.
4. Defender was a US Marine.

an armed civilian. The majority—twenty-one incidents—didn't involve mass-shooting scenarios. Instead, they were knife attacks, gun-brandishing episodes where the weapon was never fired, armed robberies where the criminals never tried to execute the customers present, and shootings that didn't involve enough targeted victims to constitute a mass shooting. It's no wonder that when one pro-gun blogger at the *Washington Post* wrote an article identifying ten instances of citizens with guns stopping mass shootings, he had to couch his examples with a variety of qualifiers such as: "it's not certain whether [the gunman] would have killed other people" (to describe an attack by an unstable person who specifically targeted two of his healthcare providers—and passed on shooting others—because, of all reasons, they prohibited him from bringing his firearms to therapy); and "it's possible that the criminal wasn't planning on killing anyone" (to describe an incident where a mentally disturbed man frustrated with his church entered the house of worship and brandished his weapon without firing it, even though he had ample opportunity to do so).[114]

Of the thirty-six incidents, only fifteen were actual mass-shooting situations (as defined in chapter 2). Out of this subset, the armed intervenor in five of these incidents was a law enforcement officer (not a private citizen). In two cases, armed civilians drew their weapons and helped detain the perpetrators, but only after the shootings had concluded. (Neither defender in these two incidents actually used his weapon to end the rampage.) In four shootings, the attempted defensive gun uses failed to stop the attacks, with the armed intervenors shot in two of these instances.

When these cases are thoroughly assessed, it becomes abundantly clear that the real figure is not thirty-six successful interventions. The real figure is four.

Nearly 90 percent of the interventions commonly cited by gun-rights advocates as evidence that armed civilians bring shooting sprees to a halt are false positives. Only four of their examples are actually successful defensive gun uses. Even here, one of the armed citizens was a US Marine and another was a retired police officer serving as her church's security guard. If one assumes that there have been at least 300 *attempted* mass shootings in the United States per year over the past quarter century—a rather-conservative assumption given that there have been, on average, nearly 350 *actual* mass shootings per year in the past three years—then the rate of a private citizen employing a firearm to stop a potential or actual mass shooting is at most one in 1,875, or 0.05 percent.[115] And in all probability, given that there have only been four such interventions in recent history, the odds of an armed citizen successfully stopping a mass shooting are likely lower.

What all this data tells us is that, if someone went on a rampage tomorrow, there's at a minimum a 99.95 percent chance that the attack will not be stopped by an armed civilian.

There doesn't seem to be lots of support for Lott's theories.[116] Of particular relevance to mass shootings, it's pretty clear that gun-free and gun-restricting zones don't have much influence on target selection. So, then, what does? The answer is something a bit more personal.

If it's true that mass shooters deliberately select gun-free zones to attack because they want to be able to kill as many people as possible before being stopped, then we should see a great deal of shootings targeting locations and victims to which the perpetrators have no direct connection. In other words, most gun rampages should be random shootings. In this context, we are told that the key question that helps shooters decide where to strike is, Where can I go to spill the most blood? And according to commentators like John Lott, the answer is a gun-free zone where a lot of potential victims will be present—and unarmed.

Of course, we now know from the review above that well over 80 percent of gun massacres don't occur in gun-restricting zones, let alone gun-free zones. When we dig even deeper into the facts of each gun massacre from the past fifty years, another pattern jumps out: Very few high-fatality mass shooters strike easy, arbitrary targets. Specifically, out of the 109 gun attacks in my data set where the nature of the relationship between the perpetrator and the victims can be discerned, ninety-four incidents (86 percent) involved perpetrators who had a direct prior connection to the target or the victims.[117] The remaining fifteen incidents (14 percent) appear to have been random.[118]

Over 40 percent of gun massacres involved a family or domestic element, claiming the life of at least one relative, partner (current or former), or presumed paramour. Furthermore, 56 percent of these high-fatality mass shootings took place, in whole or in part, in a residential setting. Again, this is what we would expect if target selection is personal as opposed to random. It's also worth noting, residences are not gun-free zones. As a result, this further undermines the idea that mass shooters intentionally go on rampages in places where civilians are prohibited from carrying personal firearms. In fact, the second most common targets were commercial establishments, which tend to be selected because gunmen have workplace or customer grievances (see table 5.6). Here, too, way more often than not, these locales are gun-allowing zones.

Table 5.6. Types of Locales Targeted in Gun Massacres, 1966–2015.

Locale Type	Number of Incidents	Number That Were in Gun-Free Zones	Number That Were in Gun-Restricting Zones
Residential	64	0	0
Business/Commercial	33	7	0
Public/Transportation	12	0	0
School/University	8	3	2
Government/Military	5	2	3
Religious	4	1	0
Nonprofit	2	0	0

Note: The number of incidents in this table exceeds the 111 gun massacres since 1966 because fifteen incidents occurred in multiple locales. Of the fifteen multiple-locale incidents, thirteen occurred in two locale types and the remaining two occurred in three locale types. All fifteen multiple-locale incidents took place, in part, in a residential locale.

One of the surprising findings of this research is that, despite the media fixation with school shootings, only eight of the 111 incidents in my data set (7 percent) involved schools—and of those only three were bona fide gun-free zones: the massacres at Red Lake High School,

Oikos University, and Sandy Hook Elementary School. Columbine High School had an armed school resource officer on site and Virginia Tech had an armed police force, making them both gun-restricting zones. The other schools that were victimized by gun massacres—the University of Texas at Austin, California State University at Fullerton, and Umpqua Community College—were all gun-allowing zones.[119]

Another noteworthy finding is that just twelve attacks (11 percent) occurred in public spaces (including public transportation), without a single such incident involving a gun-free or gun-restricting zone. The remaining eleven targets were government/military sites, religious institutions, and nonprofit organizations. While all the governmental targets were gun-restricting zones, only three of the remaining eleven mass-shooting sites were gun-free zones.

The above findings go hand-in-hand and establish that gun-restricting and gun-free zones don't play a significant role in target selection. Instead, as suggested by the 3P model of mass violence presented in chapter 4, the most important factor in determining where and whom to attack is a result of something that directly provokes a gunman. Or, to put it in simpler terms, mass shootings tend to be personal.

THE FOG OF RAMPAGE AT THE NAVY YARD

Despite the evidence that gun-allowing zones don't deter mass shootings, the number of places where people can legally bear arms in the United States seems to be growing. For certain, due in large part to a concerted push by gun-rights organizations, the number of states that are right-to-carry and open-carry states is on the rise. And that's creating dilemmas for public safety. Let's do a simple exercise to see what I mean.

Here are two scenarios. Which one involves a good guy with a gun, and which one involves a bad guy with a gun? In scenario A, you are standing in line waiting to check a bag at an airport ticket counter when you suddenly glance toward the main entrance and notice a man carrying an assault rifle loaded with a one-hundred-round magazine. In scenario B, you are walking down a city street and spot a man across the street armed with an assault rifle and a holstered semiautomatic handgun. Quick, which one is the bad guy? Hint: It's only one of them.

This might strike you as a silly test, given that I have provided you with very little information. But the scenarios I just described mirror reality in that people, abruptly confronted with armed individuals in their presence, often have split seconds to decide whether or not their lives are in danger—and all they have to go on is what's directly visible to them.

These scenarios mirror reality in another manner as well. They actually happened. In June 2015, a self-described open-carry activist accompanied his daughter to Atlanta's Hartsfield-Jackson International Airport. Saying good-bye to loved ones before they board a plane is a fairly routine occurrence. What made this drop-off unique was that the man was toting an AR-15 assault rifle, armed with a one-hundred-round magazine similar to the one used by James Holmes in the Aurora theater massacre. It turns out that under Georgia law, bringing a loaded firearm into the ticket-counter area of an airport terminal is perfectly legal, as travelers who panicked and alerted the police soon discovered. Despite the objections of many in the terminal, there was nothing that authorities could do. The armed man was lawfully exercising his right to protect himself and his daughter. As he explained, "You never know where something might happen."[120]

A few months later, in November, a man in his midthirties was standing on a Colorado Springs street, armed with an AR-15 assault rifle, a 9mm semiautomatic pistol, and a .357 revolver. When a neighbor looked out her window and spotted him, she immediately phoned 911. Like the concerned travelers at the Atlanta airport, the caller was informed that the individual was completely within his rights to be carrying weapons in public. Feeling uneasy, but also realizing that there wasn't much more she could do, she hung up and kept watch from inside her house. But moments later, she was back on the phone with 911, hysterically pleading with the operator to dispatch police to the scene, where the man was now executing passers-by.[121]

After the fact, it's of course quite easy to distinguish between the good guy and the bad guy. But it's extremely difficult to tell the difference before the shooting starts. There's often just too much uncertainty and ambiguity to make sound judgments in situations where guns are present—and that can result in disastrous consequences.

∗ ∗ ∗

Writing in the 1800s, the noted Prussian strategist Carl von Clause-witz observed that, in combat, there are always unexpected twists and moments of mayhem that can undermine success. "War is the realm of uncertainty," he cautioned.[122] "Three-quarters of the factors on which action in war is based are wrapped in a fog of greater or lesser uncertainty." Basically, military accidents, setbacks, and fail-ures often result from muddled and messy situations. Over the years, this concept has come to be known as the "fog of war."[123]

Shootings are also muddled and messy, clouded by the fog of rampage. Readily ignoring this, critics of gun-free zones fixate only on the upside of allowing people to carry firearms in the event that they are suddenly confronted by a mass shooter. But what could go wrong? Not much, according to John Lott. Recall, he maintains that never once has a police officer mistaken an armed civilian inter-venor for the spree gunman and accidentally shot him; nor has an innocent bystander ever been shot by a concealed-handgun permit holder firing back in self-defense during a mass shooting.[124]

Once again, Lott's claims are inaccurate.

There are indeed examples of armed citizens intervening with unfortunate consequences. For starters, there are several instances where a private civilian decided to draw his weapon and confront a rampage gunman, only to be shot instead. In 1973, William Bonner tried to rob the Liquorama Liquor Store in Los Angeles while on a murder spree.[125] When the owner's stepson Roosevelt Jenkins drew his weapon and shot at Bonner, the gunman returned fire, wounding Jenkins. As often happens in these rapid-action ambushes, not a single one of the six shots fired by Jenkins hit Bonner amidst the chaos of the situation.

In 2005, David Arroyo attacked his ex-wife and son as they were approaching the Smith County Courthouse in Tyler, Texas, for a child-support hearing.[126] Police officers on location immediately engaged Arroyo, who wounded three of them. Mark Wilson, a resi-dent living nearby, heard the gunshots, grabbed his pistol, and ran to assist. Wilson was able to hit Arroyo, perhaps saving the life of

Arroyo's son. But the gunman was wearing a bulletproof vest. Able to return fire, Arroyo killed Wilson before fleeing the scene.

In another high-profile rampage later that year, twenty-year-old Dominick Maldonado laid siege to the Tacoma Mall in Tacoma, Washington. Armed citizen Dan McKown intervened, instructing the gunman to put down his weapon. Instead, Maldonado spun around and shot McKown, leaving him paralyzed.[127] Finally, in 2014, two right-wing extremists, Jared and Amanda Miller, executed two Las Vegas police officers while they were eating lunch at a pizzeria. From there, the married couple proceeded to a nearby Walmart, where Jared Miller fired his weapon in an attempt to draw in and ambush responding officers. Fearful for the safety of shoppers, concealed-carry permit holder Joseph Wilcox drew his handgun and attempted to disarm Jared Miller, a move that resulted in Amanda Miller surprising Wilcox and killing him.[128]

Over the years, the presence of armed civilians has also complicated police operations aimed at stopping active shooters. In one of the most famous instances from 1966—often considered the first gun massacre of the modern era—Austinites rallied to calls over AM radio for assistance in trying to neutralize University of Texas Tower sniper Charles Whitman.[129] Perched atop Austin's tallest landmark, Whitman picked off his initial victims at a rate of roughly one person every two minutes. Those with personal firearms who came to help took up positions throughout the campus and unleashed a hail of bullets aimed at Whitman. While the counterassault no doubt provided first responders and good Samaritans the cover they needed to rescue wounded victims and drag them to safety, it failed to stop Whitman, who was well protected by the observation deck's stone parapet. Whitman was ultimately stopped by two Austin police officers who were able to climb the tower, break through Whitman's barricade, and shoot him. But because of all the gunfire constantly bombarding the tower, the counterattack was excessively risky, almost killing the officers.

Ruben Torres's attempt to stop William Cruse's rampage at a Palm Bay, Florida, supermarket in 1987 provides another example.[130] Officers pulling up to the parking lot were met by a man firing his gun into the store. Amidst the confusion of the situation, police mistook Torres for one of the active shooters and arrested him, briefly drawing attention away from the real perpetrator, who was inside executing customers.

And, in perhaps the most tragic example stemming again from William Bonner's shooting spree across South-Central Los Angeles in 1973, Versell Bennett, a private security guard, attempted to prevent Bonner from carjacking a getaway vehicle after Bonner crashed his car. Bennett opened fire on Bonner at the exact moment that police officers were arriving on scene. Seeing the armed Bennett shooting, the policemen mistook him for the rampage gunman and killed him.[131]

Disastrous consequences have also followed when gun owners have fired their weapons in self-defense, although the downside of defensive gun use seems to be glossed over by those who favor an armed society. Take Donald Trump's views on the issue. When he addressed the 2015 Paris attacks that left scores of concert attendees at the Bataclan theater dead, he suggested that if only the victims had been armed, then it "would have been the shootout at the O.K. Corral."[132] The 2016 Republican presidential candidate stated that as if it would have been a good thing. But the increased risk to bystanders getting caught in the cross fire is another problem with defensive gun use during a mass shooting.

The most obvious—and tragic—illustration is the shootout that erupted between motorcycle clubs at a Waco, Texas, restaurant in 2015. With over one hundred bikers carrying weapons, an exchange of gunfire between rival gangs left nine people dead and another eighteen injured. The feud, caught on video surveillance cameras, was nothing short of an exercise in complete and utter pandemonium. People, unaware of where bullets were coming from, returned fire wildly. Even the presence of law enforcement just feet away—stationed outside the restaurant as a precaution—did absolutely nothing to deter the outbreak of violence.[133]

There are several other examples as well, including the 2012 murder of a man at a Jackson, Tennessee, nightclub, which resulted in his friends firing back in self-defense, leaving eighteen people wounded from the exchange of rounds; and the 2015 mass shooting that left four people wounded after a fight involving roughly one hundred people outside a bar in Elkhart, Indiana, escalated from words to weapons.[134] In Waco, Jackson, and Elkhart, people were shot as a result of being caught in the cross fire between those seeking to kill foes and those seeking to defend themselves.[135]

And it's not just armed civilians. Police officers also accidentally shoot innocent bystanders. Case in point: the NYPD officers who tried to arrest a man following a gun attack at the Empire State Building in 2012. When two policemen confronted the perpetrator on the street as he was fleeing, the man drew his weapon. The officers fired a combined sixteen rounds, striking and killing the man—along with nine pedestrians who were in the vicinity.[136]

Police officers are trained for high-stress, life-or-death encounters. Yet, as the Empire State Building shooting demonstrates, even those qualified in the use of lethal force commit harmful mistakes. Here's a statistic to put things in perspective. RAND, a policy think tank, assessed the effectiveness of NYPD officers in firearm incidents. After reviewing all officer-involved gunfights between 1998 and 2006, RAND found that NYPD officers hit their intended targets only 18 percent of the time.[137] In other words, over four out of five bullets fired by NYPD officers during a shooting missed their targets. It's no wonder that, in a recent shootout with an alleged armed robber, NYPD officers had to fire eighty-four bullets before finally striking the suspect.[138]

When gun-rights advocates press their case for the elimination of restrictions of carrying personal firearms, it's premised on an assumption that defensive gun use during an active shooting situation will be successful in prematurely ending the attack and saving lives. But that's one overly confident assumption. If those who are substantially proficient in firearms use have such a high miss rate, why should we expect better results from those who lack the equivalent training?

Think of it in a slightly different manner. Have you ever found yourself in a situation that raised your anxiety levels or made you extremely nervous? Flying in an airplane? Meeting your potential in-laws? How about something as simple as taking a test? Recollect what a mess you were trying to write an essay or answer a set of tough questions within a confined period of time. Now take that level of apprehension and increase it exponentially. Do you think if you were in the Aurora movie theater—in the darkness, with smoke obstructing your sight, people fleeing all around you, and bullets whizzing by you—that you would have been able to calmly and collectively position yourself for a clean shot at James Holmes? Could you be certain that, in the fog of rampage, you would have hit Holmes as opposed to an innocent person? Or, for that matter, that you would have killed Holmes before he killed you?

The point is not to deny that armed civilians can stop mass shootings. It's certainly within the realm of possibility. The point is, instead, to put that possibility in perspective. Gun-rights advocates have labored to research and identify instances where private citizens carrying firearms successfully intervened in mass shootings. Yet, despite their hard work, they have been able to identify only four such cases—and even of those, one involved a US Marine and the other a retired police officer who was serving as an armed security guard, two people who were trained to handle such high-stress and dangerous situations. As we just read, the number of unsuccessful interventions is more than double those that were successful. But here, too, the overall number of unsuccessful interventions is low. The clear lesson is that just as there can be rare instances where things go right, there can also be rare instances where things go wrong. Either way, defensive gun uses in mass shootings are rare—which means we shouldn't put much faith in armed civilians coming to the rescue of those in the crosshairs of a rampage gunman.

The case against gun-free zones claims that these areas are "magnets" for mass shootings. According to the theory, the presence of people with guns would deter such attacks, as shooters would opt instead to target places where they will avoid armed resistance; and, should deterrence fail, those carrying firearms could intervene and stop a rampage early, sparing at least some lives.

The evidence from gun massacres fails to support this theory. In the vast majority of cases, the targeted areas were neither gun-free nor gun-restricting. The attack sites of most gun massacres were, contrary to the theory, places where people were not prohibited from carrying firearms. Furthermore, in many of the locations where massacres have occurred in the past fifty years, guns not only were permitted but were present. The Washington Navy Yard is an exemplar case.

John Lott and numerous other proponents of expanded gun rights have argued that Aaron Alexis laid siege to the navy yard because it was a gun-free zone. The problem with this assertion is that it wasn't a gun-free zone, as substantiated by the stationing of armed security guards inside the very same structure that Alexis attacked. The presence of firearms played no role whatsoever in deterring Alexis. Nor did the theory's corollary—that people with guns can disrupt an attack mid-rampage—factor much into events.

Armed defenders failed to stop Alexis before he had expended the ammunition he had brought with him, *and* he actively sought out confrontations with them. Even when presented with an opportunity for safe exit, Alexis chose to re-arm and continue hunting security guards and law enforcement officials. As a result, Alexis prolonged his rampage by an extra fifty minutes. In that hectic time frame—which must have seemed like an eternity to first responders—Alexis used a security guard's pistol to shoot a civilian employee and two police officers. In fact, according to a police after-action report, Alexis engaged armed personnel on no less than five occasions.[139] Does this sound like an individual keen on avoiding armed resistance?[140]

Like most rampage gunmen, Aaron Alexis struggled with mental illness. The former navy petty officer had a long history of misconduct during his military service—"insubordination, disorderly conduct, unauthorized absences from work and at least one instance of drunkenness"—but he still received an honorable discharge in 2011.[141] Among his troubles, he had multiple run-ins with law enforcement. Two of these incidents involved a firearm.[142] On one occasion, while still in uniform, Alexis accidentally fired a bullet through the ceiling of his Fort Worth apartment. The police arrested Alexis on a misdemeanor charge of discharging a firearm within city limits. However, Alexis assured the district attorney that his gun went off accidentally while he was cleaning it. As a result, the prosecutor declined to take the matter to trial.[143] In the other firearms-related episode, Alexis shot out the tires of a car belonging to a member of a construction crew that was working near his Seattle residence. When questioned by detectives, Alexis confessed to the act but stated that he didn't remember firing his .45-caliber semiautomatic handgun until over an hour later, as he had blacked out during the actual incident. While the construction workers told authorities that Alexis had been giving them dirty stares for about a month before the shooting, Alexis explained that the men had tampered with his car and disrespected him. He implied that his angry outburst was fueled by post-traumatic stress disorder associated with participating in rescue efforts at the World Trade Center in the immediate aftermath of 9/11—a claim which Alexis's father confirmed to police. In a classic example of bureaucratic bungle, the police forwarded the matter to prosecutors for a determination of whether or not to bring a criminal case against Alexis, but somehow the paperwork was misplaced and the issue was never given proper consideration.[144]

After leaving the navy, Alexis worked as a subcontractor, performing various information-technology projects for the military. During this time in his life, his mental health began deteriorating. For example, while on assignment at the naval station in Newport, Rhode Island, naval police were summoned to Alexis's hotel room after a clerk raised concerns that he was acting bizarrely. When officers arrived, they discovered that "Alexis had taken apart his bed, believing someone was hiding under it."[145] They also noted that "Alexis had taped a microphone to the ceiling to record the voices of people that were following him." When questioned, Alexis explained that a microchip had been inserted into his head and microwave signals were disturbing him, preventing him from sleeping through the night. Sleep deprivation was something that Alexis complained about in two separate visits to Veterans Administration medical centers. Both times, Alexis was prescribed medication to help him sleep and sent on his way.[146]

The warning signs were evident. Something was clearly off with Alexis. But his condition never received serious attention, let alone treatment.

When Alexis executed his heinous crime on the morning of September 16, 2013, he used a shotgun that carried several messages etched into the weapon: "Not what y'all say!" "End to the torment!" "Better off this way!" One carving read, "My ELF weapon." It was a reference to extremely low frequency radio waves that are utilized in communicating with submarines, and which many conspiracy theorists believe are used by the government to manipulate people.[147]

According to the FBI, Alexis suffered from "the delusional belief that he was being controlled or influenced" by these submarine communications. In the course of their investigation, law enforcement officials discovered a message that Alexis had left behind: "Ultra low frequency attack is what I've been subject to for the last 3 months."[148] Alexis took up arms and attacked the navy yard—the facility where submarines were designed—to bring an end to the "attack" he felt the government was perpetrating against him.

Like the Fort Hood shooting committed by Nidal Hasan and the San Bernardino massacre committed by Syed Farook and his wife, Tashfeen Malik, the armed assault on the Washington Navy Yard was an act of terrorism, as defined by the United States Criminal Code.[149] But it was also an act of workplace violence, as—just like Hasan and Farook—Aaron Alexis was taking his grievance with the government out on his colleagues. The mere fact that Alexis laid siege to a military facility established that his attack was political. Yet, as with the vast majority of rampages, it was also personal.

As mentioned earlier, the night of the Washington Navy Yard shooting, CNN's Piers Morgan hosted John Lott on his program. Conservative on-air personality Ben Ferguson appeared alongside Lott, and both men made a concerted effort to lay some of the blame on gun-free zones. Morgan tried to argue that the navy yard was not a gun-free zone because there were armed guards present: "after . . . Sandy Hook, after Aurora, you wanted armed guards at movie theaters, armed guards at schools, there were armed guards at the naval base."[150] Morgan insisted that "it made absolutely no difference."

Ferguson retorted that armed guards aren't enough. "This is the reason why we're not calling for armed guards, because they cannot work and today is proof of that," Ferguson told the audience. "We are saying that if you were in the United States Navy and we trust you with navy ships and war, why the hell wouldn't we trust you to carry your weapon to work with you?"[151]

What Ferguson didn't realize was that the exact type of person he felt should be armed at the military installations like the Washington Navy Yard was Aaron Alexis to a tee.

If rampage gunmen select targets based on the degree of armed resistance they are likely to encounter, the Washington Navy Yard would have been one of the last places that Aaron Alexis would have attacked. Yet gun-rights advocates continue to blame gun-free zones for America's growing mass-shooting problem, ignoring the fact that most attacks are not opportunistic. They're personal. That, in turn, means gun massacres can occur anywhere. Whether a home, a business, a school, a church, or even a military base, no place in America is safe from rampage violence.

The trinity of violence informs our understanding of mass shootings by helping us focus on why people go on rampages and why they strike where they do. As a framework, it can also shed light on why the carnage has reached unprecedented levels. But, in order to better comprehend the increase in lethality, we have to shift our attention away from the perpetrators and the targets to the third prong of the trinity: the weapons.

CHAPTER SIX

GUNS KILL, SOME MORE THAN OTHERS

T hursday, July 19, 2012, was one of the happiest days in Ashley Moser's life. The twenty-five-year-old was pretty sure she was pregnant.[1] That afternoon, she had a scheduled ultrasound, which she hoped would confirm her prenatal status. Moser already had a six-year-old daughter, Veronica Moser-Sullivan, from a previous marriage. But that relationship had ended in divorce when Veronica was three. A baby offered a new beginning for Ashley and her boyfriend, Jamison Toews.

Toews was excited too. Earlier, he had asked his little cousin if she and her friend would babysit Veronica for a few hours while he and Moser went for the sonogram. The two thirteen-year-old girls readily agreed.

At the doctor's office, they received great news: Moser was indeed pregnant. Looking at the monitor, Moser and Toews saw the first images of their child. By all indications, their baby seemed to be developing just fine. The young couple decided that news of a healthy pregnancy called for celebration. Veronica and her babysitters would be treated to pizza for dinner. As they were eating, Toews's cousin suggested that they continue the merriment by going to the movies. *The Dark Knight Rises*, the final installment of director Christopher Nolan's highly acclaimed Batman trilogy, was opening that night. Moser didn't know much about the movie, but it was summer and she saw no reason why Veronica shouldn't go to the midnight premiere. So all five hopped into the car and made their way to the Century 16 cinema in Aurora, Colorado. They got to the theater early, knowing that the show might sell out. It paid off. They not only got tickets but also secured what were arguably the best seats in the 415-seat auditorium: four rows up in the stadium-seating section, middle of the row.

Veronica was thrilled to be at the movies, at a midnight showing, no less. She was cuddled up to her mom, sitting on her lap in the moments prior to the screening. After a while, however, Veronica's body was digging into Moser's abdomen, which became uncomfortable for the pregnant mother. Just prior to the theater going dark, Moser placed her daughter in the seat next to her and told her she needed to sit there during the movie.

The film was scheduled to start at 12:05 a.m. But with previews, it didn't begin until 12:20. Shortly afterward, a young man stood up from his front-row seat and made his way toward the emergency-exit door at the front, right side of the theater. Exiting auditorium number 9, he nonchalantly wedged a bracket clip between the door and the frame to keep the door ajar.

Once outside in the parking-lot area, the young man made his way over to his vehicle, where he started suiting up: a tactical ammunition vest; tactical gloves; throat, arm, and groin protectors; ballistic leggings; a ballistic helmet; a gas mask; gas canisters; a Taser disguised as a cellphone; pocket knives; a 12-gauge shotgun; an AR-15 assault rifle; a .40-caliber semiautomatic handgun; numerous extended-capacity magazines; and hundreds of rounds of live ammunition. Moments later, he returned to Theater 9 through the emergency-exit door.

The initial reaction of most moviegoers who could make out the young man in the dark auditorium was that he was in costume for the premiere, possibly dressed as the film's protagonist himself— Batman—who is also known as the Caped Crusader. Even after he lobbed a gas canister over the heads of those sitting in the stadium-seating section of the theater, many continued to think that this was either a publicity stunt or a prank. As one witness recalled, "I thought it was showmanship. I didn't think it was real."[2]

Suddenly, everything changed.

The young man drew his 12-gauge Remington 870 Express Tactical shotgun and fired into the ceiling. The loud bang and bright flash startled most of the spectators. He then leveled his aim and unleashed five more shotgun rounds, spraying the audience with hundreds of pellets in just seconds, before switching to his semiautomatic assault rifle.

As the dark auditorium filled with an irritating smoke that smelled like pepper, people's vision became further obscured. Startled and confused, Ashley Moser tried to make sense of what was happening. She, too, initially suspected that this was a teenager pulling off some sort of elaborate practical joke. At first, she thought the smoke canister that exploded right behind her might have been a stink bomb.[3] She also mistook the shotgun blasts that filled the theater with luminous bursts of light for fireworks. But as soon as she heard the rapid fire of the assault rifle, her parental instinct kicked in: she needed to grab her daughter and leave.

Moser reached for Veronica's hand but she "couldn't feel it."[4] So she got to her feet and turned to look at her daughter. "As soon as I stood up," Moser recalled, "I just remember getting hit in my chest. And I remember falling and landing on top of [Veronica]."[5] Knocked down, laying atop of her daughter, Moser still thought that what struck her was a firework of some type. It wasn't until a few seconds later, when she tried to move and couldn't, that she realized this was no prank.

At exactly 12:38 a.m., the first call came into 911. "There's some guy . . . after us," Kevin Quinonez screamed into his cell phone. It was difficult for the emergency dispatcher to make out what Quinonez was saying because of all the commotion in the background. But one distinct sound stood out: semiautomatic gunfire. At least thirty rounds were fired during the short twenty-seven-second call, many coming in bursts of five or six at time.[6]

Ashley Moser had not been struck by some sort of bottle rocket or firecracker. She had been hit by a bullet. And she wasn't struck just once. She had been shot three times. The impact she felt was a round penetrating her back and exiting through her chest. The punch of the projectile was so powerful that it numbed her to the pain of being hit twice more within a mere second—once in the shoulder, causing the bullet to ricochet inside her and lodge in her spine, and once in the thigh. Her daughter, who was pinned underneath her and not breathing, had also been shot. The same green-tipped, armor-piercing bullets that struck her mother managed to travel through the seats in front of Veronica and slice through her four-foot, four-inch, fifty-eight-pound frame in four separate locations: her abdomen, pelvis, arm, and knee. Her tiny body was no match for the powerful "enhanced" rounds that impaled her. It was later determined that one bullet traveled through the little girl's buttocks, hip, bladder, and iliac artery and vein before coming to rest inside her. Another bullet entered her right side and tore through her liver, spleen, kidney, and pancreas, causing tissue to bleed into her heart and lungs.[7]

As the gunman fired indiscriminately on the panicked crowd, some tried to run toward the nearest exit. Others tried to take cover on the floor. It didn't make much of a difference to those who found themselves in the path of the shooter's bullets, which were designed to perforate steel and Kevlar. No barrier in the movie theater was strong enough to stop such firepower, as Ashley Moser, her daughter, and dozens of other gunshot victims discovered.

One of the unfortunate spectators was twenty-three-year-old Caleb Medley, who was attending the movie with his wife, Katie, and their friend. The trio had picked seats located close to an exit—the same exit that figured into the gunman's plan of attack. Katie Medley was nine-months pregnant and concerned about going into labor during the movie. She insisted on being near the aisle in case she needed to exit the theater quickly.

While the events of that night were chaotic, Katie Medley vividly remembers how the rampage unfolded, beginning with the sliver of light that crept into the theater as the perpetrator re-entered through the emergency exit. Seconds later, she heard a hissing sound as a gas canister was hurled over their heads. Like Ashley Moser and scores of others, she too initially thought it was a prank, and that it was going to be "really funny."[8] Then the gunman, standing between the front row and the screen, opened fire. "It was clear. It was gunshots—a lot of them."[9] Instinctively, Katie Medley fell to the floor to shield herself and her unborn baby. She turned to look at her husband, but he wasn't on the ground next to her. "That's when I saw that he was still sitting in his chair. . . . I saw his feet on the floor and I couldn't understand why he was sitting in his chair when someone was shooting," she would later testify. "That's when I saw blood pouring from his face."[10] Her immediate thought upon seeing the head wound was "*He's dead.*"[11]

For the duration of the attack, Katie Medley remained on the floor. But after the shooting stopped, she rose to her feet. As she recalled, "It was hard to stay crouched because I was so pregnant."[12] Despite a powerful fear that the shooter wasn't finished and that he might now walk through the auditorium row by row to execute survivors, she decided to stand up and tend to her husband. Caleb had blood "pouring into his mouth and he was actually choking on his blood."[13] But he was still breathing.

Katie Medley did the best she could to comfort her seriously wounded husband, including washing the blood off his face and talking to him. Being inside the theater was, nevertheless, growing difficult. She remembers, "The air was very thick. It was hard to breathe."[14] When Aurora police officers finally breached the auditorium and began escorting moviegoers to safety, she knew she had to leave her husband and go outside to save their child. Thinking it would be the last time she would see Caleb alive, Katie took his hand, kissed him, and told him that she loved him and "would take care of our baby if he didn't make it[15]."

Caleb Medley squeezed her hand in acknowledgment.

★ ★ ★

Police officers began arriving on scene within two to three minutes of Kevin Quinonez's call to 911. Jason Oviatt, who had been on patrol nearby, was one of the first officers to reach the movie theater. As he sprang out of his squad car, Oviatt noticed several gunshot victims in the parking lot. He knew instantly that the city of Aurora had an active-shooter incident on its hands. He and a fellow officer spotted a trail of blood and followed it. It led them to the rear of the cinema complex.

As the officers approached, people were still filing out of the emergency exits, some crying and screaming. Amidst all the pandemonium, there was one individual who stood out, standing next to a white Hyundai parked not far from the emergency exit for auditorium number 9. At first glance, Oviatt observed that he was wearing black tactical gear, including a gas mask and a ballistic helmet. Oviatt initially mistook him for a fellow law enforcement officer. But his extremely composed demeanor tipped off Oviatt that something about this guy was amiss. "Everyone was urgently doing something. This person was very relaxed, standing by the car, not really doing anything at all," Oviatt would later testify in court. "I knew that he had to be involved in the shooting."[16]

As he approached the man, Oviatt spotted a handgun atop the vehicle. Oviatt drew his weapon and ordered the man to put his hands in the air. The man readily complied. After looking over the car to make sure no one was inside, waiting to ambush the officers, they handcuffed him and escorted him away from the fleeing crowd to a nearby trash-bin area. They then proceeded to pat him down for weapons—a search that produced two knives and two large-capacity ammunition magazines.

With the suspect secure, the officers removed the man's helmet and mask, revealing a young, white male with bright-orange hair. Oviatt's colleague asked the bizarre-looking individual if there were other gunmen. "It's just me," he replied in a calm tone.[17] A more thorough search of the subject would later reveal that, according to his driver's license, he was twenty-four-year-old Aurora resident James Holmes.

★ ★ ★

Aurora police officer Justin Grizzle had less than thirty minutes left on his shift when he received the dispatcher's call of a shooting at the Century 16 cinema. As he was nearing the complex, a request for assistance from a fellow officer at the rear of the theater came over the radio. By this point, theater patrons were spilling out everywhere into the parking lot, and the police cars that were on scene had blocked numerous access lanes. Grizzle hopped the curb and drove down the sidewalk to reach the rear parking area. His recollection of that evening as he arrived on scene was that it was "complete chaos. Everybody running. People covered in blood."[18]

As Grizzle exited his vehicle, he looked over and saw what looked like his colleagues in uniform struggling with a SWAT team member. He ran over and helped pin down the man's legs as his fellow officers handcuffed him. When they stood up the detainee, he realized that this wasn't a fellow cop. This was the gunman.

After Grizzle helped place the subject in the back of a squad car and made sure that there wasn't a second shooter, he looked over and realized, "People were still coming out screaming, 'Help! Help! Help!'"[19] He dashed to the theater to help evacuate the trapped and the injured. As he entered, he nearly fell down from slipping in all the blood on the ground. Inside, the alarm was wailing, strobe lights were flashing, and cell phones were ringing nonstop, as area residents were getting word of the gun attack and wanted to make sure their loved ones who were in attendance at the midnight premiere were alright. Grizzle remembers his first impression as he looked into the seats. "It was horrendous. It was a nightmare. It looked like a war scene."[20] People were screaming, crying, trying to crawl to safety. He remembers spotting gunshot victims whose wounds were so awful that they were hardly recognizable; some literally had "holes" in their limbs.[21]

After the initial shock passed, Grizzle's training kicked in and he went into triage mode, checking the injured for a pulse and, for those seriously wounded, flipping them onto their sides so that they wouldn't asphyxiate on their own blood. "Some," he recalled, "you just knew were dead and there was no point in checking."[22] One person whom he skipped over was six-year-old Veronica Moser-Sullivan. He knew, just from looking at her, that she was gone.

But her mother Ashley was still alive. When Grizzle came upon her, he made a snap decision that she needed urgent medical care, that he couldn't wait for paramedics to arrive and transport her to a hospital. "I didn't want anyone else to die," Grizzle recalled.[23] So he sprinted to his vehicle, frantically cleared out the seats, and raced back into the theater. Ordering the distraught but unharmed Jamison Toews to follow him out, Grizzle swept Ashley Moser off the ground and carried her to his patrol car.

As she lay in the back seat, fighting for her life, Moser stopped breathing. This happened several times. Each time, Grizzle and Toews would start screaming at her. And each time, she responded by breathing again. The drive to the hospital took only a few minutes, but Grizzle also had to deal with Toews, who was in the front passenger seat and suffering from a fit of hysteria. While they were en route, Toews kept insisting that they return to the theater to rescue his daughter as well. At one point, he even tried to jump out of the speeding patrol car so that he could get back to Veronica; Grizzle grabbed him by the shirt and held him inside the vehicle until he calmed down. Moments later, they arrived at the emergency-room entrance. After he helped hospital personnel get Moser onto a waiting stretcher, Grizzle jumped back into his patrol car and returned to the theater complex to help evacuate additional victims who were in dire need of medical attention.

One of the wounded whom Grizzle transported to the hospital was Caleb Medley, who had been shot in the head. Grizzle understood that time was of the essence if Medley was to survive. Grizzle harks back to the car ride vividly. During the quick drive to the hospital, Medley kept making "the most God-awful sound."[24] He was "gurgling on his own blood."[25] At one point, he fell silent and Grizzle began screaming at him: "Don't you fucking die on me! Don't you fucking die on me!"[26] As horrible as that sound was, Grizzle breathed a sigh of relief when Medley resumed making it. It was a good sign. He was breathing again.

Grizzle made four separate runs to local emergency rooms that night, transporting a total of six patients. By the end of his shift, his vehicle was covered in blood—on the seats, headrests, dashboard, ceiling, floor; it was practically everywhere. "There was so much blood, I could hear it sloshing in the back of my car," he would later testify.[27] His determination and efforts paid off, however. Every single person Grizzle transported to the hospital survived.

Six-year-old Veronica Moser-Sullivan did not survive. She was one of twelve people killed by James Holmes. In addition, Holmes's rampage left another seventy theater patrons injured—fifty-eight of them as a result of gunshot wounds. Many of those who were struck by gunfire that evening will never fully recover, including both Caleb Medley and Ashley Moser, who are wheelchair-bound. Caleb Medley is now the proud father of a little boy, who was born while Caleb was on the operating table. Unfortunately, Caleb's brain trauma makes it difficult for him to communicate and interact with his child. Ashley Moser's fate is equally tragic. She not only lost her daughter, she also miscarried while in surgery. She survived, but she remains paralyzed, never to walk again.[28]

Investigators required ten days to process the crime scenes at the Century 16 cinema complex. The entire first day was devoted to removing the bodies of the ten people who died inside the theater. (Two of the twelve mortally wounded were pronounced dead at area hospitals.) Authorities spent the following nine days gathering evidence and taking photographs. Crime-scene investigators amassed 123 items inside auditorium number 9, largely weapons-related materials, although several bone fragments were among the articles recovered. The collection of evidence was so enormous that field technicians ran out of markers, forcing them to use folded business cards to denote the location of objects.

Expended bullet casings accounted for over half of the items recovered: seventy-six in total—six spent shotgun shells, sixty-five spent .223-caliber casings, and five spent .40-caliber casings. Based on a forensic analysis, it was determined that twenty-four of the seventy gunshot victims were hit in the initial barrage of shotgun fire, two of them fatally. The majority of casualties were caused by

Holmes's semiautomatic assault rifle. The force with which the enhanced bullets were discharged from the AR-15 was so powerful that several rounds punctured through the drywall, striking three moviegoers in the adjacent theater. In fact, crime-scene investigators identified 240 ballistic impacts on the floor, walls, and seats in auditorium number 9, as well as an additional sixteen impact points in auditorium number 8.

Every single one of the .223-caliber bullets were fed into the assault rifle by a unique one-hundred-round extended-capacity magazine known as a "drum." Eventually, the drum jammed, forcing Holmes to switch to his Glock .40-caliber semiautomatic handgun. However, perhaps as a result of rampage weariness akin to that seen in the Columbine, Virginia Tech, and Sandy Hook massacres, Holmes stopped shooting after firing just five rounds from his pistol. He then left the theater and walked over to his parked vehicle, where he awaited the arrival of law enforcement.

With seventy gunshot victims, the rampage in Aurora is one of the highest-casualty mass shootings in American history. What's particularly disturbing about James Holmes's attack is his strike ratio. He shot seventy people with seventy-six rounds. That's practically one person hit for every pull of the trigger, a feat made possible in part because Holmes used an AR-15 assault rifle armed with a one-hundred-round drum that allowed him to fire sixty-five .223-caliber armor-piercing cartridges into the crowd of over four hundred theater patrons in under one minute. As this fact made its way into news accounts, it was only natural that politicians and commentators began blaming the AR-15 for the magnitude of carnage.[29]

AMERICA'S GUN

In the aftermath of the Aurora multiplex massacre, gun-control advocates highlighted the unique lethality of the AR-15: "This shooter was planning a military style assault and he chose a rifle that was designed for just such an attack," decried Dennis Henigan of the Brady Campaign to Reduce Gun Violence.[30] Opponents of the AR-15 stressed that the assault rifle has one primary purpose: to kill human

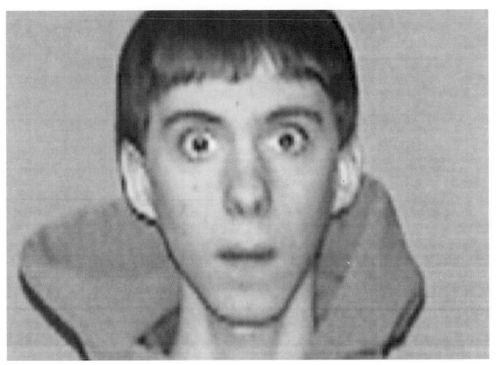

Newtown gunman Adam Lanza's Western Connecticut State University student ID photo.

AR-15 assault rifle used to perpetrate the mass shooting at Sandy Hook Elementary School.
Photo by Det. Michael Tranquillo, Connecticut State Police.

Memorial bench dedicated to the victims of the massacre in Copley Township, Ohio. *Photo by Frank Karnavas.*

Fort Hood mass shooter Nidal Malik Hasan. *Photo from the US Army.*

Fort Hood mass-shooting victim being transported to safety. *Photo by Sgt. Jason R. Krawczyk, US Army photographer.*

President George W. Bush consoles a Virginia Tech student at a memorial service for shooting victims. *Photo by Eric Draper, White House photographer.*

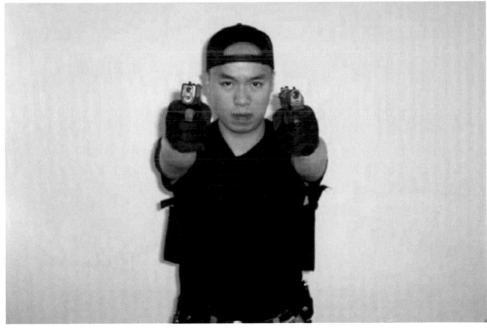

Virginia Tech gunman Seung Hui Cho.

CCTV footage of Washington Navy Yard gunman Aaron Alexis prowling for victims to shoot. *Photo from the US Navy.*

Etchings on the side of the shotgun employed by Washington Navy Yard mass shooter Aaron Alexis denoting "My ELF Weapon!" which is a reference to Extremely Low Frequency radio waves. *Photo from the Federal Bureau of Investigation.*

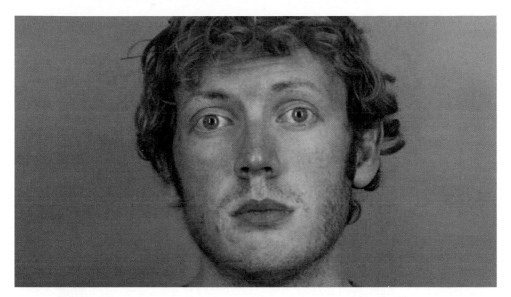

Arapahoe County, Colorado, Sheriff´s Department booking photo of Aurora theater massacre gunman James Holmes.

Crime-scene investigation bullet trajectory markers from inside Auditorium 9 of the Century 16 movie theater. *Photo from the Office of the District Attorney, Arapahoe County, Colorado.*

President Barack Obama meets with mass-shooting victims and their family members in the White House. *Photo by Pete Souza, White House photographer.*

beings. "Our own American weapon of mass destruction" was how one Missouri state legislator referred to it following James Holmes's rampage.[31] A member of the editorial advisory board at the *Daily Camera* in nearby Boulder, Colorado, pointedly asked, "Does anyone hunt ducks, deer or elk with an AR15?"[32] This question drove home a particular theme emphasized by critics: civilians have no legitimate reason to possess AR-15s and other similar assault weapons. In their view, AR-15s belong only in the hands of the military and law enforcement. "If you want access to assault weapons, join the National Guard," the *Daily Camera* editor admonished.[33]

Several members of Congress immediately took to the airwaves to propose a reinstatement of the federal Assault Weapons Ban, which had expired in 2004 after being in effect for only a decade. Leading the charge were Representative Carolyn McCarthy (D-NY), who lost her husband in the 1993 Long Island Rail Road rampage, and Senator Diane Feinstein (D-CA), who was the primary sponsor of the original ban in 1994. Appearing on *Fox News Sunday* just two days after the massacre, Feinstein railed against assault rifles like the AR-15:

> My thoughts are these—pure and simple—weapons of war don't belong on the streets. . . . [T]hese are weapons that you are only going to be using to kill people in close combat. That's the purpose of that weapon. . . .
>
> I believe that people use these weapons because they can get them. I believe that a revolver and a rifle and shotgun isn't going to do the damage. . . . Why do you need this? You don't need it for hunting. . . . You don't need it for self-defense. Why do you need it? Why do we make it available?[34]

She took the opportunity to call for a new ban on assault weapons: "I think that these weapons ought to be stopped," she told the show's host.[35] Over on CBS's *Face the Nation*, Aurora's congressman Ed Perlmutter (D-CO) echoed Feinstein. When prompted for ideas about how to reduce the carnage of mass shootings, he suggested that imposing restrictions on the availability of AR-15s and other similar firearms is "where it starts."[36]

Most in Congress are, nevertheless, reluctant to embrace gun control as a way to reduce rampage violence. In fact, the same program that hosted Feinstein also featured her colleague from across the aisle, Senator Ron Johnson (R-WI). An ardent advocate for gun rights, Johnson took exception to Feinstein's position. In rebuttal, he insisted that a free society can't prevent the mentally ill and evil from obtaining weapons and going on killing sprees. "Somebody who wants to purposely harm another individual is going to find a method of doing it," he maintained. "This isn't an issue about guns. This is just really an issue about sick, demented individuals."[37]

Johnson also challenged Feinstein's attempt to label the AR-15 an "assault rifle." Instead, he asserted that the AR-15 is basically a hunting rifle, claiming that, in his home state of Wisconsin, that's how his constituents utilize AR-15s. Johnson insisted that the types of firearms Feinstein wants to prohibit are "just common all over the place." In his view, an assault weapons ban would infringe on the Second Amendment rights of Americans. He urged citizens to exercise skepticism regarding any attempts to restrict ownership of AR-15s and similar "hunting rifles." As he put it, "I really would hate to see a tragedy like this used to promote a political agenda to reduce Americans' freedoms. Enough have been taken away and we don't want to lose any more."[38]

Less than five months after the Aurora massacre, the AR-15 was back in the spotlight, this time as the weapon Adam Lanza used to murder twenty-six women and children at Sandy Hook Elementary School. Again, there were fervent calls to ban this particular rifle. Again, the emotional pleas fell on deaf ears in the nation's capital.

What is it about the AR-15 that makes it such a lightning rod for controversy? The danger it poses to American society seems obvious: It's been the weapon of choice in two of the deadliest mass shootings in recent history. But why are there so many people on the other side of the debate who serve as the rifle's biggest advocates? What is it about the AR-15 that makes it so popular among gun owners?

The AR-15 wasn't always favored by gun enthusiasts and outdoor sportsmen. Most firearms purists, indeed, associated it with its original purpose, as a battlefield armament. And for decades, they shunned the so-called black rifle as a weapon that had no place in a civilized society.[39]

The irony is that one of the biggest opponents of war from the past quarter century is also the man responsible for helping to launch the AR-15 into stardom: former secretary of defense Robert McNamara.

* * *

After winning the presidential election in 1960, John F. Kennedy set out on a mission to place some of the smartest people in the country in positions of authority within the executive branch. The late historian David Halberstam dubbed these men appointed by Kennedy to serve as his senior advisors "the best and the brightest."[40] One of those individuals was former Harvard Business School professor and Ford Motor Company president Robert McNamara. As one of the so-called Whiz Kids, McNamara was instrumental in bringing management science models to the US military during World War II. The goal of this approach was to study patterns and determine optimal ways to improve an organization's efficiency and effectiveness. (In today's academic parlance, this practice is often referred to as "operations research.") When the war ended, he brought this form of design and modeling to Ford, with impressive results, taking a money-losing entity and turning it around into a highly profitable corporation. One of McNamara's secrets was to downsize Ford's vehicles while at the same time making them safer and cheaper. Under his guidance, Ford launched the exceptionally popular Ford Falcon and Lincoln Continental, transforming the American automobile market.[41]

When McNamara took the helm at the Pentagon, he brought along with him several members of his team at Ford. This new generation of Whiz Kids tried to revolutionize the Department of Defense the same way they did the Ford Motor Company. One of their projects was replacing the army's standard-issue rifle—the M14—with a more efficient weapon. In 1961, the US military had soldiers in Southeast Asia serving as advisors to the South Vietnamese armed forces. But with the war in Indo-China escalating following the withdrawal of France, the Kennedy administration concluded that preventing communist forces from seizing control of Vietnam was a vital national interest. The fighting, however, was taking place in a new type of environment, one that was starkly different from the battlefronts of World Wars I and II as well as Korea, with which American armed forces were familiar. The guerilla skirmishes that came to characterize the Vietnam War often occurred in rural villages and the jungle. This new form of firefight required a new form of firearm—something lighter, more controllable in close-combat situations, and more efficient in target acquisition.[42]

A few years earlier, a group of engineers set up a tiny outfit within the larger Fairchild Engine and Airplane Corporation. The division, named ArmaLite, was tasked with creating the next-generation military rifle. After numerous failures, the team came up with a prototype in 1959 that proved reliable and effective, able to fire smaller-caliber bullets with greater force in one of three forms: spray, burst, and single rounds. That prototype: the ArmaLite Rifle 15—or AR-15, for short. Shortly afterward, the designs for the AR-15 were sold to Colt, which in turn started mass producing it in 1962 as the M16 rifle for the US military. While there was initial hesitation to embrace the M16, following a series of successful field tests, the army adopted the new rifle platform.[43] The benefits became evident almost immediately:

Troops loved the new gun because of its ergonomic design and easy handling, vastly preferring it to the Army brass' beloved M14. The newfangled plastic, aluminum, and stamped-steel gun, which looked like something out of *Buck Rogers*, was so much easier to use than the M14 that in marksmanship tests troops were able to qualify as expert marksmen at a dramatically higher rate given the same amount of training time. The AR-15's step-function improvement in individual usability gave a significant boost to squad-level battlefield performance. Army studies showed that a five-man squad armed with AR-15s had as much kill potential as an 11-man squad armed with the M14.[44]

After US forces left Vietnam following the conclusion of the war, the military's demand for M16s declined. Then in the late 1970s, gas shortages produced pandemonium in the country. This was followed in 1979 by the Soviet Union's invasion of Afghanistan, which seemed to breathe new life into the Cold War. Suddenly, Americans began to worry about what the future held, which in turn spawned the survivalist movement. And with that came a new opportunity for manufacturers of assault rifles. By making a semiautomatic version of the M16—the AR-15—the firearms industry was able to tap into a whole new profit stream: civilians.[45]

★ ★ ★

Today, civilians in the United States own approximately six million AR-15s.[46] While it accounts for only about 2 percent of the overall civilian firearms inventory, which is estimated to be at least 320 million, the AR-15's market share is rapidly growing. What was once the exclusive purview of Colt is now a profit generator for over thirty firearms manufacturers.[47] Normally ranging in price from $1,000 to $2,000, gun dealers sell about eight hundred thousand AR-15s each year, resulting in annual revenues of at least $800 million. In the words of one federally licensed firearms seller, "The AR-15 now is probably the economic engine of the gun industry."[48] For some gun stores, AR-15s and their accessories account for 80–85 percent of all sales, bringing in as much as $1 million a month.

Why the growing love affair with the AR-15? The National Shooting Sports Foundation—the predominant trade association for the firearms industry—maintains that its primary function is as a "modern sporting rifle" for use particularly in hunting: "their cartridges are standard hunting calibers, useful for game up to and including deer."[49] While some outdoorsmen stalk and kill animals with AR-15s, the truth is that these guns are better suited for hunting small vermin than they are for taking down sizeable game.

No, the AR-15's real allure is something else: protection.

Testifying before a Senate committee on gun violence following the tragedy in Newtown, National Rifle Association executive vice president Wayne LaPierre explained why powerful weapons like the AR-15 are embraced by many of his organization's members:

> What people all over the country fear today is being abandoned by their government if a tornado hits, if a hurricane hits, if a riot occurs, that they're going to be out there alone. And the only way they're going to protect themselves in the cold, in the dark, when they're vulnerable, is with a firearm.[50]

In post-9/11 and post-Katrina America, the survivalist cause took on a new life. And for these so-called doomsday preppers, the AR-15 has become more than the weapon of choice. It's also become a symbol of their movement: the last line of defense between freedom and tyranny, between life and death.

What better weapon to hunker down with during the onset of the apocalypse than the civilian version of what American soldiers rely on in combat? The "black rifle" designed for the battlefields of Vietnam has now become a defender of the homestead. It's this new purpose that has led to the AR-15's meteoric rise, making it, in the words of the CNBC business news network, "America's gun."

It's easy to see why the AR-15 has become a favorite of those who are on the firing end of the rifle. It's fairly reliable, practically effortless to wield, and straightforward to use. Even someone who has little experience with firearms will be able to shoot an AR-15 with a decent degree of accuracy. And let's not forget perhaps the most rudimentary reason gun enthusiasts love the AR-15: It's fun to shoot. As one commentator described it, "much of what's 'fun' about shooting an assault weapon is that it feels masculine; it's an implicit expression of male sexuality."[51] Indeed, some observers have gone so far as to suggest that it empowers people's heroic, role-playing fantasies: "You can be this soldier but you don't have to enlist."[52]

By the same token, it's also easy to see why those on the receiving end of an AR-15 are its biggest foes. Emergency-room physician Comilla Sasson is one of those individuals who has seen, first hand, the damage that the "black rifle" is capable of inflicting. Sasson was on duty at the University of Colorado Medical Center the evening of the Aurora massacre. One of the first mass-shooting patients she treated that night was Farrah Soudani. The twenty-two-year-old Soudani was brought in with, among other gunshot injuries, a gaping wound on her side. After being hit by a .223 round from Holmes's AR-15, her stomach and intestines literally spilled out of her body, forcing her to hold them in her hands as she was transported to the hospital in a police cruiser. "I've seen a lot of gunshot wounds in my life but those were absolutely, completely different than anything else I've ever seen," Dr. Sasson remembered.[53] "These are the kinds of wounds that our folks over in Afghanistan are seeing, and here I am sitting in Aurora, Colorado, seeing these kinds of things."[54]

Soudani is one of the fifty-eight gunshot victims who survived the mass shooting. Looking back, she believes that the outcome would have been "absolutely" different had Holmes not been armed with an AR-15. She suspects that Holmes would have still gone on a rampage even if he didn't possess an AR-15. But in that circumstance, she thinks he "would've . . . maybe had more handguns" instead. "Hopefully, [fewer] people could've gotten hurt."[55]

But would that have actually been the case? Is the AR-15 the real culprit? Or are things a little more nuanced?

LOW IN WEIGHT, HIGH IN CAPACITY

It's one thing to read or hear about a shooting. It's quite another to see it with your own eyes. When high-profile attacks like Virginia Tech, Aurora, Sandy Hook, the Washington Navy Yard, and Charleston occur, we get a sense of the tragedy from reading newspaper headlines or catching brief overviews from television-news broadcasts. Occasionally, there are criminal trials, as in the prosecution of James Holmes, which last months and feature gruesome testimony. Few people, however, follow legal proceedings closely enough to truly grasp the horror of being a victim of a rampage. As a result, the vast majority of Americans has a very limited—and heavily fil-tered—experience with such extreme acts of gun violence.

On August 26, 2015, this sheltered comprehension was shat-tered as Americans turned on their television sets and perused their social-media accounts to be shocked by raw video of a multiple-victim shooting that was captured by two different cameras and broadcast on live television. In a dreadful and appalling manner, people witnessed a rampage unfold from start to finish. They saw how simple, quick, and effortless it is to take the lives of others—and how vulnerable and help-less we all are when ambushed by someone armed with a gun.

That morning, Alison Parker, a reporter at CBS-affiliate WDBJ in Roanoke, Virginia, was interviewing Vicki Gardner of the Smith Mountain Lake Regional Chamber of Commerce in a live segment for *Mornin'*—the station's early-morning news program that serves as a lead-in to the nationally televised *CBS This Morning*. Carrying a handgun, disgruntled former WDBJ employee Vester Lee Fla-nagan (a.k.a. Bryce Williams) nonchalantly walked up to Parker and cameraman Adam Ward and shot them, squeezing off eight initial rounds in under four seconds. The two journalists were instantly hit and collapsed.[56] Gardner also fell to the ground and curled up into a fetal position. Although not hit in the initial barrage, Gardner played dead. Seconds later, the video records seven more shots before cutting out. They were "insurance rounds," Flanagan fired into both Parker and Ward to ensure that they wouldn't survive. (One of the seven insurance rounds entered Gardner's back, leaving her with a serious albeit nonlethal injury.)[57]

The whole incident lasted just fifteen seconds. Armed with a fifteen-round 9mm semiautomatic handgun, Flanagan riddled Parker and Ward with bullets. His weapon was so easy to handle that he was able to fire it successfully with just one hand. In fact, the pistol was so light and the recoil so minor that Flanagan was able to employ his other hand to hold his smartphone, which he used to record the attack.[58] Afterward, he posted the video on his Twitter and Facebook pages for the world to see, contributing to what journalist Steven Neumann calls the gun violence "participation mystique"—the phe-nomenon whereby viewers experience what it feels like to be both hunter and prey.[59] "America's first social-media murder" will, no doubt, leave a lasting impression on those who witnessed it on their high-definition flat-screens, computers, tablets, and smartphones.[60] "It can't be unseen," Neumann correctly noted. "It can't be unfelt."[61]

Beyond the vicarious and sickening sense of placing us there at the crime, the video of the WDBJ shooting also provides a unique look into why gun violence has become deadlier. It boils down to two elements: (1) the ease with which a gunman can shoot a modern-day weapon and (2) the number of bullets he can fire without interruption. These "improvements" in marksmanship and killing power, in turn, correspond with two "advances" in firearms technology: (1) plastic bodies and (2) extended-capacity magazines. It's these two factors that allow novice shooters like Vester Lee Flanagan to become proficient assassins with little to no training—and it's these two factors that explain the growing casualty tolls in mass shootings.

It's strange to think that the creation of plastic guns begins with the invention of women's nylon stockings, but it's true. During the period between World War I and World War II, the DuPont chemical company set out on an ambitious task of discovering an alternative to silk. The problem with silk was that it was largely produced in Asia, making supplies relatively expensive and subject to the whims of diplomatic dispute. As economic relations began deteriorating between the United States and Japan during the 1930s, the leadership at DuPont saw an opportunity for making money by developing a silk substitute that would be cheaper to manufacture and readily available to American consumers.[62] Funneling resources into a research-and-development lab devoted to the creation of a new form of industrial plastics known as polymers, DuPont began producing polyesters that it hoped would do the trick. But every material the engineers came up with was a bust because they all had low melting points. This meant they couldn't be washed in hot water, nor could they be ironed.[63]

In 1934, under the leadership of former Harvard lecturer Wallace Carothers, a team of researchers at DuPont had a major breakthrough when they created a fiber that had the elasticity of polyester but could withstand much higher temperatures: nylon. By the end of the decade, DuPont was capable of producing millions of pounds of nylon annually. Polyamide 6,6—as the nylon was known internally—offered lots of market opportunities.[64] DuPont initially produced it for use as toothbrush bristles, fishing line, and surgical sutures.[65] But the chemical giant also had its eyes on one prize in particular: the women's hosiery market.[66]

At the time, Americans were spending over $70 million a year on silk stockings. DuPont's revolutionary fiber offered women a more affordable product that was promoted as lasting longer than traditional stockings.[67] It was a smashing success. By 1945, the demand for nylon stockings was so strong that women were lining up by the thousands to purchase them in what became known as the "nylon riots."[68] In one instance that makes today's iPhone cues look tame, on June 12, 1946, an estimated forty thousand women formed a line that extended a mile long in Pittsburgh, hoping to get their hands on just one of the thirteen thousand pairs of stockings available for sale at the Masterwoven Hosiery Shop.[69] As chance would have it, stockings were just the starting point.

After Japan attacked the United States in 1941, Washington became desperate for parachutes, which were traditionally made of silk. However, with silk suddenly in shortage, the military brass turned to DuPont for help with the design and manufacture of nylon parachutes. Soon, DuPont found itself developing new uses for nylon. By the war's denouement, nylon had become a crucial component in flak jackets, tents, tie cords, tow ropes, shoelaces, hammocks, and mosquito netting.[70] Nylon was clearly a versatile product—and, as national needs shifted, it became a critical "fiber" of the defense industry.[71]

Nylon also came to the rescue of the firearms industry. As a result of the Great Depression, Remington Arms suffered through a period of financial setback that left it wanting for significant cash infusion. Seeing an opportunity to expand its holdings, in 1933, the DuPont corporation purchased a majority interest in Remington—giving America's oldest rifle maker much-needed outside investment while giving the chemical firm a foothold in the national-defense and personal-defense markets.[72] It was only natural, then, that the first synergy between plastics and firearms would occur at Remington.

As the number of arms manufacturers catering to the civilian market started to grow following World War II, Remington found itself facing stiff competition. The executives at the firearms company knew that to get back in the game, they would have to lower production costs of at least one of their popular rifles. An improved weapon that cost less to make would translate into greater profit. Given DuPont's involvement in national security, Remington approached its majority stakeholder and asked for help in developing a midpriced .22-caliber rifle. The chemical engineers at DuPont proposed that, instead of manufacturing the rifle's receiver and stock with steel, Remington utilize the same industrial plastic that allowed DuPont to dominate the hosiery market.[73]

Moldable nylon allowed the research-and-development team at DuPont to produce a single-piece receiver and stock combination. Remington took this cheaper, lighter unit and covered its center in low-cost formed steel to give it the appearance of a more traditional rifle. But this was no ordinary rifle. The Remington Nylon 66—aptly named for the polyamide 6,6 that served as its core material—was a revolution in small-arms design. It held the promise of increased reliability and accuracy—not to mention increased profits.[74]

After going through a variety of tests in the factory, Remington provided its field representatives with two prototypes of the new nylon rifle in 1958, and they were instructed to test-fire it in adverse conditions. Salesman Delbert Connor took the assignment to heart. He disliked the firearms from the moment he received them: "My first impression of these guns was that they were just toys—or maybe air rifles for Buck Rogers. I doubt that the color or material will make much difference on the first showings. The public will refer to them as plastic."[75] Motivated by such disdain, he set out to put the rifles through a series of tests that were so extreme, failure would be certain: firing the weapons from a variety of positions, including upside-down; firing them at different rate of speed (including fanning the trigger at such a high-rate that the barrel overheated); and firing them in adverse weather conditions, including a blinding sandstorm. Conner even took one rifle, ran it over with his station wagon, then sank it (fully loaded) into a lake. When he pulled it back out and drained it of water, he shot one hundred rounds without a single glitch. He even threw it off of a structure onto concrete pavement, causing it to crack. It had no significant impact on the rifle, which continued to operate flawlessly.[76]

In all, Conner fired around two thousand rounds of various brands of ammunition in his Nylon 66 rifles. When the time came to communicate his findings back to corporate headquarters, he summed up his experience this way: "Looks like a plastic toy—performance and accuracy unbelievable." Conner added a personal request at the end of his report: "I would surely like to have one back—charged to my sample account—if and when available."[77]After winning over even the toughest critics in the development stage, the Nylon 66 went on sale to the general public in 1959, with Remington guaranteeing that "this stock will not warp, crack, chip, fade or peel for the life of the rifle, or we will replace it free."[78] That same year, competitive shooter Tom Frye set out to break the world record of shooting 2.5-inch wood blocks as they were tossed in the air. Using three Nylon 66 rifles, he fired an average of one shot every four seconds over a period of thirteen straight eight-hour days. Smashing the previous record of 72,500 hits, Frye successfully shot 100,004 out of 100,010 blocks. In other words, his hit rate was 99.994 percent. He only missed six out of the 100,010 shots he fired. Remington couldn't have asked for better marketing than this. As word of Frye's accomplishments spread among hunters and firearms enthusiasts, demand for the new gun grew. By 1991, when production of the Nylon 66 was discontinued, it had become the bestselling .22-caliber weapon in Remington's history, with over one million of the plastic rifles sold.[79]

The Nylon 66 ushered in a new era. Seeing the success Remington achieved, other gun manufacturers decided to pursue research and development of similar weapons. Within a few decades, practically every major gunmaker was producing plastic firearms for sale to civilians.

✳ ✳ ✳

Polymers are typically industrial plastics. Today, synthetic polymers are often injection-molded, meaning they can be cast into a variety of shapes, sizes, and colors.[80] Polymers share four basic characteristics:

1. Adaptability: They can be molded into endless configurations;
2. Durability: They are generally not susceptible to harsh elements, including extreme temperatures and corrosion;
3. Insulation: They exhibit high degrees of thermal and electrical resistance; and
4. Light Mass: They are light in weight.[81]

Polymer products are everywhere in our everyday lives: nylon stockings, toothbrushes, microwave-safe cookware, disposable plates and cups, plumbing pipes, cell phones, computers, automobiles, . . . and firearms.

When the chemical engineers at DuPont were given their charge for the development of a plastic .22-caliber rifle, Remington provided them with a long list of specifications. The new rifle stock had to be made of a material that was malleable. It had to maintain its permanent color. It had to have an easily repairable finish. It had to resist abrasion, corrosion, and distortion. It had to be heavy-duty, with high tensile-impact and bend strength. It had to operate in extreme cold and heat. It had to be impervious to "solvents, oils, mild acids, alkalis, fungus, rodents and insects."[82] And it had to be lightweight.

In 1970, the German armaments company Heckler & Koch introduced the VP70—the first polymer handgun.[83] The core concept behind this new weapon was to replicate the traits of the Remington Nylon 66 and the ArmaLite AR-15 rifles in an easy-to-use, durable, and more affordable semiautomatic pistol.[84] Prior to this, handguns were generally made of steel or alloy. Not only are metal guns heavier, making them harder to wield, but they are also readily subject to corrosion and malfunction if not properly maintained.[85] Polymer firearms, by contrast, are far more resilient, resistant to environmental elements such as sun, rain, snow, and mud.[86] In fact, contact with water—even saltwater—will not necessarily impact a polymer gun in a negative manner. This means that, generally, polymer weapons will not rust. It also means that, in a time of high-stress, perspiration will not cause a polymer gun to fail.[87] Moreover, because they can be molded and fitted in a variety of ways, polymer firearms offer numerous ergonomic advantages that traditional blued steel and alloy firearms cannot offer.[88] For instance, Glock semiautomatic handguns—some of the bestselling polymer pistols on the market—are extremely popular in part because they feature rough-textured surfaces and finger grooves that provide shooters with a more comfortable and secure grip.[89]

There are two additional design features that make polymer firearms easier to shoot. First, because they are made of lightweight, elastic plastic, polymer guns—especially polymer handguns—do a much more superior job of absorbing the recoil pulse than more traditional steel and alloy guns. This results in smoother shooting.[90] As Paul Barrett, the biographer of the Glock pistol, describes it, "The steel slide striking the plastic frame produces less jarring force and vibration than the metal-on-metal impact of other pistols."[91]

Second, manufacturers of polymer firearms have made significant advances in trigger pull. For instance, traditional handguns (both revolvers and semiautomatics) have heavier triggers that require stronger and lengthier pulls. Typically, steel handguns have about twelve-pound trigger pulls, requiring that the trigger travel over one inch to fire a round.[92] Glock introduced handguns with only five-pound trigger pulls. Barrett captured the importance of this design breakthrough by comparing the Glock 9mm to a .38 revolver: "The Glock is easy to shoot and does not demand great strength. A .38-caliber Smith & Wesson, by contrast, requires a real tug—and rewards you with a firm kick."[93] Moreover, Glock shrank the trigger travel distance to half an inch. This lighter trigger action makes for quicker and more consistent shooting. With the first trigger pull in metal semiautomatic handguns being heavy but the subsequent pulls being lighter, many shooters tend to strike below their point of aim on the first shot and above their point of aim on the second shot. Enhanced trigger dynamics made polymer pistols not only easier to use but also more accurate. This was certainly the case with the Glock 17: "Poor marksmen became adequate; moderately skilled shooters begin grouping rounds in small bunches near dead center of the target. The pistol's gentle five-pound trigger action doesn't require the sort of muscular squeeze that can cause the user to jerk the gun off target."[94]

To understand how plastic firearms like the AR-15 and the Glock 17 revolutionized marksmanship, all you need to do is go online to YouTube and search for gun bloopers. You're sure to find video clips of people firing traditional long guns and handguns and either getting knocked to ground or injured as a result of recoil. After you've done this, search out people shooting polymer guns. The contrast is stark. Shooting such weapons is relatively effortless. That makes them more efficient, accurate, and lethal. So lethal, in fact, that Vester Lee Flanagan, holding his polymer Glock 9mm with just one hand, killed his former WDBJ newsroom colleagues with ease.[95]

Lightweight, easy-to-fire polymer firearms explain why the lethality of rampages has risen significantly in the past fifty years, especially of late. But plastic guns offer only a partial explanation. As mentioned earlier, there's another factor that arguably makes a more significant contribution to the growing bloodshed: extended-capacity magazines.

Let's go back to the WDBJ shooting and try to reimagine the attack involving a .38-caliber revolver instead of a 9mm pistol. For starters, the gunman—who was holding his weapon with only one hand—would have experienced greater recoil, which might have sent some of his shots astray. He would have also had to stop to reload after five or six shots.[96] As he fired on the reporter first, recoil and reloading might have provided the other two victims a chance to flee or fight back. Even an experienced marksman needs several seconds to empty a revolver of used casings and then refill it with live rounds.[97] At the very least, that would have provided time for Vicki Gardner, the interview subject who was not hit in the initial barrage of gunfire, to run away.

Extended-capacity magazines are arguably the biggest game changers in rampage violence. They allow gunmen the opportunity to fire on their targets without interruption. It's actually quite straightforward: the more bullets a mass shooter has in his firearm, the more gunshot wounds he can inflict. Recall that the impetus for the M16 was the military's desire for a lighter weapon that was capable of holding more ammunition, which translated into greater "kill potential."[98] Extended-capacity magazines are force multipliers when it comes to kill potential.[99]

Extended-capacity magazines provide other advantages as well. Offensively, they provide a gunman with rapid-fire capability. As the name implies, large-scale magazines when inserted into either a semiautomatic or a fully automatic weapon, allow the shooter to fire off rounds at an extremely quick rate. This comes in handy, for example, when a target is in a gunman's line of sight for only a few seconds. A decent shooter who is able to squeeze off three rounds a second can, with rapid-fire capability, shoot nine bullets in just three seconds. That's nine chances to hit a target in a very short window of opportunity.

Defensively, high-capacity magazines provide gunmen with extended cover. Think back to some memorable shoot-outs from your favorite war or crime films. When soldiers or cops are pinned down and need to make lengthy sprints to reach safety or to get to the bad guy, they often ask for cover so that they can dart to their destinations without being shot in the process. Put yourself in the position of the individual making a dash for it. Would you rather that the person providing you with cover have a six-shot or a thirty-shot firearm? If the distance you need to run will take you over ten seconds to traverse, you'll likely want your partner to be armed with a weapon loaded with an extended-capacity magazine that allows him or her to fire lots of rounds without interruption.

In much the same way, high-capacity magazines provide an additional defensive advantage—this one directly to shooters. For any gunman, there is always the possibility that someone will rush him and try to tackle him (or at the very least try to wrestle his weapon away from him). The longer a shooter can fire without interruption, the longer he can keep defenders at bay. And the longer defenders are kept from physically confronting a gunman, the more opportunity there is for inflicting damage—which is, after all, the immediate objective of most active shooters on a rampage.

The mass shooting that targeted Arizona congresswoman Gabrielle "Gabby" Giffords and her constituents offers a powerful illustration of the difference an extended-capacity magazine makes. As Giffords was holding a "Congress on Your Corner" event at a Tucson-area shopping center on the morning of January 8, 2011, twenty-two-year-old Jared Loughner approached her and fired a single round point-blank into her head, just above her left eye. Loughner then turned his Glock 19 handgun fitted with a fully loaded thirty-three-bullet high-capacity magazine on those in the immediate vicinity. First he shot the chief judge of the federal district court in Arizona, John Roll, who had stopped by to discuss a matter with Giffords and happened to be right next to her at the moment Loughner commenced his attack. Loughner then hit three of the congresswoman's staffers. From there, he went after those standing in line to meet Giffords. Walking from front to back, Loughner opened fire on the crowd. One by one, he shot fourteen more victims. The entire rampage was over in just fifteen seconds. In that brief moment of time, Jared Loughner had discharged thirty-three rounds and wounded nineteen people, six of them fatally.[100]

One of those murdered that day was Christina-Taylor Green. Even though she was only nine years old, Christina had an interest in politics. Her neighbor had decided to take her to the political meet and greet so that she could make the acquaintance of her congressional representative. Christina was so excited about the opportunity to engage in a civic exchange with a Washington politician that she had prepared a question about the BP oil spill in the Gulf of Mexico. Before she could ask Giffords what the federal government was doing to help protect the environment, Loughner tragically cut the little girl down with a direct hit to her chest.[101] Appearing before a Senate committee on gun violence, Giffords's husband, astronaut Mark Kelly, testified, "The first bullet went into Gabby's head. Bullet number thirteen went into a nine-year-old girl named Christina-Taylor Green, who was very interested in democracy and our government, and really deserved a full life committed to advancing those ideas. . . . I contend that if . . . [Loughner] did not have access to a high-capacity magazine . . . Christina-Taylor Green would be alive today."[102]

How do you tell someone that his or her loved one would be alive today if only the killer hadn't been armed with an extended-capacity magazine?

★ ★ ★

Skeptics unfamiliar with the details of the Tucson mass shooting might suggest that even if Loughner's Glock were armed with multiple ten-round magazines instead of a thirty-three-round magazine, he would have just quickly swapped out magazines and resumed his attack. Either way, Christina-Taylor Green's life would have been cut short. But this is to presume that the rampage gunman would not have been physically confronted by bystanders during those precious moments that he needed to reload ammunition.

Here's an indisputable fact: during an active shooting, the perpetrator is either firing his gun or not firing his gun. While pulling the trigger, it's difficult to accost a gunman head on. But if he runs out of bullets, there is downtime in the shooting. That's precious time that affords those under fire with a chance to fight back (or, at the very least, to flee, as the Sandy Hook first-graders who pushed their way past Adam Lanza while he was replacing magazines taught us).

Until a gunman can successfully reload, he is vulnerable to counterattack by those nearby. Case in point: Jared Loughner.

When Loughner emptied his thirty-three-round magazine, he quickly ejected it and reached into his pocket for a second thirty-three-round magazine. Maybe his fingers were sweaty and it slipped from his hand. Or maybe it was wedged in his pants in such a way that it bumped the pocket liner as it was being removed, causing him to fumble it. Or perhaps he sensed he was about to be assaulted and panicked. Regardless, Loughner dropped his reload ammunition. Before he could bend down and pick it up, he was brought to the pavement by one of his victims. Even though he had been grazed in the head by a bullet, Bill Badger saw an opportunity to subdue the shooter as he paused to restock his weapon with bullets—and Badger took it. Grabbing Loughner by the arm, Badger forced the shooter to the ground. Another bystander dug his knee so sharply into Loughner's back that it elicited cries of "Ow! Ow! You're hurting me!"[103]

What's to say that, if Loughner were using ten-round instead of thirty-three-round magazines, he wouldn't have been stopped by those in the waiting line after firing his tenth shot rather than his thirty-third? If so, think of how many people would have been spared that day. In all likelihood, the casualty toll would have been, at the very least, cut in half. And Christina-Taylor Green would still be with us.

For a rampage gunman set on amassing a high casualty toll, the more bullets he can fire, the more blood he is likely to shed and the less likely it is that he will be confronted before he has to pause or stop shooting. Semiautomatic firearms coupled with extended-capacity magazines facilitate gun massacres by increasing an active shooter's rate of fire while simultaneously limiting his downtime. To demonstrate this, let's imagine a simple experiment. Let's take two gunmen—one an expert marksman and the other an average shooter—and let's give them three different weapons to test-fire: a six-shot revolver, a semiautomatic handgun with two different magazine configurations (ten-round and thirty-round), and a semiautomatic assault rifle with a one-hundred-round drum. How many bullets can they discharge in exactly one minute, using the different firearms? Moreover, in those sixty seconds, how much time is spent pulling the trigger and how much is spent not actively shooting because they have to stop and reload?[104]

The calculations are pretty clear-cut (see table 6.1).[105] Limited-capacity revolvers provide the lowest rate of fire and the highest amount of downtime. A gunman with average shooting skills and armed with a six-shot revolver is likely to get off only eighteen rounds in one minute, leaving him vulnerable to counterattack for over two-thirds of the minute, as he pauses to reload. As bullet capacity goes up and reload time goes down, the rate of fire increases and the downtime decreases. The one-hundred-round drum clearly transforms an assault rifle into the most dangerous of the weapons in this scenario. It not only results in 150 rounds being fired by a well-trained gunman in sixty seconds but also leaves the smallest window of opportunity (only ten seconds) for confronting the shooter when he's out of bullets. For fifty seconds out of the entire minute, it's practically impossible for defenders to fight back. It's this factor—ammunition capacity—that makes semiautomatic firearms, particularly assault rifles like the AR-15 that can hold one-hundred-round drums, extremely lethal.

Table 6.1. Comparison of Firearm Capabilities.

Average Shooter

Firearm	Six-Shot Revolver	Semi-Auto Handgun (Ten-Round Magazines)	Semi-Auto Handgun (Thirty-Round Magazines)	Assault Rifle (One-Hundred-Round Drums)
Firing Rate	1 Shot per Second	2 Shots per Second	2 Shots per Second	2 Shots per Second
Reload Rate	20 Seconds	10 Seconds	10 Seconds	15 Seconds
Time Shooting	18 Seconds	20 Seconds	40 Seconds	50 Seconds
Time Not Shooting	42 Seconds	40 Seconds	20 Seconds	10 Seconds
Bullets Fired	18 Rounds	40 Rounds	80 Rounds	100 Rounds

Expert Shooter

Firearm	Six-Shot Revolver	Semi-Auto Handgun (Ten-Round Magazines)	Semi-Auto Handgun (Thirty-Round Magazines)	Assault Rifle (One-Hundred-Round Drums)
Firing Rate	1.5 Shots per Second	3 Shots per Second	3 Shots per Second	3 Shots per Second
Reload Rate	10 Seconds	5 Seconds	5 Seconds	10 Seconds
Time Shooting	20 Seconds	25 Seconds	40 Seconds	50 Seconds
Time Not Shooting	40 Seconds	35 Seconds	20 Seconds	10 Seconds
Bullets Fired	24 Rounds	75 Rounds	120 Rounds	150 Rounds

THE AURORA THEATER MASSACRE ARSENAL

Following the Aurora theater massacre, the Colorado legislature enacted three sweeping gun-control bills that, among other things, banned the sale of ammunition magazines with a capacity larger than fifteen bullets. Avid Second Amendment advocates revolted against these laws. In a blunt attempt to punish two major proponents of these public-safety measures, the gun-rights movement organized a recall campaign. On September 10, 2013, State Senate President John Morse and State Senator Angela Giron—both Democrats—were removed from office and replaced by pro-gun Republicans.[106]

State Senator Bernie Herpin was one of those who ascended to office in the wake of the recall, replacing Morse. In February 2014, during a Senate committee hearing on a bill Herpin sponsored to repeal the ban on extended-capacity magazines, one of his Democratic colleagues questioned the utility of his proposal: "My understanding is that James Holmes bought his 100-round capacity magazine legally. So in fact, [the 2013 high-capacity magazine ban] would have stopped James Holmes from purchasing a 100-round magazine. I was wondering if you agree with me."[107] Herpin, in what was clearly a poorly thought-out response, replied: "As it turned out, that was maybe a good thing that he had a 100-round magazine, because it jammed. If he had four, five, six 15-round magazines, there's no telling how much damage he could have done until a good guy with a gun showed up." Herpin was trying to suggest that the larger the capacity of the magazine, the more likely it is that the magazine might jam. But to the families of the victims, Herpin's suggestion that the public should put its faith in product defects as a means to ensure its safety came across as stupid and insensitive.

The AR-15 that James Holmes fired at the Century 16 multiplex did, in fact, jam. But not before it discharged sixty-five rounds. As we have already seen, one-hundred-round drums provide greater kill potential than smaller-capacity magazines. Had Holmes—at best, an average shooter by his own admission—been using thirty-round magazines, it would have provided theater patrons with approximately two additional ten-second windows to escape or to confront Holmes before he could have gotten off sixty-five shots.[108] And had he been using ten-round magazines, the shooting downtime would have increased to six ten-second windows—a full minute.

Contrary to the suggestion floated by Herpin, the one-hundred-round drum used by James Holmes played a critical role in making the Aurora theater massacre one of the highest-casualty mass shootings in American history.[109]

James Holmes's arsenal—particularly his polymer AR-15 assault rifle armed with a one-hundred-round drum—lends credence to the proposition that, as firearms become lighter and their ammunition capacities become larger, they become more lethal. But that's the anecdotal takeaway from one gun massacre (albeit one that registered an extremely high casualty toll). What about the weapons used in other gun massacres?

If all firearms were equal, we would find that, on average, they produced similar outcomes, especially similar fatality tolls. In practice, however, that's not the case. After examining the firearms used in the 111 gun massacres in my data set, it's clear that there is a significant difference between attacks that involve semiautomatic weapons and those that do not. Those massacres where there was no evidence that the weapons used were semiautomatic firearms resulted, on average, in fewer deaths per attack. In fact, those high-fatality mass shootings accounted for 27 percent of the 111 incidents in my data set, but for only 23 percent of the 904 cumulative deaths resulting from those incidents (see table 6.2). On the other hand, gun massacres involving semiautomatic firearms produced, on average, higher death tolls. Semiautomatic firearm attacks accounted for 73 percent of all the incidents in my data set, but 77 percent of the fatalities resulting from those incidents. The conclusion is unambiguous: semiautomatic firearms, when used in mass shootings, increase the lethality of such attacks.[110]

Table 6.2. Percentage of Gun-Massacre Incidents and Cumulative Fatalities by Firearm Type.

Gun Massacres between 1966 and 2015...	Percentage of All Incidents (N = 111)	Percentage of All Deaths (N = 904)	Difference (in Percentage)
...Not Involving Semi-Autos	27	23	−4
...Involving Semi-Autos	73	77	+4
...Involving Assault Weapons	25	29	+4
...Involving ECMs	47	55	+8
...Involving Polymer Guns	34	42	+8
...Involving Assault Weapons + ECMs	22	27	+5
...Involving ECMs + Polymer Guns	30	38	+8
...Involving Polymer Assault Weapons + ECMs	12	15	+3

Note: There is no separate category for polymer assault weapons without extended-capacity magazines (ECMs) as every gun massacre involving polymer assault weapons also involved ECMs.

This finding is particularly troubling because, over the course of the past fifty years, semiautomatic firearms have become more prevalent in high-fatality mass shootings (see figure 6.1). Their use in gun massacres has consistently increased decade after decade. The shift is particularly drastic when the first ten-year period of the past fifty years is compared to the most recent ten-year period. During the period 1966–1975, semiautomatic firearms were involved in 47 percent of all gun massacres. Jump forward to the present and you'll see that they have been involved in 92 percent of all gun massacres that have occurred in the past ten years. A similar pattern exists in terms of deaths resulting from semiautomatic firearm use in high-fatality mass shootings (see figure 6.2). During the period 1966–1975, semiautomatic firearm massacres accounted for 48 percent of all gun-massacre fatalities. In the past ten years, they have accounted for 95 percent of fatalities. It's also worth noting that, forty to fifty years ago, the range in the average number of deaths per gun massacre between those not involving semi-automatic weapons and those involving such weapons was relatively close: 7.1–7.3 (see figure 6.3). In the past decade, however, that difference has grown to its widest margin, with the former producing, on average, six fatalities per attack and the latter over nine deaths. In fact, in the past twenty years, the average death toll for incidents not involving semiautomatic firearms has bottomed out at six deaths—the minimum number of fatalities required for a shooting to meet the definition of a gun massacre.[111]

As discussed in chapter 3, gun massacres escalated extensively between the time periods 1966–1975 and 1976–1985. Afterward, they waned in both occurrence and lethality, reaching new lows in the 1990s, before spiking to unprecedented levels in the past ten years (see table 6.3). The use of semiautomatic firearms in such incidents has also grown to unprecedented levels of late.

Following the Aurora massacre, assault weapons seemed to bear the brunt of the blame. But, as I argued earlier in this chapter, polymer firearms and extended-capacity magazines are also considerably responsible for the increased bloodshed. A review of the data supports this assessment. In fact, the two factors that have correlated with the highest differential in death tolls are polymer guns and large-capacity magazines (see table 6.2). Assault weapons, on their own, were involved

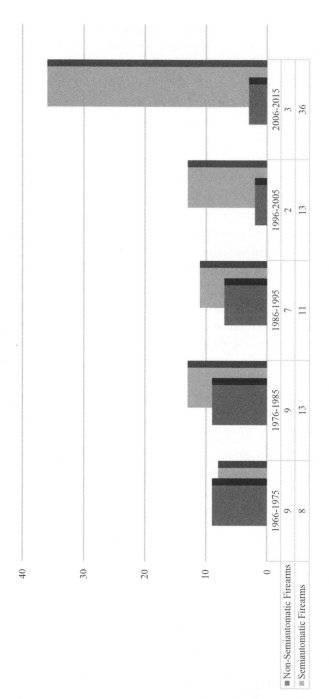

Fig. 6.1. Number of Gun Massacres per Decade (Massacres Involving Semiautomatic Firearms versus Massacres Not Involving Semiautomatic Firearms).

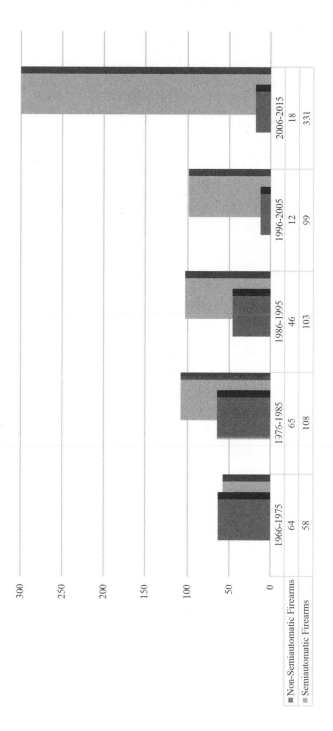

Fig. 6.2. Number of Deaths Resulting From Gun Massacres per Decade (Massacres Involving Semiautomatic Firearms versus Massacres Not Involving Semiautomatic Firearms).

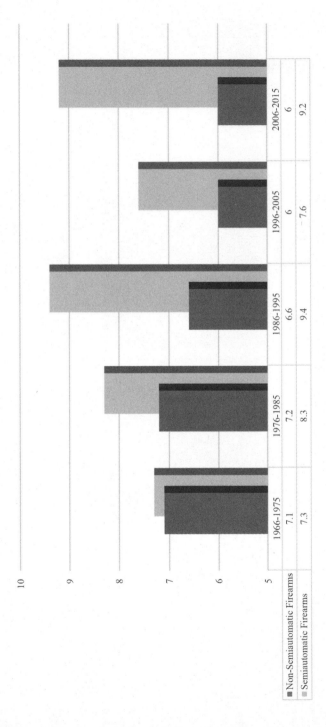

Fig. 6.3. Average Number of Deaths per Gun Massacre by Decade
(Massacres Involving Semiautomatic Firearms versus Massacres Not Involving Semiautomatic Firearms).

	1966-1975	1976-1985	1986-1995	1996-2005	2006-2015
Non-Semiautomatic Firearms	7.1	7.2	6.6	6	6
Semiautomatic Firearms	7.3	8.3	9.4	7.6	9.2

Table 6.3. Gun-Massacre Incidents and Fatalities by Firearm Type.

	1966–1975	1976–1985	1986–1995	1996–2005	2006–2015	Total
All Gun Massacres						
Incidents	17	22	18	15	39	111
Deaths	122	173	149	111	349	904
Average Death Toll	7.2	7.9	8.3	7.4	8.9	8.1
Gun Massacres Not Involving Semiautomatics						
Incidents	9	9	7	2	3	30
Deaths	64	65	46	12	18	205
Average Death Toll	7.1	7.2	6.6	6.0	6.0	6.8
Gun Massacres Involving Semiautomatics						
Incidents	8	13	11	13	36	81
Deaths	58	108	103	99	331	699
Average Death Toll	7.3	8.3	9.4	7.6	9.2	8.6
Gun Massacres Involving Assault Weapons						
Incidents	3	6	6	3	10	28
Deaths	26	58	44	26	110	264
Average Death Toll	8.7	9.7	7.3	8.7	11.0	9.4
Gun Massacres Involving ECMs						
Incidents	3	5	9	9	26	52
Deaths	26	53	82	72	261	494
Average Death Toll	8.7	10.6	9.1	8.0	10.0	9.5
Gun Massacres Involving Polymer Guns						
Incidents	1	2	3	7	25	38
Deaths	6	19	38	61	253	377
Average Death Toll	6.0	9.5	12.7	8.7	10.1	9.9
Gun Massacres Involving Assault Weapons + ECMs						
Incidents	3	3	6	2	10	24
Deaths	26	40	44	20	110	240
Average Death Toll	8.7	13.3	7.3	10.0	11.0	10.0
Gun Massacres Involving ECMs + Polymer Guns						
Incidents	1	2	3	6	21	33
Deaths	6	19	38	52	226	341
Average Death Toll	6.0	9.5	12.7	8.7	10.8	10.3
Gun Massacres Involving Polymer Assault Weapons + ECMs						
Incidents	1	2	2	1	7	13
Deaths	6	19	15	13	87	140
Average Death Toll	6.0	9.5	7.5	13.0	12.4	10.8

Note: There is no separate category for polymer assault weapons without extended-capacity magazines (ECMs) as every gun massacre involving polymer assault weapons also involved ECMs.

in only 25 percent of all gun massacres from the past fifty years, and those incidents accounted for 29 percent of all gun-massacre fatalities. The bigger impact results from using polymer guns and high-capacity magazines. The former were employed in 34 percent of all gun massacres, yet those attacks accounted for 42 percent of all gun-massacre fatalities. That's an 8 percent differential. The latter resulted in an identical percentage differential (47 percent of all massacres and 55 percent of all fatalities), although the larger overall tallies provide reason to find the use of extended-capacity magazines even more disconcerting than the use of polymer firearms.

One of the impressions that someone might form after hearing critics fault assault weapons like the AR-15 is that these potent firearms are used fairly often to perpetrate gun massacres. The data, however, do not support such a conclusion. On the contrary, assault weapons were used in only a quarter of the gun massacres from the past fifty years (see tables 6.2 and 6.3). Even in the past ten years, they were used in only ten attacks (again roughly 25 percent of all attacks in the past decade).

The same can be said for polymer guns and extended-capacity magazines. They, too, were involved in less than half of all gun massacres from the past fifty years (see tables 6.2 and 6.3). Nonetheless, unlike assault weapons, high-capacity magazines and polymer guns stand apart in their prevalence of late. Assault weapons have only been used in roughly one-fourth of all gun massacres since 2006. Extended-capacity magazines and polymer guns, on the other hand, have been used in about two-thirds of all such gun massacres. Indeed, a comparison with the earliest and most recent ten-year periods of my data set shows that, while the use of assault weapons increased by a factor of nearly three, the use of large-capacity magazines has increased by a factor of nearly nine, and the use of polymer firearms has increased by a factor of twenty-five.

Another relationship worth investigating is the frequency and lethality of these three elements—assault weapons, extended-capacity magazines, and polymer firearms—when employed in combination. Again, across the entire fifty-year time frame, their use remains limited, but their impact lethal (see tables 6.2 and 6.3). This becomes indisputable when the different firearms are assessed by the average number of fatalities that result when they are involved in gun massacres (see figure 6.4). In general, the average death toll since 1966 has been 8.1. When gunmen don't shoot their victims with semiautomatic firearms, this average falls 17 percent to 6.8 deaths per incident.[112] The employment of semiautomatic firearms makes the average death toll per incident rise 5 percent to 8.6. The jumps are more profound when the shootings are broken down into those involving assault weapons, extended-capacity magazines, and polymer guns. Each of these elements result in, respectively, 16 percent, 17 percent, and 22 percent increases. The largest growth in average death toll, however, results when mass shooters attack with polymer assault weapons armed with extended-capacity magazines— all three elements in one. Those instances result in an average of 10.8 deaths per attack—a 33 percent increase from the 8.1 baseline.

When the comparisons are limited to just the past decade—when gun massacres almost always involved semiautomatic firearms—the most lethal outcome again results from attacks involving all three elements: polymer assault weapons armed with extended-capacity magazines. In the past ten years, the increase from the baseline average of number deaths per incident soars from 8.9 to 12.8 (see figure 6.4). That's an enormous 39 percent upsurge in the average number of fatalities when all three elements are involved in a gun massacre— and at a time when modern medicine has drastically reduced the likelihood of dying from gunshot wounds, no less.

One final question worth addressing: Do gun massacres employing more than one firearm or involving more than one perpetrator result in higher death tolls? It makes sense that if you have more weapons, you can produce more bloodshed. And the data support such a conclusion as it pertains to high-fatality mass shootings (see table 6.4). The average death toll when a perpetrator is armed with only a single weapon is 6.9 fatalities per incident (see table 6.5). That number jumps to 9.2 fatalities per incident when a gunman is armed with multiple firearms. That's higher than the average death toll for all 111 incidents in the data set but less than the average death toll resulting from incidents involving assault weapons, extended-capacity magazines, or polymer firearms (compare tables 6.3 and 6.5). A breakdown of the data clearly establishes that, while mass shootings involving two or more guns often

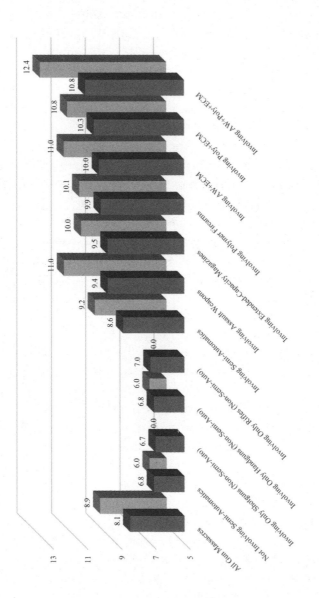

■ 1966–2015 ■ 2006–2015

Fig. 6.4. Average Number of Fatalities per Gun Massacre by Firearm Type (1966–2015 Compared to 2006–2015).
Note: There is no separate category for polymer assault weapons without extended-capacity magazines (ECMs)
as every gun massacre involving polymer assault weapons also involved ECMs.

result in increased carnage, the impact is driven more by the use of enhanced weapons (especially polymer guns equipped with extended-capacity magazines) than by the use of multiple firearms.

Table 6.4. Percentage of Gun-Massacre Incidents and Cumulative Fatalities by Number of Firearms and Shooters.

Gun Massacres between 1966 and 2015 ...	Percentage of All Incidents (N = 111)	Percentage of All Deaths (N = 904)	Difference (in Percentage)
. . . Involving Only One Gun	47	40	–7
. . . Involving Multiple Guns	53	60	+7
. . . Involving Only One Shooter	86	86	0
. . . Involving Multiple Shooters	14	14	0

Unlike the sizeable difference that results from using multiple weapons, gun massacres involving more than one shooter don't result in significantly more fatalities (see table 6.4). When gun massacres are perpetrated by more than one gunman, the increase in fatalities per incident increases only 2 percent—from 8.1 to 8.3 fatalities per incident (see table 6.6).[113] Even more surprising, massacres involving two gunmen have produced higher average death tolls than those involving three or more gunmen. The former have claimed an average of 9.1 lives per attack, whereas the latter have claimed 6.3 lives per attack. This suggests that the number of perpetrators, per se, doesn't significantly impact the extent of the bloodshed.

For those of you who are not data wonks, all of the statistics in the previous subsection might have left you a bit overwhelmed. The picture they paint is, nevertheless, pretty simple and straightforward. Most gun massacres involve semiautomatic firearms. The perpetrators of these murder sprees have not historically relied on assault rifles to pull off their attacks. Nor have they turned to polymer guns and large-capacity

Table 6.5. Gun-Massacre Incidents and Fatalities by Number of Firearms.

	Total
All Gun Massacres	
Incidents	111
Deaths	904
Average Death Toll	8.1
Gun Massacres Involving Only One Gun	
Incidents	52
Deaths	359
Average Death Toll	6.9
Gun Massacres Involving Multiple Guns	
Incidents	59
Deaths	545
Average Death Toll	9.2
Gun Massacres Involving Multiple Guns But Not Involving Semi-Autos	
Incidents	13
Deaths	92
Average Death Toll	7.1
Gun Massacres Involving Multiple Guns and Semi-Autos	
Incidents	46
Deaths	453
Average Death Toll	9.8
Gun Massacres Involving Multiple Guns and Assault Weapons	
Incidents	20
Deaths	204
Average Death Toll	10.2
Gun Massacres Involving Multiple Guns and ECMs	
Incidents	30
Deaths	336
Average Death Toll	11.2
Gun Massacres Involving Multiple Guns and Polymer Guns	
Incidents	22
Deaths	257
Average Death Toll	11.7
Gun Massacres Involving Multiple Guns and Assault Weapons + ECMs	
Incidents	16
Deaths	180
Average Death Toll	11.3
Gun Massacres Involving Multiple Guns and ECMs + Polymer Guns	
Incidents	19
Deaths	236
Average Death Toll	12.4
Gun Massacres Involving Multiple Guns and Polymer Assault Weapons + ECMs	
Incidents	9
Deaths	108
Average Death Toll	12.0

Note: There is no separate category for polymer assault weapons without extended-capacity magazines (ECMs) as every gun massacre involving polymer assault weapons also involved ECMs.

magazines. But—and this is a huge *but*—when they have utilized these types of guns, they have generated far greater bloodshed. The critical elements that seem to compound the carnage are, in particular, plastic weapons and large-scale ammunition-feeding devices. Assault weapons certainly contribute to the escalation of death tolls, but not quite as much as polymer guns and extended-capacity magazines do. That said, the most lethal outcomes tend to result, on average, when rampage gunmen use polymer assault weapons loaded with extended-capacity magazines. No doubt, James Holmes's decision to rely predominantly on a lightweight, ergonomically designed, high-capacity weapon made it extremely easy for him to achieve his self-professed goal of shooting "as many people as possible."[114] As it turned out, this amounted to upwards of seventy people in under three minutes.

Table 6.6. Gun-Massacre Incidents and Fatalities by Number of Shooters.

	Total
All Gun Massacres	
Incidents	111
Deaths	904
Average Death Toll	8.1
Gun Massacres Involving Only One Shooter	
Incidents	96
Deaths	779
Average Death Toll	8.1
Gun Massacres Involving Multiple Shooters (Two or More Shooters)	
Incidents	15
Deaths	125
Average Death Toll	8.3
Gun Massacres Involving Exactly Two Shooters	
Incidents	10
Deaths	91
Average Death Toll	9.1
Gun Massacres Involving More Than Two Shooters	
Incidents	5
Deaths	34
Average Death Toll	6.8

★ ★ ★

By guiding attention to the three elements of any act of violence, the trinity-of-violence framework allows us to better understand who perpetrates mass shootings and why they do it, what they tend to target and where they tend to strike, as well as how they employ weapons and which features produces more lethal consequences. As the chapters in the section demonstrate, most perpetrators are men of working age who suffer from mental illness. Moreover, as a result of unstable high self-esteem, they are easily provoked into violent action, primed by guns to shoot their problems away. Generally, they tend to target locations and victims to which they have a personal connection, and the presence of armed people does little to deter them. And, given the growing availability of lightweight, polymer semiautomatic firearms that can hold extended-capacity magazines, the damage they can do presents a genuine threat to public safety.

But just as the trinity of violence helps us better understand rampage violence, it also points us toward solutions for reducing the bloodshed. The next section draws on the trinity framework to generate suggestions for safeguarding the American public from mass shootings.

PART 3

PRESCRIPTION

CHAPTER SEVEN

BREAKING THE TRINITY

"**I**'ve been shot! We've been shot! Oh my God, help!" Those were the last words of First Officer Ray Andress's mayday call on May 7, 1964, seconds before Oakland Air Traffic Control lost contact with Pacific Air Lines Flight 773, bound for San Francisco.[1] A few moments later, a United Airlines flight in the vicinity of Flight 773's last known location reported, "There's a black cloud of smoke coming up through the undercast."[2] It was coming from what was left of Flight 773 after it had slammed into a hillside near San Ramon, California, killing all forty-four people on board the twin-engine aircraft.

A subsequent investigation determined that Francisco Gonzales, a mentally disturbed passenger, entered the cockpit of Flight 773 and shot the pilot and copilot with a .357 revolver.[3]

When I read of the downing of Pacific Air Lines 773, the first question that went through my mind was: How did Gonzales get a gun on board the plane?

Think of the safety measures that we routinely pass through these days in order to get on an airplane: Transportation Security Administration (TSA) representatives bark out instructions as we near security lines. *Dispose of any liquids you might have before going through the metal detectors. Remove your laptop from your carry-on bag and place it in a separate bin for inspection. Take off your coat, hat, belt, and shoes and run them through the machine for screening.* It's hard to sneak a firearm past an airport checkpoint, especially in light of the stringent regulations in effect since 9/11.

Turns out that back in 1964, airline passengers weren't subjected to preboarding screening. I don't mean that they weren't forced to take off their coats and shoes. Or that they weren't made to throw away their coffees. I mean they weren't screened at all.[4]

In 1964, if you wanted to bring a handgun onto a plane, you just had to conceal it in a hidden holster or place it in a carry-on bag. There was no system in place to check for firearms. In fact, metal detectors weren't installed at American airports until 1973.[5] Prior to that, it was pretty easy to bring a weapon on board an airplane.[6]

Francisco Gonzales had repeatedly told family members that he would kill himself, and he threatened to take others with him. He even told a few acquaintances that his last day on Earth would be either May 6 or May 7. The writing was clearly on the wall.[7]

His friends and family knew the twenty-seven-year-old San Francisco resident was struggling. He had hit hard times. Only four years earlier, he had proudly represented the Philippines in the Olympics as a member of the national yacht team. But by 1964, his marriage was falling apart, his financial position was in ruins due in large part to an accumulation of massive debt, and his mental health was deteriorating.[8]

On May 6, 1964, Gonzales legally purchased a Smith & Wesson .357 magnum revolver and decided to head out to Reno, Nevada, for a night of gambling.[9] Back then, Harrah's and Harold's Club casinos worked in partnership with Pacific Air Lines, offering a special $25.99 round-trip fare that brought customers from San Francisco to Reno in the evening, with a return flight out early the next day. It was quite the incentive for the binge gambler: two free drinks, a free buffet dinner, and a reimbursement of $15 toward the airfare.[10]

Arriving early for his flight to Reno, Gonzales purchased $105,000 in air-accident insurance and then proudly displayed his new revolver to people at San Francisco International Airport, while he waited to board his flight. He supposedly even told one person that he planned to kill himself with the gun.[11] Maybe if someone reported Gonzales to authorities, he might have been prevented from getting on the plane. Instead, nobody said a word.

In Reno, Gonzales decided to go for broke. According to news accounts, he had a run of bad luck at the tables. But losing his money didn't seem to faze him. As he reportedly told one dealer, "it won't make any difference after tomorrow."[12] Ready to die, on the morning of May 7, Gonzales boarded the return flight home, selecting a seat immediately behind the cockpit door. After a brief stop-over in Stockton, where two passengers deplaned and another ten boarded, Flight 773 took off for San Francisco. But exactly ten minutes into the flight, Gonzales entered the cockpit and shot the pilot and copilot before turning the gun on himself. With the pilots incapacitated, the Fairchild F-27A turboprop aircraft went into a steep descent, slamming into the ground at nearly a 90-degree angle moments later.[13]

Executing a cockpit crew was unprecedented until Gonzales's midair rampage in 1964. But the downing of Pacific Air Lines Flight 773 was a distressing wake-up call that passenger airplanes were extremely vulnerable to attack by anyone traveling with a weapon on his person. It forced federal regulators to come up with ways to prevent similar disasters in the future.

Let's say you're a policymaker back in 1964. What would you recommend to avert another attack like the assault on Flight 773?

The trinity of violence reminds us that every act of violence involves a perpetrator, a target, and a weapon. Without all three of these components, you can't have an attack. Applying this model sheds insight into why, where, and how hostile strikes might occur. But it also serves another equally valuable function: It offers solutions for how to prevent—or at least minimize—violence.

If every act of violence requires all three elements of the trinity to converge, then, to avoid an attack, all we need to do is take away *one* of the three elements. No perpetrator willing to commit an act of criminal aggression? No attack. No target that can be struck? No attack. No weapon by which to carry out the hit? No attack. Eliminate one corner of the trinity and you eliminate the act of violence.

This is called *breaking the trinity.*

Strategy has its origins in the study of diplomacy and warfare. Drawing on the lessons from the fields of international relations and security studies, we are able to identify three prominent approaches that often work in conjunction with each other to help keep nations safe. Each of these strategies happens to loosely correspond with a component of the trinity of violence: dissuade the perpetrators, defend the targets, and deny the weapons.[14]

Dissuasion

Regarding perpetrators, one of the most valued strategies is dissuasion. If you can persuade heads of state that launching attacks will result in disastrous consequences that won't be worth it, you can deter unwanted acts of violence. Of course, deterrence requires a credible threat if it's to be effective. Take nuclear brinkmanship, where one nuclear power tries to dissuade another by making what's known as a mutually assured destruction (MAD) argument: *If you launch a large-scale nuclear strike against us, we'll immediately retaliate with a full-blown counterstrike against you. Your attack might eliminate our country from the face of the planet, but what good will it do you if we, in kind, eliminate you?* A nuclear first-strike under such circumstances isn't just MAD, it's mad. Reason dictates that only the mentally unsound or suicidal would attack when facing the near certain possibility of death.

Let's come back to our earlier question: What safety measures would you recommend to prevent another gun rampage on an airplane? The strategy of dissuasion works by convincing a potential shooter that an attack won't be worth it. But what could you do to alter the calculus of someone who is prepared to kill the flight-deck crew in an effort to bring down a plane? You can warn him that, if he attempts such an attack, he'll be killed. That's not likely to make a difference, though. After all, that's often the objective of mass murderers: to die and take a whole bunch of other people with them in the process. And it's probably safe to assume that, if the threat of death won't be an effective deterrent, then the threat of arrest and imprisonment after the fact won't have much of an impact either.

Defense

When deterrence fails—and sometimes it does—countries fall back on defense. If a potential target can be hardened or fortified to the point that an attack against it will do little to no significant damage, then the attack, should it occur, will fail in its objective. Protection is the next best outcome to prevention. Again, to draw on an example from international politics, in the summer of 1990 the United States issued a "clear and repeated warning"[15] to Iraq that, if it invaded neighboring Kuwait, it would be met with war. Saddam Hussein, the Iraqi dictator at the time, thought that the United States was bluffing. So on August 2, 1990, Iraq invaded Kuwait. But the response of the US-led coalition was swift and substantial. In combat that lasted just one hundred hours, coalition forces successfully liberated Kuwait, handing Iraq a costly and humiliating defeat in the process. The attack wasn't averted, but its damage was successfully minimized to an acceptable level.

Returning to aviation security, protecting the aircraft and the people on board is likely a better strategy. Perhaps the solution might be something as simple as requiring cockpit doors to remain locked during the duration of a flight? As an added measure, you can recommend fortifying cockpit doors so that they're impenetrable and bulletproof as well, making it impossible for a gunman to shoot the flight-deck crew through a closed door. But, in the pre-9/11 world, couldn't an attacker just kill one flight attendant or passenger every minute until the captain opens the cockpit door? Of course, in the post-9/11 era, pilots are trained not to open the door in such a situation. But one problem that remains is that, from time to time, pilots need to exit the flight deck. What happens when the pilot needs to go to the rest room? Couldn't an attacker storm the cockpit when the door opens to allow the crew entry and exit? These days, you might notice that when a pilot needs a bathroom break, a flight attendant wheels a beverage cart in front of the cockpit door to serve as an obstacle to anyone intent on rushing the flight deck. But if someone is armed, he could easily shoot the crew before they could shut the door.

Maybe the solution is to arm the pilots? That way, if anyone breaches the cockpit door, one of the pilots could defend the plane by shooting the assailant before the assailant shoots him or her. On the other hand, isn't it extremely unlikely that the pilots will have enough time to locate his or her firearm, ready it, and spin around to aim and fire it before the attacker puts a bullet in the pilot? Remember, in an ambush, the victim has about a second to react before being shot. The odds seem stacked against the pilots in this scenario. Maybe the answer is to have armed air marshals aboard flights? But, here too, the only way to guarantee their effectiveness would be to have air marshals on every single flight. Given that daily there are well over twenty-five thousand passenger flights that cross American airspace, that would require an exorbitant commitment of resources and manpower.[16] So, what about allowing passengers to defend the aircraft with their personal firearms? That way, if a bad guy pulls out a gun, some good guys can draw their weapons and neutralize the threat before it brings down the plane? Of course, that assumes that nobody gets hurt in the cross fire and that none of the bullets flying around the cabin penetrate the plane's fuselage, causing a sudden drop in air pressure that sends the aircraft into a fatal dive.

Denial

Dissuasion and defense are, of course, strategies that focus primarily on ends. Denial of weapons highlights the importance of means. The logic that underpins this is actually quite simple. Achieving ends requires means. If you can deprive potential threats the means that they require to accomplish their ends, you can make their ends unattainable. Staying with examples from statecraft, the strategy of denial often manifests itself in disarmament. Think of it this way: one of the biggest threats to global security is the proliferation of nuclear weapons. If a rogue state gets nuclear capabilities, it can use its new power to conquer or, worse, annihilate other countries. But if you preclude that state from acquiring nuclear weapons, then you eliminate the existential threat it can pose. After all, a crazed leader on the world stage can't launch a nuclear strike if he doesn't have nukes to launch. Basically, no weapons, no threat, no worries.

The truth is that many dissuasion- and defense-based measures are now in effect to keep us safe in the sky. Criminal laws threaten prosecution of anyone who attempts an act of violence aboard an airliner. Fortified cockpit doors are kept shut for nearly the entire duration of a flight. And air marshals do accompany many, although far from all, flights. But as the above discussion notes, measures aimed at dissuasion and defense are far from perfect. It's not that they don't contribute to aviation safety. Obviously, they do. However, there's a third strategy—one of denial—that offers greater security: turning commercial airplanes into gun-restricting zones.

Here's a simple question: Would you feel safer flying on an airplane if passengers were allowed to carry firearms on board, or if they were precluded from doing so? I suspect most Americans would like to keep weapons off of planes. But not everyone feels this way. After 9/11, the head of Gun Owners of America, the second largest gun-rights organization in the United States, endorsed the idea of allowing individuals with concealed-carry permits to bring their personal firearms onto flights.[17] And he was not the only person pushing for such a measure.[18]

The Federal Aviation Administration has long gone the other way. In the early 1970s, it mandated that metal detectors be installed at all airports.[19] By employing technologies to spot hazardous materials, authorities are now able to seize firearms before they're brought onto airplanes. At its core, it's a strategy of denial—depriving access to lethal weapons. It might not make the perpetrators any less bad, but it certainly helps make them less dangerous.

A TALE OF TWO BOMBINGS

Let's forget about guns for a moment and examine another weapon that has posed a significant threat to American society in the past: bombs. Large-scale explosive devices are capable of claiming hundreds of lives in the single push of a button or lighting of a fuse. Bombs have been used to blow up planes, trains, ships, cars, and buildings. Overseas, the United States has certainly been victimized by its fair share of high-profile bombings: the truck bombing of the

Marine barracks in Beirut, Lebanon, in 1983; the downing of Pan Am Flight 103 over Lockerbie, Scotland, in 1988; the explosion at the Khobar Towers in Saudi Arabia in 1996; the dual strike against the American embassies in Kenya and Tanzania in 1998; and the assault on the USS *Cole* in Yemen in 2000.

The United States has also experienced deadly bombings on American soil. But generally attacks inside our borders have been of a lesser magnitude than those perpetrated overseas—with one exception: the bombing of the Alfred P. Murrah Federal Building in Oklahoma City, on the morning of April 19, 1995, by right-wing extremist Timothy McVeigh.

After loading a rented twenty-foot-long Ryder truck with a massive fertilizer bomb, McVeigh drove his vehicle to the Murrah Building and parked in the drop-off area, directly below the building's daycare center. McVeigh then lit two slow-burning fuses, locked the truck, and made his way over to a waiting getaway car. Moments later, the nearly five thousand-pound bomb detonated, leaving only a portion of the building standing. The damage was of such a large scale that rescue and recovery efforts lasted seventeen days. In the worst act of domestic terrorism in American history until 9/11, the attack—planned by McVeigh and his co-conspirator Terry Nichols—left 168 dead and nearly seven hundred injured. Among the dead were nineteen children who were in the building's daycare center that morning.[20]

Once the perpetrators were captured and their motives uncovered, the focus turned to how they were able to pull off such a mammoth attack. Officials soon discovered that the materials required to build a truck bomb were readily available: basically, explosives-grade ammonium nitrate mixed with fuel oil. Fearing similar attacks in the future, the federal government responded by heavily restricting the availability of precursor explosive materials.[21]

Explosive devices typically have four components: the explosive material; the initiator; the switch; and the power supply.[22] As with breaking the trinity, if you can take away one of these elements, you should be able to avert a bombing. Of course, some of these components are so commonplace in society that restricting access to them is sure to be a failing effort. Take cell phones, which can serve as switches, and batteries, which can power initiators and switches. On the other hand, precursor chemicals like explosives-grade ammonium nitrate as well as initiators like blasting caps can be—and are being—successfully regulated. In the aftermath of the Oklahoma City attack, the federal government instituted a series of controls that reduced the concentration of dangerous chemicals in common consumer products (for example, ammonium nitrate in fertilizer) and tightened access to precursor chemicals, explosives, and detonators (for example, requiring a license to purchase certain materials). The results have been impressive.[23]

Let's fast-forward to May 1, 2010. Faisal Shahzad, a young man angry with American military policy in the Middle East and South Asia, loaded an IED into his Nissan Pathfinder and parked it in Times Square. As he exited the vehicle, Shahzad lit several M-88 firecrackers, which he rigged to serve as the initial triggering device of his homemade bomb, which also consisted of gunpowder, gasoline, propane canisters, and urea-based fertilizer.[24] Within moments, the M-88s began exploding. There was fire . . . popping . . . smoke. And then . . . nothing. Shahzad's attempt to strike at the heart of New York City failed miserably. Why? Because explosives-grade fertilizers and blasting caps are no longer available for purchase in the United States without a special license.[25]

The regulations instituted following the Oklahoma City bombing worked; so well, indeed, that there has not been a mass-fatality bombing on American soil since 1995. It's not that there haven't been bombings. The Boston Marathon attack shows that people can still make IEDs and cause damage. But the destruction is now limited. The Tsarnaev brothers killed three people with two devices—one IED killed two people and the other IED killed one person. Because of the restrictions currently in place, the best that would-be bombers can do is to create pipe bombs and crude IEDs like the pressure-cooker bombs that were constructed by the Tsarnaevs. These devices can still maim and kill, but they can't produce catastrophic destruction like the Oklahoma City truck bomb did. Those days are behind us—and regulatory schemes are to thank.

✯ ✯ ✯

The above vignettes illustrate that there is a preferred way of reducing threats to public safety: denying weapons to potential perpetrators. By preventing high-risk individuals from acquiring dangerous weapons or by hindering them from employing such weapons, government can keep its citizens safe.

In a way, homeland security is akin to George Orwell's *Animal Farm*. All strategies proposed by the trinity of violence are equal, but some are more equal than others. It's not that dissuasion and defense aren't valuable. They are. After all, we still criminalize bombings and erect barricades in front of important structures. But laws, on their own, often fail to dissuade homicidal and suicidal individuals. And blast barriers can't be erected everywhere. There are just too many potential perpetrators and targets for these strategies to be effective on their own. In open societies where resources are limited, securing public safety depends primarily on a strategy of denial to break the trinity of violence.

The success of the United States in countering aviation attacks and bombings by restricting access to, and use of, weapons raises an important question: If the deprivation of weapons works in these areas, couldn't it also serve as an effective strategy in reducing gun violence?

THE AMERICAN EXPERIENCE

The United States has been exemplary in safeguarding its citizenry from a host of deadly threats: accidents, environmental hazards, pandemics, hijackings, bombings, even weapons of mass destruction. Through successful regulation of hazardous products—almost all with little to no public controversy—the different levels of government all work hand in hand to keep us safe from a plethora of dangers.[26] But when it comes to protecting us from gun violence, the government's record has been abysmal.[27] In fact, the United States is in a class all by itself. No other advanced, Western democracy experiences the magnitude of gun violence that presently afflicts American society.[28] This is particularly true when it comes to mass shootings.[29]

The United States does little to regulate firearms, especially at the federal level.[30] While it goes to great lengths to restrict access to WMDs and IEDs, the same can't be said for its efforts to keep firearms out of the hands of high-risk individuals. Indeed, the American experience with gun control nationwide is so limited that it can actually be chronicled in a few bullet points:

- The National Firearms Act of 1934: Heavily regulated machine guns, short-barrel rifles and shotguns, and silencers.
- The Federal Firearms Act of 1938: Established a federal licensing system to regulate manufacturers, importers, and dealers of firearms.
- The Omnibus Crime Control and Safe Streets Act of 1968: Prohibited anyone under twenty-one years of age from purchasing a handgun.
- The Gun Control Act of 1968: Required that all interstate firearms transfers or sales be made through a federally licensed firearms dealer and prohibited certain categories of people— felons (indicted or convicted), fugitives, drug abusers, mentally ill persons (as determined by adjudication), illegal aliens, dishonorably discharged servicemen, US-citizenship renouncers, and domestic abusers—from possessing firearms.[31]
- The Firearm Owners Protection Act of 1986: Barred the purchase or transfer of automatic weapons without government approval.
- The Undetectable Firearms Act of 1988: Required that all firearms have at least 3.7 oz. of metal that can be detected by a metal detector.
- The Gun-Free School Zones Act of 1990: Criminalized possession or discharge of a firearm in a school zone.
- The Brady Handgun Violence Prevention Act of 1993: Required

that anyone attempting to purchase a firearm from a federally licensed dealer pass a background check.[32]

- The Federal Assault Weapons Ban of 1994: Banned the sale and possession of semiautomatic assault weapons and extended-capacity magazines not grandfathered prior to the enactment of the law.[33]

Of all of these measures, the National Firearms Act of 1934 and the Assault Weapons Ban of 1994 (AWB) were the only ones instituted primarily in an effort to reduce the carnage of mass shootings. The former was passed in response to a series of bloody gangland executions, including the infamous 1929 St. Valentine's Day massacre in Chicago.[34] While there are still machine guns in circulation, the National Firearm Act, in conjunction with the Firearm Owners Protection Act of 1986, sharply cut the availability of machine guns, which likely explains the complete elimination of massacres perpetrated with such automatic-fire weapons.

Like the National Firearms Act, the AWB was introduced following several high-profile mass shootings in the early 1990s: the Luby's restaurant, 101 California Street office complex, and Long Island Railroad train car massacres.[35] Signed into law by President Bill Clinton, the AWB went into effect on September 13, 1994. At the insistence of the gun-rights lobby, however, the bill contained a ten-year sunset provision. As Congress never renewed the ban, it automatically expired on September 13, 2004.

The decade the law was in effect nonetheless resulted in a unique experiment, allowing us to discern what impact, if any, the ban had on gun violence in general and mass shootings in particular. As to the former, the academic consensus seems to be that the AWB had a minimal impact on reducing violent crime.[36] This hardly comes as a surprise. After all, most crimes don't involve assault weapons. The real test should be: Did it succeed in its intended purpose of reducing rampage violence? The answer is a resounding yes.

Let's take a closer look.

The best way to assess the impact of something is to conduct what, in social science, we commonly refer to as a time-series analysis. Basically, that's a fancy name for a before-and-after test. Figures 7.1

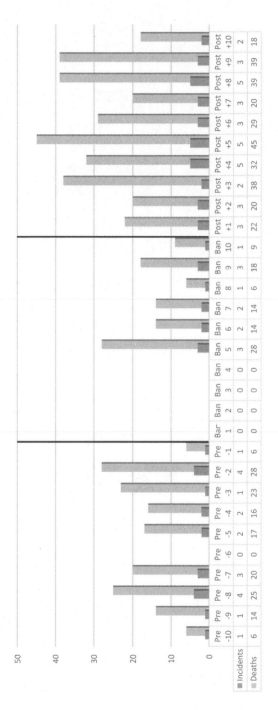

Fig. 7.1. Gun Massacres Before, During, and After the Assault Weapons Ban of 1994.

Note: The lines in the graph demarcate the start and end points of the Assault Weapons Ban, which was in effect from September 13, 1994, through September 12, 2004. The data are drawn from Table 3.2.

	Pre -10	Pre -9	Pre -8	Pre -7	Pre -6	Pre -5	Pre -4	Pre -3	Pre -2	Pre -1	Ban 1	Ban 2	Ban 3	Ban 4	Ban 5	Ban 6	Ban 7	Ban 8	Ban 9	Ban 10	Post +1	Post +2	Post +3	Post +4	Post +5	Post +6	Post +7	Post +8	Post +9	Post +10
Incidents	1	1	4	3	0	2	2	1	4	1	0	0	0	0	3	2	2	1	3	1	3	2	2	5	5	3	3	5	3	2
Deaths	6	14	25	20	0	17	16	23	28	6	0	0	0	28	14	14	6	18	9	22	20	38	32	45	29	20	39	39	18

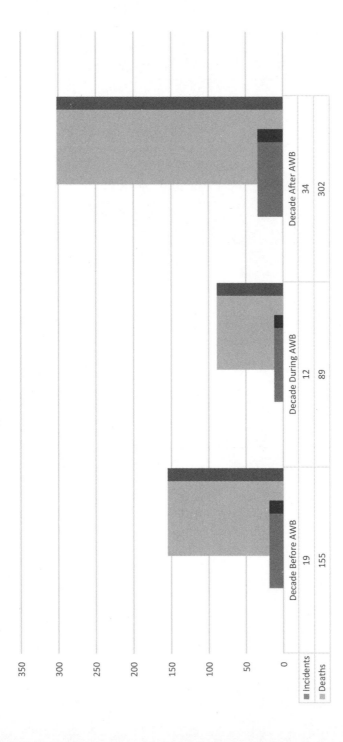

Fig. 7.2. Gun Massacres by Decade Before, During, and After the Assault Weapons Ban of 1994.
Note: The Assault Weapons Ban was in effect from September 13, 1994, through September 12, 2004.
The data are drawn from Table 3.2.

and 7.2 provide a look at the before-and-after pictures. In the decade prior to the enactment of the AWB, the United States experienced nineteen gun massacres that resulted in 155 cumulative deaths, for an average death toll of 8.2 fatalities per incident. During the ten-year period that the AWB was in effect, the numbers declined substantially, with only twelve gun massacres, resulting in eighty-nine deaths, for an average of 7.4 fatalities per incident.[37] What's particularly astounding about this time period is that during the first four and a half years of the ban, there wasn't a single gun massacre in the United States. Not one. This is unprecedented in modern American history.[38] Since 1966, the longest streaks without a gun massacre prior to era of the AWB were two instances of consecutive years (1969–1970 and 1979–1980).[39] Then, all of a sudden, from September 1994 to April 1999, the country experienced a long calm. As further evidence of the AWB's effectiveness, once it expired, rampages returned with a vengeance. In the ten years after the ban, the number of gun massacres nearly tripled to thirty-four incidents, sending the total number of deaths skyrocketing to 302, for an average of 8.9 fatalities per incident.[40] These numbers paint a clear picture: America's experiment, while short-lived, was also extremely successful.[41]

ZEROING OUT GUN MASSACRES

The biggest takeaway from America's experience with a ban on assault weapons and extended-capacity magazines is that gun-control legislation can save lives. But is there a way to get to zero? Is there a way to eliminate gun massacres once and for all? For that, we have to look overseas for insights.

One of the biggest obstacles to successful gun control is the ability to transport firearms across open, contiguous borders. In the United States, it's a problem that allows guns to flow freely from states with lax laws into states with strict laws. A common complaint frequently leveled by elected officials in places like California, Illinois, Maryland, New York, and Massachusetts is that people just need to drive across a state line and they can readily obtain firearms that they can then easily—if perhaps illegally—bring back into their jurisdictions.[42] That was certainly the case in the Washington Navy Yard massacre. Unable to purchase a shotgun in the District of Columbia, given its strict gun laws that seriously restrict weapons possession by nonresidents, Aaron Alexis took a twenty-minute drive to Newington, Virginia, and secured his instrument of mass murder with little complication.[43]

And it's not just the United States. Continental Europe, which has eliminated passport and customs controls between most nations in an effort to create a common market, facilitates the transport and transfer of goods—both benign and dangerous. The November 2015 Paris terrorist attacks, which claimed 130 lives, serve as a prominent example of how, despite strict national gun regulations, France was unable to stop the importation of automatic weapons into the country. What happened in Paris is a terrifying reminder that disparate laws and open borders can be a recipe for disaster.[44]

It again raises another fascinating question: What about areas that can control the flow of people and products across their borders? When those entities pass tough, nationally uniform firearms restrictions, do they see significant declines in the type of violence they are trying to reduce? And, more to the point, have such jurisdictions had success in curbing gun massacres?

What better cases to examine than water-locked countries that, as a result of geography, don't share contiguous, open borders? They provide for the perfect natural experiment.

★ ★ ★

Great Britain illustrates that being encircled by water doesn't make a country immune to gun violence. The island nation has certainly experienced its share of crime and bloodshed, including some horrific instances of rampage violence. One of England's most disturbing mass murders occurred on the afternoon of August 19, 1987, when twenty-seven-year-old Michael Robert Ryan went on a shooting spree in the town of Hungerford. Armed with a semiautomatic handgun and two assault rifles—all legally owned and equipped with extended-capacity magazines—Ryan killed sixteen people and wounded another fifteen before finally taking his own life. At the time, it was the deadliest gun massacre in modern British history.[45]

The British government reacted by passing the 1988 Firearms Act, which banned most semiautomatic rifles and burst-fire weapons, and tightened restrictions on certain shotguns. However, after deliberation, legislators opted to forego enacting a large-scale ban on handguns, leaving them largely available within the confines of the country's licensing scheme.[46]

Nearly a decade later, on March 13, 1996, Great Britain again fell victim to a horrific rampage. Armed with four legally owned handguns—two of them extended-capacity semiautomatic pistols—and nearly 750 rounds of ammunition, forty-three-year-old Scout leader Thomas Hamilton attacked an elementary school in Dunblane, Scotland. Storming the school's gymnasium, where physical-education classes were in progress, Hamilton gunned down a group of students and their teachers before firing a fatal round into his head.[47]

The national tragedy, which claimed seventeen innocent lives—sixteen of them children between the ages of five and six—and left fifteen others wounded, created an uproar in Great Britain. Feeling intense public pressure to further curtail the availability of weapons, the British Parliament passed two Firearms Acts in 1997 that essentially banned private ownership of handguns.[48]

Despite these legislative efforts to control firearms, on June 2, 2010, fifty-two-year-old taxi driver Derrick Bird perpetrated a series of ambush attacks across thirty different crime scenes in the English county of Cumbria. Equipped with a bolt-action rifle and a double-barrel shotgun that he was licensed to own for purposes of pest control and sport, Bird killed twelve and injured another eleven. While harder to slaughter scores of people without semiautomatic firearms, the Cumbria massacre demonstrates that it can be done if perpetrated in piecemeal fashion against unsuspecting victims across a variety of locations.[49]

The British experience with mass shootings can be seen in two different ways. On the one hand, despite the implementation of strict gun-safety measures following the Hungerford and Dunblane massacres, the nation has not been rampage-free. On the other hand, the island of approximately sixty-three million residents has come pretty close to zeroing out high-fatality mass shootings, suffering only one gun massacre since 1996. By comparison, the United States, which is roughly five times the population of Great Britain, has experienced fifty-four times the number of gun massacres over the same twenty-year time period.

Given such a stark contrast, it's hard to escape the conclusion that gun control contributes tremendously to a reduction in rampage violence.

* * *

Australia is another advanced democracy that is no stranger to rampage violence. In the 1980s and early 1990s, the water-locked continent was being victimized by gun massacres at a rate of roughly one every two years.[50] Compared to the United States, this may not seem like a lot of high-fatality mass shootings. However, when you take into consideration the fact that Australia has a population comparable to the state of New York, the country's gun-violence problem stands out. Between 1981 and 1996, Australia was experiencing gun massacres at a rate that was roughly four times that of New York.

The deadliest of all Australian gun massacres occurred in 1996, when twenty-eight-year-old Martin Bryant went on a shooting spree in the Tasmanian town of Port Arthur. Armed with two semiautomatic assault rifles that were equipped with extended-capacity magazines, the mentally disturbed Bryant killed thirty-five people and wounded another twenty-three before being captured by authorities. Given a patchwork of disparate gun laws across Australia's six states and two territories, Bryant was able to buy his arsenal from licensed firearm dealers in Tasmania, where, in general, assault rifles were legally available for purchase.[51]

Just twelve days after the tragedy in Port Arthur, the conservative government of Prime Minister John Howard clamped down on guns nationwide by enacting the National Firearms Agreement of 1996 (NFA). Among other things, the NFA imposed a ban on all semiautomatic rifles and implemented an unprecedented mandatory weapons buy-back program. In what became known as "the big melt," the government bought back close to 650,000 firearms, which it then destroyed.[52]

As happened in Great Britain following the Hungerford massacre, handguns were excepted from strict restriction. The handgun loophole allowed a mentally unstable student to legally acquire multiple handguns and attack his classmates and professor at Monash University in 2002.[53] While the gunman killed only two of his victims—preventing the shooting from rising to the level of a massacre—it raised enough concern that Parliament reacted by banning handguns. Today, while there still remain classes of firearms that are legal in Australia, the most dangerous ones have been taken out of circulation.[54]

Australia's successful fair-market value buy-back program serves as a model for bolstering public safety by taking dangerous weapons off the streets. Not only has there not been another gun massacre on the continent in over a decade, but since 1996 the strict restrictions imposed on gun possession have also drastically decreased both firearm homicides and suicides—indicating that efforts to prevent mass murder can generate additional payoffs in other areas of violence reduction as well.[55]

The Australian experience is an exemplar of effective firearms regulation, demonstrating that gun massacres can indeed be zeroed out.

Could it be that Americans are inherently more evil than British and Australian nationals? Is the explanation for our mass-shooting problem that simple? No. It's that Americans own a lot more firearms than citizens of other democracies do—and the United States has done little to emulate the regulatory successes that the remainder of the advanced world has used to control dangerous weapons and keep their societies secure.

Offering some wisdom from his own efforts to curtail rampage violence in Australia, John Howard reminds us that—despite opposition for hard-core firearms enthusiasts—the security benefits of regulating weapons far outweigh the political costs. Sharing his insights following the massacre in Newtown, Connecticut, Howard noted, "Few Australians would deny that their country is safer today as a consequence of gun control."[56]

Australia teaches us that if we're looking to break the trinity of rampage violence, it can be done. The trick is to privilege and promote one strategy—deprivation of weapons—over the others. After all, you can't have a gun massacre without a gun.

CHAPTER EIGHT

THE BAD MAN'S AWE

It was September 11, 2008—the seventh anniversary of the 9/11 attack—and Meleanie Hain decided that she wasn't going to take any chances. The central Pennsylvania mother of three was determined to protect her family, especially against an assault seeking to commemorate the worst act of terrorism in American history. She knew one way to decrease the odds of her children being victimized was to have them stay home. But Hain's five-year-old daughter had a soccer game that day. She couldn't let her little girl down like that. So Hain came up with Plan B: she would attend her child's match armed. If anything went wrong, she could at least intervene and eliminate the threat before it got her.[1]

Her decision to pace the sidelines with a holstered semiautomatic pistol on her hip didn't go over well with the other parents. After numerous complaints were lodged following the game, the Lebanon County sheriff revoked Hain's permit to carry a concealed firearm.[2] Hain, however, felt that the sheriff's actions infringed on her constitutional right to bear arms, so she fought back.[3] After bringing a civil suit against the sheriff, a state court judge ordered that her concealed-carry permit be reinstated. Emboldened by her day in court, Hain returned to the pitch packing heat.[4]

Finding herself suddenly cast into the national spotlight, the strapped soccer mom became a fresh face in the gun-rights movement. It was an opportunity Hain seized on to become a vocal proponent of the Second Amendment right to self-defense. As she put it in a response to her critics, "People who say, 'You do not need a gun at a soccer field,' . . . I wonder if they could tell me when I will need it? That way I could just avoid that time and place."[5]

✯ ✯ ✯

As Meleanie Hain's words remind us, rampage violence can occur at any time and in any place. For gun-rights supporters, the answer is to always be prepared, to fight gunfire with gunfire. Measures that reduce the number of guns in our society only endanger us further, they tell us. We need more guns, not fewer. That, in turn, means we need less regulation.

It's a message that was sent loud and clear following the massacre in Newtown. Addressing the tragedy in a press conference a week after it happened, NRA executive vice president Wayne LaPierre laid blame on the mental-health system, Hollywood, the video-game industry, the news media, criminals, and gun-control advocates, among others. Every factor that could be tied to a mass shooting was mentioned by LaPierre—with one exception: guns. Here, he offered a different perspective. Guns aren't the problem. They're the solution.

It was a point he tried to drive home by asking, "Since when did the word 'gun' automatically become a bad word?"[6] He was being rhetorical:

> A gun in the hands of a Secret Service agent protecting the President isn't a bad word. A gun in the hands of a soldier protecting the United States isn't a bad word. And when you hear the glass breaking in your living room at 3 a.m. and call 911, you won't be able to pray hard enough for a gun in the hands of a good guy to get there fast enough to protect you.[7]

The NRA was telling us, if we want to make America safer, we need to stop demonizing guns. An important step in this direction is to stop perpetuating "the dangerous notion that one more gun ban—or one more law imposed on peaceful, lawful people—will protect us where 20,000 others have failed!"[8] It was a twist on an old NRA adage: Guns don't kill people; people kill people. Now we were being told that gun-control measures kill people too.

When seen through the prism of the trinity of violence, the NRA's position is defense-heavy. That is, for the NRA, the solution to rampage violence is to protect the target. It has little faith in dissuading the perpetrator. "The truth is that our society is populated by an unknown number of genuine monsters—people so deranged, so evil, so possessed by voices and driven by demons that no sane person can possibly ever comprehend them," LaPierre warned us. "They walk among us every day. And does anybody really believe that the next Adam Lanza isn't planning his attack on a school he's already identified at this very moment?"[9] With so many of these "monsters" among us, there's little that new laws can do to deter most of them from committing heinous acts of violence, LaPierre argues.

You can also forget about depriving the weapon. This is anathema to the NRA's core beliefs. In his press conference, LaPierre asserted that those who try to single out firearms as the culprit "don't know what they're talking about!"[10]

Breaking the trinity of rampage violence is simple for the NRA. "The only way to stop a monster from killing our kids is to be personally involved and invested in a plan of absolute protection."[11] That means privileging one strategy above all others: defending the target. Or as LaPierre put it, "The *only* thing that stops a bad guy with a gun is a good guy with a gun."[12]

Wayne LaPierre's infamous speech was more than an attempt to propose policy prescriptions for reducing the carnage of mass shootings. He was also trying to stave off additional restrictions on gun ownership and use. In a way, LaPierre's address was a direct response to President Barack Obama, who just days earlier in a White House press conference announced that Vice President Joe Biden would spearhead a national response to gun massacres, one focused on another prong of the trinity of violence—the weapon.

IF NOT NOW, WHEN?

A month after the murder of twenty-seven people in Newtown, President Obama and Vice President Biden unveiled their Now Is the Time initiative—a national strategy aimed at reducing gun violence, particularly mass shootings. Speaking from the White House, the president stated, "If America worked harder to keep guns out of the hands of dangerous people, there would be fewer atrocities like the one that occurred in Newtown."[13] The president then went on to identify three specific proposals that he called on Congress to endorse:

(1) the enactment of universal background checks that would require all gun sales and transfers to be subject to preauthorization;
(2) the reinstatement of the federal Assault Weapons Ban; and
(3) the appropriation of additional resources to law enforcement so that it can crack down on illicit gun trafficking and straw purchases.[14]

The president concluded his remarks by warning that some forces in American society would resist his efforts to institute gun-safety measures: "There will be pundits and politicians and special interest lobbyists publicly warning of a tyrannical, all-out assault on liberty. . . . And behind the scenes, they'll do everything they can to block any commonsense reform and make sure nothing changes whatsoever."[15] He was referring to the NRA and other pro-gun organizations. He knew that the gun-rights movement would put up a fierce fight. But he felt that, despite the uphill battle, his agenda would be enacted, given the national sentiment at the time.

He was wrong.

Almost three months to the day after the White House unveiled its Now Is the Time plan, the Democrat-controlled Senate failed to secure the requisite number of votes needed to debate a bill that would have required universal background checks. To be clear, this wasn't a vote on whether or not to close the so-called gun-show loophole by making all gun purchases and transfers subject to a background check. This was merely a vote on whether or not to discuss such proposed legislation. Pursuant to a Senate rule, sixty votes are needed to debate a pending bill on the chamber's floor. Only fifty-four senators agreed to bring the universal-background-check bill forth. The president's agenda never even got out of the gate. A small group of Democratic senators teamed up with their Republican colleagues to kill the bill.[16]

In an emotional press conference on the White House lawn afterward, President Obama stood in front of visibly shaken victims who had lost loved ones to mass shootings, and he lambasted Congress for its inaction. Calling it "a pretty shameful day for Washington," the president vowed to continue pressing for tighter regulation of firearms.[17] Three years later, not a single piece of the president's legislative package has been passed.[18] If gun reforms couldn't be implemented following the tragedy at Sandy Hook, could they ever be implemented? Many pundits commenting on the defeat of universal background checks—a policy prescription that, at the time, was supported by 90 percent of the American public—declared that the NRA is just too powerful to get any sort of gun-safety measure enacted at the federal level.[19]

Gun control was pronounced dead at 4:04 p.m. on April 17, 2013.[20]

One problem though: those who were quick to write gun-control's obituary ignored the lessons of history.

★ ★ ★

If there is one theme that has been constant in American history, it's that social progress always begins with political setback. This is the story of the abolition of slavery, the empowerment of women, the protection of minorities, and the equality of marriage. It's also a theme repeated time and time again in efforts to protect society from all sorts of hazardous consumer products. Just to offer one prominent example, let's take a quick look at automobiles.

In 1965, consumer-safety advocate Ralph Nader published *Unsafe at Any Speed: The Designed-In Dangers of the American Automobile.* The book amounted to an indictment of the automobile industry for its failure to equip new cars with, among other standard safety features, seat belts.[21] At the time, seat belts were standard in planes and race cars, but not in passenger vehicles—despite years of calls for such protections following a series of well-publicized accidents, beginning with the death of actor James Dean in 1955. With around fifty thousand people dying each year as a result of auto accidents, Nader demanded legislation to make cars safer.[22]

While seat belts were commonplace in Europe during the early 1960s, in Detroit there was strong resistance to making passenger restraints standard.[23] Fearful of the significant costs that would be incurred if all new cars had to be equipped with additional safety features like the seat belt, auto makers engaged in a public-relations campaign that placed blame for motor vehicle deaths on drivers and road engineers—not cars. Even though the industry never used this language, what they were really saying was something akin to what would later become the rally cry of the gun-rights movement: cars don't kill people; people kill people.[24] Nader's contribution to the building criticism helped. Following the deaths of comedian and actor Ernie Kovacs and Chicago Bears running back Willie Galimore—both killed in automobile accidents as a result of not wearing seat belts—Congress, in 1966, authorized the executive branch to require seat belts in all new cars. Two years later, the Department of Transportation officially mandated that all American vehicles be equipped with passenger restraints, a step taken on the heels of the high-profile car crash that claimed the life of actress Jayne Mansfield.[25]

Despite the availability of safety belts, as late as 1981 the Centers for Disease Control and Prevention (CDC) found that only 11 percent of the population was wearing seat belts.[26] The low numbers were in part the result of a continuing campaign against seat belts, peppered with myths about their use—for example, it's safer to be thrown from a car than to be restrained inside it, and seat belts trap passengers when cars are submerged underwater.[27] At the core of the opposition was a belief that mandating seat-belt use infringed on an individual's right to liberty. In the words of Derek Kieper, who eventually became one of the more vocal opponents of automobile safety restraints, "No law, or set of laws, has made the government more intrusive and ridiculous than seat belt legislation."[28]

It took a combination of "click it or ticket" laws and a decades-long public-education campaign to get use up to 86 percent, where it is presently.[29] Department of Transportation statistics clearly show that seat belts save well over ten thousand lives annually.[30] Indeed, over half of all people killed each year in motor vehicle accidents are unrestrained.[31] And as to that myth that being ejected from a car is safer, the CDC has found that 75 percent of all passengers thrown from cars in accidents die—with the seat belt pretty much being the difference between life and death, given that passengers are thirty times more likely to be ejected if they are unrestrained.[32]

The obvious moral of this story is that regulation has saved countless lives. But there are other lessons as well, among them: Congress is reluctant to embrace reform when it conflicts with the interests of industries that feed campaign coffers; when individual rights clash with public safety, society can be slow to come around to reform; and the tipping points tend to be two high-profile events—often tragedies—that bookend the process, with the initial event stimulating reform proposals and the subsequent event impelling politicians to enact change. Of course, as the tale of seat belts shows, even after legislation is passed, there can still be resistance from some quarters—and only a combination of education and enforcement can overcome it.

Just like the high-profile deaths of Hollywood legends James Dean and Jayne Mansfield served as tipping points triggering major reform in automobile safety, past gun safety reforms have also been bookended by high-profile tragedies. For example, the Gun Control Act of 1968 was spurred by the assassination of President John F. Kennedy in 1963, but it took the assassination of his younger brother Senator Robert F. Kennedy to tip it into law.[33] Similarly, the idea for requiring background checks was largely prompted by the assassination attempt on President Ronald Reagan in 1981, which left his press secretary James Brady partially paralyzed from a bullet wound to the brain. Twelve years later, partly in response to Gian Luigi Ferri's rampage at a law firm in San Francisco, Congress passed the Brady Handgun Violence Prevention Act of 1993.[34]

Some of these changes took over a decade to implement. And numerous Americans died in the interim as a result of government inaction. But, despite initial political resistance and compounding heartbreak, reform eventually took hold.

If history is a guide, then it seems likely that the attack on Sandy Hook is the start of the next major reform in gun safety. What is arguably the most disturbing shooting in American history kick-started a national dialogue on firearms and it prompted President Obama's Now Is the Time initiative for reducing the carnage of rampage violence. What we don't know is what will be the subsequent tragedy that jolts Congress out of its complacency. But sadly it will likely take another gun massacre on par with Newtown before change is enacted.

As those who fought for automobile and gun safety in the past can attest, now might not be the time, but soon it will be.

THE WAY FORWARD

One of the criticisms that President Obama's Now Is the Time agenda continues to face is that, considering it was a plan occasioned by the Newtown massacre, its implementation would likely have not stopped Adam Lanza's attack.[35] Recalling the three main components of the initiative—universal background checks, an assault weapons ban, and a crackdown on illegal gun trafficking and straw purchases—opponents note that none of these would've kept Lanza from getting his hands on firearms. For starters, the guns used in the attack were all legally acquired by his mother after she passed a background check. Moreover, while an assault weapons ban might stem the manufacture of certain military-style rifles in the future, the president's current proposal (like the 1994 ban) would grandfather older models already in circulation, meaning that the AR-15 used by Lanza would have been legal. And, as the AR-15 was not straw-purchased for him, tighter enforcement of gun-trafficking laws also would have not prevented the Sandy Hook slayings.

The Obama administration's plan is a good starting point—especially for purposes of curbing gun violence in general. There are obviously scores of firearms that are employed by criminals that have been obtained without background checks or through illegal transactions.[36] In addition, while closing the gun-show loophole wouldn't have kept firearms out of Adam Lanza's hands, other rampage gunmen like the Columbine killers, who exploited this loophole, would have been prevented from acquiring weapons.[37] Wanting to prevent another circumvention of the Brady Act is certainly a wise policy position. Furthermore, going forward, a ban on assault weapons—even one with gaping loopholes—is still likely to stem some of the bloodshed of rampage violence, as the 1994 AWB did. So, no matter how you see it, the president's proposals are, overall, solid ideas.

However, if the federal government is serious about addressing mass shootings, it must do more. That means instituting gun-safety measures that will go well beyond those that form the centerpiece of the Now Is the Time initiative. Toward this end, there are eight reforms that can be powerful forces in breaking the trinity of rampage violence through weapons deprivation.

1. *Banning and buying back all extended-capacity magazines.* Some gun-control advocates might envision an America where all assault weapons—and perhaps all polymer guns—are banned. Given that there's currently at least one gun in circulation for every American in the population, this is a pipe dream.[38] But there is one measure—controversial as it may be—that, if it were to be implemented, would sharply curtail rampage violence: a ban on extended-capacity magazines. Recall from chapter 6, the factor most associated with high death tolls in gun massacres is the use of a magazine holding more than ten bullets. If such magazines were completely removed from circulation, the bloodshed would be drastically reduced. Nothing facilitates a shooter's ability to spray people with bullets more than being armed with a firearm equipped with twenty, thirty, and, in the case of James Holmes, one hundred bullets. No one needs that kind of capability. Not even for self-defense.[39]

   To do this, however, would entail more than just a ban on extended-capacity magazines. It would require a mandatory buy-back program, like Australia's, that would recoup magazines that were not retrofitted to a ten-round cap. Bans are suboptimal if prohibited items are grandfathered, allowing those already possessed by lawful owners to remain in circulation. At the same time, it would be unjust to seize firearm components without compensating owners with fair-market value for their weapons. While a buy-back regime sounds logistically burdensome, Australia demonstrates that such programs are actually fairly simple to administer. One way to execute such a plan would be over a period of three years, with people receiving full value plus a 10 percent bonus if extended-capacity magazines are turned in during the first year; full value, the second year; and 50 percent value, the third year. After that, anyone possessing a banned magazine would be committing a felony and would lose all future gun-ownership rights. Such a program could cost upward of $500 million over several years. But this is roughly the same amount the United States spent training five Syrian men—yes, five men—to fight ISIS.[40] Unlike the failed counter-ISIS program, however, the extended-capacity magazine buy-back program would undoubtedly save countless lives, making the $500 million a price worth paying.[41]

2. *Expanding prohibitions on gun ownership.* Currently, under federal law, convicted felons, fugitives from justice, domestic abusers, unlawful drug users, persons adjudicated to be mentally ill, illegal aliens, former Americans who have renounced their US citizenship, and dishonorably discharged soldiers are barred from possessing firearms. However, the fact that many people go on shooting sprees with legally obtained weapons indicates that there are still many dangerous people who are able to slip through the cracks. There are two categories of people, in particular, whom the government could do a better of job of disarming: people with a history of criminal violence that doesn't rise to the level of a felony, and suspected terrorists. Washington Navy Yard mass shooter Aaron Alexis had a history of misdemeanor-level violence, destroying night-club furniture in a fit of rage and, in an even more disturbing exhibition of troubling behavior, shooting out the tires of a vehicle belonging to a construction crew that he felt had disrespected him.[42] This is exactly the kind of violent behavior that should ban someone from being a gun owner—before they grad-

uate to deadlier uses of force.[43] Preempting would-be terrorists is also another prudent measure Congress should adopt. According to the Government Accountability Office, between 2004 and 2014, over two thousand people on the FBI's terrorism watch list successfully cleared a background check and purchased a firearm.[44] It seems pretty reasonable to insist that, if you aren't allowed to board a plane, you shouldn't be allowed to buy a gun.

Beyond creating two new categories of prohibited gun owners, the federal government needs to also expand two of the existing categories to include many of the types of people who have gone on to commit mass shootings in the past. Specifically, the definition of domestic abusers must be broadened to include anyone who has perpetrated or threatened an act of violence against a romantic partner, a partner's family, or his or her own family. The current law in effect allows boyfriends and stalkers to evade firearms restrictions. The same holds for children who abuse their siblings or parents.[45] By expanding the category to include any sort of domestic violence or criminal harassment that can result in a civil order of protection, the law can disarm dangerous pursuers like Richard Farley who, in 1988, killed seven at his place of employment in Sunnyvale, California, after his coworker applied for a restraining order to prevent his unwanted advances and prowling.[46] As most mass shootings involve a domestic element, this could help significantly reduce rampage violence. In addition, as the law currently stands, only those deemed to be "mentally defective" by a court of law are barred from possessing weapons. This needs to be widened to authorize medical professionals to make similar determinations—and to allow those professionals to file their determinations with all relevant federal and state agencies that conduct firearms background checks. This would allow psychiatrists to bring any person who is under treatment—whether involuntary or voluntary, in-patient or out-patient—to the attention of the appropriate authorities.[47] Such a modification to the law might have prevented the Aurora and Newtown gunmen from possessing firearms, as both had been receiving psychiatric care.[48] With the most common characteristic of mass shooters being mental illness, this adjustment is arguably one of the most important steps that lawmakers can take to help keep society safe from rampage violence.

3. *Closing the default proceed loophole.* Under current federal law, a background check for a firearms purchase must be completed within three business days. After the three-day period lapses, the sale is allowed to go through even if the review has not been completed. It's known as the default proceed loophole. In 2015, it received national attention when a South Carolina gun dealer went ahead and sold a Glock .45-caliber semiautomatic handgun to Dylann Roof after the FBI failed to complete the background check within the allotted time frame. Later, the FBI determined that Roof's admission of drug use following a narcotics arrest disqualified him from purchasing the firearm. However, because the three-day period had passed, Roof legally acquired the pistol—the same weapon he later used to slaughter nine parishioners at Charleston's historic Emanuel AME Church.[49] There is no reason why this window can't be widened to fifteen business days, to allow authorities to properly vet someone. To the purchaser, it's a matter of inconvenience. To the public, it's a matter of life or death.

4. *Instituting gun courts.* Just like many jurisdictions have family, juvenile, and even drug courts—specialized courts where the judges and lawyers are trained in dealing with the unique issues that appear on the docket—American society would benefit from the establishment of gun courts.[50] The idea is to have experts trained in behavioral science and Second Amendment law. The jurisdiction of these courts would be twofold. In criminal matters, gun courts could hear all misdemeanor firearms offenses. One of the key functions of such a court would be to order the confiscation and (eventual) destruction of any weapons used to commit a violent crime. Further-

more, such a court could revoke the gun rights of any defendant in return for a sentence reduction (or as an alternative to incarceration). In civil matters, they would handle cases involving gun rights and ownership. In particular, such courts would hear emergency petitions for what are known as gun violence restraining orders (GVROs)—which are temporary orders requested by government officials or family members seeking to remove guns from the possession of an unstable person believed to be a threat to themselves or others, until such time as the subject's mental health returns to normal. Regardless of whether hearing criminal or civil cases, one of the purposes of a gun court is to expedite the judicial process, hearing cases that involve weapons seizures within seventy-two hours.[51] Tucson mass murderer Jared Loughner offers an example of someone who made school officials uncomfortable as his mental health deteriorated.[52] Had Arizona had a gun-court system with the authority to issue GVROs, it could have intervened and prevented Loughner from having access to the firearm he used to kill six and wound thirteen others.

5. *Promoting disarmament in plea bargains.* Related to the creation of gun courts, prosecutors need to be trained in how to handle pending felony cases. Under federal law, anyone convicted of a felony loses his or her right to own a firearm. However, as district attorneys are constantly trying to cut their caseloads, they're often willing to let defendants plead to reduced charges. The problem is that, when the lesser crime is a misdemeanor, dangerous offenders escape having to give up their weapons as a result of their plea bargains. Six relatives of Ronald Lee Haskell's ex-wife might be alive today if prosecutors had not allowed Haskell to plead down a violent attack to a misdemeanor simple assault charge. As a result, Haskell was not prohibited from purchasing firearms, which allowed him to buy the large quantity of 9mm ammunition and extended-capacity magazines that he used in 2014 to execute his former sister-in-law, her husband, and four of their five children in Spring, Texas.[53] It's vital that prosecutors accept pleas that

reduce felonies to misdemeanors only if the defendants agree to relinquish their gun rights in return.

6. *Establishing gun-recovery squads.* Expecting every dangerous person to surrender his or her firearms voluntarily will likely prove to be a losing strategy for ensuring public safety. Even when ordered to relinquish their weapons, some individuals refuse to comply. The only way to guarantee that unauthorized persons are disarmed is to have police officers recover any and all guns possessed in violation of the law. A model unit in this regard is California's Armed and Prohibited Persons System (APPS). The APPS is a part of the state's Bureau of Firearms—which is a law enforcement agency under the California Department of Justice. Funded largely from a $19 fee imposed on all firearms sales and transfers conducted in the state, APPS special agents have recovered over ten thousand illegal guns in the ten years the program has been in existence.[54] Such agencies can serve three functions. First, they can regularly cross-check databases of prohibited persons against gun-ownership records and, if there are any hits, they can obtain a recovery warrant from a gun court and seize unlawfully possessed weapons. Second, they can serve GVROs and deprive dangerous people of their firearms. Third, they can recover guns when gun rights are surrendered as part of a criminal conviction or plea bargain.

7. *Converting Joint Terrorism Task Forces into Joint Threat Task Forces.* One of the greatest resources that can be utilized to prevent mass shootings already exists. The Joint Terrorism Task Forces (JTTFs) are staffed by a combination of federal, state, and local law enforcement and intelligence agents who investigate terrorism threats. With over seventy task forces operating across the country, the JTTFs are well positioned to monitor potentially dangerous activities such as online threats to commit mass shootings, assassination plots, and large-scale ammunition purchases.[55] As the JTTFs are already manned with FBI, ATF, and Secret Service agents, their size, resources,

and mandate should be expanded to investigate all potential violent attacks, including active-shooter threats.[56]

8. *Enhancing gun-storage laws.* Some of the most prominent gun massacres have been the result of perpetrators helping themselves to their relatives' firearms and using them to go on murder sprees. The mass shootings perpetrated by Jeffrey Weise, Robert Hawkins, and Adam Lanza are examples of rampages that could have been avoided if family members had securely stored their firearms, depriving the killers access to weapons. The easiest way to avoid such calamities from occurring in the future is to require that all firearms in the home—unless in use on the owner's person—must be locked away in a gun safe (or a similar storage device), accessible only by the owner (and perhaps the owner's spouse). To ensure compliance, owners should be subject to civil liability and criminal prosecution when their weapons are used by someone else to commit an act of violence. It doesn't matter if a gun is loaned out or negligently stored. If it's used to shoot innocent people, then the lawful owner must answer for the attack as well.[57]

Mass shootings currently pose the most credible threat to American public safety. The key to addressing this growing danger begins with acknowledging the security risk of rampage violence—and the central role guns play in facilitating that threat. From here, we can proceed to break the trinity of rampage violence by adopting prudent gun-control measures like the policy recommendations proposed above. If we value the welfare of our fellow citizens, then we should welcome the regulation of firearms, for in today's day and age, public safety requires gun safety. There's no sensible way to achieve the former without the latter.

IT'S THE GUNS, STUPID

Take a moment and plan a deadly rampage—an attack intended to kill multiple victims. Pick your motive. Maybe you're mad at your boss for passing you over on your long-due promotion. Maybe you're tired of your teacher being hypercritical of your work. Maybe you're heartbroken over a recent divorce and blame your ex's family. Or maybe you're furious with the foreign policies of the United States. Next, pick your target. Your decision will likely be driven by your motive. If it's one of the motives just mentioned, your target might respectively be your place of employment, your school, your former in-law's residence, or the general public. Finally, pick your weapon. You can't get your hands on weapons of mass destruction and you can't build a bomb, so you'll be forced to select something more readily available. Here are four options: a blunt instrument, a knife, a vehicle, and a gun. Pick one.

It's an uncomfortable exercise, isn't it? For most people whose inhibitions don't get in the way of designing a mass-casualty attack, they opt for guns. They understand that guns are the easiest way to kill scores of people. This was certainly the conclusion Aurora gunman James Holmes reached. As he wrote in his infamous notebook, bombs were "too regulated & suspicious" to employ.[58] He also ruled out the use of a biological weapon as it "requires extensive knowledge, chemicals and equipment." He instead chose mass murder, which he noted produces "maximum casualties, easily performed w[ith] firearms." Sandy Hook killer Adam Lanza held a similar opinion: "I just can't get into vehicular slaughterers. It seem[s] to [*sic*] mediated, like using remote explosives (too hot). And knives stray too far from the whole 'mass' aspect (too cold). The aesthetic of pistols tends to be just right."[59]

It's not that Americans don't go on rampages with other weapons. It's that rampages perpetrated with weapons other than guns don't rise to the level of a massacre. Take Damien Robins's hammer attack against residents of Clark County, Nevada, or Ricky Aldrich's golf-club attack in Lebanon, Oregon. Both assaults targeted numerous victims—but neither managed to kill anyone.[60] It's the same with knives. Dylan Quick's X-Acto knife attack against Lone Star Community College students left fourteen people slashed, and Alex Hribal's stabbing spree at Franklin Regional High School wounded twenty fellow students and a school security officer.[61] Again, despite the large number of victims, no one died. It's even hard to commit mass murder when running people down with vehicles weighing thousands of pounds—as Nathan Campbell and Lakeisha Holloway did. Each of these car rampages killed one person despite seventeen being hit by Campbell and thirty-eight being struck by Holloway.[62]

Irate perpetrators or vulnerable targets on their own don't necessarily result in mass murder. The key to killing on a large-scale is the instrument of force employed. And, looking at the slew of recent slaughters, the lethal factor that nearly all have in common is the weapon. Quite simply, guns are at the root of most of today's deadly rampages. Guns prime the perpetrators. Guns penetrate the targets. And guns produce the carnage.[63]

Enhancing our security through measures aimed at regulating guns stands at the opposite end of the spectrum from what the NRA advises we do to reduce rampage violence. America's largest gun-rights organization continues to push for more guns, not fewer. As Wayne LaPierre asserts, "the only thing that stops a bad guy with a gun is a good guy with a gun."[64] We of course know from previous chapters, this couldn't be further from the truth.

If we're looking for certainties, there's only one: a bad guy without a gun is always better than a bad guy with a gun.

While we can't prevent every act of violence, implementing the policy prescriptions advanced above will substantially reduce the occurrence and lethality of mass shootings. And if there's a good chance we can save the next Christina-Taylor Green from the next Jared Loughner or the next Jesse Lewis from the next Adam Lanza, don't we owe it to them to try? Don't we owe it to all Americans—any one of whom can be the next victim of a preventable death—to try our best to keep them safe? It's something that seat-belt opponent Derek Kieper and gun-control opponent Meleanie Hain might now answer in the affirmative but for the fact that Kieper was killed as a result of being ejected from his car in a weather-related accident and Hain was shot dead by her husband in a murder-suicide. Holding firm to their principles at the time of their deaths, Kieper was unrestrained in his vehicle and Hain was surrounded by numerous firearms that she kept at home—decisions that preserved their liberties and cost them their lives.[65]

If only they subscribed to Philip Massinger's famous axiom: "The good need fear no law; it is his safety, and the bad man's awe."[66]

CHAPTER NINE

THE NEW NORMAL

On the morning of September 25, 1982, I was waiting for the bus to pick me up and take me to my junior high school's stadium, so that I could suit up for a football game, when a group of police cars—lights flashing, sirens blaring—tore by me. I'd never seen such a massive law enforcement response in my hometown of Wilkes-Barre, Pennsylvania. After the game, I remember our head coach, visibly upset, telling us that there had been a tragic event in our city and that our parents could tell us more when we got home.

Later I learned that a former prison guard named George Banks had gone on a shooting spree in town during the early morning, perpetrating one of the deadliest gun rampages in American history. One of the thirteen people Banks killed that day was my coach's friend, and the older brother of one of my classmates.[1]

As a community, we were shocked and horrified. Yet, reactions following the slaughter stand in sharp contrast to the way we react today. People didn't create large-scale makeshift memorials. The media didn't besiege our city. There was no national moment of silence. American flags weren't lowered to half-mast nationwide in the aftermath. And the president of the United States didn't visit, let alone propose any kind of significant policy reforms, even though seven of the thirteen victims were children.

We did talk about the rampage, though. In hallways, diners, offices, and homes, people were asking, who was George Banks, and why did he do it? We also discussed the victims. Those poor, innocent kids. How could Banks target precious children as young as a year old? What did they do to deserve such an awful fate?

But I don't recall a single conversation about the weapon. Banks used an AR-15 with extended-capacity magazines, which he had no problem purchasing despite having been previously convicted of armed robbery, as there were no background checks back then. Today, such information would be front-page material and run nonstop along the ticker of twenty-four-hour cable news channels. Three decades ago, though, the gun was simply not a topic of much conversation.

That was then.

Jump forward three decades to Sandy Hook. People in all fifty states shed a tear on December 14, 2012. Strangers drove to Newtown to leave flowers, cards, and stuffed animals. The media clogged all roads in and out of Newtown. Around the country, people bowed their heads in silence a week later as flags flew at half-mast in honor of the victims. President Obama flew to Connecticut, met with parents of the victims, and spoke at a memorial service held at nearby Newtown High School. And when he addressed the crowd, the president tacitly blamed guns for the string of mass shootings that have occurred since he took office.

It's a cultural script that has become so commonplace, President Obama has begun wondering if gun massacres—and our standard reactions to them—have become "the new normal."[2] And he's certainly justified in feeling disillusioned with the growing problem of rampage violence. Over 25 percent of all gun massacres in the past five decades have occurred since he took office in 2009. With so much carnage under his watch, he has observed, "Somehow this has become routine." As he noted after an attack at an Oregon community college in 2015 killed nine, "The reporting is routine. My response here at this podium ends up being routine. . . . We've become numb to this. We talked about this after Columbine and Blacksburg, after Tucson, after Newtown, after Aurora, after Charleston. It cannot be this easy for somebody who wants to inflict harm on other people to get his or her hands on a gun."[3]

★ ★ ★

Active shooter. Lockdown. Safe room. Shelter in place. This is the new vocabulary of the current era. In a country where there's now, on average, one mass shooting—and over one lockdown—per day, preparing for the next gun rampage seems to have become a new way of life.

When I was a child, we participated in civil-defense exercises out of fear that the Soviet Union would launch a nuclear strike. Are you old enough to remember "duck-and-cover" drills? That was the phrase drilled into students' minds during the height of the Cold War, the mantra for saving people from the biggest threat of that day and age. Today, the instruction is "run, hide, fight." It's the "duck and cover" of the current era—aimed to protect us from the biggest danger that we now face: mass shootings.

The most realistic violent threat to the American people no longer comes out of the sky on the tip of a missile. It now comes out of the barrel of a gun. As a nation, we need to arrest the growing risk posed by firearms—especially lightweight polymer semiautomatic firearms loaded with extended-capacity magazines—falling into the hands of dangerous people. It's incumbent on us that we reject the notion that gun massacres are the new normal. We need to break free from the "routine" that President Obama mentions. Doing so is possible, but it will require adopting a series of sensible measures—like those outlined in this book—aimed at breaking the trinity of rampage violence. It's something that needs to happen, and happen fast—before the next group of theater patrons, holiday shoppers, work colleagues, schoolchildren, or family members is slaughtered by a gunman on a shooting spree.

Ask yourself: when you hear the word *Columbine,* what's the first thought that comes to your mind? How about *Aurora? Oak Creek? Newtown? San Bernardino?* These are no longer communities and cities just like those where we live and work. They're now infamous crime scenes and massacre sites—seared into our collective memory—in what has become a rampage nation.

A THEORETICAL PROFILE OF SEUNG HUI CHO

FROM THE PERSPECTIVE OF A FORENSIC BEHAVIORAL SCIENTIST BY ROGER L. DEPUE, PhD[1]

W hen a shocking and horrendous crime has been committed an immediate response is, "Why?" It is human nature to seek an answer to that question, some feasible explanation for the motivation behind the crime. We will never know for certain what motivated Seung Hui Cho to go on a murderous rampage on April 16, 2007. But professionals experienced in the study of multiple victim murderers have noted some patterns of personality and behavior that are pertinent here. As a result of 33 years of experience in the analysis of crimes of violence, including the study of violent fantasies, I have developed the following theory about what drove Cho to do what he did. I begin with a general observation.

Most assassinations in the United States are not politically motivated. Instead they are often the work of inadequate persons who do not see any kind of meaningful life for them ahead. As a consequence of any of several types of mental disorders, they have come to the realization that they will never become important persons, such as significant contributors to their society and therefore, memorable persons in history. Some feel so poorly about themselves they do not believe they can even cope with the ordinary responsibilities of life. They feel powerless over their destinies and are helpless victims of their unfulfilled needs. They begin to build a fantasy where they can be achievers and persons who can change the course of history not in a beneficial way, but perhaps as an outcast. There is something significant they can do.

These killers target a particular person or persons. They can do away with one of those very people who are functioning well, coping with life's stresses and requirements all the while achieving success. They can kill one of those people who have risen to a position of accomplishment, influence and prominence. Then they will be forever recognized as the person who shot the president, the movie star, or the famous athlete. They begin to plan the event. They read books and magazines about assassinations of the past. Like John W. Hin[c]kley, Jr., they have their photograph taken in front of Ford's Theatre and the White House. They write of their plan in essays and journals. They want to make sure that history properly records their most significant event. And if they are killed in the assassination effort it will be worth it. It will be a sacrifice. They can go down in history as a great assassin.

Their act will thus be twofold: they will have a place in history as a major player (on the world scene) if the victim is important enough, and they will be killing that which they can not have for their own by virtue of ability, talent and achievement.

Similarly, some multiple victim killers act out of a distorted sense of unfairness and disappointment stemming from their own actual inadequacies and unsatisfied needs for attention, adulation, power and control. Perhaps, such was the case of Seung Hui Cho.

If one examines the life of Cho along the five dimensions of human growth and development, his inadequacies become apparent. Physically Cho was average to below average. He was frail and sick as an infant toddler. Even the autopsy report remarked about his lack of muscle for the body of a 23-year-old male. Emotionally, his growth was stunted as a result of his "selective mutism." Spiritually, he showed little interest and dropped out of his church before experiencing a growth in faith. Socially, he could not function at all. He was virtually devoid of social skills due to his extreme social anxiety disorder. Intellectually, which was his strongest attribute, he was average to above average in his academic pursuits but even these afforded him little or no consistent or positive sense of achievement based on the feedback from his peers or others.

Cho lived a life of quiet solitude, extreme quiet and solitude. For all of his 23 years of life the most frequent observation made by anyone about him was that Seung Hui Cho had absolutely no social life. During all of his school years he had no real friends. He had no interest in being with others. In fact, he shied away from other people and seemed to prefer his own company to the company of others. His few attempts to reach out to females at college were inappropriate and frightened them.

Cho was quiet and uncommunicative even in his own family. This led his parents to repeatedly discuss this abnormal characteristic with extended family members, church leaders, schoolteachers, counselors and medical practitioners. It was all to no avail. It appeared this boy could not voluntarily participate in the social arena under any circumstances, regardless of any advice, threats or rewards. Not even the medication he took for a year or the several years of therapy seemed to correct this serious handicap.

As a result of this condition of solitude, he grew into a joyless, socially invisible loner. But this condition in no way masked his desire to be somebody. He did well in school in spite of his lack of interaction. He was intelligent and worked hard to complete his assignments so that he could convince his teachers that he had a good grasp of the subject matter presented, even though he was orally mute. He simply did it all alone and with as little oral communication as was absolutely necessary. There are many problems that accompany such a lifestyle. One of the big problems with being a loner is that one does not get helpful reality checks from people who can challenge disordered thinking. Once a loner cuts off outsiders he automatically takes himself out of the game where he could grow, with help, out of his inadequacies. He inadvertently condemns himself to ongoing inadequacy and compensatory fantasies.

It was in his second and third year of college that he began to find what he thought would be his niche, his special talent that would set him apart from the sea of other students at the university. He would become a great writer. He changed his major from computer technology to English. He began to write in earnest banging out composition after composition on his computer keyboard. He began seriously to believe that his original material and unique style were very good. He sent a book proposal to a publisher with great expectations. When it was returned stamped "rejected" he probably was devastated.

He internalized this rejection for months. His sister tried to console him and offered to edit his work, but he would not let her even see the document. He tried to impress his English professors with his writing assignments but only one or two saw any particular talent. In fact many of his professors as well as his fellow students reacted negatively to his stories that were often laden with horror and violence. Cho's dream was slipping away because of people— people who could not see and appreciate his desperate need to be recognized as somebody of importance. Once again he could not function successfully in the real world of people and normal expectations. These rejections were devastating to him and he fantasized about getting revenge from a world he perceived as rejecting him, people who had not satisfied so many of his powerful needs. He felt this way despite the fact that many of his teachers, counselors, and family members had extended themselves to him out of a desire to help him succeed and be happy.

At the same time, he realized that his parents had made great sacrifices for him so that he could attend college. He never asked them for anything yet they always asked him if he needed anything. They paid for his tuition, books, and expenses, and tried to give him whatever money he needed despite their own lack of education and low level of employment and earning potential. Perhaps he resented the fact that his parents worked and sacrificed so much and obtained so little in return. Meanwhile he was constantly aware of his classmates taking from their affluent parents and squandering their money on luxuries and alcohol. He perceived that these students had no appreciation for hard work and sacrifice. He saw them as spoiled and wasteful. They drove their BMW's [sic], dressed in stylish clothes and consumed the best food and drink. They had parties where sex and alcohol were plentiful. These students whom he once secretly wished to join were now considered evil and his peers were conspicuously privileged. They were engaging in "debauchery" and they needed to be taught a lesson.

Cho began to fantasize about punishing the "haves" for their stupidity and insensitivity toward him and others like him—the "have nots." He remembered how Eric and Dylan (in his fantasy he was on a first name basis with Harris and Klebold, the Columbine killers) had extracted their revenge while cheating society out of ever having the opportunity of arresting and punishing them by committing suicide at the end of their massacre.

His fantasies began to come out in his writings as he authored plays about violence and revenge. Gradually, he realized he could extract a measure of revenge against the evil all around him. He began to plan. Simply by signing his name, he easily got a credit card to begin to make his purchases. He began to purchase the instruments and munitions he would need. He knew that he would never have to pay for these purchases because he would be dead. Like Eric and Dylan, he would kill as many of them as possible and then commit suicide. But his plan would be even better than theirs. He would plan a killing that would go down in history as the greatest school massacre ever. He would be remembered as the savior of the oppressed, the downtrodden, the poor, and the rejected.

There was pleasure in planning such a grand demonstration of "justice." He began to write about his plan and the rationale for it. He videotaped himself as he performed his role and read from the script he had written. He began to feel a power he had never felt before, and a freedom from his burden of inadequacy. He experienced a freedom to express the fantasies long held in abeyance. Whatever inhibitions he may have had against committing such an act were easily slipping away. He rented a vehicle. He purchased his weapons and ammunition, and began to practice for the big day. The excitement mounted as he moved closer to the day of reckoning.

Graduation was only weeks away but for Cho it was not an occasion for joy. Rather it was a time of fear and dread. He had never held a job in his life, not even during summer vacations from school. He did not want to go to graduate school as his parents had urged. The educational institution did not appreciate him. He would soon be facing the job market as a mediocre English major whose ideas and compositions as a writer had been rejected, while all those around him were planning careers with enthusiasm and great expectations. What would he ever do once he was out of the intellectual environment of college where his brain had at least some success? He would be turned out into the world of work, finances, responsibilities, and a family. What a frightening prospect. As graduation loomed ahead he felt even more inadequate. There was the probability of only more rejection ahead.

By this time Cho may have become submerged (immersed) into a state of self-pity and paranoia, and could not distinguish between constructive planning for the future and the need for destructive vengeance and retaliation. His thought processes were so distorted that he began arguing to himself that his evil plan was actually doing good. His destructive fantasy was now becoming an obsession. He had become a person driven by a need for vengeance and would now strike out against "injustice" and rejection. He would become the source of punishment, the avenger, against those he perceived as the insensitive hypocrites and cruel oppressors. He didn't need specific targets. His mission was to destroy them all. In his distorted fantasy world, he himself had actually become that which he seemed to despise most. He had become the instrument for the destruction of human dignity and precious potential.

POSTSCRIPT

Just days before this book was scheduled to be delivered to the printer, a gunman entered Pulse, an Orlando, Florida, nightclub known for welcoming the gay community, and opened fire on the bar's patrons. As I write this postscript, the death toll from the attack stands at forty-nine (not including the shooter, who was killed by police). Another fifty-three individuals were wounded and taken to local hospitals for treatment. Given that several of these victims remain in grave condition, it's possible that the number of fatalities will increase in the days and weeks ahead.

While it's still early in the investigation, the perpetrator has been identified as twenty-nine-year-old Omar Mateen. A natural-born American citizen from Port Saint Lucie, Florida, Mateen was a self-radicalized, jihadist terrorist who swore his allegiance to ISIS in a phone call placed to 911 during his rampage. According to statements made by his father to the news media, Mateen displayed an animosity toward the LGBT community—an animosity fueled by ISIS, which is notorious for brutally murdering gay people. Based on this information, authorities have begun treating the incident as both a hate crime and an act of terrorism.

Consistent with the findings of this book, preliminary indications are:

- the gunman was a working-age, mentally unstable, violent male who had a grievance against certain segments of American society;
- he was not deterred from attacking a location where a uniformed police presence was providing armed security (nor was he stopped early in his rampage despite exchanging gunfire

with three police officers in the initial moments of what would become a three-hour siege and hostage standoff); and

- he was armed with two polymer semiautomatic firearms—a 9mm handgun and a .223-caliber assault rifle—equipped with extended-capacity magazines that provided him with the ability to inflict over one hundred casualties.

The Orlando nightclub massacre has now become the deadliest shooting rampage in American history. As such, it confirms an additional finding of this book: the threat posed by mass shootings continues to grow.

June 14, 2016

NOTES

CHAPTER ONE: SANDY HOOK

1. The details of the Newtown massacre are drawn predominantly from an online repository created by the Connecticut State Police: http://cspsandy hookreport.ct.gov (accessed March 27, 2014). This website contains all of the state police's publicly available evidence, reports, files, and media. Additional information is drawn from *Report of the State's Attorney for the Judicial District of Danbury on the Shootings at Sandy Hook Elementary and 36 Yogananda Street, Newtown, Connecticut, on December 14, 2012,* released on November 25, 2013 (*Sandy Hook Final Report* hereinafter), http://www.ct.gov/csao/cwp/view.asp?a=1801&q=535784 (accessed March 27, 2014). The audio recordings from the Newtown 911 call center are available at https://soundcloud.com/nydailynews/sets/sandy-hook -911-audio-1 (accessed March 27, 2014). When necessary, information from official sources is supplemented by news media accounts. In those instances, specific citations are provided.

2. All times of day in this chapter, unless otherwise denoted, are a.m.

3. Andrew Solomon, "The Reckoning: The Father of the Sandy Hook Killer Searches for Answers," *New Yorker,* March 17, 2014, http://www.newyorker.com/ reporting/2014/03/17/140317fa_fact_solomon (accessed April 19, 2014).

4. Adam Lanza was armed as follows: a Saiga 12-gauge semiautomatic shotgun (including two magazines loaded to full capacity with ten rounds of 12-gauge shotgun cartridges each), a Bushmaster .223 AR-15-type semiautomatic assault rifle (including ten magazines loaded to full capacity with thirty rounds of 5.56mm cartridges each), a Glock 20SF 10mm semiautomatic handgun (including six magazines loaded to full capacity with fifteen rounds of 10mm cartridges each), and a SigSauer P226 9mm semiautomatic handgun (including four magazines loaded to full capacity with twenty rounds of 9mm cartridges each and two magazines loaded to full capacity with eighteen rounds of 9mm cartridges each). In addition, Lanza had three loose rounds with him (one extra 5.56mm cartridge and two 12-gauge shotgun cartridges). Lanza fired a total of 156 rounds at Sandy Hook Elementary School: 154 5.56mm rounds and two 10mm rounds.

5. As he exited the vehicle, Adam Lanza left behind the loaded 12-gauge shotgun. The shotgun was loaded with a 10-round magazine. Lanza also left behind an additional magazine loaded with ten shotgun cartridges. While some commentators have speculated that he left the shotgun in the car in preparation for a subsequent firefight with police officers on the exterior grounds of Sandy Hook, his decision to die inside the school casts doubt on this scenario. A more likely theory is that the nearly eight-pound shotgun prohibitively weighed down Lanza, forcing him to leave it behind. For more on the ambush theory, see Dave Altimari and Steven Goode, "Details Emerge on Sandy Hook Shooting, Items Found in Lanza Rooms," *Hartford Courant*, October 19, 2013, http://articles .courant.com/2013-10-19/news/hc-sandy-hook-shooting-details-20131018_1 _nancy-lanza-adam-lanza-20-first-graders (accessed April 19, 2014); and Matthew Lysiak, *Newtown: An American Tragedy* (New York: Gallery, 2013), p. 89.

6. I use the past tense to describe the school building because Sandy Hook Elementary was razed in 2013.

7. Given the chaos of the situation, recollections of how events inside the school unfolded are sometimes slightly different, leading to conflicting accounts in police reports. When presented with conflicting accounts, I tried to present details in a manner that made the most logical sense, especially in light of other evidence that supports such an interpretation.

8. Kaitlin Roig's statements are from an interview she granted to ABC News. See "Connecticut Shooting: Teacher Kaitlin Roig Protected Her Students," ABC News, December 14, 2012, http://abcnews.go.com/WNT/video/connecticut -shooting-teacher-kaitlin-roig-protected-students-17978970 (accessed April 19, 2014).

9. The details of Jesse Lewis's heroism and death are not recollected in any publicly available reports. They emanate from interviews his mother has given. The specifics were relayed to her by police investigators. See, for example, Michael Melia, "Mom: Newtown Victim Shouted for Classmates to Run," Associated Press, October 18, 2013, http://bigstory.ap.org/article/mom-newtown-victim-shouted -classmates-run (accessed April 19, 2014).

10. Two of Victoria Soto's students managed to hide in the bathroom, undetected by Adam Lanza. They both survived.

11. The statements of Laura Esposito and Kerri Sommer as well as that of the female student provide some of the most valuable evidence as to the movements of Adam Lanza inside the school. In particular, their testimony helps establish that he attacked Room 10 prior to Room 8.

12. The quotes from Room 8 are verbatim from police witness statements collected from the three people sheltering in place in Room 6. The attribution

of specific quotes as well as the precise timeline is based on my assessment of how events *likely* unfolded during Adam Lanza's attack on Lauren Rousseau's class.

13. The coroner's autopsy of Adam Lanza revealed that he weighed 112 pounds at the time of his death. The forensics lab assessed the weight of the different weaponry Lanza had on his person when he entered Sandy Hook Elementary School, and found that the firearms, magazines, and ammunition weighed a combined 30.5 pounds.

14. Dave Cullen, *Columbine* (New York: Twelve, 2009), p. 351.

15. It's possible that Adam Lanza entered Room 6, the classroom adjacent to Room 8, after exiting Lauren Rousseau's classroom. The three people hiding in the bathroom in Room 6 recall hearing movement in their classroom, but they're uncertain if what they heard was Lanza entering or police officers clearing the room. In any event, the room was adequately locked down and, if Lanza had entered, he wouldn't have seen anyone in the room, which would have given him reason to move on.

16. Cullen, p. 350.

17. Of the twenty-eight innocent people Adam Lanza shot inside Sandy Hook Elementary School, twenty-six died. Only teachers Natalie Hammond and Deborah Pisani survived.

CHAPTER TWO: THE BEGINNING OF WISDOM

1. Details of the Simon Bolivar shooting are drawn from the following sources: Danny Monteverde, "Shooting of 5 on Simon Bolivar Came on Day of Family Celebrations," *Times–Picayune*, May 30, 2012, http://www.nola.com/crime/index.ssf/2012/05/shooting_of_5_on_simon_bolivar.html (accessed September 15, 2014); Mary Foster, "Bloody Hour Leaves 4 Dead—Including 5-Year-Old," Associated Press, May 30, 2012, http://www.goerie.com/apps/pbcs.dll/article?AID=/20120530/APN/1205300928 (accessed September 15, 2014); Leslie Williams, "Girl, 5, Woman Killed in Central City Shooting; 3 Other Injured," *Times–Picayune*, May 31, 2012, http://www.nola.com/crime/index.ssf/2012/05/girl_7_woman_killed_in_central.html (September 15, 2014). The three gunmen—Sam Newman, Demond Sandifer, and Tyron Harden—were subsequently convicted of the murders and sentenced to life in prison. John Simerman, "Mayor Landrieu in Courtroom as Judge Hands Life Sentences to Gangland Killers of Shawanna Pierce 5-Year-Old Briana Allen," *New Orleans Advocate*, November 17, 2015, http://www.theneworleansadvocate.com/news/13905390-93/mayor-landrieu-in-courtroom-as (accessed April 15, 2015); and Ken Daley, "Mayor Mitch Landrieu, Police Chief

Watch as Killers of Briana Allen, Shawanna Pierce Handed Life Sentences," *Times–Picayune*, November 18, 2015, http://www.nola.com/crime/index.ssf/2015/11/mayor_police_chief_watch_as_ki.html (accessed December 13, 2015). The driver of the vehicle, Stanton Guillory, is awaiting trial for his role in the ambush. John Simerman, "Alleged Accomplice in Briana Allen Murder Tied to Contract Killing of Federal Witness," *New Orleans Advocate*, February 15, 2015, http://www.theneworleansadvocate.com/news/11612105-171/alleged-accomplice-in-briana-allen (accessed December 13, 2015). Tyron Harden was identified as the shooter of the AK-47 after he bragged, "I killed a whole baby!" See Ramon Antonio Vargas, "Boasts about Little Briana Allen's Murder Allegedly Led to Suspect," *Times–Picayune*, April 22, 2013, http://www.nola.com/crime/index.ssf/2013/04/boasts_about_little_briana_all.html (accessed September 15, 2014).

2. Quoted in Foster, "Bloody Hour Leaves 4 Dead."

3. Quoted in Danielle Dreilinger, "Mother's Day Shooting Victim, 10, Lost Cousin Briana Allen and Father to Violence," *Times–Picayune*, May 14, 2013, http://www.nola.com/crime/index.ssf/2013/05/mothers_day_shooting_victim_10.html (accessed September 15, 2014). See also "WDSU, Hotel Grant Birthday Wish to Parade Shooting Victim," WDSU, May 15, 2013, http://www.wdsu.com/news/local-news/new-orleans/boy-hurt-in-parade-shooting-victim-gets-birthday-wish/20167654 (accessed September 15, 2014); and Naomi Martin, "What Happens to Ka'Nard Allen," *Times–Picayune*, May 10, 2014, http://www.nola.com/crime/index.ssf/2014/05/kanard_allen_mothers_day_shoot.html (accessed September 15, 2014).

4. Details of the Mother's Day Parade shooting are drawn from the following sources: "Mother's Day Second-Line Shooting on Frenchmen Street Injures at least 19 People," *Times–Picayune*, May 13, 2013, http://www.nola.com/crime/index.ssf/2013/05/mothers_day_second-line_shooti.html (accessed September 15, 2014); Helen Freund, "3 Still in Critical Condition at Mother's Day Second-Line Shooting," *Times–Picayune*, May 13, 2013, http://www.nola.com/crime/index.ssf/2013/05/3_still_in_critical_condition.html (accessed September 15, 2014); Naomi Martin, "Mother's Day Turns into Nightmare for Mass Shooting Victims' Families," *Times–Picayune*, May 13, 2013, http://www.nola.com/crime/index.ssf/2013/05/mothers_day_turns_into_nightma.html (accessed September 15, 2014); Patrick Jonsson, "New Orleans Parade Shooting: Arrests Show City Reworked Approach to Policing," *Christian Science Monitor*, May 17, 2013, http://www.csmonitor.com/USA/Justice/2013/0517/New-Orleans-parade-shooting-Arrests-show-city-s-reworked-approach-to-policing (accessed September 15, 2014); Naomi Martin, "Accustomed to Handling Shootings, New Orleans Emergency Responders Snapped into Action Amid Mother's Day Carnage,"

Times–Picayune, April 3, 2013, http://www.nola.com/crime/index.ssf/2013/05/accustomed_to_handling_shootin.html (accessed September 15, 2014); John Simerman, "Indictments Leveled, Record Bonds Set in Mother's Day Shooting Spree," *New Orleans Advocate*, July 13, 2013, http://theadvocate.com/news/neworleans/6489651-148/indictments-leveled-record-bonds-set (accessed September 15, 2014); Claire Galofaro, "Shootings Part of a Larger Drug Feud, Documents Allege," *New Orleans Advocate*, January 9, 2014, http://theadvocate.com/news/neworleans/8007181-148/mothers-day-shootings-part-of (accessed September 15, 2014); Richard A. Webster, "After Mother's Day Shooting, a Push for Progress amid Relentless Violence," *Times–Picayune*, May 10, 2014, http://www.nola.com/crime/index.ssf/2014/05/mothers_day_shooting_neighborh.html (accessed September 15, 2014); Naomi Martin, "Mother's Day Shooting: Gang Feud behind Last Year's Violence Target of Authorities," *Times–Picayune*, May 11, 2014, http://www.nola.com/crime/index.ssf/2014/05/mothers_day_shooting_the_gang.html (accessed September 15, 2014); and Andy Grimm, "In Mother's Day Shooting Case, First Gang Member Pleads Guilty," *Times–Picayune*, August 26, 2014, http://www.nola.com/crime/index.ssf/2014/08/mothers_day_shooters_co-defend.html (accessed September 15, 2014).

5. The radio transmissions of first responders are quoted in Martin, "Accustomed to Handling Shootings."

6. Quoted in ibid.

7. As another spectator put it, "Mothers should not have to be crying any day no less Mother's Day." Quoted in "Mother's Day Second-Line Shooting on Frenchmen Street."

8. I use the term *casualties* to refer to nonfatal injuries as well as fatalities.

9. All searches of news media coverage that are discussed in this chapter were conducted on August 25, 2014.

10. Like the search for stories on Ka'Nard Allen, a search for reports mentioning his five-year-old cousin Briana Allen also generated no hits in the *New York Times*, *USA Today*, or CNN.

11. The Scott brothers were eventually apprehended. Their prosecution was ceded to the US Attorney's office as part of a larger gang-activity and drug-dealing case. See Helen Freund, "After Feds Take over Mother's Day Shooting Case, DA Drops State Charges," *Times–Picayune*, May 9, 2014, http://www.nola.com/crime/index.ssf/2014/03/after_feds_take_over_da_drops.html (accessed September 15, 2014). In September 2015, the brothers entered guilty pleas on charges stemming from their involvement in racketeering, conspiracy, and five gang-related shootings, including the Mother's Day Parade shooting. In March 2016, Akein Scott was sentenced to life in prison and his brother Shawn was sentenced to

forty years behind bars. See Andy Grimm, "Mother's Day Shooting Gunmen Plead Guilty to Federal Charges," *Times–Picayune*, September 15, 2015, http://www.nola .com/crime/index.ssf/2015/09/mothers_day_shooting_suspects_4.html (accessed September 17, 2015); and Emily Lane, "Mother's Day Gunman Imprisoned for Life; Brothers Also Sentenced," *Times–Picayune*, March 29, 2016, http://www.nola .com/crime/index.ssf/2016/03/mothers_day_shooting_sentence.html (accessed April 15, 2016).

12. The disparity in recognition also extends to familiarity with the perpetrators. For instance, many Americans have heard of Jared Loughner and Adam Lanza. But few have ever heard of the Simon Bolivar or Mother's Day Parade shooters.

13. Christopher Ingraham, "There Have Been 1,001 Mass Shootings in America since 2013," *Washington Post*, October 12, 2015, https://www.washington post.com/news/wonk/wp/2015/10/12/there-have-been-1001-mass-shootings-in -america-since-2013 (accessed December 13, 2015).

14. Philip J. Cook and Kristin A. Goss, *The Gun Debate: What Everyone Needs to Know* (New York: Oxford University Press, 2014). See also Nicholas Kristof, "How Could We Blow This One?" *New York Times*, July 3, 2013, http://www.nytimes .com/2013/07/04/opinion/kristof-how-could-we-blow-this-one.html (accessed April 30, 2015); and Sue Miller, "When Did Mass Shootings Become So Frighteningly Mundane in America?" *Guardian*, June 11, 2014, http://www .theguardian.com/commentisfree/2014/jun/11/mass-shootings-america-2014 -killing (accessed April 30, 2015).

15. See, for example, Marilyn Miller and David Scott, "Copley Residents Still on Edge after Deadly Rampage," *Akron Beacon Journal*, August 13, 2011, http:// www.ohio.com/news/local/copley-residents-still-on-edge-after-deadly-rampage -1.229652 (accessed September 20, 2014).

16. Details of the Copley massacre are drawn from the following sources: Kathy Antoniotti, Marilyn Miller, Rick Armon, and Betty Lin-Fisher, "Last Moments Futile for Boy Slain in Copley Mass Shooting," *Akron Beacon Journal*, August 8, 2011, http://www.ohio.com/news/break-news/last-moments-futile-for-boy-slain -in-copley-mass-shooting-1.228840 (accessed September 20, 2014); Kevin Begos and Andrew Welsh-Huggins, "Ohio Gunman Was in Property Dispute, Neighbors Say," Associated Press, August 9, 2011, http://news.yahoo.com/ohio-gunman -property-dispute-neighbors-222022501.html (accessed September 20, 2014); Jim Carney, "Copley Neighbor Helps Woman Dealing with Unimaginable Horror," *Akron Beacon Journal*, August 9, 2011, http://www.ohio.com/news/local/copley -neighbor-helps-woman-dealing-with-unimaginable-horror-1.229059 (accessed September 20, 2014); Rick Armon, Kathy Antoniotti, and Ed Meyer, "Copley

Shooter Bought Gun Five Days before Killing Spree," *Akron Beacon Journal,* August 10, 2011, http://www.ohio.com/news/local/copley-shooter-bought-gun-five-days-before-killing-spree-1.229130 (accessed September 20, 2014); "Cause of Deaths Released for Copley Victims and Shooter," *Akron Beacon Journal,* August 10, 2011, http://www.ohio.com/news/break-news/cause-of-deaths-released-for-copley-victims-and-shooter-1.229181 (accessed September 20, 2014); Rick Armon and Jim Carney, "Copley Mass Killer Leaves Unanswered Questions, Community in Grief," *Akron Beacon Journal,* August 13, 2011, http://www.ohio.com/news/local/copley-mass-killer-leaves-unanswered-questions-community-in-grief-1.229732 (accessed September 20, 2014); Phil Trexler, "Copley Mother Recalls Terror of Facing Mass Killer," *Akron Beacon Journal,* August 27, 2011, http://www.ohio.com/news/copley-mother-recalls-terror-of-facing-mass-killer-1.231890 (accessed September 20, 2014); Phil Trexler, "Prosecutor Clears Copley Officer in Shooting of Mass Killer," *Akron Beacon Journal,* September 21, 2011, http://www.ohio.com/news/break-news/prosecutor-clears-copley-officer-in-shooting-of-mass-killer-1.236157 (accessed September 20, 2014); Phil Trexler, "Family Suggests Copley Gunman Had Untreated Mental Issues," *Akron Beacon Journal,* October 7, 2011, http://www.ohio.com/news/break-news/family-suggests-copley-gunman-had-untreated-mental-issues-1.239054 (accessed September 20, 2014); and Jim Carney, "Becky Dieter Remembers Being Shot," *Akron Beacon Journal,* August 8, 2012, http://www.ohio.com/news/local/becky-dieter-remembers-being-shot-we-lost-many-great-people-that-day-1.325380 (accessed September 20, 2014).

17. Quoted in Carney, "Copley Neighbor Helps Woman."

18. Quoted in ibid.

19. Quoted in Trexler, "Family Suggests Copley Gunman."

20. Quoted in Begos and Welsh-Huggins, "Ohio Gunman Was in Property Dispute."

21. Quoted in Trexler, "Copley Mother Recalls."

22. Michael Johnson survived the rampage by running upstairs and exiting the Bagley house through a window while Hance was in the basement, hunting down Scott Dieter. Ibid.

23. Gary Kleck, *Targeting Guns: Firearms and Their Control* (Hawthorne, NY: Aldine de Gruyter, 1997), pp. 124–25, 144. In subsequent analyses, he employed a slightly broader conceptualization that defined mass shootings as "all shooting incidents involving more than six victims shot (fatally or nonfatally, not including the offenders)." See "Declaration of Gary Kleck in Support of Motion for Preliminary Injunction" in *Fyock et al. v. City of Sunnyvale,* filed on December 23, 2013, in the United States District Court for the Northern District of California, San Jose Division (Case Number: CV13–05807 RMW), p. 6, http://michellawyers

.com/wp-content/uploads/2013/12/Fyock-v.-Sunnyvale_Conformed-Declaration
-of-Gary-Kleck-In-Support-of-Motion-for-Preliminary-Injunction.pdf (accessed
September 25, 2014).

24. In the aftermath of the 1999 massacre at Columbine High School, the *New York Times* published a detailed analysis of mass shootings—the first of its kind in the mainstream press. To identify appropriate incidents, the newspaper set aside Kleck's six-or-more-killed prerequisite and defined rampages as follows: "The crimes had to have had multiple victims, at least one of whom died, and [had] to have occurred substantially at one time and in a place where people gather—a workplace, a school, a mall, a restaurant, a train. Multiple killings that were a result of domestic strife, robbery or political terrorism were excluded, as were serial killings." Ford Fessenden, "They Threaten, Seethe and Unhinge, Then Kill in Quantity," *New York Times*, April 9, 2000, http://www.nytimes.com/2000/04/09/us/they-threaten-seethe-and-unhinge-then-kill-in-quantity.html (accessed September 25, 2014). The groundbreaking study was based on an analysis of ninety-nine rampage murders that had occurred between 1949 and 1999. A few years later, a team of researchers led by one of Kleck's former students, Grant Duwe, published a study on large-scale gun attacks in *Homicide Studies*. The article sought to assess the impact of certain laws on mass shootings, which the authors defined as "incidents in which four or more people are fatally shot in a public place." Unlike the somewhat more restrictive approach taken by the *New York Times*, the only shootings that were excluded in this study were attacks occurring at home as well as those in which *both* the shooter(s) and the victims were involved in illegal activities "such as organized crime, gang activities, and drug sales." Grant Duwe, Tomislav Kovandzic, and Carlisle E. Moody, "The Impact of Right-to-Carry Concealed Firearm Laws on Mass Public Shootings," *Homicide Studies* 6 (November 2002): 271–96. Duwe has continued to maintain a data set of mass public shootings, and it now covers the time period 1915–2012. I am grateful to him for sharing his data set with me.

25. Mark Follman, Gavin Aronsen, and Deanna Pan, "U.S. Mass Shootings, 1982–2016: Data from *Mother Jones*' Investigation," *Mother Jones*, April 18, 2016, http://www.motherjones.com/politics/2012/12/mass-shootings-mother-jones-full-data (accessed April 26, 2016). See also Mark Follman, "What Exactly Is a Mass Shooting?" *Mother Jones*, August 24, 2012, http://www.motherjones.com/mojo/2012/08/what-is-a-mass-shooting (accessed March 14, 2015); and Mark Follman, "Why Mass Shootings Deserve Deeper Investigation," *Mother Jones*, January 30, 2013, http://www.motherjones.com/politics/2013/01/mass-shootings-james-alan-fox (accessed March 14, 2015).

26. Follman, Aronsen, and Pan, "U.S. Mass Shootings, 1982–2016." The *Mother Jones* fatality tallies include the shooters who died at the scene.

27. "Behind the Bloodshed: The Untold Story of America's Mass Killings," *USA Today*, http://usatoday30.usatoday.com/news/nation/mass-killings/index .html (accessed March 14, 2015). See also William M. Welch and Meghan Hoyer, "30 Mass Killings, 137 Victims: A Typical Year," *USA Today*, December 16, 2013, http://www.usatoday.com/story/news/nation/2013/12/15/mass-killings-main/ 3821897/ (accessed March 14, 2015).

28. William J. Krouse and Daniel J. Richardson, *Mass Murder with Firearms: Incidents and Victims, 1999–2013*, CRS Report R44126 (Washington, DC: Congressional Research Service, July 30, 2015), p. 10, https://fas.org/sgp/crs/misc/ R44126.pdf (accessed December 13, 2015). Based on this definition, CRS identified 317 mass shootings between 1999 and 2013. Ibid., p. 12. In a 2013 report, which has not been retracted, CRS used a slightly more restrictive definition of mass shootings: "incidents occurring in relatively public places, involving four or more deaths—not including the shooter(s)—and gunmen who select victims indiscriminately." The earlier CRS study excluded any acts where the use of force was "a means to an end such as robbery or terrorism." Based on the more restrictive definition, which is similar to the conceptualization employed by *Mother Jones*, the 2013 CRS report identified only seventy-eight mass shootings between 1983 and 2012. Jerome P. Bjelopera et al., *Public Mass Shootings in the United States: Selected Implications for Federal Public Health and Safety Policy*, CRS Report R43004 (Washington, DC: Congressional Research Service, March 18, 2013), pp. 3–7, http://fas.org/sgp/crs/misc/R43004.pdf (accessed September 25, 2014).

29. John Paparazzo, Christine Eith, and Jennifer Tocco, *Strategic Approaches to Preventing Multiple Casualty Violence: Report on the National Summit on Multiple Casualty Shootings* (Washington, DC: US Department of Justice, Office of Community Oriented Policing Services, 2013), http://ric-zai-inc.com/Publications/cops -p269-pub.pdf (accessed September 25, 2014). While the COPS report identified only twenty-four incidents since 1949, the summit wasn't trying to generate a comprehensive list. It should also be noted that in 2014, the FBI issued a report on active-shooter incidents. The report defined active shootings as acts of firearm violence wherein individuals are "actively engaged in killing or attempting to kill people in a . . . populated area." Assuming that a populated area is any space with people in it, an active-shooter incident is practically indistinguishable from an attempted shooting, in general. In fact, four of the 160 active shooter incidents that the report identified from 2000 to 2013 resulted in no casualties. In all fairness to the FBI, however, the report expressly states, "This is not a study of mass killings or mass shootings." J. Pete Blair and Katherine W. Schweit, *A Study of Active Shooter Incidents, 2000–2013* (Washington, DC: US Department of Justice, Federal Bureau of Investigation, 2014), http://www.fbi.gov/news/stories/2014/september/fbi

-releases-study-on-active-shooter-incidents/fbi-releases-study-on-active-shooter
-incidents (accessed September 25, 2014).

30. One of the most common misrepresentations repeated time and time again in the media is that the FBI defines mass shootings as acts of gun violence resulting in four of more deaths. One prominent authority who has promoted this erroneous claim is Mark Follman, the national affairs editor at *Mother Jones* who oversees the magazine's mass-shooting project. Mark Follman, "How Many Mass Shootings Are There, Really?" *New York Times*, December 3, 2015, http://www .nytimes.com/2015/12/04/opinion/how-many-mass-shootings-are-there-really .html (accessed December 13, 2015). The problem stems from a misreading of an FBI report that recommended that 'mass murder' be defined as "a number of murders (four or more) occurring during the same incident, with no distinctive time period between the murders." The term *mass shooting*, however, never appears in the report. Behavioral Analysis Unit, Federal Bureau of Investigation, *Serial Murder: Multi-Disciplinary Perspectives for Investigators* (Washington, DC: US Department of Justice, Federal Bureau of Investigation, 2005), pp. 8–9, http:// www.fbi.gov/stats-services/publications/serial-murder (accessed September 25, 2014). See also James Alan Fox, "You're Not about to Die in a Mass Shooting," *USA Today*, December 7, 2015, http://www.usatoday.com/story/opinion/2015/12/07/ mass-shooting-fbi-statistics-sanbernardino-terrorism-column/76892404 (accessed December 13, 2015).

31. Kleck doesn't include the Mother's Day and Copley Township shootings in his data set of mass shootings, even though both clearly meet his current definition of at least seven victims shot. Kleck's most recent data set is available in the appendix of "Declaration of Gary Kleck."

32. Only *USA Today* considers the Copley massacre to have been a mass shooting. After reviewing the data set that formed the foundation of the Duwe et al. analysis in *Homicide Studies*, I noticed that the authors determined that the Copley attack failed to meet its definition of a mass public shooting. Applying the *New York Times*, *Mother Jones*, COPS, and 2013 CRS definitions also leads to the exclusion of the Copley shooting.

33. Tryon Edwards, *A Dictionary of Thoughts* (Detroit, MI: F. B. Dickerson, 1908), p. 88, https://archive.org/stream/dictionaryofthou007549mbp#page/n7/ mode/2up (accessed April 15, 2016).

34. See Follman, Aronsen, and Pan, "U.S. Mass Shootings, 1982–2016."

35. Ibid.

36. Ibid.

37. The arbitrary approach employed by *Mother Jones* provided an open invitation for academic criticism. See, for example, James Alan Fox, "Mass

Shootings Not Trending," *Crime and Punishment* (blog), January 23, 2013, http://www.boston.com/community/blogs/crime_punishment/2013/01/mass_shootings_not_trending.html (accessed September 25, 2014).

38. A few of the other analyses seem to have made similar choices when forced to dismiss certain obvious incidents because of their selected preconditions. For instance, like *Mother Jones*, both the Duwe and CRS data sets include the murder of Nancy Lanza and two students at a Virginia Tech dormitory as part of their mass *public* shooting fatality counts. The original CRS data set—which was part of a 2013 report on mass shootings—also included the massacre at Brown's Chicken and Pasta in Palatine, Illinois, even though the restaurant was robbed during the attack. Moreover, COPS, in its report, identified the gun attacks at a US Army base in Fort Hood, Texas, and a Sikh temple in Oak Creek, Wisconsin, as multiple-casualty shootings despite the fact that the Obama administration deemed both massacres to be acts of terrorism—a motive that should disqualify both incidents from consideration pursuant to the COPS definition. On the identification of the these two shootings as terrorist attacks, see, for example, Caroline Bankoff, "Eric Holder Calls Sikh Temple Shooting a Hate Crime at Memorial," *New York Magazine*, August 10, 2012, http://nymag.com/daily/intelligencer/2012/08/holder-calls-sikh-temple-shooting-a-hate-crime.html (accessed April 24, 2016); and John T. Bennett, "Obama: 'New Phase' of Terror, a 'Cancer That Has No Immediate Cure,'" *Roll Call*, December 6, 2015, http://www.rollcall.com/news/home/obama-no-evidence-california-shooters-directed-isis (accessed April 26, 2016).

39. Bjelopera et al., *Public Mass Shootings in the United States*, p. 5.

40. In 2013, a group of Reddit users started a crowdsourcing project called the Mass Shooting Tracker. As will be discussed further in chapter 3, they began collecting data on every mass shooting in the United States that met their definition of the term: "A mass shooting is when four or more people are shot in an event, or related series of events, likely without a cooling off period." The definition can be found on their Reddit page, https://www.reddit.com/r/GunsAreCool/wiki/2015massshootings (accessed December 13, 2015). The definition of mass shooting that I employ in this book is a slightly modified version of the Mass Shooting Tracker's definition. Like the Mass Shooting Tracker team, I believe that mass shootings shouldn't be limited to mass murders involving a firearm. For examples of how the Mass Shooting Tracker's definition is becoming increasingly accepted by the mainstream media following the string of high-profile mass shootings in 2015 that culminated with the massacre at the Inland Regional Center in San Bernardino, see Sharon LaFraniere, Sarah Cohen, and Richard A. Oppel Jr., "How Often Do Mass Shootings Occur? On Average, Every Day, Records

Show," *New York Times*, December 2, 2015, http://www.nytimes.com/2015/12/03/us/how-often-do-mass-shootings-occur-on-average-every-day-records-show.html (accessed December 13, 2015); Christopher Ingraham, "What Makes a 'Mass Shooting' in America," *Washington Post*, December 3, 2015, https://www.washingtonpost.com/news/wonk/wp/2015/12/03/what-makes-a-mass-shooting-in-america (accessed December 13, 2015); Paul Thornton, "That Period of Nonpolitical Mourning after a Shooting? We're Past That Now," *Los Angeles Times*, December 3, 2015, http://www.latimes.com/opinion/opinion-la/la-ol-san-bernardino-shooting-readers-react-20151203-story.html (accessed December 17, 2015); and German Lopez, "The San Bernardino Shooting Is America's 1,044th Mass Shooting in 1,066 Days," *Vox*, December 3, 2015, http://www.vox.com/policy-and-politics/2015/12/3/9843254/san-bernardino-mass-shootings (accessed December 13, 2015). The Mass Shooting Tracker definition has also been prominently referenced on CNN and MSNBC. For criticisms of the Mass Shooting Tracker definition, see Follman, "How Many Mass Shootings Are There, Really?" and James Alan Fox, "You're Not about to Die in a Mass Shooting."

41. I realize that the four-casualty threshold is, in itself, arbitrary. After all, why not two casualties? Or three? However, it's impossible to identify mass shootings without some baseline.

42. Again, to be clear, this doesn't mean that firearm barrages that don't rise to the fatality-level of a gun massacre aren't also mass shootings; just that gun massacres resulting in more than five people murdered are generally more disturbing than gun attacks that result in fewer deaths.

43. A discussion of the origins of this adage, which is often attributed to Socrates, can be found at the AskPhilosophers online forum, posted May 23, 2013, http://www.askphilosophers.org/question/5187(accessed April 15, 2016).

CHAPTER THREE: A GROWING THREAT

1. The background material on Bill Iffrig is drawn predominantly from the short documentary *The Finish Line*, http://www.sportsonearth.com/video/v32073955/2013-boston-marathon-runner-bill-iffrig-tells-all (accessed February 7, 2015). See also Bill Sheets, "Lake Everett Runner Just Feet from Blast in Boston," *Herald* (Everett), April 15, 2013, http://www.heraldnet.com/article/20130415/NEWS01/704159868 (accessed February 7, 2015); Chris Erskine, "Bomb Blast Couldn't Keep Him Down in Boston," *Los Angeles Times*, April 25, 2013, http://articles.latimes.com/2013/apr/25/sports/la-sp-0426-erskine-bill-iffrig-20130426 (accessed February 7, 2015); and Josh Brant, "Back on His Feet," *Runner's World*,

June 3, 2013, http://www.runnersworld.com/boston-marathon/back-on-his-feet (accessed February 7, 2015).

2. See, for example, Deborah Hastings, "Boston Marathon Bombing May Be Linked to Domestic Atrocity Anniversaries: Experts," *New York Daily News*, April 18, 2013, http://www.nydailynews.com/news/crime/boston-marathon-bombing-linked -domestic-atrocity-anniversaries-experts-article-1.1320993 (accessed October 21, 2014). See also Cara Maresca, "Waco, Oklahoma City, Boston: What's the Deal with Patriots Day?" MSNBC, April 15, 2013, http://www.msnbc.com/msnbc/waco-oklahoma-city -boston-whats-the-deal (accessed October 21, 2014); Emanuella Grinberg, "Boston, Oklahoma City, Waco: Why Patriots Day?" CNN, April 16, 2013, http://www.cnn .com/2013/04/15/us/patriots-day-boston-bombing (accessed October 21, 2014); and Alex Spillius, "Boston Marathon Bombs: The Early Theories," April 16, 2013, *Telegraph* (London), http://www.telegraph.co.uk/news/worldnews/northamerica/ usa/9997156/Boston-Marathon-bombs-the-early -theories.html (accessed October 21, 2014).

3. Most of the information on the Tsarnaevs is drawn from Scott Russell and Jenna Helman, *Long Mile Home: Boston under Attack, the City's Courageous Recovery, and the Epic Hunt for Justice* (New York: Dutton, 2014); and "The Fall of the House of Tsarnaev," *Boston Globe*, December 15, 2013, http://www.bostonglobe.com/ Page/Boston/2011-2020/WebGraphics/Metro/BostonGlobe.com/2013/12/ 15tsarnaev/tsarnaev.html (accessed October 21, 2014).

4. Deborah Sontag, David S. Herszenhorn, and Serge F. Kovelski. "A Battered Dream, Then a Violent Path," *New York Times*, April 27, 2013, http://www .nytimes.com/2013/04/28/us/shot-at-boxing-title-denied-tamerlan-tsarnaev-reeled .html (accessed October 21, 2014).

5. Holly Bailey, "The Mystery of Tamerlan's Widow," *Yahoo News*, April 14, 2013, http://news.yahoo.com/katherine-russell-tsarnaev-boston-marathon -bombing-210147523.html (accessed October 21, 2014).

6. "Fall of the House of Tsarnaev."

7. Alan Cullison, "Boston Bombing Suspect Was Steeped in Conspiracies," *Wall Street Journal*, August 6, 2013, http://www.wsj.com/articles/SB1000142412788 73234206045786498307822194440 (accessed October 21, 2014).

8. Ellen Barry, "Boston Bomb Inquiry Looks Closely at Russia Trip," *New York Times*, May 8, 2013, http://www.nytimes.com/2013/05/09/world/europe/boston -bombing-inquiry-looks-closely-at-russia-trip.html (accessed October 21, 2014).

9. "Fall of the House of Tsarnaev."

10. Michael Levenson, "Cambridge Wrestling Coach Recalls Dzhokhar Tsarnaev as 'Dedicated Kid,'" *Boston Globe*, April 19, 2013, http://www.boston.com/ metrodesk/2013/04/19/cambridge-wrestling-coach-recalls-dzhokhar-tsarnaev -dedicated-kid/WjY1NDVadrsVFI2IhyHsLI/story.html (accessed October 26, 2014).

11. Janet Reitman, "Jahar's World," *Rolling Stone*, July 17, 2013, http://www
.rollingstone.com/culture/news/jahars-world-20130717 (accessed October 26,
2014).

12. Michael Wines and Ian Lovett, "The Dark Side, Carefully Masked," *New
York Times*, May 4, 2013, http://www.nytimes.com/2013/05/05/us/dzhokhar
-tsarnaevs-dark-side-carefully-masked.html (accessed October 26, 2014).

13. Ibid.

14. Ibid.

15. The article from *Inspire* magazine continues to remain readily available on
the Internet.

16. Eric Schmitt, Mark Mazzetti, Michael S. Schmidt, and Scott Shane,
"Boston Plotters Said to Initially Target July 4 for Attack," *New York Times*, May 2,
2013, http://www.nytimes.com/2013/05/03/us/Boston-bombing-suspects
-planned-july-fourth-attack.html (accessed October 27, 2014).

17. Estimates of the number of people injured by the bombings have
exceeded three hundred in some reports. The *Boston Globe* made a concerted effort
to identify those seriously injured at the marathon and came up with sixty-one
individuals. The full list is available here: http://www.boston.com/news/local/
massachusetts/specials/boston_marathon_bombing_victim_list (accessed February
7, 2015). It seems that many of the injuries were minor, like small abrasions and
ringing of the ears. This would explain the high initial injury tally. See James F.
Tracy, "The Boston Marathon Bombings Inflated Injury Tallies," *Memory Hole*
(blog), May 11, 2013, http://memoryholeblog.com/2013/05/11/the-boston
-marathon-bombings-inflated-injury-tallies (accessed February 7, 2015).

18. In December 2014, as part of a plea bargain with federal prosecutors,
Dzhokhar's former classmate Stephen Silva admitted that he had provided Dzhokhar
with the 9mm semiautomatic handgun used to kill Massachusetts Institute of
Technology police officer Sean Collier and to engage law enforcement during the
shootout in Watertown. Patricia Wen, "Tsarnaev Friend Pleads Guilty to Heroin,
Gun Charges," *Boston Globe*, December 19, 2014, http://www.bostonglobe.com/
metro/2014/12/19/dzhokhar-tsarnaev-friend-federal-court-enter-guilty-plea-heroin
-gun-charge/agln5etCEvaA8nunI1bCoN/story.html (accessed February 18, 2015).

19. The coroner listed Tamerlan Tsarnaev's cause of death as "gunshot
wounds" from the firefight with police and "blunt trauma" from being run over by
his brother. Jess Bidgood, "Autopsy Says Boston Bombing Suspect Died of Gunshot
Wounds and Blunt Trauma," *New York Times*, May 4, 2013, http://www.nytimes
.com/2013/05/05/us/autopsy-says-boston-bombing-suspect-died-of-gunshot
-wounds-and-blunt-trauma.html (accessed April 30, 2015). In the criminal trial
against Dzhokhar Tsarnaev, the prosecution introduced testimony that the blunt

trauma contributed to Tamerlan's death more than the gunshot wounds. Kevin Cullen, "In Watertown, One Brother's Decision Led to Death of Another," *Boston Globe*, March 15, 2015, http://www.bostonglobe.com/metro/2015/03/16/turn -makes-martyr/xWp8hj4Wx01mrKUglRF93J/story.html (accessed April 30, 2015).

20. Portions of Dzhokhar Tsarnaev's note are reproduced in the Government's Opposition to Defendant's Motion to Suppress Statements, filed in the US District Court of Massachusetts on May 21, 2014, p. 4, http://c.o0bg .com/rw/Boston/2011-2020/2014/05/22/BostonGlobe.com/Metro/Graphics/ tsarnaev1.pdf (accessed October 27, 2014).

21. This is the definition that the National Counter-Terrorism Center (NCTC) employs in determining whether an attack—domestic or foreign—qualifies as an act of terrorism. The definition is found at 22 USC § 2656f(d)(2). The other prominent definition of terrorism is located in the US Criminal Code at 18 USC. § 2331(5). It defines "domestic terrorism" as activities that "(A) involve acts dangerous to human life that are a violation of the criminal laws of the United States or of any State; (B) appear to be intended (i) to intimidate or coerce a civilian population; (ii) to influence the policy of a government by intimidation or coercion; or (iii) to affect the conduct of a government by mass destruction, assassination, or kidnapping; and (C) occur primarily within the territorial jurisdiction of the United States."

22. See, for example, Alana Semuels, "At Boston Marathon Bombing Site, All Signs Point to Normality," *Los Angeles Times*, April 13, 2014, http://www.latimes .com/nation/la-na-boston-bombing-boylston-20140413-dto-htmlstory.html (accessed October 27, 2014); Josh Levs, " 'We Are America, We, We Own the Finish Line,' Biden Says at Boston Bombing Memorial," CNN, April 16, 2014, http:// www.cnn.com/2014/04/15/us/boston-marathon-bombing-anniversary (accessed October 27, 2014); and Bob Nightengale, "One Year Later, Red Sox Reflect on 'Small' Recovery Role," *USA Today*, April 20, 2014, dhttp://www.usatoday.com/ story/sports/mlb/2014/04/20/boston-marathon-bombing-anniversary-fenway -park-ceremony/7949893 (accessed October 27, 2014).

23. Many details pertaining to the Fort Hood massacre are drawn from court testimony. Carlos Saucedo blogged from the courtroom daily during Nidal Hasan's Article 32 hearing. His informative posts are available at http://www.kwtx.com/ home/misc/Stories-And-Blogs-From-October-2010-Article-32-Hearing-214670881 .html (accessed October 30, 2014). Jeremy Schwartz of the *Austin American-Statesman* also reported on the legal proceedings daily. See Jeremy Schwartz, "Soldiers Testify about Bloodbath at Fort Hood Shooting," *Austin American-Statesman*, October 14, 2010, http://www.statesman.com/news/news/local/soldiers-testify-about-bloodbath -during-fort-hoo-1/nRygp (accessed October 30 2014); Jeremy Schwartz, "On Second

Day of Testimony in Fort Hood Shooting Hearing, Harrowing Tales of Survival,"
Austin American-Statesman, October 14, 2010, http://www.statesman.com/
news/news/state-regional/on-second-day-of-testimony-in-fort-hood-shooting-h/
nRyh2 (accessed October 30 2014); Jeremy Schwartz, "Witnesses in Fort Hood
Shooting Hearing Say Hasan Returned to Shoot Same Victims Over and Over,"
Austin American-Statesman, October 15, 2010, http://www.statesman.com/news/
news/state-regional/witnesses-in-fort-hood-shooting-hearing-say-hasan-/nRykN
(accessed October 30 2014); Jeremy Schwartz, "Witness: Man's Face Was 'Blank'
During Fort Hood Shooting," *Austin American-Statesman*, October 18, 2010, http://
www.statesman.com/news/news/local/witness-mans-face-was-blank-during-fort-hood
-shoot/nRyq9 (accessed October 30 2014); Jeremy Schwartz, "Witness: Hasan Visited
Shooting Site a Week Earlier, Refused Immunization," *Austin American-Statesman*,
October 19, 2010, http://www.statesman.com/news/news/local/witness-hasan
-visited-shooting-site-a-week-earlier/nRyrX (accessed October 30 2014); Jeremy
Schwartz, "Police Recall a Torrent of Bullets at Fort Hood," *Austin American
-Statesman*, October 21, 2010, http://www.statesman.com/news/news/state-regional/
police-recall-a-torrent-of-bullets-at-fort-hood/nRys3 (accessed October 30 2014); and
Jeremy Schwartz, "Witness: Hasan Spent Weeks before Fort Hood Shooting at Local
Range," *Austin American-Statesman*, October 21, 2010, http://www.statesman
.com/news/news/local/witnesses-hasan-spent-weeks-before-fort-hood-shoot/
nRytp (accessed October 30, 2014). Additional details are drawn from the following
sources: Ana Campoy, Peter Sanders, and Russell Gold, "Hash Browns, Then 4
Minutes of Chaos," *Wall Street Journal*, November 9, 2009, http://www.wsj.com/
articles/SB125750297355533413 (accessed October 30 2014); "Wounded Fort Hood
Soldier: 'Blood Just Everywhere,'" CNN, November 12, 2009, http://www.cnn
.com/2009/US/11/12/fort.hood.wounded.soldier/index.html (accessed October
30 2014). Unless otherwise stated, background material on the Fort Hood mass
murder comes from the above sources.

24. Saucedo, "Hasan Hearing Blog Tuesday Oct. 19, 2010."

25. Molly Hennessy-Fiske, "Officer Describes Shooting, Triage," *Los Angeles
Times*, August 9, 2013, http://articles.latimes.com/2013/aug/09/nation/la-na-fort
-hood-20130809 (accessed November 11, 2014).

26. Philip Jankowski, "Hasan Grinned as He Fired, Witness Testifies," *Daily
Herald* (Killeen), August 13, 2013, http://kdhnews.com/military/hasan_trial/
hasan-grinned-as-he-fired-witness-testifies/article_93c962be-03cb-11e3-8def
-001a4bcf6878.html (accessed November 11, 2014).

27. David Zucchino, "Police Officers Describe Fort Hood Gunfight," *Los
Angeles Times*, October 21, 2010, http://articles.latimes.com/2010/oct/21/nation/
la-na-fort-hood-20101021 (accessed November 11, 2014). See also Sig Christenson,

"Officer Recounts Gun Battle with Hasan," *San Antonio Express-News*, August 16, 2013, http://www.mysanantonio.com/news/local/article/Officer-recounts-gun -battle-with-Hasan-4738456.php (accessed November 11, 2014).

28. Zucchino, "Police Officers Describe."

29. Charley Keyes, "Witnesses Recount Bloody Scenes at Fort Hood Hearing," CNN, October 20, 2010, http://www.cnn.com/2010/CRIME/10/19/texas.fort .hood.shootings (accessed November 11, 2014).

30. There were also numerous others who were injured while taking cover or fleeing the attack.

31. Scott Huddleston, "Fort Hood Shooter Had 177 Unspent Rounds," *Military City* (blog), October 20, 2010, http://blog.mysanantonio.com/military/ 2010/10/fort-hood-shooter-had-177-unspent-rounds (accessed November 11, 2014). Hasan also had five additional loose 5.7mm rounds in his pants at the time of his arrest. Ibid. Reportedly, Hasan had a revolver in his pocket, but I have been unable to find specific information on this weapon. See Jeremy Schwartz, "Prosecution Rests in Fort Hood Shooting Case," *Austin American-Statesman*, August 20, 2013, http://www.statesman.com/news/news/local/prosecution-calls-final -witnesses-in-hasan-trial/nZTDR (accessed November 11, 2014).

32. Tim McGirk, "Hasan's Therapy: Could 'Secondary Trauma' Have Driven Him to Shooting?" *Time*, November 7, 2009, http://content.time.com/time/ nation/article/0,8599,1936407,00.html (accessed November 14, 2014). See also "Troubling Portrait Emerges of Shooting Suspect," NBC News, November 5, 2009, http://www.nbcnews.com/id/33695256/ns/us_news-tragedy_at_fort_hood/t/ troubling-portrait-emerges-shooting-suspect (accessed November 14, 2014).

33. Dana Priest, "Fort Hood Suspect Warned on Threats within the Ranks," *Washington Post*, November 10, 2009, http://www.washingtonpost.com/wp-dyn/ content/story/2009/11/09/ST2009110903704.html (accessed November 14, 2014).

34. Mariah Blake, "Internal Documents Reveal How the FBI Blew Fort Hood," *Mother Jones*, August 27, 2013, http://www.motherjones.com/politics/2013/08/ nidal-hasan-anwar-awlaki-emails-fbi-fort-hood (accessed November 14, 2014). See also Larry Shaughnessy, "Hasan's Email Exchange with al-Awlaki; Islam, Money and Matchmaking," *Security Clearance* (blog), July 20, 2012, http://security.blogs .cnn.com/2012/07/20/hasans-e-mail-exchange-with-al-awlaki-islam-money-and -matchmaking (accessed November 14, 2014).

35. James Dao, "Suspect Was 'Mortified' about Deployment," *New York Times*, November 5, 2009, http://www.nytimes.com/2009/11/06/us/06suspect.html (accessed November 14, 2014). Mary Pat Flaherty, William Wan, and Christian Davenport, "Suspect in Fort Hood Shooting, a Muslim, Asked Army to Discharge Him, Aunt Said," *Washington Post*, November 6, 2009, http://www.washingtonpost

.com/wp-dyn/content/article/2009/11/05/AR2009110505216.html (accessed November 14, 2014).

36. "Fort Hood Suspect Said Methodical Goodbyes," CBS News, November 6, 2009, http://www.cbsnews.com/news/fort-hood-suspect-said-methodical-goodbyes (accessed November 14, 2014).

37. Joseph Rhee, Mary-Rose Abraham, Anna Schecter, and Brian Ross, "Officials: Major Hasan Sought 'War Crimes' Prosecution of US Soldiers," ABC News, November 16, 2009, http://abcnews.go.com/Blotter/officials-major-hasan-sought-war-crimes-prosecution-us/story?id=9019904 (accessed November 14, 2014); Brooks Egerton, "Fort Hood Captain: Hasan Wanted Patients to Face War Crimes Charges," *Dallas Morning News*, November 17, 2009, http://www.dallasnews.com/news/20091117-Fort-Hood-captain-Hasan-wanted-9439.ece (accessed November 14, 2014); and James Dao and Dan Frosch, "Military Rules Said to Hinder Therapy," *New York Times*, December 6, 2009, http://www.nytimes.com/2009/12/07/us/07 therapists.html (accessed November 14, 2014). Copies of some of the e-mails Hasan sent to his superiors, requesting judicial investigations of some of his patients, were obtained by the *New York Times*. See "Emails from Maj. Nidal Malik Hasan," *New York Times*, August 20, 2013, http://www.nytimes.com/interactive/2013/08/21/us/21hasan-emails-document.html (accessed November 14, 2014).

38. David Zucchino, "Suspect in Ft. Hood Rampage Sought High-Tech Gun, Salesman Says," *Los Angeles Times*, October 21 2010, http://articles.latimes.com/2010/oct/21/nation/la-na-fort-hood-20101022 (accessed November 14, 2014).

39. Earlier, the NCTC had inferred that the Fort Hood shooting was an act of terrorism under the statutory definition of terrorism, and cataloged the attack as such in its Worldwide Incidents Tracking System (WITS). National Counterterrorism Center, *2009 Report on Terrorism* (Washington, DC: National Counterterrorism Center, April 30, 2010), p. 61, http://www.riskintel.com/wp-content/uploads/downloads/2011/10/2009_report_on_terrorism.pdf (accessed February 14, 2015).

40. Manny Fernandez, "Fort Hood Suspect Says Rampage Was to Defend Afghan Taliban Leaders," *New York Times*, June 4, 2013, http://www.nytimes.com/2013/06/05/us/fort-hood-suspect-says-he-was-defending-taliban-leaders.html (accessed November 17, 2014). The following week, the presiding judge rejected Hasan's defense on grounds that it lacked legal merit. See Manny Fernandez, "Judge Rejects Fort Hood Shooting Suspect's Defense Strategy," *New York Times*, June 4, 2013, http://www.nytimes.com/2013/06/15/us/judge-rejects-fort-hood-shooting-suspects-defense-strategy.html (accessed November 17, 2014).

41. Catherine Herridge and Pamela Browne, "Accused Fort Hood Shooter Releases Statement to Fox News," Fox News, July 26, 2013, http://www.foxnews

.com/politics/2013/07/26/accused-fort-hood-shooter-claims-us-military-at-war
-with-his-religion (accessed November 17, 2014); and Catherine Herridge and
Pamela Browne, "Hasan Sends Writings to Fox News ahead of Fort Hood Shooting
Trial," Fox News, August 1, 2013, http://www.foxnews.com/politics/2013/08/01/
hasan-sends-writings-ahead-fort-hood-shooting-trial (accessed November 17, 2014).

42. Billy Kenber, "Nidal Hasan Convicted of Fort Hood Killings," *Washington Post*, August 23, 2013, http://www.washingtonpost.com/world/national-security/ nidal-hasan-convictcd-of-fort-hood-killings/2013/08/23/39c468c8-0c03-11e3-9941 -6711ed662e71_story.html (accessed November 17, 2014); and Billy Kenber, "Nidal Hasan Sentenced to Death for Fort Hood Shooting Rampage," *Washington Post*, August 28, 2013, http://www.washingtonpost.com/world/national-security/nidal -hasan-sentenced-to-death-for-fort-hood-shooting-rampage/2013/08/28/aad28de2 -0ffa-11e3-bdf6-e4fc677d94a1_story.html (accessed November 17, 2014).

43. Catherine Herridge, "Fort Hood Shooter Sends Letter to Pope Francis Espousing 'Jihad,'" Fox News, October 10, 2014, http://www.foxnews.com/ politics/2014/10/09/fort-hood-shooter-sends-letter-to-pope-francis-espousing -jihad (accessed November 17, 2014).

44. As this book was going to press, authorities announced that they were ruling out weather-related and accidental factors as the cause of a fire and ensuing explosion at a West, Texas, fertilizer plant in April 2013. Fifteen people lost their lives as a result of the tragedy: three who were killed in the initial blast, and another twelve first responders who were killed trying to combat the flames. Investigators determined that "the only hypothesis that could not be eliminated is incendiary." In other words, law enforcement now suspects that this incident was an act of arson. While the police do not presently have a suspect or a motive, they indicated that they believe they are "headed in the right direction" by treating the fire as having been "intentionally set." Should the continuing investigation conclude with certainty that was indeed a criminal act, it would qualify as the one of the deadliest acts of intentional violence from the past decade (2006–2015), joining the eighteen mass shootings in table 3.1. For more information, see Sue Ambrose, "Fire That Triggered West Blast Was a Criminal Act, Government Officials Say," *Dallas Morning News*, May 11, 2016, http://thescoopblog.dallasnews .com/2016/05/fire-caused-fire-that-triggered-west-explosion-government -investigators-say.html (accessed May 11, 2016); Asher Price and Jeremy Schwartz, "Arson Blamed by Investigators for West Fertilizer Co. Explosion," *Austin American-Statesman*, May 11, 2016, http://www.statesman.com/news/news/announcement -on-cause-of-west-fertilizer-co-explos/nrLNn (accessed May 11, 2016); and Tommy Witherspoon, "West Explosion Investigators Say Someone Started Fire," *Waco Tribune-Herald*, May 11, 2016, http://www.wacotrib.com/news/west_explosion/

west-explosion-investigators-say-someone-started-fire/article_45c7fe83-3664-57d8
-8cc8-4d65e7990317.html (accessed May 11, 2016).

45. See Centers for Disease Control, "FastStats: Assault or Homicide," http://
www.cdc.gov/nchs/fastats/homicide.htm (accessed February 7, 2015).

46. Emily Miller, "Obama Tells Americans to 'Obsess' over Rare Mass
Shootings," *Washington Times*, September 25, 2013, http://www.washingtontimes
.com/news/2013/sep/25/miller-obama-tells-americans-to-obsess-over-the-sh
(accessed October 27, 2014).

47. John Fund, "The Facts about Mass Shootings," *National Review Online*,
December 16, 2012, http://www.nationalreview.com/articles/335739/facts-about
-mass-shootings-john-fund (accessed October 27, 2014).

48. Daniel Kahneman, *Thinking Fast and Slow* (New York: Farrar, Straus, and
Giroux, 2011), p. 138.

49. High-profile gun rampages can dominate news coverage. For example,
the Newtown and Aurora shootings were two of the five most followed stories of
2012. The Newtown massacre, in fact, came in second, behind only the presidential
election, outranking every other story of 2012, even though it occurred with two
just weeks left in the calendar year. Pew Research Center, "Elections, Tragedies
Dominate Top Stories of 2012," December 20, 2012, http://www.people-press
.org/2012/12/20/election-tragedies-dominate-top-stories-of-2012 (accessed July
25, 2013). Mass shootings were also identified as the leading news topic of 2012
in the annual Associated Press survey of news editors. "Poll Ranks Top 10 News
Stories on 2012," *USA Today*, December 20, 2012, http://www.usatoday.com/story/
news/2012/12/20/year-top-news/1783303 (accessed July 25, 2013). Furthermore,
reporting on gun violence accounted for eight of the top ten crime evening news
stories in 2012 and seven of the top ten in 2013. Remarkably, in 2012, continuing
coverage of the Tucson rampage that involved former Congresswoman Gabrielle
Giffords came in at seventh place—even though the shooting occurred in January
2011. See "Top Ten Crimes Stories 2012," *Tyndall Report: Year in Review 2012*,
http://tyndallreport.com/yearinreview2012/crime (accessed July 25, 2014);
and "Top Ten Crimes Stories 2013," *Tyndall Report: Year in Review 2013*, http://
tyndallreport.com/yearinreview2013/crime (accessed July 25, 2014).

50. Louis Klarevas, "Trends in Terrorism since 9/11: Is Terrorism Still a
Threat to the United States?" *Georgetown Journal of International Affairs* 12 (Winter/
Spring 2011): 76–88, http://papers.ssrn.com/sol3/papers.cfm?abstract
_id=2163208 (accessed October 27, 2014).

51. On the near impossibility of terrorists acquiring nuclear weapons, see
John Mueller, *Atomic Obsession: Nuclear Alarmism from Hiroshima to Al-Qaeda* (New
York: Oxford University Press, 2012).

52. For an overview of the two competing sides of the gun debate, see Adam Winkler, *Gunfight: The Battle of the Right to Bear Arms in America* (New York: W. W. Norton, 2013).

53. Mark Follman, Gavin Aronsen, and Deanna Pan, "U.S. Mass Shootings, 1982–2016: Data from *Mother Jones*' Investigation," *Mother Jones*, April 18, 2016, http://www.motherjones.com/politics/2012/12/mass-shootings-mother-jones-full-data (accessed April 26, 2016). The *Mother Jones* fatality tallies include the shooters who died at the scene.

54. Amy P. Cohen, Deborah Azrael, and Matthew Miller, "Rate of Mass Shootings Has Tripled Since 2011, Harvard Research Shows," *Mother Jones*, October 15, 2014, http://www.motherjones.com/politics/2014/10/mass-shootings-increasing-harvard-research (accessed October 27, 2014).

55. Out of the 133 mass shootings that left four or more victims dead, Everytown found that 86 involved four fatalities and 23 involved five fatalities. The remaining 24 incidents (18 percent of the total data set) in the Everytown report are gun massacres. These 24 high-fatality mass shootings accounted for 214 of the 673 cumulative deaths (32 percent). Everytown for Gun Safety, *Analysis of Recent Mass Shootings*, August 2015, http://everytownresearch.org/documents/2015/09/analysis-mass-shootings.pdf (accessed December 13, 2015). The data that served as the basis of this report is available separately at http://everytownresearch.org/wp-content/uploads/2015/12/Everytown-Mass-Shooting-Analysis-Data-07-14-2015-4.xlsx (accessed December 13, 2015).

56. Glenn Beck, *Control: Exposing the Truth about Guns* (New York: Threshold Editions / Mercury Radio Arts, 2013), pp. 32, 34.

57. Ibid., p. 35. Beck adds, "The *Mother Jones* methodology was created to ensure that only a very specific set of killings would be generated." Ibid.

58. Ibid., p. 33.

59. James Alan Fox, "No Increase in Mass Shootings," *Crime and Punishment* (blog), August 6, 2012, http://www.boston.com/community/blogs/crime_punishment/2012/08/no_increase_in_mass_shootings.html (accessed October 27, 2014).

60. Fox implies that building a data set of mass shootings strictly from news accounts is suspect, suggesting that such endeavors are "based on unofficial data of questionable reliability." James Alan Fox, "You're Not about to Die in a Mass Shooting," *USA Today*, December 7, 2015, http://www.usatoday.com/story/opinion/2015/12/07/mass-shooting-fbi-statistics-sanbernardino-terrorism-column/76892404 (accessed December 13, 2015).

61. Paul Overberg, Jodi Upton, and Meghan Hoyer, "*USA Today* Research Reveals Flaws in Mass-Killing Data," *USA Today*, December 3, 2013, http://www.

usatoday.com/story/news/nation/2013/12/03/fbi-mass-killing-data
-inaccurate/3666953 (accessed December 16, 2014).

62. Jason Kissner, "The Sandy Hook School Massacre and FBI Data Anomalies," *Global Research Newsletter*, September 27, 2014, http://www.globalresearch.ca/
the-sandy-hook-school-massacre-and-fbi-data-anomalies/5404658 (accessed April
30, 2015).

63. From 1976 to 2011, eighty-seven gun massacres resulting in the murder
of six or more victims were cataloged in the SHR data sets. Of those, twenty-three
were erroneous. That means only sixty-four of the high-fatality mass shootings
in the SHR data sets were verifiable. That's an error rate of 26 percent. But that
speaks only to erroneous incidents entered into the system. There were also
nineteen gun massacres I documented in table 3.2 that were omitted from the
SHR data sets. When those missing incidents are accounted for, the error rate
jumps to 40 percent. In other words, the accuracy rate for gun massacres in the
SHR data sets is only 60 percent. Similarly, *USA Today*, in its own examination of
mass killings since 2006, found that the SHR data sets had an accuracy rate of
only 57 percent. Meghan Hoyer, "In FBI Murder Data, Mass Killings Often Go
Missing," *USA Today*, September 10, 2014, http://www.usatoday.com/story/news/
nation/2014/09/10/mass-killings-missing-data/12990815 (accessed December 16,
2014).

64. In all fairness, Fox has acknowledged the limitations of working with SHR
data. Fox has introduced a few statistical corrections to the overall data set, but
none of the techniques that he recommends for filling in the gaps can generate
accurate numbers pertaining to gun massacres. James Alan Fox, "Missing Data
Problems in the SHR: Imputing Offender and Relationship Characteristics,"
Homicide Studies 8 (August 2004): 214–54.

65. John Lott is certainly a polemic figure in the gun debate, often referred
to as a "discredited scholar" and even accused of unethical conduct. For more on
the controversies surrounding Lott, see chapter 5. Also, see Evan DeFilippis and
Devin Hughes, "Shooting Down the Gun Lobby's Favorite 'Academic': A Lott of
Lies," *Armed with Reason*, December 1, 2014, http://www.armedwithreason.com/
shooting-down-the-gun-lobbys-favorite-academic-a-lott-of-lies (accessed December
16, 2014).

66. The argument that an increase in gun ownership results in less crime is
based predominantly on John Lott, *More Guns, Less Crime: Understanding Crime and
Gun Control Laws*, 3rd ed. (Chicago: University of Chicago Press, 2000).

67. Lott's report utilized the same fatality threshold as the Everytown report:
a minimum of four victims shot to death. John R. Lott Jr., *The Myths about Mass
Public Shootings: Analysis*, Report of the Crime Prevention Research Center,

October 9, 2014, p. 4, http://crimepreventionresearchcenter.org/wp-content/
uploads/2014/10/CPRC-Mass-Shooting-Analysis-Bloomberg2.pdf (accessed
October 27, 2014).

68. Ibid., p. 5.

69. Ibid., p. 19.

70. Beck also cites the research of criminologist Grant Duwe, who suggests
that mass shootings might have actually decreased in the recent past. As the *Los
Angeles Times* noted, "The 26 public shooting massacres [Duwe] tallied between
2000 and 2009 were significantly down from the 43 cases he counted in the 1990s."
Matt Pearce, "2012 Is Tragic, but Mass Shootings Not Increasing, Experts Say,"
Los Angeles Times, December 18, 2012, http://articles.latimes.com/2012/dec/18/
nation/la-na-nn-mass-shootings-common-20121218 (accessed October 27, 2014).
Unlike Fox, Duwe excludes certain mass shootings that were motivated by criminal
enterprise or occurred in private, making his conclusions subject to some of the
same limitations associated with the *Mother Jones* analysis.

71. "Findings of Fact, Conclusions of Law, and Order," *Colorado Outfitters
Association et al. v. Hickenlooper,* Civil Action No. 13–cv–01300–MSK–MJW, US
District Court for the District of Colorado, June 26, 2014, http://michellawyers.
com/wp-content/uploads/2013/05/Cooke-v.-Hickenlooper_Findings-of-Fact
-Conclusions-of-Law-and-Order.pdf (accessed November 23, 2014).

72. "Reporter's Transcript: Trial to Court—Day Three," *Colorado Outfitters
Association et al. v. Hickenlooper,* Civil Action No. 13–cv–01300–MSK–MJW, US
District Court for the District of Colorado, April 2, 2014, p. 529, http://michel
lawyers.com/wp-content/uploads/2013/05/Cooke-v.-Hickenlooper_Reporters
-Transcript-Trial-to-Court-Day-Three.pdf (accessed November 23, 2014). Kleck
elaborated on his reasoning for opposing a ban on magazine capacity in a *Wall
Street Journal* op-ed:

> The availability of large-capacity magazines is certainly irrelevant to ordi-
> nary gun violence, which usually involves few or no shots fired, but it is
> even irrelevant to virtually all mass shootings, because the shooters either
> have multiple guns, making it easy to fire many rounds without reloading,
> or they have ample time and opportunity to reload because there is no one
> present willing to stop them while they reload. . . .
>
> When there are willing interveners, it limits how much death and
> injury a shooter can inflict with the initial magazine; the smaller the maga-
> zine, the fewer the victims. Unfortunately, these conditions almost never
> prevail in mass shootings. . . .
>
> Any restrictions that limit the availability of guns for criminal purposes

also limit their availability for self-protection. . . . Making guns unavailable for self-defense can therefore cost lives, and this cost must be taken into account when considering the possible slight benefit of measures that would prevent only the rarest of crimes.

Gary Kleck, "Mass Shootings Aren't the Real Gun Problem," *Wall Street Journal*, January 15, 2011, http://www.wsj.com/articles/SB1000142405274870395910457608 1910062180664 (accessed November 23, 2014).

73. Kleck has served as an expert witness in at least five other gun rights cases: *Heller v. District of Columbia; Fyock v. Sunnyvale; San Francisco Veteran Police Officers Association v. San Francisco; Tardy v. O'Malley;* and *Shew v. Malloy.* See "Reporter's Transcript: Trial to Court—Day Three," pp. 582–83.

74. Gary Kleck, *Targeting Guns: Firearms and Their Control* (Hawthorne, NY: Aldine de Gruyter, 1997), pp. 124–25.

75. "Reporter's Transcript: Trial to Court—Day Three," p. 529.

76. Ibid.

77. Ibid., p. 580.

78. "Reporter's Transcript: Trial to Court—Day Five," *Colorado Outfitters Association et al. v. Hickenlooper,* Civil Action No. 13–cv–01300–MSK–MJW, US District Court for the District of Colorado, April 4, 2014, p. 975 (emphasis added), http://michellawyers.com/wp-content/uploads/2013/05/Cooke-v.-Hickenlooper _Reporters-Transcript-Trial-to-Court-Day-Five.pdf (accessed November 23, 2014).

79. Ibid., pp. 977–78.

80. The forty-five-minute time frame was reported in Megan Gallegos, "Data Questioned in Gun Control Trial," *Courthouse News Service,* April 6, 2014, http://www .courthousenews.com/2014/04/06/66817.htm (accessed November 23, 2014).

81. "Reporter's Transcript: Trial to Court—Day Five," p. 993.

82. Ibid., p. 995.

83. "Findings of Fact, Conclusions of Law, and Order," p. 35. In fact, the judge's opinion upholding Colorado's law noted, "The General Assembly considered evidence that mass shootings occur with alarming frequency and often involve use of large-capacity magazines." Ibid., p. 32. In March 2016, the US Court of Appeals for the Tenth Circuit vacated the district court's ruling on the grounds that the plaintiffs lacked standing to bring their legal action. The result was the same: the lawsuit was dismissed. *Colorado Outfitters Association et al. v. Hickenlooper,* Nos. 14-1290 and 14-1292, March 22, 2016, https://www.ca10.uscourts.gov/ opinions/14/14-1290.pdf (accessed April 17, 2016).

84. Because research funding was not available to me, I didn't have the resources to search out and catalog every mass shooting—at least four people shot in

a single incident—that occurred in the United States since 1966. Just tracking down the mass shootings where five people were shot to death would have likely more than doubled my data set. *USA Today* found a similar pattern. Between January 1, 2006, and June 30, 2015, the newspaper identified 39 mass shootings resulting in six or more deaths. Shifting the baseline to five or more deaths increased the data set by more than double (42 additional incidents), to 81 such mass shootings. When the newspaper included shootings resulting in four or more deaths, the tally jumped by 130 incidents to 211 total mass shootings. The *USA Today* mass murder data set can be accessed at http://www.usatoday.com/story/news/nation/2013/09/16/mass-killings-data-map/2820423 (accessed December 13, 2015).

85. As figure 3.1 illustrates, there were three quasi-flatline periods when total deaths in gun massacres were accumulating at a rate of zero or close to zero (1968–1972, 1977–1980, and 1993–1998). The past decade, however, has exhibited no such pattern.

86. The ten-year period 1996–2005 was the decade with the least number of gun massacres as well as the least number of cumulative deaths resulting from such attacks. A possible explanation for this decline is offered in chapter 7.

87. By "five-plus-shooting-year," I mean a calendar year with five or more gun massacres. Similarly, by "four-plus-shooting-year," I mean a calendar year with four or more gun massacres.

88. Gary Fields and Cameron McWhirter, "In Medical Triumph, Homicides Fall Despite Soaring Gun Violence," *Wall Street Journal*, December 8, 2012, http://www.wsj.com/articles/SB10001424127887324712504578131360684277812 (accessed February 10, 2015).

89. Since 1973, the National Opinion Research Center at the University of Chicago has been surveying how many households have firearms. These gun-ownership rates are compiled roughly every two years by the General Social Survey. The data from 1973 to 2012 are available in Tom W. Smith, Faith Laken, and Jaesok Son, *Gun Ownership in the United States: Measurement Issues and Trends*, General Social Survey Methodological Report No. 123 (Chicago: National Opinion Research Center, 2014), http://publicdata.norc.org:41000/gss/documents//MTRT/MR123%20Gun%20Ownership.pdf (accessed March 17, 2015). The data for 2014 are reported in "Gun Ownership among Americans at a Record Low, Survey Finds," *Chicago Tribune*, March 10, 2015, http://www.chicagotribune.com/news/local/breaking/chi-gun-ownership-record-low-20150310-story.html (accessed March 17, 2015).

90. Since 1973, when the General Social Survey began probing household gun-ownerships rates, the number of households in the United States has nearly doubled from 68 million to 124 million. Yet the absolute number of armed

households has remained fairly constant at an average of 40 million. The lowest number of households with guns was recorded in 1973 (approximately 33 million) and the highest number was recorded in 1989 (approximately 46 million). In 2014, the number of households in the United States with firearms is again roughly 40 million. Annual data on the number of households in the United States is drawn from "Number of Households in the U.S. from 1960 to 2013," *Statista*, http://www .statista.com/statistics/183635/number-of-households-in-the-us (accessed March 17, 2015). As the data only extends to 2013, the number of households in the United States in 2014 has been estimated to be 124 million, based on a projection from previous years. The absolute number of armed households was calculated by multiplying the number of households by the percentage of households that the General Social Survey found had guns at home.

91. Todd C. Frankel, "Why the CDC Still Isn't Researching Gun Violence, Despite the Ban Being Lifted Two Years Ago," *Washington Post*, January 14, 2015, http://www.washingtonpost.com/news/storyline/wp/2015/01/14/why-the -cdc-still-isnt-researching-gun-violence-despite-the-ban-being-lifted-two-years-ago (accessed February 10, 2015).

92. The list of incidents is available online at massshootingtracker.org as well at the sub-Reddit /r/GunsAreCool. Every incident listed in the Mass Shooting Tracker contains a link to a news media account that allows for verification of the shooting. The incidents—attacks involving four or more victims shot—include the gunmen in the number of people shot. Therefore, an unknown portion of these incidents actually involved three innocent people being shot alongside the perpetrator, for a total of four killed or wounded by gunfire.

93. National Weather Service, "How Dangerous Is Lightning?" http://www .lightningsafety.noaa.gov/odds.htm (accessed February 18, 2015).

94. In a December 2015 CBS News / *New York Times* poll conducted in the immediate aftermath of the terrorist attack in San Bernardino, respondents identified terrorism as the most important problem facing the United States. In addition, 79 percent of respondents indicated that they felt there would likely be another terrorist attack on American soil within the next few months. Anthony Salvanto et al., "Poll: After San Bernardino Attacks, American Concern about Terror Threat Rises," CBS News, December 10, 2015, http://www.cbsnews.com/ news/poll-after-san-bernardino-attacks-american-concern-about-terror-threat-rises (accessed December 13, 2015).

95. Klarevas, "Trends in Terrorism," p. 80.

96. In the past decade, there have been seven lethal terrorist attacks perpe-trated by jihadists on American soil. These seven attacks resulted in a total of forty-two fatalities. Louis Klarevas, "Almost Every Fatal Terrorist Attack in America

Since 9/11 Has Involved Guns," *Vice*, December 4, 2015, http://www.vice.com/
read/almost-every-fatal-terrorist-attack-in-america-since-911-has-involved-guns-123
(accessed December 13, 2015). At a time when Americans are particularly
concerned about becoming the victim of an ISIS-inspired act of terrorism, it's
valuable to identify the odds of that happening. Basically, in any given year, the odds
of being killed in an act of jihadist terrorism on American soil are around one in
eighty million, an astronomically lesser chance than being killed in a mass shooting
on American soil, which has a likelihood of about one in 700,000. These odds
were calculated by dividing the current estimated population of the United States
(320 million people) by the average number of people killed in the United States
annually in jihadist terrorist attacks (four people) and mass shootings (433 people).

CHAPTER FOUR: UNSTABLE, ANGRY, ARMED MEN

1. Unless otherwise noted, all the information on the Virginia Tech massacre
is drawn from Virginia Tech Review Panel, *Mass Shootings at Virginia Tech, April 16,
2007: Report of the Review Panel*, August 2007, http://www.washingtonpost.com/
wp-srv/metro/documents/vatechreport.pdf (accessed May 2, 2015).

2. Ibid., p. 34.

3. Quoted in ibid., p. 35.

4. Quoted in ibid., p. 37.

5. Quoted in ibid., p. 42.

6. Quoted in ibid., p. 50.

7. Quoted in ibid., p. 50.

8. Quoted in ibid., p. 47.

9. Quoted in ibid., p. 48.

10. 18 USC § 922(g)(4).

11. Of the sixty-two occupants in the four classrooms Cho breached, only
thirteen avoided being shot; ten of them as a result of jumping from the second-
floor window and the other three presumably by playing dead.

12. Six more students were hurt as a result of jumping out of the windows in
Professor's Librescu's classroom.

13. "Killer's Manifesto: 'You Forced Me into a Corner,'" CNN, April 18, 2007,
http://edition.cnn.com/2007/US/04/18/vtech.shooting/index.html (accessed
May 2, 2015).

14. Ibid. See also M. Alex Johnson, "Gunman Sent Package to NBC News,"
NBC News, April 19, 2007, http://www.nbcnews.com/id/18195423#.VdC
-Mvmqqkp (accessed May 2, 2015).

15. "Seung Hui Cho's 'Manifesto,'" https://schoolshooters.info/sites/default/files/cho_manifesto_1.1.pdf (accessed May 2, 2015).

16. Ibid.

17. Interview on NBC's *Today* show, April 19, 2007, transcript available through Lexis-Nexis (accessed May 3, 2015).

18. *NBC Nightly News*, April 18, 2007, transcript available through LexisNexis (accessed May 3, 2015).

19. *NBC Nightly News*, April 19, 2007, transcript available through LexisNexis (accessed May 3, 2015).

20. See, for example, *American Morning* (CNN), April 19, 2007, transcript available through LexisNexis (accessed May 3, 2015); *The Big Story with John Gibson* (Fox News), April 19, 2007, transcript available through LexisNexis (accessed May 3, 2015); *Glenn Beck* (CNN), April 19, 2007, transcript available through LexisNexis (accessed May 3, 2015); *Hannity & Colmes* (Fox News), April 19, 2007, transcript available through LexisNexis (accessed May 3, 2015); *Lou Dobbs Tonight* (CNN), April 19, 2007, transcript available through LexisNexis (accessed May 3, 2015); *The O'Reilly Factor* (Fox News), April 19, 2007, transcript available through LexisNexis (accessed May 3, 2015); *Showbiz Tonight* (CNN), April 19, 2007, transcript available through LexisNexis (accessed May 3, 2015); and *Glenn Beck* (CNN), April 20, 2007, transcript available through LexisNexis (accessed May 3, 2015).

21. Interview on *Hannity & Colmes* (Fox News), April 19, 2007, transcript available through LexisNexis (accessed May 3, 2015).

22. Interview on *Glenn Beck* (CNN), April 19, 2007, transcript available through LexisNexis (accessed May 3, 2015).

23. Interview on *Larry King Live* (CNN), April 21, 2007, transcript available through LexisNexis (accessed May 3, 2015).

24. David Brooks, "The Morality Line," *New York Times*, April 19, 2007, http://www.nytimes.com/2007/04/19/opinion/19brooks.html (accessed May 3, 2015).

25. Some in the general public lashed out against the Korean-American community, attributing the violence to Cho's ethnicity. Fortunately, this absurd—and racist—factor quickly faded away. See, for example, Jennifer Steinhauer, "Korean-Americans Brace for Problems in Wake of Killings," *New York Times*, April 19, 2007, http://www.nytimes.com/2007/04/19/us/19korea.html (accessed May 3, 2015); Adrian Hong, "Koreans Aren't to Blame," *Washington Post*, April 20, 2007, http://www.washingtonpost.com/wp-dyn/content/article/2007/04/19/AR2007041902942.html (accessed May 3, 2015); and DeWayne Wickham, "Madman, Not Koreans, to Blame for Shootings," *USA Today*, June 23, 2007, http://usatoday30.usatoday.com/news/opinion/columnist/wickham/2007-04-23-wickham_N.htm (accessed May 3, 2015).

26. Matt Apuzzo and Sharon Cohen, "Shooter Fitting Profile: Awkward, Shy, Bullied," *Pittsburgh Post-Gazette*, April 20, 2007, p. A10.

27. "Bullied Cho's 'HS Death List,'" *New York Post*, April 20, 2007, http://nypost.com/2007/04/20/bullied-chos-hs-death-list/ (accessed May 3, 2015).

28. Khristopher Brooks, "Va. Tech Psychology Professor Discusses Massacre, Gunman," *Bristol Herald Courier*, April 21, 2007, available through LexisNexis (accessed May 3, 2015).

29. Matt Apuzzo, "A Day of Mourning," *Charleston Daily Mail*, April 20, 2007, p. 3A.

30. Mike Musgrove, "Va. Tech: Dr. Phil & Jack Thompson Blame Video Games," *Washington Post*, April 17, 2007, http://voices.washingtonpost.com/posttech/2007/04/va_tech_dr_phil_jack_thompson.html (accessed May 3, 2015). Two days later, the *New York Post* published yet another rumor that Cho loved to play *Counter-Strike*—a first-person shooter video game. Leela De Crester, "Psycho Penned Poison Plays," *New York Post*, April 18, 2007, http://nypost.com/2007/04/18/psycho-penned-poison-plays/ (accessed May 3, 2015). Thompson seized this news report and subsequently began blaming *Counter-Strike*. Winda Benedetti, "Were Video Games to Blame for Massacre?" NBC News, April 20, 2007, http://www.nbcnews.com/id/18220228/ns/technology_and_science-games/t/were-video-games-blame-massacre/#.VdDKS_mqqko (accessed May 3, 2015).

31. Interview on *Larry King Live* (CNN), April 16, 2007, http://transcripts.cnn.com/TRANSCRIPTS/0704/16/lkl.01.html (accessed May 3, 2015).

32. Mike Nizza, "Updates on Virginia Tech," *New York Times*, April 18, 2007, http://thelede.blogs.nytimes.com/2007/04/18/updates-on-virginia-tech/ (accessed May 3, 2015).

33. Jake Coyle, "Bloody Movie Could Have Inspired Killer," *Record* (Bergen County), April 20, 2007, p. A10.

34. Stephen Hunter, "Cinematic Clues to Understand the Slaughter," *Washington Post*, April 20, 2007, http://www.washingtonpost.com/wp-dyn/content/article/2007/04/19/AR2007041901817.html (accessed May 3, 2015).

35. Ibid.

36. Katharine Lackey, "Timeline: Germanwings Flight 9525 Crashes into Alps," *USA Today*, March 28, 2015, http://www.usatoday.com/story/news/world/2015/03/26/germanwings-9525-alps-crash-timeline/70490808/ (accessed May 9, 2015).

37. Brian Murphy, "Reports: Desperate Pilot Used Ax on Locked Cockpit Door of Doomed Plane," *Washington Post*, March 28, 2015, https://www.washingtonpost.com/world/reports-desperate-pilot-used-ax-on-locked-cockpit-door-of-doomed-plane/2015/03/27/d89a10a2-d492-11e4-ab77-9646eea6a4c7_story.html (accessed May 9, 2015).

38. Steve Almasy and Laura Smith-Spark, "Reports: Antidepressants Found at Home of Co-Pilot Andreas Lubitz," CNN, March 28, 2015, http://edition .cnn.com/2015/03/28/europe/france-germanwings-plane-crash-main/index .html (accessed May 9, 2015); Henry Samuel, "Germanwings Crash: Andreas Lubitz Searched Online for Suicide and Cockpit Doors," *Telegraph* (London), April 2, 2015, http://www.telegraph.co.uk/news/worldnews/germanwings -plane-crash/11512137/Germanwings-crash-Andreas-Lubitz-searched-online -for-suicide-and-cockpit-doors.html (accessed May 9, 2015); Patrick Sawer and Raziye Akkoc, "Andreas Lubitz: Everything We Know about Germanwings Plane Crash Co-Pilot," *Telegraph* (London), May 6, 2015, http://www.telegraph.co.uk/ news/worldnews/europe/france/11496066/Andreas-Lubitz-Everything-we-know -about-Germanwings-plane-crash-co-pilot.html (accessed May 9, 2015); and Ben Mathis-Lilley, "Germanwings Crash Pilot, Paranoid about Going Blind, Saw 41 Doctors in Five Years," *Slate*, June 11, 2015, http://www.slate.com/blogs/the_ slatest/2015/06/11/andreas_lubitz_41_doctors_in_five_years_thought_he_was_ going_blind.html (accessed June 11, 2015).

39. "Troubled Pilot," *Time*, March 1, 1982, p. 33.

40. Murray Sayle, "Confucius in the Cockpit," *Spectator* (London), March 6, 1982, pp. 11–13.

41. Ibid.

42. Ibid.

43. Ibid., p. 12.

44. Eric Malnic, William C. Rempel, and Ricardo Alonso-Zaldivar, "Egypt Air Co-Pilot Caused '99 Jet Crash, NTSB to Say," *Los Angeles Times*, March 15, 2002, http://articles.latimes.com/2002/mar/15/news/mn-32955 (accessed May 10, 2015).

45. Ibid.

46. Ibid.

47. Ibid.

48. Clive Williams, "Pilot Suicide Cases Few and Far Between," *Sydney Morning Herald*, April 8, 2014, http://www.smh.com.au/it-pro/pilot-suicide-cases-few-and-far-between-20140408-zqs8w.html (accessed May 10, 2015).

49. "Moroccan Pilot's Failed Love Affair Blamed for Crash," *Los Angeles Times*, April 26, 1994, http://articles.latimes.com/1994-08-26/news/mn-31366_1_love-affair (accessed May 10, 2015).

50. Richard C. Paddock, "A Jet Crash That Defies Resolution," *Los Angeles Times*, September 5, 2001, http://articles.latimes.com/2001/sep/05/news/ mn-42336 (accessed May 10, 2015).

51. While my data set is composed of 111 gun massacres, the perpetrators

of three of these attacks remain undetermined. Therefore, all data in this section is limited to the 108 gun massacres in which the perpetrators were known to authorities.

52. While beyond the scope of this study, it is well-established that a primary reason why men are generally more violent than women has to do with hormones; testosterone, in particular. For a sampling of studies examining the relationship between testosterone and aggression, see Allen Mazur and Theodore A. Lamb, "Testosterone, Status, and Mood in Human Males," *Hormones and Behavior* 14 (September 1980), pp. 236–46; Alan Booth et al., "Testosterone, and Winning and Losing in Human Competition," *Hormones and Behavior* 23 (December 1989): 556–71; Brian A. Gladue, Michael Boechler, and Kevin D. McCaul, "Hormonal Response to Competition in Human Males," *Aggressive Behavior* 15 (November– December 1989): 409–22; John Archer, "The Influence of Testosterone on Human Aggression," *British Journal of Psychology* 82 (February 1991): 1–28; and Dov Cohen et al., "Insult, Aggression, and the Southern Culture of Honor: An 'Experimental Ethnography,'" *Journal of Personality and Social Psychology* 70 (May 1996): 945–60.

53. A prominent example of a senior-citizen active-shooter situation was seventy-three-year-old Frazier Glenn Miller's hate-inspired gun attack at a Jewish Community Center and a nearby Jewish retirement community in Overland Park, Kansas, in 2014. The fatal assault left three people dead, missing the four-victim definitional bar of a mass shooting. Had Miller encountered a fourth potential victim before being apprehended, there is every reason to believe he would have shot that person as well, given his statements regarding the murders. For more on the shooting, see Rick Jervis, "Shootings at Jewish Centers in Kansas Leave 3 Dead," *USA Today*, April 14, 2014, http://www.usatoday.com/story/news/ nation/2014/04/13/suburban-kansas-city-shooting/7674747/ (accessed May 14, 2015); and Judy L. Thomas, "F. Glenn Miller Jr. Talks for the First Time about the Killings at Jewish Centers," *Kansas City Star*, November 15, 2014, http://www .kansascity.com/news/local/crime/article3955528.html (accessed May 14, 2015). Another well-known instance was eighty-nine-year-old James von Brunn's gun attack at the United States Holocaust Memorial Museum in Washington, DC, in 2009. Von Brunn entered the museum and opened fire on a security guard, killing him. Two other security guards were able to return fire, striking von Brunn before he could get off additional rounds. (Von Brunn ultimately died in prison while awaiting trial.) For more on the shooting, see Michael E. Ruane, Paul Duggan, and Clarence Williams, "At a Monument of Sorrow, a Burst of Deadly Violence," *Washington Post*, June 11, 2009, http://www.washingtonpost.com/wp-dyn/content/ article/2009/06/10/AR2009061001768.html (accessed May 14, 2015); and Del Quentin Wilber, "Von Brunn, White Supremacist Holocaust Museum Shooter,

Dies," *Washington Post*, January 7, 2010, http://www.washingtonpost.com/wp-dyn/content/article/2010/01/06/AR2010010604095.html (accessed May 14, 2015).

54. The reason why most high-fatality mass shooters are in their twenties, and why few are older than their fifties, might be related to testosterone levels in adult males. Testosterone peaks in many men during their twenties and then starts to decrease to the point that, by their sixties, most men have significantly lower testosterone levels. See, for example, Dominique Simon et al., "The Influence of Aging on Plasma Sex Hormones in Men: The Telecom Study," *American Journal of Epidemiology* 135 (April 1, 1992): 783–91.

55. See, for example, David J. Leonard, "The Unbearable Invisibility of White Masculinity: Innocence in the Age of White Male Mass Shootings," *Gawker*, January 12, 2013, http://gawker.com/5973485/the-unbearable-invisibility-of-white-masculinity-innocence-in-the-age-of-white-male-mass-shootings (accessed May 14, 2015); Tiffany Xie, "Mass Shooters Have a Gender and Race: A Closer Look at White Male Privilege," Political Research Associates, June 19, 2014, http://www.politicalresearch.org/2014/06/19/mass-shooters-have-a-gender-and-a-race/ (accessed May 14, 2015); and Josiah M. Hesse, "Why Are So Many Mass Shootings Committed by Young White Men?" *Vice*, June 23, 2015, http://www.vice.com/read/why-are-so-many-mass-shootings-committed-by-young-white-men-623 (accessed June 27, 2015).

56. The seventy-four people categorized as white includes three shooters of Middle Eastern and North African descent. Currently, the US Census Bureau treats people of Middle Eastern and North African descent as Caucasians. This may nevertheless change in the 2020 census. Jeff Karoub, "Census Bureau May Count Arab-Americans for the First Time in 2020," PBS *News Hour*, January 30, 2015, http://www.pbs.org/newshour/rundown/census-bureau-considering-new-category-arab-americans-2020-count/ (accessed May 14, 2015). Hispanics are also categorized across racial groups. However, the federal government regularly provides demographic data that separate out Hispanics, and as such I have treated them as a separate group for purposes of my study. For more information, see Karen R. Humes, Nicholas A. Jones, and Roberto R. Ramirez, *Overview of Race and Hispanic Origin: 2010* (Washington, DC: US Census Bureau, March 2011), http://www.census.gov/prod/cen2010/briefs/c2010br-02.pdf (accessed May 14, 2015).

57. Consistent with the practices of the US Census Bureau, the racial category for Asians includes individuals of Pacific Island descent, and the racial category for Native Americans includes individuals of Native Alaskan descent. See US Census Bureau, "Explanation of Race and Hispanic Origin Categories," September 15, 1999, http://www.census.gov/population/estimates/rho.txt (accessed May 14, 2015).

58. Quoted in Sari Horwitz et al., "What We Know So Far about Charleston Church Shooting Suspect Dylann Roof," *Washington Post*, June 20, 2015, http://www

.washingtonpost.com/news/post-nation/wp/2015/06/20/what-we-know-so-far-about
-charleston-church-shooting-suspect-dylann-roof/ (accessed June 27, 2015).

59. Quoted in Erik Ortiz F. Brinley Bruton, "Charleston Church Shooting: Suspect Dylann Roof Captured in North Carolina," NBC News, June 18, 2015, http://www.nbcnews.com/storyline/charleston-church-shooting/charleston-church-shooting
-suspect-dylann-roof-captured-north-carolina-n377546 (accessed June 27, 2015).

60. Matthew Lysiak, "Charleston Massacre: Mental Illness Common Thread for Mass Shootings," *Newsweek*, June 19, 2015, http://www.newsweek.com/charleston-massacre-mental-illness-common-thread-mass-shootings-344789 (accessed June 27, 2015).

61. Keith Ablow, "Charleston: Why Didn't Anyone Help Dylann Roof?" Fox News, June 22, 2015, http://www.foxnews.com/opinion/2015/06/22/charleston
-why-didnt-anyone-help-dylann-roof.html (accessed June 27, 2015).

62. Arthur Chu, "It's Not about Mental Illness: The Big Lie That Always Follows Mass Shootings by White Males," *Slate*, June 19, 2015, http://www.salon
.com/2015/06/18/its_not_about_mental_illness_the_big_lie_that_always_follows
_mass_shootings_by_white_males/?utm_source=facebook&utm_medium
=socialflow (accessed June 27, 2015).

63. See, for example, German Lopez, "Everybody Blames Mental Illness for Mass Shootings. But What If That's Wrong?" *Vox*, June 23, 2015, http://www.vox.com/2015/6/23/8833529/mental-illness-mass-shootings (accessed June 27, 2015); and David Crary, "Mental Health Experts Respond Carefully to Mass Killings," Associated Press, June 27, 2015, http://bigstory.ap.org/article/e60b31a60d4d453bab1ddd6e7af9f3a0/mental-health-experts-respond-carefully
-mass-killings (accessed June 27, 2015).

64. Julia Craven, "Racism Is Not a Mental Illness," *Huffington Post*, June 22, 2015, http://www.huffingtonpost.com/2015/06/18/charleston-shooting-mental
-health_n_7616460.html (accessed June 27, 2015).

65. See, for example, Jonathan M. Metzl, "Why Are the Mentally Ill Still Bearing Arms?" *Lancet*, June 25, 2011, http://www.thelancet.com/journals/lancet/article/PIIS0140-6736(11)60950-1/fulltext (accessed June 27, 2015); James L. Knoll, IV, "Mass Shootings: Research and Lessons," *Psychiatric Times* 30 (February 2013): 7; Aaron Levin, "Capitol Hill Gets Straight Story on Gun Violence, Mental Illness," *Psychiatric News*, March 1, 2013, http://psychnews.psychiatryonline.org/doi/10.1176/appi.pn.2013.3a5 (accessed June 27, 2015); and Dennis Grantham, "Mass Shootings, Criminal Violence: Cant' Be Predicted, But Can Be Mitigated," *Behavioral Healthcare* 33, no. 3 (May/June 2013): 46–48, http://csgjusticecenter
.org/mental-health/media-clips/mass-shootings-criminal-violence-cant-be
-predicted-but-can-be-mitigated/ (accessed June 27, 2015).

66. Jonathan M. Metzl and Kenneth T. MacLeish, "Mental Illness, Mass Shootings, and the Politics of American Firearms," *American Journal of Public Health* 105, no. 2 (February 2015), p. 241.

67. Sarah L. Desmarais et al., "Community Violence Perpetration and Victimization among Adults with Mental Illnesses," *American Journal of Public Health* 104 (December 2014): 2342–49.

68. Metzl and MacLeish, p. 242.

69. See, for example, Peter Langman, "Rampage School Shooters: A Typology," *Aggression and Violent Behavior* 14 (January/February 2009): 79–86; Peter Langman, *Why Kids Kill: Inside the Minds of School Shooters* (New York: St. Martin's Griffin, 2010); James L. Knoll IV, "The 'Pseudocommando' Mass Murderer: Part I, the Psychology of Revenge and Obliteration," *Journal of the American Academy of Psychiatry and the Law* 38 (March 2010): 87–94; James L. Knoll IV, "The 'Pseudocommando' Mass Murderer: Part II, The Language of Revenge," *Journal of the American Academy of Psychiatry and the Law* 38 (June 2010): 263–72; James L. Knoll IV, "Mass Murder: Causes, Classification, and Prevention," *Psychiatric Clinics of North America* 35 (December 2012): 757–80; and Donald G. Dutton, Katherine R. White, and Dan Fogarty, "Paranoid Thinking in Mass Shooters," *Aggression and Violent Behavior* 18 (September/October 2013): 548–53. For a few examples that draw from less prominent case studies, see Paul E. Mullen, "The Autogenic (Self-Generated) Massacre," *Behavioral Sciences and the Law* 22 (May/June 2004): 311–23; and W. Walter Menninger, "Uncontained Rage: A Psychoanalytic Perspective on Violence," *Bulletin of the Menninger Clinic* 71 (Spring 2007): 115–31.

70. Because mental health professionals are often unable to interview and examine violent criminals, especially those who die during the commission of their acts, the best alternative for assessing offenders' mental states is to draw on observations made by family, friends, and acquaintances, and perform what is known as a "distance diagnosis." For more on this practice, see Amy L. Saborsky and Katherine Ramsland, "Distance Diagnosis: Can We Really Tell Whether Dahmer Had Asperger's Disorder?" *Forensic Examiner* 22 (Summer 2013): 42–48.

71. Suicidal behavior is considered a mental disorder by the medical community. See, for example, David J. Kupfer, "DSM-5's New Approach to Suicide Risk, Behavior," *Huffington Post*, October 10, 2013, http://www.huffingtonpost.com/david-j-kupfer-md/dsm-5-suicide_b_3731260.html (accessed May 22, 2015).

72. Alcohol and substance abuse are considered Axis I mental disorders by the medical community. See, for example, John M. Grohol, "DSM Diagnostic Codes for Mental Disorders," Psych Central, October 9, 2013, http://psychcentral.com/disorders/dsmcodes.htm (accessed May 22, 2015).

73. While my data set consists of 111 gun massacres, the perpetrators of three

of the attacks remain undetermined. Therefore, my examination of perpetrators is limited to the 108 gun massacres where authorities have publicly identified the perpetrators. In 102 of these 108 shootings, I was able to document some evidence of mental illness (including serious substance abuse problems); thus, 94 percent. It's possible that the remaining six gun massacres also involved gunmen with mental illness. However, my search of news reports and documents related to these six attacks failed to uncover any evidence that would support such a conclusion. The six cases from table 3.2 are the gun massacres dated May 2, 1981; February 17, 1982; February 5, 1987; September 25, 1987; January 26, 1991; and January 15, 2003.

74. See, for example, Jarvis DeBarry, "New Orleans Crimes and Murders Leave Us at a Loss for Words," *Times–Picayune*, May 21, 2013, http://www.nola .com/opinions/index.ssf/2013/05/murders_in_new_orleans_leave_u.html (accessed May 22, 2015). There have been numerous studies suggesting that most gang members suffer from some degree of mental illness. In particular, there is evidence that antisocial personality disorder is prevalent among gang members, as is anxiety disorder and substance abuse. To a lesser degree, one study found that a quarter of its sample screened positive for psychosis. Interestingly, the number of gang members who suffered from depression was below the societal average, making it a mental disorder relatively uncommon among gang members. For more on this, see Jeremy W. Cold et al., "Gang Membership, Violence, and Psychiatric Morbidity," *American Journal of Psychiatry* 170 (September 2013): 985–93. See also Vincent Egan and Matthew Beadman, "Personality and Gang Embeddedness," *Personality and Individual Differences* 51 (October 2011): 748–53.

75. John Caniglia, "Copley Shooter Michael Hance Was Eccentric, But also Helpful to Neighbors in Akron," *Plain-Dealer*, August 9, 2011, http://blog .cleveland.com/metro/2011/08/shooter_described_as_eccentric.html (accessed September 20, 2014).

76. Tim McGirk, "Hasan's Therapy: Could 'Secondary Trauma' Have Driven Him to Shooting?" *Time*, November 7, 2009, http://content.time.com/time/ nation/article/0,8599,1936407,00.html (accessed November 14, 2014). See also "Troubling Portrait Emerges of Shooting Suspect," NBC News, November 5, 2009, http://www.nbcnews.com/id/33695256/ns/us_news-tragedy_at_fort_hood/t/ troubling-portrait-emerges-shooting-suspect/ (accessed November 14, 2014); Daniel Zwerdling, "Walter Reed Officials Asked: Was Hasan Psychotic?" National Public Radio, November 11, 2011, http://www.npr.org/templates/story/story .php?storyId=120313570 (accessed November 14, 2014); and Manny Fernandez, "Fort Hood Gunman Told Panel That Death Would Make Him a Martyr," *New York Times*, August 12, 2013, http://www.nytimes.com/2013/08/13/us/fort-hood -gunman-told-panel-that-death-would-make-him-a-martyr.html (accessed November

14, 2014). On January 13, 2011, the Sanity Board impaneled to assess Nidal Hasan's competence for purposes of his court-martial produced a report for the court. Excerpts of that report were leaked to the press. Those excerpts can be found at https://s3.amazonaws.com/s3.documentcloud.org/documents/750594/hasan-document.pdf (accessed November 14, 2014).

77. "The Fall of the House of Tsarnaev," *Boston Globe*, December 15, 2013, http://www.bostonglobe.com/Page/Boston/2011-2020/WebGraphics/Metro/BostonGlobe.com/2013/12/15tsarnaev/tsarnaev.html (accessed October 21, 2014); and Sayle, "Confucius in the Cockpit," p. 12.

78. Jay Richards, "How Many Victims to Come, How Many Himizu's to Surface? A Clinical Understanding of Dylann Roof's Role in the Emanuel Church Massacre" *Psychology Today*, June 24, 2015, https://www.psychologytoday.com/blog/the-violent-mind/201506/how-many-victims-come-how-many-himizus-surface (accessed June 27, 2014). See also, Kylie Cheung, "The Differences between Sociopaths & Psychopaths Might Not Be Immediately Clear—But There Are Crucial Distinctions," *Bustle*, July 6, 2015, http://www.bustle.com/articles/94802-the-differences-between-sociopaths-psychopaths-might-not-be-immediately-clear-but-there-are-crucial (accessed July 7, 2015).

79. Ken Duckworth, "Mental Illness: Facts and Numbers," National Alliance on Mental Illness, March 2013, http://www2.nami.org/factsheets/mentalillness_factsheet.pdf (accessed May 22, 2015).

80. National Institute of Mental Health, "Serious Mental Illness (SMI) among U.S. Adults," National Institute of Mental Health, n.d., http://www.nimh.nih.gov/health/statistics/prevalence/serious-mental-illness-smi-among-us-adults.shtml (accessed May 22, 2015).

81. Centers for Disease Control and Prevention, "Mental Illness Surveillance among Adults in the United States," Centers for Disease Control and Prevention, December 2, 2011, http://www.cdc.gov/mentalhealthsurveillance/fact_sheet.html (accessed May 22, 2015).

82. How mental illness clouds the judgment of mass shooters and which specific disorders tend to be associated with mass violence are two topics that are beyond the scope of my book. However, as more funding becomes available to study mass violence, especially mass shootings, these two topics will hopefully become the subjects of further investigation.

83. Leonard Berkowitz, "Is Criminal Violence Normative Behavior? Hostile and Instrumental Aggression in Violent Incidents," *Journal of Research in Crime and Delinquency* 15 (July 1978): 151.

84. Ibid., pp. 148–49.

85. Ibid., p. 158.

86. Ibid.

87. Ibid., p. 159. Berkowitz added, "Their goal was to hurt, and whatever injury they inflicted was the immediate reinforcement that maintained their aggressiveness."

88. For a review of this literature, see Roy F. Baumeister, Laura Smart, and Joseph M. Boden, "Relation of Threatened Egotism to Violence and Aggression: The Dark Side of High Self-Esteem," *Psychological Review* 103 (January 1996): 6–7; and Michael K. Ostrowsky, "Are Violent People More Likely to Have Low Self-Esteem or High Self-Esteem?" *Aggression and Violent Behavior* 15 (January 2010): 70–71.

89. Baumeister, Smart, and Boden, "Relation of Threatened Egotism to Violence and Aggression," p. 7.

90. Ibid., pp. 7–9.

91. Michael H. Kernis, Bruce D. Grannemann, and Lynda C. Barclay, "Stability and Level of Self-Esteem as Predictors of Anger Arousal and Hostility," *Journal of Personality and Social Psychology* 56 (June 1989): 1013–22. See also Michael H. Kernis, "Measuring Self-Esteem in Context: The Importance of Stability of Self-Esteem in Psychological Functioning," *Journal of Personality* 73 (December 2005): 1569–1605.

92. Baumeister, Smart, and Boden, "Relation of Threatened Egotism to Violence and Aggression," p. 12.

93. Ibid., p. 8.

94. The original experiment is reported in Brad J. Bushman and Roy F. Baumeister, "Threatened Egotism, Narcissism, Self-Esteem, and Direct and Displaced Aggression: Does Self-Love or Self-Hate Lead to Violence?" *Journal of Personality and Social Psychology* 75 (July 1998): 219–29. The experiment was replicated and improved upon (in particular properly assessing the nexus between self-esteem and aggression) in a follow-up study. The second set of results is reported in Brad J. Bushman et al., "Looking Again, and Harder, for a Link between Low Self-Esteem and Aggression," *Journal of Personality* 77 (April 2009): 427–46. In the words of Baumeister, Smart, and Boden, "violence is perpetrated by a small subset of people with favorable views of themselves." Baumeister, Smart, and Boden, "Relation of Threatened Egotism to Violence and Aggression," p. 26.

95. Bushman and Baumeister, "Threatened Egotism, Narcissism, Self-Esteem, and Direct and Displaced Aggression," p. 222.

96. Bushman and his colleagues also examined the role that narcissism plays in contributing to aggression. What they found is that when combined with high self-esteem, narcissism can correlate with aggression. But narcissism, on its own, did not necessarily fuel aggression. The mediating factor was the level of self-esteem. If it was not high, narcissism's impact was insignificant: "The covert or low-self-

esteem variety of narcissism appears not to foster aggressive responding. In contrast, narcissists with high self-esteem, which is to say the so-called overt narcissists, appear to be exceptionally aggressive when criticized." Bushman et al., "Looking Again, and Harder, for a Link between Low Self-Esteem and Aggression," p. 444.

97. Other studies, using similar experiments, have confirmed an analogous, albeit not identical, pattern, wherein high levels of narcissism correlate with aggression. See, for example, Tanja S. Stucke and Siegfried L. Sporer, "When a Grandiose Self-Image Is Threatened: Narcissism and Self-Concept Clarity as Predictors of Negative Self-Emotions and Aggression Following Ego-Threat," *Journal of Personality* 70 (August 2002): 509–32; and Jean M. Twenge and W. Keith Campbell, "'Isn't It Fun to Get the Respect That We're Going to Deserve?' Narcissism, Social Rejection, and Aggression," *Personality and Social Psychology Bulletin* 29 (February 2003): 261–72. Again, it is important to emphasize that Bushman and his colleagues were able to further tease out this relationship and uncovered that it is the combination of narcissism with high self-esteem (as opposed to narcissism coupled with low self-esteem) that seems to be driving force behind aggression in these instances of response to ego threat.

98. In their explication of this theory, Baumeister, Smart, and Boden concluded:

> Aggressors seem to believe that they are superior, capable beings. Signs of low self-esteem, such as self-deprecation, humility, modesty, and self-effacing mannerisms, seem to be rare (underrepresented) among violent criminals and other aggressors. The typical, self-defining statements by both groups and individuals who aggress indicate a belief in their superiority, not inferiority. Violent and criminal individuals have been repeatedly characterized as arrogant, confident, narcissistic, egotistical, assertive, proud, and the like. . . .
>
> In all spheres we examined, we found that violence emerged from threatened egotism, whether this was labeled as wounded pride, disrespect, verbal abuse, insults, anger manipulations, status inconsistency, or something else.

Baumeister, Smart, and Boden, "Relation of Threatened Egotism to Violence and Aggression," p. 26. One important factor to keep in mind is that this dynamic applies to mass shooters who seem to be acting in support of a group to which they belong. Therefore, gang members like the Scott brothers and terrorists like Nidal Hasan are acting in response to an ego threat as well. However, in cases involving groups, the individual's identity is directly tied to a group's identity. A threat to the group with which a person identifies passionately (or zealously) can be readily internalized as a direct ego threat to that individual. For more on how this plays out with regard to groups, see ibid., pp. 21–26.

99. While the 111 gun massacres in my data set are the result of 111 unique motives, I will analyze the attacks by category in chapter 5, which examines the targets and locations.

100. For a sampling of studies that have confirmed the existence of what is commonly known as "the weapons effect," see Leonard Berkowitz and Anthony Lepage, "Weapons as Aggression-Eliciting Stimuli," *Journal of Personality and Social Psychology* 7 (October 1967): 202–207; Craig A. Anderson, Arlin J. Benjamin Jr., and Bruce D. Bartholow, "Does the Gun Pull the Trigger? Automatic Priming Effects of Weapon Pictures and Weapon Names," *Psychological Science* 9 (July 1998): 308–14; and Bruce D. Bartholow et al., Interactive Effects of Life Experience and Situational Cues on Aggression: The Weapons Priming Effect in Hunters and Non-Hunters," *Journal of Experimental Social Psychology* 41 (January 2005): 48–60.

101. In a seminal study dating back to the late 1960s in the service of the National Commission on the Causes and Prevention of Violence, Donald Newman interviewed violent criminals who used guns while perpetrating their offenses. He found that "the gun to these men is many things. It can in a single individual play a variety of roles and have a variety of meanings. To some it was a source of omnipotent power, while to others it was an equalizer." He went on to conclude, "The gun puts distance between the victim and the assailant. It exaggerates conflict and escalates violence. It is both a source of fear and fascination, and for some it takes on a magical quality." Donald E. Newman, "Firearms and Violent Crime: Conversations with Protagonists," in George D. Newton Jr. and Franklin E. Zimring, eds., *Firearms and Violence in American Life* (Washington, DC: GPO, 1969), p. 194. Psychoanalyzing the impact of guns on men, W. Walter Menninger argues, "On its face, the gun is an instrument of power and aggression. . . . Literally and figuratively, the gun symbolizes masculine power, with a striking parallel to the male sex organ; it is an eternally erect phallus that can achieve great pleasure through an explosively powerful projection. . . ." W. Walter Menninger, "Uncontained Rage: A Psychoanalytic Perspective on Violence," *Bulletin of the Menninger Clinic* 71 (Spring 2007): 127.

102. Michael C. Monuteaux et al., "Firearm Ownership and Violent Crime in the U.S.: An Ecologic Study," *American Journal of Preventive Medicine* 49 (August 2015): 210.

103. Anderson, Benjamin, and Bartholow, "Does the Gun Pull the Trigger?" p. 308.

104. Jennifer Klinesmith, Tim Kasser, and Francis T. McAndrew, "Guns, Testosterone, and Aggression: An Experimental Test of a Mediational Hypothesis," *Psychological Science* 17 (2006): 568–71.

105. Ibid.

106. Ibid., p. 570.

107. For excerpts of Holmes's statements to the court-appointed psychiatrist pertaining specifically to the impact of his weapons on his planning, see Noelle Phillips, "Aurora Theater Shooting Trial, the Latest from Day 21," *Denver Post*, May 29, 2015, http://www.denverpost.com/theater-shooting-trial/ci_28213308/aurora -theater-shooting-trial-latest-from-day-21 (accessed August 29, 2015); and Jordan Steffen, "Aurora Theater Shooting Trial, the Latest from Day 25," *Denver Post*, June 4, 2015, http://www.denverpost.com/theater-shooting-trial/ci_28250708/aurora -theater-shooting-trial-latest-from-day-25 (accessed August 29, 2015).

108. Ibid.

109. Ibid.

110. For more on the Aurora theater massacre, see chapter 6.

111. As more and more scholars study mass violence, perhaps they will be able to come up with novel approaches for better testing this framework in a more systematic fashion.

112. Just a reminder: while the mean as well as median age of high-fatality mass shooters was thirty-three, most shooters were in their twenties.

113. See, for example, Emanuel Tanay, "Virginia Tech Mass Murder: A Forensic Psychiatrist's Perspective," *Journal of the American Academy of Psychiatry and the Law* 35 (2007): 152; Langman, "Rampage School Shooters," p. 83; and Dutton, White, and Fogarty, "Paranoid Thinking in Mass Shooters," pp. 549–50.

114. Virginia Tech Review Panel, *Mass Shootings at Virginia Tech*, pp. N3–N5.

115. "Seung Hui Cho's 'Manifesto.'"

116. Ibid.

117. Ibid.

118. Ibid.

119. Baumeister, Smart, and Boden, "Relation of Threatened Egotism to Violence and Aggression," p. 11. Baumeister and his colleagues add, "aggression can be regarded as a crude technique of affect regulation." Ibid., p. 10.

120. Ibid., p. 11.

121. Dave Cullen, *Columbine* (New York: Twelve, 2010).

122. Virginia Tech Review Panel, *Mass Shootings at Virginia Tech*, p. 37.

123. Ibid., p. 42.

124. "Transcript of Omar Thornton's 911 Call," *Hartford Courant*, August 5, 2010, http://articles.courant.com/2010-08-05/community/hc-connecticut -shooting-911-call-tran20100805_1_dispatcher-yeah-treat (accessed June 2, 2015).

125. Explaining this phenomenon further, psychologists have noted that "once a person becomes familiar with the emotional distress of losing self-esteem, he or

she may become watchful for potential or incipient threats and may react strongly to what observers would regard as slight or trivial offenses." Baumeister, Smart, and Boden, "Relation of Threatened Egotism to Violence and Aggression," p. 11. This seems to match up with Omar Thornton's gun rampage. After the shooting, the police investigated Thornton's allegations of severe mistreatment and found no evidence to support his claims. "Police Rebut Killer's Claim of Bias on Job," *New York Times*, May 12, 2011, http://www.nytimes.com/2011/05/13/nyregion/worker-who-killed-8-in-2010-was-not-bias-victim-police-say.html (accessed June 2, 2015).

126. See, for example, Jim Nolan, "The Outcasts Crazed Butchers Wanted Spotlight Teen Gunmen Constantly Searched for Identity," *Philadelphia Daily News*, April 22, 1999, p. 5; and Peter Wilkinson with Matt Hendrickson, "Before Columbine, Humiliation and Hate: The Chilling Story of Two Young Rebels, Reb and VoDkA," *National Post*, June 5, 1999, p. B1.

127. "Movies Related to Columbine," Cult of Columbine, January 30, 2014, http://cultofcolumbine.tumblr.com/post/74998723153/movies-related-to-columbine-the-full-list of (accessed June 2, 2015).

128. "Video Games Related to Columbine," Cult of Columbine, February 2, 2014, http://cultofcolumbine.tumblr.com/post/75340934832/video-games-related-to-columbine-the-full-list (accessed June 2, 2015).

129. In September 2013, Fox News published a four-part series on its website that reviewed some of the arguments that linked violent entertainment with mass violence. See Mike Jaccarino, "'Training Simulation': Mass Killers Often Share Obsession with Violent Video Games," Fox News, September 12, 2013, http://www.foxnews.com/tech/2013/09/12/training-simulation-mass-killers-often-share-obsession-with-violent-video-games/ (accessed June 2, 2015); Mike Jaccarino, "'Frag Him': Video Games Ratchet Up Violence, Blur Line between Fantasy and Reality," Fox News, September 12, 2013, http://www.foxnews.com/tech/2013/09/13/with-today-ultraviolent-video-games-how-real-is-too-real/ (accessed June 2, 2015); John Brandon, "'Watch This': How Ultraviolent Video Games and Ultraviolent Films Differ," Fox News, September 14, 2013, http://www.foxnews.com/tech/2013/09/14/ultraviolent-video-games-different-ultraviolent-films/ (accessed June 2, 2015); and Adam Shaw, "Has 'Grand Theft Auto V' Grown Up?" Fox News, September 16, 2013, http://www.foxnews.com/tech/2013/09/16/has-grand-theft-auto-grown-up/ (accessed June 2, 2015).

130. Glenn Beck, *Control: Exposing the Truth about Guns* (New York: Threshold Editions / Mercury Radio Arts, 2013), p. 134.

131. In addition to the unsupported claims that *Natural Born Killers* fueled the Columbine killers' attack on their high school and that *Oldboy* drove Seung Hui Cho to commit the Virginia Tech massacre, another popular claim asserts

that James Holmes's murderous rampage at a movie theater in Aurora, Colorado, in 2012 was the by-product of two movies: *Batman: The Dark Night Rises* and *The Suffocator of Sins*. See, for example, Corky Siemaszko, "Aurora Massacre Suspect James Holmes May Have Been Inspired by Darker and More Twisted Take on the Batman Story," *New York Daily News*, August 2, 2012, http://www.nydailynews.com/news/national/aurora-massacre-suspect-james-holmes-inspired-darker-twisted-batman-story-article-1.1127531 (accessed June 2, 2015); and Stephen Singular and Joyce Singular, *The Spiral Notebook: The Aurora Theater Shooter and the Epidemic of Mass Violence Committed by American Youth* (Berkeley, CA: Counterpoint, 2015).

132. Another expectation might be that we should see violent movie makers and video game designers over-represented among those who commit heinous crimes. But to the best of my knowledge, there is little indication that those who create violent entertainment allow their realities to imitate their art.

133. Christopher J. Ferguson, Mark Coulson, and Jane Barnett, "Psychological Profiles of School Shooters: Positive Directions and One Big Wrong Turn," *Journal of Police Crisis Negotiations* 11 (2011): 145–46.

134. Ibid., p. 148. Christopher J. Ferguson has written extensively on the topic of violent entertainment and criminal violence, often as a contributor to *Time* magazine. For a sampling of his commentaries (which frequently review the current state of academic research on the topic), see "Video Games Don't Make Kids Violent," *Time*, December 7, 2011, http://ideas.time.com/2011/12/07/video-games-dont-make-kids-violent/ (accessed June 2, 2015); "Don't Link Video Games with Mass Shootings," *Time*, September 20, 2013, http://edition.cnn.com/2013/09/20/opinion/ferguson-video-games/index.html (accessed June 2, 2015); and "Parents, Relax: Movie Violence Up, Real Violence Down," *Time*, November 12, 2013, http://ideas.time.com/2013/11/12/parents-relax-movie-violence-up-real-violence-down/ (accessed June 2, 2015).

135. In an effort to shift blame away from the availability of guns and toward the prevalence of violent entertainment and virtual (online) communication, Beck asserts:

> Common sense tells us that maybe this isn't about the gun after all. Maybe it's about the person holding it.
>
> That means we have an issue with our society and with our families and our schools. We have issues with parenting and mentoring and bullying and the way we treat depression and anxiety. We have an issue with kids' finding pleasure and solace by playing video games in darkened bedrooms and basements instead of running around outside with friends. We have an issue with kids' spending hours on their phones and computers texting

and posting on Facebook instead of having real, personal connections and conversations with others. We have an issue with kids' having unfettered access to the worst the Internet has to offer instead of the best that our communities can provide.

We have a lot of new issues in America, but access to guns isn't one of them.

Beck, *Control,* p. 126.

136. Virginia Tech Review Panel, *Mass Shootings at Virginia Tech,* p. 51.

CHAPTER FIVE: NO PLACE IS SAFE

1. "Navy Yard Shooting: Remembering the Victims," *Washington Post,* September 17, 2013, http://www.washingtonpost.com/wp-srv/special/local/navy -yard-shooting-victims (accessed August 3, 2013).

2. Ibid.

3. Unless otherwise noted, all the information on the Washington Navy Yard massacre is drawn from District of Columbia Metropolitan Police Department, *After Action Report: Washington Navy Yard, September 16, 2013* (Washington, DC: Metropolitan Police Department, July 2014), http://mpdc.dc.gov/sites/default/ files/dc/sites/mpdc/publication/attachments/MPD%20AAR_Navy%20Yard _Posting_07-2014.pdf (accessed August 3, 2015).

4. Kevin Johnson, Donna Leinwand Leger, and Doug Stanglin, "Gunman Believed to Have Assembled Shotgun in Men's Room," *USA Today,* September 17, 2013, http://www.usatoday.com/story/news/nation/2013/09/17/navy-yard -shooting-aaron-alexis-washington/2824793 (accessed August 3, 2015).

5. The MPD *After Action Report* claims that Alexis initially tried to purchase an AR-15 at Sharpshooters gun store in Newington, Virginia, but he was denied an instant sale because he was a Texas resident. An investigation by the *Washington Post* found that Alexis did not actually attempt to buy an assault weapon. He did, however, test fire an AR-15 at the Sharpshooters range. Ultimately, he settled on the Remington 870 pump-action shotgun. It's possible that, if Alexis indeed wanted an AR-15, he was discouraged from making the purchase by the difference in price, given that an AR-15 would have cost about three times as much as the shotgun. See Tom Jackman, "Inside Sharpshooters, the Newington Gun Store Where Aaron Alexis Bought His Shotgun," *Washington Post,* September 18, 2013, https://www.washingtonpost.com/blogs/local/wp/2013/09/18/inside -sharpshooters-the-newington-gun-store-where-aaron-alexis-bought-his-shotgun (accessed August 3, 2015).

6. Alexis did manage to shoot one woman, Jennifer Bennett, whom he encountered in the stairwell. The woman, who was in a group of people trying to flee from a floor above where Alexis was shooting, was hit in the shoulder. With the assistance of her colleagues, she managed to get upstairs to the roof. From there, they dropped a note to the ground requesting medical assistance, which was spotted by a responding police officer. She was ultimately airlifted to safety by a US Park Police helicopter. For more on Bennett and her recovery, see DeNeen L. Brown, "'I'm a Warrior and Survivor,'" *Washington Post*, September 6, 2014, http:// www.washingtonpost.com/sf/local/2014/09/06/im-a-warrior-and-a-survivor (accessed August 3, 2015).

7. Jirus gave several interviews to media the day of the shooting. See, for example, Jennifer Bendery, "Navy Commander Describes 'Running for My Life' as Man Killed Next to Him," *Huffington Post*, September 16, 2013, http://www .huffingtonpost.com/2013/09/16/tim-jirus-navy-yard-shooting_n_3936426.html (accessed August 3, 2015); Dion Nissenbaum, "Navy Commander: Man Next to Me Was Shot in the Head," *Wall Street Journal*, September 16, 2013, http://blogs .wsj.com/washwire/2013/09/16/navy-commander-man-next-to-me-was-shot -in-head (accessed August 3, 2015); Michael D. Shear and Michael S. Schmidt, "Gunman and 12 Victims Killed in Shooting at D.C. Navy Yard," *New York Times*, September 16, 2013, http://www.nytimes.com/2013/09/17/us/shooting-reported -at-washington-navy-yard.html (accessed August 3, 2015); Bartholomew Sullivan, "Navy Yard Shooting: Navy Commander Tim Jirus Narrowly Escapes Death," KNXV, September 16, 2013, http://www.abc15.com/news/national/navy-yard -shooting-navy-commander-tim-jirus-narrowly-escapes-death (accessed August 3, 2015); and Alan Duke, "7 Victims from the Navy Yard Shooting Identified," CNN, September 17, 2013, http://www.cnn.com/2013/09/16/us/dc-navy-yard-victims (accessed August 3, 2015). That Proctor was the person shot and killed in the alley was confirmed a few days later. See Tom Ichniowski, "NAVFAC Supervisor, Contract Guard Are among Navy Yard Shooting Victims," *Engineering News-Record*, September 20, 2013, http://www.enr.com/articles/7637-navfac-supervisor-contract-guard-are -among-navy-yard-shooting-victims (accessed August 3, 2015).

8. Additional details on the shootout between Alexis and police are drawn from Peter Hermann, "Officer Who Shot Navy Yard Gunman Says It 'Needed to Be Done,'" *Washington Post*, September 14, 2014, https://www.washingtonpost .com/local/crime/officer-who-shot-navy-yard-gunman-says-it-needed-to-be -done/2014/09/14/5aeaf8f0-384e-11e4-8601-97ba88884ffd_story.html (accessed August 3, 2015).

9. Ibid.

10. Ibid.

11. Ibid.

12. Ibid.

13. *Piers Morgan Live* (CNN), transcript from show airing September 16, 2013, http://transcripts.cnn.com/TRANSCRIPTS/1309/16/pmt.01.html (accessed April 18, 2016).

14. Ibid.

15. Ibid.

16. Quoted in Courtland Milloy, "Self-Described 'Pastor for the Gun People' Braces for Blow Back after Navy Yard Rampage," *Washington Post*, September 17, 2013, https://www.washingtonpost.com/local/self-described-pastor-for-the-gun -people-bracing-for-blowback-after-mondays-rampage/2013/09/17/55870acc-1f48 -11e3-94a2-6c66b668ea55_story.html (accessed August 7, 2015).

17. Quoted in John Surico and Tamer El-Ghobashy, "Danger Seen in Gun Sales via Internet," *Wall Street Journal*, September 18, 2013, http://www.wsj.com/articles/ SB10001424127887323808204579083540940729158 (accessed August 7, 2015).

18. Tweet posted by @TedNugent, Twitter, September 16, 2013, https:// twitter.com/TedNugent/status/379748864787369985 (accessed August 7, 2015).

19. J. D. Tuccille, "Washington Navy Yard Already Suffers the Restrictions That Gun Control Advocates Favor," *Reason*, September 17, 2013, https://reason .com/blog/2013/09/17/navy-yard-already-suffered-the-restricti (accessed August 7, 2015).

20. A. W. R. Hawkins, "Piers Morgan Throws Tantrum: Navy Yard 'Is Not a Gun Free Zone,'" *Breitbart*, September 16, 2013, http://www.breitbart.com/big -journalism/2013/09/16/piers-morgan-throws-tantrum-navy-yard-is-not-a-gun-free -zone (accessed August 7, 2015).

21. Jim Treacher, "Why Is It That Mass Shootings Tend to Happen in the Places with the Strictest Gun Laws?" *Daily Caller*, September 16, 2013, http:// dailycaller.com/2013/09/16/why-is-it-that-mass-shootings-tend-to-happen-in -places-with-the-strictest-gun-laws (accessed August 7, 2015).

22. Steve Watson, "Navy Yard Shooting: Did Gun Free Zone Enable Killer?" *Infowars*, September 16, 2013, http://www.infowars.com/navy-yard-shooting-did -gun-free-zone-enable-killers (accessed August 7, 2015).

23. For a video clip of the news segment, see Matt Gertz, "Right-Wing Media Rush to Politicize Washington Navy Yard Shooting," *Media Matters for America*, September 16, 2013, http://mediamatters.org/blog/2013/09/16/right-wing -media-rush-to-politicize-washington/195892 (accessed August 7, 2015).

24. Gallup Poll, October 7–11, 2015, http://www.pollingreport.com/guns .htm (accessed November 15, 2015).

25. John R. Lott Jr., *More Guns, Less Crime: Understanding Crime and Gun Control*

Laws, 3rd ed. (Chicago: University of Chicago Press, 2010), p. 20. The book is now in its third edition, but each subsequent edition contains the text of earlier editions.

26. Lott wasn't entirely sure why these states initially experienced a bump in mass shootings, but he offered a possible theory: "Perhaps those planning such shootings do them sooner than they otherwise would have, before too many citizens acquire concealed-handgun permits." Ibid., pp. 105–106.

27. As Lott notes, "after passage of such [nondiscretionary concealed-handgun] laws, the mean per-capita death rate from mass shootings in those states plummets by 69 percent." Ibid., p. 105.

28. In all fairness, Lott said this relationship applied only to the period 1977–1992. His data set showed that, prior to 1977, the mean death and injury rates from mass shootings "were quite low but definitely not zero." Ibid., p. 106.

29. The law is codified at 18 USC § 921 and 18 USC § 921(q). For more on the law, see Carl W. Chamberlin, "Johnny Can't Read 'Cause Jane's Got a Gun: The Effect of Guns in Schools, and Options after *Lopez*," *Cornell Journal of Law and Public Policy* 8 (Winter 1999): 281–346.

30. Michael Doyle, "Rehnquist Able to Move Court's Center to Right," *Star-News*, September 5, 2005, p. 5. In 1995, the US Supreme Court, in *United States v. Lopez*, struck down the law as an unconstitutional exercise of the commerce clause of the US Constitution. In 1996, Congress enacted an amended version of the original act to apply only to a firearm that "has moved in or otherwise affects interstate commerce"—which is practically every gun in the United States. Seth J. Safra, "The Amended Gun-Free School Zones Act: Doubt as to Its Constitutionality Remains," *Duke Law Journal* 50 (November 2000): 637–62.

31. Lott, *More Guns, Less Crime*, p. 118; emphasis in original.

32. Ibid., p. 194.

33. Ibid., pp. 195–96. Lott added, "The estimates imply that the average state passing these [right-to-carry] laws reduces the total number of murders and injuries per year [from multiple-victim public shootings] from 1.91 to .42 and the number of shootings from .42 to .14." Ibid., p. 196. In subsequent articles on the relationship between the enactment of right-to-carry laws and multiple-victim public shootings, Lott revised his findings to state that the number of such attacks fell by 60 percent, as opposed to 67 percent. See John R. Lott Jr., "Why Gun Bans Still Don't Work," Fox News, September 29, 2010, http://www.foxnews.com/opinion/2010/09/29/gun-bans-dont-work.html (accessed August 10, 2015).

34. Ibid., p. 196–97. According to Lott, "The results for multiple-victim public shootings are consistent with the central findings of this book: as the probability that victims are going to be able to defend themselves increases, the level of deterrence increases." Ibid., p. 197.

35. Ibid.

36. Ibid., pp. 322–23.

37. Ibid., p. 324.

38. Ibid., p. 325.

39. John R. Lott Jr., "'Lone Wolf' Terror Attacks: We're Sitting Ducks and Americans with Guns Are Last Line of Defense," Fox News, October 30, 2014, http://www.foxnews.com/opinion/2014/10/30/lone-wolf-terror-attacks-were -sitting-ducks-and-americans-with-guns-are-last.html (accessed August 10, 2015).

40. Ibid. Using the Aurora theater massacre as an example, Lott adds, "Armed security guards at movie theaters are rare in low crime areas, such as Aurora, especially on less crowded weeknights. And, with an audience fleeing the theater, armed guards may have experienced difficulty getting quickly inside." John R. Lott Jr., "Did Colorado Shooter Single Out Cinemark Theater Because It Banned Guns?" Fox News, September 10, 2012, http://www.foxnews.com/ opinion/2012/09/10/did-colorado-shooter-single-out-cinemark-theater.html (accessed August 10, 2015).

41. John R. Lott Jr., "Gun-Free Zones an Easy Targets for Killers," Fox News, June 18, 2015, http://www.foxnews.com/opinion/2015/06/18/gun-free-zones -easy-target-for-killers.html (accessed August 10, 2015).

42. The quote is excerpted from Rodger's 141-page manifesto. It is quoted in John R. Lott Jr., "Memo to Gun-Control Advocates: Even Elliot Rodger Believed Guns Would Have Deterred Him," Fox News, May 28, 2014, http://www.foxnews .com/opinion/2014/05/28/memo-to-gun-control-advocates-even-elliot-rodger -believed-guns-would-have.html (accessed August 10, 2015).

43. In discussions with a court-appointed psychiatrist, James Holmes explained that the reason he chose the Century 16 cinema in Aurora was because it was far enough away from his neighborhood that his friends were unlikely to be there. The sessions with the psychiatrist were videotaped and played for the jury during Holmes's murder trial. The conversation pertaining to why he selected the Century 16 multiplex can be found in the *Denver Post*'s daily blog coverage of the trial. See Jordan Steffen, "Aurora Theater Shooting Trial, the Latest from Day 23," *Denver Post*, June 2, 2015, http://www.denverpost.com/theater-shooting-trial/ci_28234621/ aurora-theater-shooting-trial-latest-from-day-23 (accessed August 29, 2015).

44. Lott, "Did Colorado Shooter."

45. John R. Lott Jr., "Uber Driver in Chicago Stops Mass Public Shooting, Compiling Other Cases Where Concealed Handgun Permit Holders Have Stopped Mass Shootings," Crime Prevention Research Center, April 21, 2015, http:// crimeresearch.org/2015/04/uber-driver-in-chicago-stops-mass-public-shooting (accessed August 10, 2015).

46. Hunter Roosevelt, "12 Times Mass Shootings Were Stopped by Good Guys with Guns," *Controversial Times*, June 23, 2015, http://controversialtimes.com/ issues/constitutional-rights/12-times-mass-shootings-were-stopped-by-good-guys -with-guns (accessed August 10, 2015). See also Eugene Volokh, "Do Citizens (Not Police Officers) with Guns Ever Stop Mass Shootings?" *Washington Post*, October 3, 2015, https://www.washingtonpost.com/news/volokh-conspiracy/ wp/2015/10/03/do-civilians-with-guns-ever-stop-mass-shootings (accessed October 3, 2015).

47. Lott, "Why Gun Bans Still Don't Work"; and John R. Lott Jr., "After Fort Hood: Should Soldiers Be Allowed to Bear Arms on Base?" Fox News, April 9, 2014, http://www.foxnews.com/opinion/2014/04/09/after-fort-hood-should -soldiers-be-allowed-to-bear-arms-on-base.html (accessed August 10, 2015).

48. Lott, "Gun-Free Zones an Easy Targets for Killers."

49. Ibid.

50. See, for example, the discussions on CNN's *Dr. Drew* (June 18, 2015) and Fox News Channel's *The Kelly File* (June 19, 2015).

51. Quoted in Christopher Ingraham, "An NRA Board Member Blamed the Pastor Killed in Charleston for the Deaths of His Members," *Washington Post*, June 19, 2015, https://www.washingtonpost.com/news/wonk/wp/2015/06/19/an-nra -board-member-blamed-a-murdered-pastor-for-the-deaths-in-charleston-yes-really (accessed August 10, 2015).

52. Molly Jackson, "FBI Director Labels Chattanooga Shooting 'Terrorism.' Does It Matter?" *Christian Science Monitor*, December 16, 2015, http://www .csmonitor.com/USA/Justice/2015/1216/FBI-director-labels-Chattanooga -shooting-terrorism.-Does-it-matter (accessed April 20, 2016).

53. John R. Lott Jr., "Chattanooga Shootings: Why Should We Make It Easy for Killers to Attack Our Military?" Fox News, July 16, 2015, http://www.foxnews.com/ opinion/2015/07/16/chattanooga-shootings-why-should-make-it-easy-for-killers-to -attack-our-military.html (accessed August 10, 2015). See also John R. Lott Jr., "Gun -Free Zones Are Killing Us," Fox News, July 28, 2015, http://www.foxnews.com/ opinion/2015/07/28/gun-free-zones-are-killing-us.html (accessed August 10, 2015).

54. See, for example, the discussions on Fox News Channel's *The O'Reilly Factor* (July 16, 2015) and Fox News Channel's *The Kelly File* (July 17, 2015).

55. Cooper Allen, "Trump Slams 'Gun-Free Zones' in Chattanooga Shooting," *USA Today*, July 17, 2015, http://onpolitics.usatoday.com/2015/07/17/ chattanooga-trump-gun-free-zones (accessed August 10, 2015).

56. Eugene Scott and Ashley Killough, "Trump Calls for End of Gun-Free Zones in Wake of Chattanooga Shooting," CNN, July 17, 2015, http://www.cnn .com/2015/07/17/politics/2016-candidates-chattanooga-shooting (accessed

August 10, 2015); Alexis Levinson, "Ted Cruz: Chattanooga Shooting Shows Need for Immigration Overhaul, Arming Military on Bases," *National Review*, July 17, 2015, http://www.nationalreview.com/article/421325/cruz-says-chattannoga -shooting-illustrates-need-immigration-overhaul-arming-military (accessed August 10, 2015); Carly Fiorina, Facebook post of July 17, 2015, https://www.facebook .com/CarlyFiorina/posts/10156188756045206 (accessed August 10, 2015); Mike Huckabee, "Gun Free Zones Are Really Just Sitting Duck Zones for Radical Islamists," Fox News, July 17, 2015, http://www.foxnews.com/ opinion/2015/07/17/lets-be-honest-gun-free-zones-are-really-sitting-duck-zones -for-radical-islamists.html (accessed August 10, 2015); "Indiana, Florida, Texas, Arkansas, Oklahoma, Louisiana to Arm Guardsmen in the Wake of Chattanooga Shootings," *Chattanooga Times Free Press*, July 18, 2015, http://www.timesfreepress .com/news/local/story/2015/jul/18/states-move-protect-military-sites-wake -chattanooga-shootings/315294 (accessed August 10, 2015); David Weigel, "Rand Paul Readying Hill Push for Guns on Military Bases and Recruiting Stations," *Washington Post*, July 20, 2015, https://www.washingtonpost.com/news/post -politics/wp/2015/07/20/rand-paul-readying-hill-push-for-guns-on-military-bases -and-in-recruiting-stations (accessed August 10, 2015); Rachelle Blidner, "Gov. Scott Walker Issues Order to Arm Wisconsin National Guard after Chattanooga Shootings," *New York Daily News*, July 21, 2015, http://www.nydailynews.com/news/ national/gov-scott-walker-issues-order-arm-wisc-national-guard-article-1.2298791 (accessed August 10, 2015); Adam Edelman, "GOP Presidential Candidate Rick Perry: 'Gun-Free Zones Are a Bad Idea . . . Enforcement of Laws Is What Seems to Be Lacking,'" *New York Daily News*, July 27, 2015, http://www.nydailynews.com/ news/politics/gop-candidate-rick-perry-gun-free-zones-bad-idea-article-1.2304751 (accessed August 10, 2015).

57. See, for example, Eugene Scott, "GOP Candidates: Gun Laws Won't Stop 'Crazies,'" CNN, October 2, 2015, http://www.cnn.com/2015/10/02/politics/ huckabee-rubio-carson-republican-candidates-gun-laws (accessed October 3, 2015).

58. Of course, the contradiction between rhetoric and reality has not been lost on some commentators, who note that these proclamations have been made at campaign rallies that bar attendees from carrying arms. Bill Barrow and Jill Colvin, "Trump and Carson Mock Gun-Free Zones at Their Gun-Free Rallies," *Talking Points Memo*, December 10, 2015, http://talkingpointsmemo.com/news/gun-free -zones-trump-carson (accessed December 11, 2015).

59. "Donald Trump to Packed House in Knoxville: Guns Could Have Prevented Paris Attacks," WATE, November 16, 2015, http://wate.com/ 2015/11/10/trump-to-visit-knoxville-monday (accessed November 21, 2015).

60. John Lott has posted a copy of his curriculum vitae online, which lists

his education and some of his previous work experiences. It is available from his personal blog at http://johnrlott.tripod.com/Lott_CV_1-19-07.pdf (accessed August 14, 2015).

61. Jon Wiener, *Historians in Trouble: Plagiarism, Fraud, and Politics in the Ivory Tower* (New York: New Press, 2004), p. 136.

62. Evan DeFilippis and Devin Hughes, "Shooting Down the Gun Lobby's Favorite 'Academic': A Lott of Lies," *Armed with Reason*, December 1, 2014, http://www.armedwithreason.com/shooting-down-the-gun-lobbys-favorite-academic-a-lott-of-lies (accessed December 16, 2014).

63. Ibid.

64. See, for example, Dean Weingarten, "*More Guns, Less Crime* Author John Lott's Testimony on Campus Carry and Gun Free Zones," Truth about Guns, November 15, 2015, http://www.thetruthaboutguns.com/2015/11/dean-weingarten/john-lotts-testimony-on-campus-carry-and-gun-free-zones-video (accessed November 21, 2015).

65. See, for example, Gary Mauser and John R. Lott Jr., *Economists' Views on Guns: Crime, Suicides, and Right-to-Carry Concealed Handgun Laws,* Report of the Crime Prevention Research Center, February 2, 2015, http://crimeresearch.org/wp-content/uploads/2015/03/Survey-of-Economists_Final.pdf (accessed August 14, 2015).

66. John R. Lott Jr., "Women Can't Be Gun-Shy about Defense," Fox News, April 30, 2002, http://www.foxnews.com/story/2002/04/30/women-cant-be-gun-shy-about-defense.html (accessed August 14, 2015); and John R. Lott Jr., "Older People Need Guns, Too," Fox News, July 21, 2015, http://www.foxnews.com/opinion/2015/07/21/have-ever-thought-letting-someone-else-manage-your-finances.html (accessed August 14, 2015).

67. John Lott, "Stand Your Ground Makes Sense: These Are Sane Laws That Protect People," *New York Daily News*, April 25, 2012, http://www.nydailynews.com/opinion/stand-ground-sense-article-1.1066823 (accessed August 14, 2015).

68. DeFilippis and Hughes, "Shooting Down the Gun Lobby's Favorite 'Academic.'"

69. A search of the websites maintained by the NRA and Gun Owners of America will result in numerous references to John Lott and his work. Just to provide two examples, see National Rifle Association-Institute for Legal Action, "John Lott to Unveil New Book at NRA Annual Meeting," NRA-ILA, May 14, 2010, https://www.nraila.org/articles/20100514/john-lott-to-unveil-new-book-at-nra-ann (accessed August 14, 2015); and Larry Pratt, "The Bias against Guns," Gun Owners of America, September 2003, https://www.gunowners.org/op0347-htm.htm (accessed August 14, 2015).

70. Grover G. Norquist and John R. Lott Jr., *Debacle: Obama's War on Jobs and Growth and What We Can Do Now to Regain Our Future* (Hoboken, NJ: Wiley, 2012).

71. See Ted Nugent book jacket blurb endorsing John R. Lott Jr., *Straight Shooting: Firearms, Economics and Public Policy* (Buffalo, NY: Merril, 2010), http://www.amazon.com/Straight-Shooting-Firearms-Economics-Public/dp/0936783478/ref=la_B001ITPMDC_1_6?s=books&ie=UTF8&qid=1410011743&sr=1-6 (accessed August 14, 2015). For a list of the Crime Prevention Research Center's Board of Directors, see Crime Prevention Research Center, "About Us," Crime Prevention Research Center, n.d., http://crimeresearch.org/about-us (accessed August 14, 2015).

72. DeFilippis and Hughes, "Shooting Down the Gun Lobby's Favorite 'Academic.'"

73. Charles F. Wellford, John V. Pepper, and Carol V. Petrie, eds., *Firearms and Violence: A Critical Review*, Committee to Improve Research Information and Data on Firearms, Committee on Law and Justice, Division of Behavioral and Social Sciences and Education, National Research Council of the National Academies (Washington, DC: National Academies, 2005), pp. 120–51. One scholar on the panel of experts, James Q. Wilson, took issue with the committee's conclusion regarding Lott's research. Wilson's "Dissent" is available in ibid., pp. 269–71. The panel responded to the dissent; see "Committee Response to Wilson's Dissent," in ibid., pp. 272–75. The entire report is available at http://www.nap.edu/catalog/10881/firearms-and-violence-a-critical-review (accessed August 14, 2015).

74. Devin Hughes and Evan DeFilippis, "A Lott More Lies: Debating *More Guns, Less Crime*," *Armed with Reason*, December 31, 2014, http://www.armedwithreason.com/a-lott-more-lies-debating-more-guns-less-crime (accessed August 14, 2015).

75. The term "defensive gun use"—sometimes abbreviated as DGU—refers to the use of a firearm in either self-defense or the defense of others.

76. Tim Lambert, "Do More Guns Cause Less Crime?" unpublished paper, November 7, 2004, http://www.cse.unsw.edu.au/~lambert/guns/lott/lott.pdf (accessed August 14, 2015).

77. Quoted in James Lindgren, "Comments on Questions about John R. Lott's Claims Regarding a 1997 Survey," unpublished assessment, January 17, 2003, http://www.cse.unsw.edu.au/~lambert/guns/lindgren.html (accessed August 14, 2015).

78. Ibid.

79. Ibid.

80. DeFilippis and Hughes, "Shooting Down the Gun Lobby's Favorite 'Academic.'"

81. The quote is from an untitled post John Lott wrote on his blog in response to an article written by Michelle Malkin criticizing him; it is available at

http://johnrlott.tripod.com/malkinsoped.html (accessed August 14, 2015). The original article that this blog post responds to is Michelle Malkin, "The Other Lott Controversy," *Town Hall*, February 5, 2003, http://townhall.com/columnists/michellemalkin/2003/02/05/the_other_lott_controversy/page/full (accessed August 14, 2015).

82. DeFilippis and Hughes, "Shooting Down the Gun Lobby's Favorite 'Academic'"; emphasis in original.

83. Wiener, *Historians in Trouble*, p. 140.

84. In full disclosure, I am an alumnus of the University of Pennsylvania, and I even took courses in criminology and legal studies through the Wharton School. But I have never met Lott, as he arrived at the school after I had graduated.

85. The archive of online posts made by John Lott under the fake account of Mary Rosh are available in Tim Lambert, "Mary Rosh's Blog," *Science Blogs*, January 21, 2003, http://scienceblogs.com/deltoid/2003/01/21/maryrosh (accessed August 14, 2015).

86. Julian Sanchez, "The Mystery of Mary Rosh: How a New Form of Journalism Investigated a Gun Research Riddle," *Reason*, May 2003, https://reason.com/archives/2003/05/01/the-mystery-of-mary-rosh (accessed August 14, 2015).

87. John Lott's e-mail confession is reproduced in Kevin Drum, "John Lott Explains," *Washington Monthly*, January 22, 2003, http://www.washingtonmonthly.com/archives/individual/2003_01/000200.php (accessed August 14, 2015).

88. John R. Lott Jr., "Research Fraud, Public Policy, and Gun Control," *Science* 300 (June 6, 2003): 1505, reproduced at http://johnrlott.tripod.com/ScienceMagLetterResp.pdf (accessed August 14, 2015).

89. Donald Kennedy, "Research Fraud, Public Policy, and Gun Control: Response," *Science*, 300, June 6, 2003, p. 1505, reproduced at: http://johnrlott.tripod.com/ScienceMagLetterResp.pdf (accessed August 14, 2015).

90. The law applies to elementary and secondary schools. The law is codified at 18 USC § 921 and 18 USC § 921(q).

91. Lott, *More Guns, Less Crime*, pp. 227–34, 321–25, and 332–36.

92. Ibid., p. 322.

93. Lott, "Memo to Gun-Control Advocates."

94. Devin Hughes and Evan DeFilippis, who maintain the blog *Armed with Reason*, are also critical of Lott for "sloppily classif[ying] ENTIRE CITIES as gun-free zones because, it is difficult to get a concealed carry permit in those cities." Citing Lott's argument that all of Boston can be characterized as a gun-free zone, they argue, "There's no objectivity or precision. [Lott] conveniently ignores facts such as Boston being a commuter city that doesn't place restrictions on people traveling into Boston with concealed carry. We also know that there are an

estimated 250,000 people with concealed carry licenses in Massachusetts, so one wonders why Lott considers Boston a 'gun-free zone.'" Hughes and DeFilippis, "A Lott More Lies"; emphasis in original.

95. Lott, "After Fort Hood"; and Lott, "Chattanooga Shootings."

96. Pursuant to my definition, if an armed guard or school resource officer routinely makes rounds on a campus, then it is not a gun-free zone. Akin to the way Lott maintains that the possibility of an armed civilian being present is the distinguishing trait that determines whether or not a location is a gun-free zone (pursuant to his definition of the term), the possibility of an armed guard or school resource officer routinely being present suffices to disqualify a location as a gun-free zone (pursuant to my definition of the term).

97. Lott, *More Guns, Less Crime*, p. 105.

98. Lott, "Gun-Free Zones an Easy Targets for Killers."

99. Lott, "Uber Driver in Chicago Stops Mass Public Shooting."

100. Lott, "Gun-Free Zones Are Killing Us."

101. Grant Duwe, Tomislav Kovandzic, and Carlisle E. Moody, "The Impact of Right-to-Carry Concealed Firearm Laws and Mass Public Shootings," *Homicide Studies* 6 (November 2002): 293.

102. Since 1966, thirty-eight states have abandoned a may-issue system in favor of a shall-issue right-to-carry system. In the past fifty years, no state has switched from shall-issue to may-issue laws.

103. The data on the adoption of right-to-carry laws for all fifty states is drawn from the following three sources: David Yamane, "The History of Concealed Weapons Laws in the United States, Part 3: The Rise of the Shall-Issue (Right-to-Carry) Era of Concealed Carry," *Gun Culture 2.0*, June 19, 2014, https://gun culture2point0.wordpress.com/2014/06/19/the-history-of-concealed-weapons -laws-in-the-united-states-part-3-the-rise-of-the-shall-issue-right-to-carry-era-of -concealed-carry (accessed August 15, 2015); Larry Arnold, "The History of Concealed Carry, 1977–2011," Texas Concealed Handgun Association, February 24, 2015, http://www.txchia.org/history.htm (accessed August 15, 2015); and Jeff Dege, "Progress in Right-to-Carry," *Radical Gun Nuttery!*, 2015, http://www.gun -nuttery.com/rtc.php (accessed August 15, 2015).

104. Duwe and his colleagues limited their data set to public mass shootings that resulted in at least four homicide fatalities. My data set is limited to gun massacres resulting in six or more homicide fatalities.

105. Lott, *More Guns, Less Crime*, p. 103.

106. The breakdown of the data that informs Lott's discussion of mass shootings in *More Guns, Less Crime* is actually not available in the book. It is, however, available in an academic working paper that Lott coauthored. John R.

Lott Jr. and William M. Landes, "Multiple Victim Public Shootings," unpublished paper, October 19, 2000, pp. 24–25. The paper is available online through the Social Science Research Network: http://papers.ssrn.com/sol3/papers .cfm?abstract_id=272929 (accessed August 10, 2015).

107. Lott, *More Guns, Less Crime*, p. 195.

108. An important point deserves mention here. In his own defense, Lott argued that the study undertaken by Duwe and his colleagues was flawed because it only looked at "a very small subset of attacks, those that left four or more victims killed." When Lott undertook his study, he used a significantly lower casualty threshold. Lott stood by his earlier calculations, and in doing so made a significant acknowledgment. He admitted that, when he too limited his data set to mass public shootings that killed at least four people, he "had also not found a statistically significant result for that one type of attack." In other words, Lott's model only supported his thesis if he stretched his conceptualization of mass shootings. Lott, *More Guns, Less Crime*, pp. 294–95.

109. John R. Lott, Jr., *The Myths about Mass Public Shootings: Analysis*, Report of the Crime Prevention Research Center, October 9, 2014, http:// crimepreventionresearchcenter.org/wp-content/uploads/2014/10/CPRC-Mass -Shooting-Analysis-Bloomberg2.pdf (accessed October 27, 2014), p. 25.

110. Open-carry laws are laws that permit citizens to carry personal firearms in public so long as they are openly visible (as opposed to concealed).

111. An alternative reading of this finding is that the nature of a target location—gun-free, gun-restricting, or gun-allowing—has no significant effect on the incidence and lethality of gun massacres. Regardless, it's a topic worthy of further study.

112. Lott and Landes, "Multiple Victim Public Shootings," p. 5.

113. On the presence of an armed civilian during the mass shooting at the Umpqua Community College, see Matt Valentine, "The Myth of the Good Guy with a Gun," *Politico Magazine*, October 5, 2015, http://www.politico.com/magazine/ story/2015/10/oregon-shooting-gun-laws-213222 (accessed November 7, 2015). On the presence of an armed civilian during the mass shooting at the Inland Regional Center, see "Transcripts: CNN Newsroom," CNN, December 3, 2015, http://edition. cnn.com/TRANSCRIPTS/1512/03/cnr.19.html (accessed December 3, 2015).

114. Volokh, "Do Citizens (Not Police Officers) with Guns."

115. These odds are calculated based on the fact that there are only four known successful defensive gun uses that have stopped mass shootings since 1991. Assuming that there has been an average of 300 *attempted* mass shootings per year over the course of the past twenty-five years, that produces a cumulative total of 7,500 attempted mass shootings since 1991. When you divide the four successful

interventions by the 7,500 total incidents, it results in a calculation of one in 1,875, or .05 percent.

116. Lott also argues that there is an instructive precedent from overseas for doing away with gun-free zones: Israel. The Middle East nation has been plagued by terrorism, often perpetrated by Arab opponents of the state. Lott asserts that, after the Israeli government began authorizing adult Jewish citizens to carry concealed weapons, terrorists stopped undertaking more conventional assaults that left them vulnerable to being shot. According to Lott, terrorists now pretty much only "resort to less effective, secretive routes of attack such as bombing." See Lott, "'Lone Wolf' Terror Attacks." While not directly related to the United States, it's still worth considering given that what works in one democracy might work in another. However, a quick glance at recent terrorist attacks in Israel provides enough anecdotal evidence to dismiss Lott's claim. In late 2015 and early 2016, Israel was confronted by a string of knife attacks—exactly the kind of up-front and close encounters of violence that Lott's insists are unlikely to occur when a sizeable portion of the citizenry is armed. See Oren Lieberman, "Israel's New Terror," CNN, November 3, 2015, http://www.cnn.com/2015/11/03/middleeast/israels -new-terror-after-jerusalem-knife-attacks (accessed November 7, 2015); and Ruth Eglash, William Booth, and Darla Cameron, "'A New Kind of Terrorism' in Israel," *Washington Post*, April 8, 2016, https://www.washingtonpost.com/graphics/world/ israel-palestine-deaths (accessed April 18, 2016).

117. This calculation is based on 109 of the 111 gun massacres in my data set. In two of the incidents—the 1968 Good Hart, Michigan, and the 1982 Craig, Alaska, murders—we have no determination as to who the perpetrators were, thus not allowing us to determine a motive, let alone whether or not there was a personal connection between the shooters and their targets and victims. Investigators looking into the 2015 Waco, Texas, biker-gang shootout that resulted in nine deaths have also refrained from publicly announcing the identities of the killers. However, because authorities have revealed that the shootout erupted as a result of a dispute between rival gangs, a relationship between the shooters and their victims can be inferred.

118. The fifteen gun massacres that involved targets or victims to which the shooter(s) didn't have a direct personal connection are New Orleans, LA, 1973; Hackettstown, NJ, 1977; Oklahoma City, OK, 1978; Manley Hot Spring, AK, 1984; San Ysidro, CA, 1984; Waddell, AZ, 1991; Killeen, TX, 1991; Fresno, CA, 1993; Garden City, NY, 1993; Seattle, WA, 2006; Indianapolis, IN, 2006; Omaha, NE, 2007; Aurora, CO, 2012; Oak Creek, WI, 2012; and Charleston, SC, 2015. The shootings fit into one of four motive categories: robbery, hate crime-terrorism, hatred of humanity, and unknown.

119. Immediately following the massacre at Umpqua Community College, many gun rights advocates—in an effort to explain why the school was targeted—asserted that the campus was a gun-free zone. This position has since been rejected. See, for example, Betsy Hammond, "Umpqua Community College Not a Gun-Free Zone: Oregon Law Prevents That," *Oregonian*, October 5, 2015, http://www.oregonlive.com/education/index.ssf/2015/10/umpqua_community _college_not_a.html (accessed November 7, 2015).

120. See "Man Raises Eyebrows Carrying Rifle through Atlanta Airport," WSB, June 2, 2015, http://www.wsbtv.com/news/news/local/man-raises-eyebrows -carrying-gun-through-atlanta-a/nmTFS (accessed November 7, 2015); and Rhonda Cook and Ernie Suggs, "Gun Rights vs. Public Discomfort in Georgia," *Atlanta Journal-Constitution*, June 6, 2015, http://www.ajc.com/news/news/state -regional-govt-politics/gun-rights-vs-public-discomfort-in-georgia/nmXLZ (accessed November 7, 2015).

121. Jesse Paul, "Open Carry Becomes Focus after Colorado Springs Shooting Rampage," *Denver Post*, November 3, 2015, http://www.denverpost.com/news/ ci_29064963/open-carry-becomes-focus-after-colorado-springs-shooting (accessed November 7, 2015); and Jakob Rodgers, "Colorado Springs Police Questioned over Response before Deadly Shooting Spree," *Colorado Spring Gazette*, November 3, 2015, http://gazette.com/colorado-springs-police-questioned-over-response -before-deadly-shooting-spree/article/1562528 (accessed November 7, 2015).

122. Carl von Clausewitz, *On War*, ed. and trans. Michael Howard and Peter Paret (Princeton, NJ: Princeton University Press, 1989), p. 101.

123. For more on the concept, see Bill Owens with Ed Offley, *Lifting the Fog of War* (Baltimore, MD: Johns Hopkins University Press, 2001).

124. John R. Lott Jr., "Gun-Free Zones Are Magnets for Murderers," *Orange County Register*, September 18, 2015, http://www.ocregister.com/articles/gun -683209-free-permit.html (accessed November 7, 2015).

125. Tom Newton and Ted Thackrey Jr., "Rampaging Gunman Leaves 6 Dead, 10 Hurt; Seized by Police," *Los Angeles Times*, April 23, 1973, p. A1; and Tendayi Kumbula, "Anger at Fiancée Blamed in Slaying of Six," *Los Angeles Times*, April 24, 1973, p. A1.

126. "Three Killed, Including Gunman in Smith County Courthouse Shoot-Out in Tyler," KLTV, February 25, 2005, http://www.kltv.com/global/story .asp?s=2994393 (accessed August 22, 2015).

127. Chris Hayes, "Mass Shooter Victim Describes Confronting Gunman," KTVI, November 6, 2013, http://fox2now.com/2013/11/04/mass-shooter-victim -describes-confronting-gunman (accessed August 22, 2015).

128. Mike Blasky et al., "Shooters Carried Arsenal, Supplies into Sunday Rampage," *Las Vegas Review-Journal*, June 9, 2014, http://www.reviewjournal.com/

news/las-vegas/shooters-carried-arsenal-supplies-sunday-rampage (accessed August 22, 2015).

129. For a discussion of the efforts of Austin's police department and its armed citizens to bring Charles Whitman's rampage to an end, see Gary M. Lavergne, *A Sniper in the Tower: The Charles Whitman Murders* (Denton: University of North Texas Press, 1997), pp. 139–222.

130. Al Truesdell, "Shopper Returns Fire but Confusion Puts Him behind Bars," *Orlando Sentinel,* April 25, 1987, http://articles.orlandosentinel.com/1987-04-25/news/0120360012_1_torres-cruse-gunman (accessed August 22, 2015).

131. "7th Person Dead in Easter Shooting," *Los Angeles Times,* April 27, 1973, p. A3. See also Newton and Thackrey, "Rampaging Gunman Leaves 6 Dead"; and Kumbula, "Anger at Fiancée Blamed in Slaying of Six."

132. "Donald Trump to Packed House in Knoxville: Guns Could Have Prevented Paris Attacks," WATE, November 16, 2015, http://wate.com/2015/11/10/trump-to-visit-knoxville-monday (accessed November 21, 2015).

133. Ann O'Neill, Ed Lavandera, and Jason Morris, "Knives, Guns, Blood and Fear: Inside the Texas Biker Shootout," CNN, October 31, 2015, http://www.cnn.com/2015/10/29/us/texas-biker-shootout-new-details (accessed November 7, 2015).

134. "Tenn. Nightclub Shooting Leaves 1 Dead, 19 Injured," *Yahoo News,* February 26, 2012, http://news.yahoo.com/tenn-nightclub-shooting-leaves-1-dead-19-injured-010738680.html (accessed November 7, 2015); and Mark Maley, "Four Shot and Injured at Overnight Brawl at the Big Easy Bar in Elkhart, Police Say," *Elkhart Truth,* October 17, 2015, http://www.elkharttruth.com/news/crime-fire-courts/2015/10/17/Four-injured-in-overnight-shooting-at-The-Big-Easy-bar-in-Elkhart.html (accessed November 7, 2015).

135. I couldn't verify whether any of those shooting back in self-defense were concealed-handgun permit holders, but in the Jackson incident, the men who initially came under attack and returned fire were never charged with a weapons violation, implying that they were lawful, licensed handgun owners. For the official facts of the shooting as presented in court, see *State of Tennessee v. Travis Lamonte Steed,* Court of Criminal Appeals of Tennessee (at Jackson), No. W2014-00146-CCA-R3-CD, May 14, 2015, http://www.tncourts.gov/sites/default/files/steedtravisopn.pdf (accessed November 7, 2015).

136. David Ariosto, "Police: All Empire State Shooting Victims Were Wounded by Officers," CNN, August 26, 2012, http://www.cnn.com/2012/08/25/justice/new-york-empire-state-shooting (accessed August 22, 2015).

137. Bernard D. Rostker et al., *Evaluation of the New York City Police Department Firearm-Training and Firearm-Discharge Review Process* (Santa Monica, CA: RAND Corporation, 2008), p. 14.

138. Rocco Parascandola et al., "Brooklyn Bandit Busted after Getting Shot in Leg by NYPD, Who Fired 84 Shots in Wild Gunfight," September 5, 2015, http:// www.nydailynews.com/new-york/nyc-crime/cops-wound-brooklyn-shooting -suspect-wild-gun-battle-article-1.2348489 (accessed October 3, 2015).

139. District of Columbia Metropolitan Police Department, *After Action Report*, pp. 12–22.

140. Some might try to argue that Alexis sought out those confrontations with armed responders because he wanted to die as a result of what is now commonly referred to as "suicide by cop." Again, the evidence doesn't support the theory. If this had truly been the case, then Alexis would have merely had to come up on an armed guard or police officer and stood there for a second or two with his weapon raised. This would have surely resulted in Alexis being killed. Instead, Alexis constantly took cover during his confrontations with armed personnel, indicating that he was not only unafraid to engage in shootouts but eager to do so in hopes of killing the people trying to neutralize him. Not the other way around.

141. Greg Botelho and Joe Sterling, "FBI: Navy Yard Shooter 'Delusional,' Said 'Low Frequency Attacks' Drove Him to Kill," CNN, September 26, 2013, http:// edition.cnn.com/2013/09/25/us/washington-navy-yard-investigation (accessed August 3, 2015). See also the *Washington Post*' s blog on the Navy Yard shooting, "Washington Navy Yard Shooting," *Washington Post*, September 17, 2013, https:// www.washingtonpost.com/blogs/liveblog-live/liveblog/shooting-at-washington -navy-yard (accessed August 3, 2015).

142. In addition to discharging a firearm on two separate occasions, Aaron Alexis was arrested for disorderly conduct following an incident where he destroyed furniture at a nightclub in DeKalb County, Georgia. Richard Serrano and David S. Cloud, "Aaron Alexis Had Extensive Disciplinary Problems, Official Says," *Los Angeles Times*, September 17, 2013, http://articles.latimes.com/2013/ sep/17/nation/la-na-nn-aaron-alexis-navy-yard-insubordination-20130917 (accessed August 3, 2015). He was also considered a person of interest, although never of arrested, after an act of vandalism that left five of his neighbors' vehicles with slashed tires in Bellevue, Washington. David Larter, "Report: Navy Yard Killings Could Have Been Prevented," *Army Times*, March 18, 2014, http://archive .armytimes.com/article/20140318/NEWS/303180061/Report-Navy-Yard-killings -could-been-prevented (accessed August 3, 2015).

143. Frank Heinz, "Aaron Alexis' History of Gun Incidents," KXAS, September 16, 2013, http://www.nbcdfw.com/news/local/Aaron-Alexis-Fort-Worth-Arrest -Report-223953911.html (accessed August 3, 2015).

144. Ibid.; and John de Leon, "SPD: Navy Yard Shooter Arrested in Seattle in 2004 for Shooting," *Seattle Times*, September 16, 2013, http://blogs.seattletimes

.com/today/2013/09/washington-navy-yard-shooter-once-lived-in-seattle (accessed August 3, 2015).

145. Tom Vanden Brook, "Report: Concerns about Navy Yard Shooter Never Reported," *USA Today*, March 18, 2014, http://www.usatoday.com/story/news/nation/2014/03/18/navy-yard-shooter-called-insider-threat/6558373 (accessed August 3, 2015).

146. Eric Tucker, "Aaron Alexis, Navy Yard Shooting Suspect, Thought People Followed Him with Microwave Machine," *Huffington Post*, November 18, 2013, http://www.huffingtonpost.com/2013/09/18/aaron-alexis-microwave-machine_n_3946916.html (accessed August 3, 2015).

147. Botelho and Sterling, "FBI: Navy Yard Shooter 'Delusional.'"

148. Ibid.

149. Pursuant to 18 USC § 2331(5), domestic terrorism refers to crimes "dangerous to human life" that occur within the United States and "appear to be intended (1) to intimidate or coerce a civilian population; (2) to influence the policy of a government by intimidation or coercion; or (3) to affect the conduct of a government by mass destruction, assassination, or kidnapping."

150. *Piers Morgan Live* (CNN), transcript from show airing September 16, 2013, http://transcripts.cnn.com/TRANSCRIPTS/1309/16/pmt.01.html (accessed April 18, 2016).

151. Ibid.

CHAPTER SIX: GUNS KILL, SOME MORE THAN OTHERS

1. Unless otherwise noted, the material in this section is drawn from the *Denver Post*'s detailed coverage of the criminal proceedings against Aurora theater shooter James Holmes. All the testimony can be found at "Aurora Theater Shooting Trial," *Denver Post*, August 26, 2015, http://theatertrial.denverpost.com (accessed August 29, 2015); and "Live Blog: The Aurora Theater Shooting Trial," *Denver Post*, August 26, 2015, http://live.denverpost.com/Event/LIVE_BLOG_The_Aurora_Theater _Shooting_Trial (accessed August 29, 2015). Denver-based NBC-affiliate KUSA also maintained a blog of the trial that was helpful in re-creating the events surrounding the theater massacre. See "Aurora Theater Trial," KUSA, http://www.9news.com/topic/a187e279-ebd5-49c0-a2b2-aeb8c35d7c98/aurora-theater-trial (accessed August 29, 2015). For brief factual overviews of the shooting as well as the trial, see Ana Cabrera, Sara Weisfeldt, and Michael Martinez, "James Holmes Murder Trial: Bullets, Fire Bombs and Those Striking Eyes," CNN, May 27, 2015, http://edition .cnn.com/2015/05/16/us/james-holmes-trial-aurora-colorado-movie-theater

-shooting (accessed August 29, 2015); and "Colorado Theater Shooting: Fast Facts," CNN, August 29, 2015, http://edition.cnn.com/2013/07/19/us/colorado-theater -shooting-fast-facts (accessed August 29, 2015).

2. Quoted in "Witness Tried to Keep Door Closed on Colo. Gunman," *Denver Post*, July 20, 2012, http://www.denverpost.com/dontmiss/ci_21118870/video -reveals-chaos-aftermath-colo-shooting (accessed July 13, 2015).

3. Anica Padilla, "Heart-Wrenching Testimony from Ashley Moser Wraps up Prosecution's Case in Trial of James Holmes," KMGH, June 19, 2015, http://www .thedenverchannel.com/news/movie-theater-shooting/prosecutors-to-finish -emotional-case-in-aurora-movie-theater-shooting-trial-of-james-holmes (accessed July 13, 2015).

4. Quoted in ibid.

5. Quoted in ibid.

6. See also Kevin Tenser, "Jury Hears First Tense 911 Call Made in Theater as Shots Are Fired by James Holmes," KMGH, May 21, 2015, http://www.thedenver channel.com/news/movie-theater-shooting/jury-hears-first-terrifying-911-call-made -in-theater-as-shots-are-fired-by-james-holmes05212015 (accessed July 13, 2015). The audio of Kevin Quinonez's phone call to 911 has been posted online by the *Denver Post*. See "Raw Audio: 911 Call from Inside Theater during Aurora Theater Shooting," May 21, 2015, https://soundcloud.com/denverpost/aurora-theater -shooting-911-call-from-inside-theater-during-shooting (accessed July 13, 2015).

7. Additional details pertaining to Ashley Moser and Veronica Moser-Sullivan are drawn from Padilla, "Heart-Wrenching Testimony from Ashley Moser."

8. Quoted in "Live Blog: The Aurora Theater Shooting Trial," *Denver Post*, April 28, 2015, http://live.denverpost.com/Event/LIVE_BLOG_The_Aurora _Theater_Shooting_Trial?Page=3 (accessed July 13, 2015).

9. Quoted in ibid.

10. Quoted in Anica Padilla, "Katie Medley Testifies on 2nd Day of Theater Shooting Trial about Choosing between Baby and Husband," KMGH, April 28, 2015, http://www.thedenverchannel.com/news/local-news/katie-medley-testifies -on-2nd-day-of-theater-shooting-trial-about-choosing-between-baby-and-husband -caleb-medley04282015 (accessed July 13, 2015).

11. Quoted in ibid.

12. Quoted in "Live Blog," April 28, 2015.

13. Quoted in ibid.

14. Quoted in ibid.

15. Quoted in ibid.

16. Quoted in Jordan Steffan, "Aurora Theater Shooting Trial, the Latest from Day 4," *Denver Post*, April 30, 2015, http://www.denverpost.com/theater

-shooting-trial/ci_28020294/aurora-theater-shooting-trial-latest-from-day-4 (accessed July 13, 2015).

17. Quoted in ibid.

18. Quoted in ibid.

19. Quoted in ibid.

20. Quoted in ibid.

21. Quoted in ibid.

22. Quoted in ibid.

23. Quoted in John Ingold, "James Holmes Preliminary Hearing: Aurora Cop Recalls, 'There Was So Much Blood,'" *Denver Post*, January 7, 2013, http://www .denverpost.com/breakingnews/ci_22326598/james-holmes-preliminary-hearing -aurora-cop-recalls-there (accessed July 13, 2015).

24. Quoted in ibid.

25. Quoted in "Live Blog: The Aurora Theater Shooting Trial," *Denver Post*, April 30, 2015, http://live.denverpost.com/Event/LIVE_BLOG_The_Aurora _Theater_Shooting_Trial?Page-17 (accessed July 13, 2015).

26. Quoted in ibid.

27. Quoted in Ingold, "James Holmes Preliminary Hearing."

28. For additional information and profiles of the victims of the Aurora theater mass shooting, see "Aurora Tragedy: List of Theater Shooting Victims," *Aurora Sentinel*, July 23, 2012, http://www.aurorasentinel.com/news/aurora-tragedy -massacre-victims-and-conditions (accessed July 13, 2015); and Anita Busch, "Aurora Theater Shooting, 3 Years Later: When Moviegoers Became Superheroes," *Deadline Hollywood*, July 1, 2015, http://deadline.com/2015/07/aurora-shooting-three-year -later-what-happened-inside-theater-1201460855/ (accessed July 13, 2015).

29. Additional information on ballistics and physical evidence is drawn from the following sources: Amanda Kost, "2nd Day of Hearings in Theater Shooting Case Covers Ballistic Evidence and Evidence Handling," KMGH, July 23, 2014, http://www.thedenverchannel.com/news/movie-theater-shooting/2nd-day-of -hearings-in-theater-shooting-case-covers-ballistic-evidence-and-evidence-handling (accessed July 13, 2015); Phil Tenser, "Aurora Police Department Crime Scene Investigators Found 76 Spent Rounds after Theater Shooting," KMGH, May 12, 2015, http://www.thedenverchannel.com/news/movie-theater-shooting/aurora -police-department-crime-scene-investigators-found-76-spent-rounds-after-theater -shooting (accessed July 13, 2015); and Phil Tenser, "240 Ballistic Impacts Found after Theater Shooting, Aurora Police CSI Testifies in Homes' Trial," KMGH, May 14, 2015, http://www.thedenverchannel.com/news/movie-theater-shooting/240 -ballistic-impacts-found-after-theater-shooting-aurora-police-csi-testifies-in-holmes -trial-051415 (accessed July 13, 2015).

30. Quoted in Matthew Dolan and Steve Eder, "Rifle in Shooting Once Was Federally Restricted," *Wall Street Journal*, July 22, 2012, http://www.wsj.com/articles/SB10000872396390443295404577543262884887188 (accessed July 19, 2015).

31. Stacey Newman, "Let's Talk about Guns," *St. Louis Post-Dispatch*, August 2, 2012, http://www.stltoday.com/news/opinion/guest-commentary-let-s-talk-about-guns/article_b06db0e2-06b6-504f-8354-63f328d79c2d.html (accessed July 19, 2015).

32. Ed Byrne, "From the Editorial Advisory Board: Aurora Shooting," *Daily Camera*, July 28, 2012, http://www.dailycamera.com/ci_21175251/from-editorial-advisory-board-aurora-shooting (accessed July 19, 2015).

33. Ibid.

34. *Fox News Sunday*, July 22, 2012. For a transcript, see http://www.foxnews.com/on-air/fox-news-sunday-chris-wallace/2012/07/22/feinstein-johnson-debate-stricter-gun-control-netanyahu-dangerous-times-middle-east#p//v/1747607229001 (accessed July 19, 2015).

35. Ibid. Rep. Carolyn McCarthy (D-NY) appeared on *CBS News This Morning* on July 21, 2012, and expressed a similar opinion about assault weapons, stating that they "probably should not be on the streets."

36. Quoted in Leigh Ann Caldwell, "Colo. Rep.: Congress Can't Avoid Gun Issue," CBS News, July 22, 2012, http://www.cbsnews.com/news/colo-rep-congress-cant-avoid-gun-issue (accessed July 19, 2015).

37. *Fox News Sunday*, July 22, 2012.

38. Ibid.

39. Natasha Singer, "The Most Wanted Gun in America," *New York Times*, February 2, 2013, http://www.nytimes.com/2013/02/03/business/the-ar-15-the-most-wanted-gun-in-america.html (accessed July 22, 2015).

40. David Halberstam, *The Best and the Brightest* (New York: Random House, 1972).

41. John A. Byrne, *The Whiz Kids: The Founding Fathers of American Business—and the Legacy They Left Us* (New York: Doubleday, 1993).

42. Jon Stokes, "The AR-15 Is More Than a Gun. It's a Gadget," *Wired*, February 25, 2013, http://www.wired.com/2013/02/ar-15 (accessed July 22, 2015); and Christian Beekman, "Here's How the AR-15 Grew to Become America's Favorite Firearm," *Task & Purpose*, September 25, 2014, http://taskandpurpose.com/heres-ar-15-grew-become-americas-favorite-firearm (accessed July 22, 2015).

43. Stokes, "The AR-15 Is More Than a Gun."

44. Ibid.

45. The AR-15 and M16 are basically identical rifles, with the key difference

being that, nowadays, "AR-15" refers to the civilian version, which fires only in semiautomatic mode, whereas "M16" refers to the military version, which is a "selective fire" weapon that can be set to shoot in automatic mode.

46. Cindy Huang, "Learning More about the AR-15 Rifle, Local Gun Culture," *Capital Gazette*, August 10, 2015, http://www.capitalgazette.com/news/for_the _record/ph-ac-cn-ar15-rifle-0810-20150809-story.html (accessed July 22, 2015).

47. "America's Gun: The Rise of the AR-15," CNBC, April 8, 2013, http://www.cnbc.com/americas-gun-the-rise-of-the-ar-15 (accessed July 22, 2015). This website accompanies a documentary with the same title that aired on CNBC. The documentary is available online at https://www.youtube.com/watch?v=OCvjoFPD5Kg (accessed July 22, 2015). When AR-15 accessories are included, the total number of companies that manufacture AR-15 or AR-15 accessories tallies up to approximately sixty. Erica Goode, "Rifle Used in Killings, America's Most Popular, Highlights Regulation Debate," *New York Times*, December 16, 2012, http://www.nytimes.com/2012/12/17/us/lanza-used-a-popular-ar -15-style-rifle-in-newtown.html (accessed July 22, 2015). See also Simon Rogers, Rob Grant, Sean Anderson, "How Many AR15 Rifles Have Been Sold in the US?" *Guardian*, December 17, 2012, http://www.theguardian.com/news/datablog/2012/dec/17/how-many-ar15-rifles-sold (accessed July 22, 2015).

48. Meghan Lisson, "Ron on Guns: AR-15 Sales Soar," CNBC, April 25, 2013, http://www.cnbc.com/id/100673826 (accessed July 22, 2015).

49. National Shooting Sports Foundation, "Fast Facts: Background Information on So-Called 'Assault Weapons,'" National Shooting Sports Foundation, 2011, http://www.nssf.org/factsheets/PDF/AssaultBG.pdf (accessed July 22, 2015).

50. Quoted in Associated Press, "Fact-Checking the Gun Control Debate," CBS News, January 30, 2013, http://www.cbsnews.com/news/fact-checking-the -gun-control-debate (accessed July 22, 2015).

51. Robert J. Spitzer, "Why Are Assault Weapons Sales Jumping? Because They're Fun to Shoot," *Los Angeles Times*, June 12, 2015, http://www.latimes.com/opinion/op-ed/la-oe-spitzer-ar15-fun-20150612-story.html (accessed July 22, 2015).

52. Tom Diaz quoted in "America's Gun."

53. Quoted in the video clip accompanying Sara Wiesenfeld, "Aurora Shooting Victim Reunites with ER Team," CNBC, April 17, 2013, http://www.cnbc.com/id/100631845 (accessed July 22, 2015). See also "America's Gun."

54. Ibid.

55. Quoted in "America's Gun."

56. The graphic footage of the shooting that was broadcast live on WDBJ is available at "BREAKING: WDBJ Shooting video FOOTAGE," YouTube video,

0:22, posted by "acdcman96fin," August 26, 2015, https://www.youtube.com/watch?v=iEH9RBxefHI (accessed October 3, 2015).

57. Matthew Diebel, "Va. TV Shooting Survivor: 'I Saw Movement. And Then Gunfire,'" *USA Today*, September 16, 2015, http://www.usatoday.com/story/news/2015/09/16/vicki-gardner-survivor–virginia-shooting–killed-two-tv-journalists-tells–playing-dead—attempt–survive/32491117 (accessed October 3, 2015).

58. The graphic footage of the shooting that was recorded by the shooter, displaying his point of view, is available at "SHOOTERS #GOPRO Live Footage of Shooters #POV #WDBJ Reporter and Camera Operator Killed," 1:33, posted by "Tyler," August 26, 2015, http://criminal-defense.usattorneys.com/shooters-gopro-live-footage-shooters-pov-wdbj-reporter-camera-operator-killed (accessed October 3, 2015).

59. Steve Neumann, "I've Developed a Paralyzing, Irrational Fear of Mass Shootings. I Bet I'm Not Alone," *Vox*, October 2, 2015, http://www.vox.com/2015/9/17/9340679/mass-shooting-fear (accessed October 3, 2015).

60. Meagan Fitzpatrick, "Why the Virginia Shooting Is Being Called the 1st 'Social Media Murder,'" CBC News, August 26, 2015, http://www.cbc.ca/news/world/virginia-shooting-social-media-1.3205123 (accessed October 3, 2015).

61. Neumann, "I've Developed a Paralyzing, Irrational Fear."

62. Charles P. Kindleberger, "Commercial Policy between the Wars," *The Cambridge Economic History of Europe*, vol. 8: *The Industrial Economies: The Development of Economic and Social Policies*, ed. Peter Mathias and Sidney Pollard (New York: Cambridge University Press, 1989), pp. 184–85.

63. Audra J. Wolfe, "Nylon: A Revolution in Textiles," *Chemical Heritage Magazine* 26 (Fall 2008), http://www.chemheritage.org/discover/media/magazine/articles/26-3-nylon-a-revolution-in-textiles.aspx (accessed July 26, 2015).

64. Ibid.

65. Wim Vanhaverbeke and Henry Chesbrough, "A Classification of Open Innovation and Open Business Models," *New Frontiers in Open Innovation*, ed. Henry Chesbrough, Wim Vanhaverbeke, and Joel West (New York: Oxford University Press, 2014), p. 56.

66. DuPont Corporation, "Innovation Starts Here," n.d., http://www.dupont.com/corporate-functions/our-company/dupont-history.html (accessed July 26, 2015).

67. Wolfe, "Nylon."

68. Emily Spivak, "Stocking Series, Part 1: Wartime Rationing and Nylon Riots," Smithsonian, September 4, 2012, http://www.smithsonianmag.com/arts-culture/stocking-series-part-1-wartime-rationing-and-nylon-riots-25391066 (accessed July 26, 2015).

69. William Cooper, "Nylon Mob, 40,000 Strong, Shrieks and Sways for Mile," *Pittsburgh Press*, June 13, 1946, pp. 1–2.

70. Wolfe, "Nylon."

71. For more on nylon, see Beth Ann Krier, "How Nylon Changed the World: 50 Years Ago Today, It Reshaped the Way We Live—and Think," *Los Angeles Times*, October 27, 1988, http://articles.latimes.com/1988-10-27/news/vw-227_1_years -ago-today (accessed July 26, 2015); and Jeremy Hill, "A Brief History of Nylon," *Mental Floss*, March 8, 2015, http://mentalfloss.com/article/61845/brief-history -nylon (accessed July 26, 2015).

72. Remington, "Company History," n.d., http://www.remington.com/pages/ our-company/company-history.aspx (accessed July 26, 2015).

73. John Gyde and Roy Marcot, "The Remington Nylon 66," *American Rifleman*, August 27, 2009, http://www.americanrifleman.org/articles/2009/8/27/ the-remington-nylon-66 (accessed July 26, 2015).

74. Ibid.

75. Ibid.

76. Ibid.

77. Ibid.

78. Quoted in ibid.

79. Ibid.

80. For a simple and easy-to-understand explanation of the injection-molding process, see Rutland Plastics Limited, "What Is the Injection-Moulding Process?" n.d., http://www.rutlandplastics.co.uk/advice/moulding_process.html (accessed July 26, 2015).

81. American Chemical Council, "The Basics: Polymer Definition and Properties," n.d., http://plastics.americanchemistry.com/Education-Resources/ Plastics-101/The-Basics-Polymer-Definition-and-Properties.html (accessed July 26, 2015).

82. Gyde and Marcot, "Remington Nylon 66."

83. For more on the Heckler and Koch VP70, see David Higginbotham, "The HK VP70: The First Polymer Framed Pistol," Guns.com, August 28, 2012, http:// www.guns.com/2012/08/28/the-hk-vp70-the-first-polymer-framed-pistol (accessed July 26, 2015); and Hilton Yam, "HK VP70: First in Polymer," *Modern Service Weapons*, March 28, 2014, http://modernserviceweapons.com/?p=7401 (accessed July 26, 2015).

84. Polymer firearms are cheaper to manufacture because the raw materials and labor cost less. Paul M. Barrett, *Glock: The Rise of America's Gun* (New York: Broadway Books 2013), p. 14.

85. Ibid., pp. 14, 99.

86. Ibid., p. 11. See also Paul Scarlata, "Shootout! Polymer Police Pistols," *Guns & Ammo Handguns*, September 24, 2010, http://www.handgunsmag.com/reviews/featured_handguns_polysh_032707 (accessed July 26, 2015).

87. Barrett, *Glock*, p. 86.

88. Ibid., p. 14.

89. Ibid., p. 263.

90. Scarlata, "Shootout!"

91. Barrett, *Glock*, p. 32.

92. Ibid., pp. 56, 142–43.

93. Ibid., p. 192.

94. Ibid., p. 56.

95. Polymer has brought such distinct advantages to firearms that gun makers have begun manufacturing polymer revolvers. See Dick Metcalf, "Polymer Revolution," *Shooting Times*, January 3, 2011, http://www.shootingtimes.com/handguns/handgun_reviews_st_polymerevo_201005 (accessed July 26, 2015).

96. Typically, .38-caliber revolvers hold five or six bullets in the cylinder.

97. Massad Ayoob, "Maximizing Semi-Auto Handgun Performance," *Daily Caller*, September 23, 2014, http://dailycaller.com/2014/09/23/massad-ayoob-maximizing-semi-auto-handgun-performance (accessed July 29, 2015). Ayoob makes an important point that, when calculating firing rates and reload times, we should not use best-case scenarios and world-record times. We should use reasonable, average times. As he notes, "World Champion Jerry Miculek is on record firing six shots from his .45 revolver, reloading with a moon clip, and firing six more in an incredible 2.99 seconds overall. There is only one Jerry Miculek. Most folks take longer to recharge a wheel gun." Ibid.

98. Stokes, "AR-15 Is More Than a Gun."

99. This subsection has benefitted from the thoughts of Kevin J. Ashton, including correspondence between us on his now-defunct blog. See Kevin Ashton, "The Physics of Mass Killing," January 24, 2013, archived at http://web.archive.org/web/20150110031240/http://kevinjashton.com/2013/01/24/the-physics-of-mass-killing (accessed July 29, 2015).

100. The details of the Tucson massacre are drawn from Gabrielle Giffords and Mark Kelly, *Enough: Our Fight to Keep America Safe from Gun Violence* (New York: Scribner, 2014), pp. 47–74.

101. Ibid.

102. "Mark Kelly Makes Case against High-Capacity Gun Magazines," ABC News, January 30, 2013, http://abcnews.go.com/Politics/video/mark-kelly-makes-case-high-capacity-gun-magazines-18356232 (accessed July 29, 2015).

103. Giffords and Kelly, *Enough*, p. 68.

104. Reload time is calculated as beginning the moment the final bullet is fired and ending the moment the first reload bullet is chambered and fired.

105. The calculations in this section are informed by Ayoob, "Maximizing Semi-Auto Handgun Performance." See also Jim Wilson, "The Revolver Speed Load," *American Rifleman*, February 10, 2012, http://www.americanrifleman.org/articles/2012/2/10/the-revolver-speed-load (accessed July 29, 2015); and Kenan Flasowski, "Semi-Automatic Handgun Reloading," *Shooting Illustrated*, October 25, 2012, http://www.shootingillustrated.com/articles/2012/10/25/semi-automatic-handgun-reloading (accessed July 29, 2015). For an article that suggests faster rates of fire than most firearms experts seem to endorse, see Brian Palmer, "How Many Times Can You Shoot a Handgun in Seven Minutes? More Than a Thousand," *Slate*, November 9, 2009, http://www.slate.com/articles/news_and_politics/explainer/2009/11/how_many_times_can_you_shoot_a_handgun_in_seven_minutes.html (accessed July 29, 2015).

106. Lynn Bartels, Kurtis Lee, and Joey Bunch, "Colorado Senate President John Morse, State Sen. Angela Giron Ousted," *Denver Post*, September 10, 2013, http://www.denverpost.com/breakingnews/ci_24066168/colorado-senate-president-john-morse-recalled-angela-giron (accessed July 31, 2015).

107. Eli Stokols, "Herpin Explains Why It Was a 'Good Thing' Holmes Had Large Ammo Magazine," KVDR, February 14, 2014, http://kdvr.com/2014/02/12/herpin-a-good-thing-that-james-holmes-had-100-round-magazine (accessed July 31, 2015). See also Kurtis Lee, "Sen. Bernie Herpin Says 'Maybe a Good Thing' Aurora Theater Gunman Had 100-Round Magazine," *Denver Post*, February 12, 2014, http://blogs.denverpost.com/thespot/2014/02/12/sen-bernie-herpin-says-maybe-good-thing-aurora-theater-gunman-100-round-magazine/105925 (accessed July 31, 2015). Herpin's repeal was defeated by the committee. Marc Stewart and Phil Tenser, "State Sen. Herpin That 'Maybe a Good Thing' That James Holmes Had a 100-Round Magazine," KMGH, February 12, 2014, http://www.thedenverchannel.com/news/politics/state-sen-herpin-suggests-it-was-maybe-a-good-thing-that-james-holmes-had-a-100-round-magazine (accessed July 31, 2015).

108. James Holmes discussed his shooting abilities in an interview with court-appointed psychiatrist Dr. William Reid. That conversation, which was videotaped, was played for the jury during Holmes's trial. See Jordan Steffan, "Aurora Theater Shooting Trial, the Latest from Day 22," *Denver Post*, June 1, 2015 http://www.denverpost.com/theater-shooting-trial/ci_28227922/aurora-theater-shooting-trial-latest-from-day-22 (accessed July 31, 2015).

109. Shortly after his gaffe, Herpin apologized to the victims' families: "There's nothing I can say to relieve their pain; I certainly didn't intend to add to their pain." Megan Schrader, "Republican Sen. Bernie Herpin Apologizes for

'Insensitive' Gun Remark," *Gazette*, February 14, 2014, http://gazette.com/
republican-sen.-bernie-herpin-apologizes-for-insensitive-gun-remark/article/
1514605 (accessed July 31, 2015).

110. The use of the term *average* in this section is a reference to the mean
average.

111. To the best of my knowledge, the impact of different types of firearms
is rarely a topic of study. One notable exception is D. C. Reedy and C. S. Koper,
"Impact of Handgun Types on Gun Assault Outcomes: A Comparison of Gun
Assaults Involving Semiautomatic Pistols and Revolvers," *Injury Prevention* 9 (June
2003): 151–55. The Reedy and Koper article, while insightful, examines all types of
criminal gun attacks that took place in one municipality: Jersey City, New Jersey. As
such, its findings do not really apply to mass shootings.

112. The use of only revolvers produces an identical average. The use of only
rifles results in an average seven deaths per incident. And the use of only shotguns
results in the lowest recorded average of 6.7 deaths per incident.

113. Out of the 111 gun massacres since 1966, ninety-six were perpetrated
by only one gunman and fifteen were perpetrated by multiple gunmen. Of those
fifteen incidents, ten involved two shooters, one involved three shooters, three
involved four shooters, and one involved more than four shooters.

114. Quoted in Steffan, "Aurora Theater Shooting Trial, the Latest from Day 22."

CHAPTER SEVEN: BREAKING THE TRINITY

1. The audio of Pacific Air Lines Flight 773's final transmission to Oakland
Air Traffic Control is available at "Pacific Air Lines Flight 773 ATC Recording
May 7, 1964," YouTube video, 0:35, posted by "starwarsfandude," March 29, 2013,
https://www.youtube.com/watch?v=L1WY1Aeuq4w (accessed December 11, 2015).

2. Civil Aeronautics Board, *Aircraft Accident Report: Pacific Air Lines, Inc.,
Fairchild F-27, N277OR, Near San Ramon, California, May 7, 1964,* November 2, 1964,
http://dotlibrary.specialcollection.net/Document?db=DOT-AIRPLANE
ACCIDENTS&query=(select+773) (accessed December 11, 2015).

3. Ibid.

4. One of the principal investigators of the crash of Pacific Air Lines Flight
773, Darrol Davison, in a KTVU "Second Look" news segment discussed how, in
1964, security provisions didn't exist to prohibit guns from being brought aboard
airplanes. The news segment is available at "Pacific Air Lines Flight 773," YouTube
video, 7:07, posted by "Tom Bailey," September 20, 2012, https://www.youtube
.com/watch?v=fpQu4Tjh-8Q (accessed December 11, 2015).

5. Jane Engle, "U.S. Aviation Security Timeline," *Los Angeles Times*, June 12, 2011, http://articles.latimes.com/2011/jun/12/travel/la-tr-airline-safety -timeline-20110612 (accessed December 11, 2015). See also Bryan Gardiner, "Off with Your Shoes: A Brief History of Airport Security," *Wired*, June 14, 2013, http://www.wired.com/2013/06/fa_planehijackings (accessed December 11, 2015).

6. Gun owners recall that in 1968 regulations were changed to prohibit carrying a firearm aboard an airplane, requiring that the weapon be checked in cargo-hold luggage. See, for example, "When Did Carrying Become Forbidden on Airplanes?" *High Road*, September 7, 2010, http://www.thehighroad.org/archive/index.php/t-540773.html (accessed December 11, 2015).

7. Civil Aeronautics Board, *Aircraft Accident Report*.

8. "Investigations: Death Wish," *Time*, November 6, 1964, http://content .time.com/time/magazine/article/0,9171,876374,00.html (accessed December 11, 2015)

9. Ibid.

10. Wallace Turner, "Pilot Reported Calling, 'I've Been Shot,' Before Crash that Killed 44 on Coast," *New York Times*, May 6, 1964, http://www.nytimes .com/1964/05/09/pilot-reported-calling-ive-been-shot-before-crash-that-killed-44 -on-coast.html (accessed December 11, 2015).

11. Civil Aeronautics Board, *Aircraft Accident Report*.

12. "Investigations: Death Wish."

13. Civil Aeronautics Board, *Aircraft Accident Report*.

14. For an excellent introduction to strategy, including a review of how dissuasion, defense, and disarmament relate to each other, see Thomas C. Schelling, *Arms and Influence*, rev. ed. (New Haven, CT: Yale University Press, 2008).

15. Keith B. Payne, *Deterrence in the Second Nuclear Age* (Lexington: University of Kentucky Press, 1996), p. 86. See also Michael Howard, "Lessons of the Cold War," *Survival* 36 (Winter 1994–95): 166.

16. Tom Walsh, "How's the Air up There?" *Barre Montpellier Times Argus*, October 14, 2015, http://www.timesargus.com/article/20151014/OPINION02/151019749 (accessed December 11, 2015).

17. Larry Pratt, "Strange Priorities," Gun Owners of America, October 2001, http://www.gunowners.org/op0136.htm (accessed December 11, 2015).

18. "Packing Heat on Planes," Fox News, February 8, 2007, http://www .foxnews.com/story/2007/02/08/packing-heat-on-planes.html (accessed December 11, 2015); Joe Sharkey, "Owners Argue Merits of Firearms on Airplanes," *New York Times*, January 2, 2012, http://www.nytimes.com/2012/01/03/business/arguing-the-merits-of-guns-on-airplanes.html (accessed December 11, 2015); Robert Farago, "'As a Pilot, I Don't Understand the Reason Why We Can't Have

Firearms and Knives on Planes,'" Truth about Guns, February 1, 2012, http://www
.thetruthaboutguns.com/2012/02/robert-farago/as-a-pilot-i-don%E2%80%99t
-understand-the-reason-why-we-can%E2%80%99t-have-firearms-and-knives-on
-planes/ (accessed December 11, 2015); and Robert Farago, "U.S. Air Marshal
System a Complete Disaster," Truth about Guns, August 18, 2015, http://www
.thetruthaboutguns.com/2015/08/robert-farago/u-s-air-marshal-system-a
-complete-disaster (accessed December 11, 2015).

19. Engle, "U.S. Aviation Security Timeline."

20. Lou Michel and Dan Herbeck, *American Terrorist: Timothy McVeigh and the
Oklahoma City Bombing* (New York: Harper, 2001).

21. John Mueller and Mark G. Stewart, *Chasing Ghosts: The Policing of Terrorism*
(New York: Oxford University Press, 2016), pp. 98–100.

22. National Forensic Science Technology Center, "A Simplified Guide to
Explosives Analysis: Principles of Explosives Analysis," A Simplified Guide to
Forensic Science, 2013, http://www.forensicsciencesimplified.org/explosives/
principles.html (accessed December 11, 2015).

23. Louis Klarevas, "The Idiot Jihadist Next Door," *Foreign Policy*, December 1,
2011, http://foreignpolicy.com/2011/12/01/the-idiot-jihadist-next-door (accessed
December 11, 2015).

24. Jana Winter, "Anatomy of a Bomb: An Inexpensive and Deadly Mishmash
of Ingredients," Fox News, May 3, 2010, http://www.foxnews.com/us/2010/
05/03/anatomy-bomb.html (accessed December 11, 2015); "Timeline—From
Parking a Car Bomb to Catching a Plane," *Reuters*, May 4, 2010, http://www
.reuters.com/article/timessquare-investigation-idUSN0411707720100504 (accessed
December 11, 2015); and Peter Grier, "Times Square Bomb: Did Pakistan Taliban
Send Its 'C' Team?" *Christian Science Monitor*, May 10, 2010, http://www.csmonitor
.com/USA/2010/0510/Times-Square-bomb-Did-Pakistan-Taliban-send-its-C-team
(accessed December 11, 2015).

25. Louis Klarevas, "Bombing on the Analysis of the Times Square Bomb
Plot," *Huffington Post*, May 25, 2011, http://www.huffingtonpost.com/louis
-klarevas/bombing-on-the-analysis-o_b_565428.html (accessed December 11,
2015).

26. David Hemenway, *While We Were Sleeping: Success Stories in Injury and Violence
Prevention* (Berkeley: University of California Press, 2009).

27. Daniel W. Webster and Jon S. Vernick, eds., *Reducing Gun Violence in
America: Informing Policy with Evidence and Analysis* (Baltimore, MD: Johns Hopkins
University Press, 2013), http://home.uchicago.edu/ludwigj/papers/Impact%20
of%20Brady%20Act%202013.pdf (accessed December 11, 2015).

28. Erin G. Richardson and David Hemenway, "Homicide, Suicide, and

Unintentional Firearm Fatality: Comparing the United States with Other High-Income Countries, 2003," *Journal of Trauma* 70 (January 2011): 238–43.

29. Sarah Kaplan, "American Exceptionalism and the 'Exceptionally American' Problem of Mass Shootings," *Washington Post*, August 27, 2015, https:// www.washingtonpost.com/news/morning-mix/wp/2015/08/27/american -exceptionalism-and-the-exceptionally-american-problem-of-mass-shootings (accessed December 11, 2015).

30. David Hemenway, *Private Guns, Public Health* (Ann Arbor: University of Michigan Press, 2006).

31. The Gun Control Act of 1968 does not apply to "antique firearms" manufactured prior to 1899. For the statutory definition of "antique firearm," see 18 USC § 921(a)(16).

32. The Brady Handgun Violence Prevention Act of 1993 does not apply to "antique firearms" manufactured prior to 1899. For the statutory definition of "antique firearm," see 18 USC § 921(a)(16).

33. Hemenway, *Private Guns, Public Health*, pp. 209–12.

34. Bureau of Alcohol, Tobacco, Firearms, and Explosives, "National Firearms Act," ATF, November 9, 2015, https://www.atf.gov/rules-and-regulations/national -firearms-act (accessed December 11, 2015).

35. Bruce H. Kobayashi and Joseph E. Olson, "In Re: 101 California Street: A Legal and Economic Analysis of Strict Liability for the Manufacture and Sale of 'Assault Weapons,'" *Stanford Law and Policy Review* 8 (Winter 1997): 41–51.

36. Christopher S. Koper, "America's Experience with the Federal Assault Weapons Ban, 1994–2004: Key Findings and Implications," in *Reducing Gun Violence in America: Informing Policy with Evidence and Analysis*, ed. Daniel W. Webster and Jon S. Vernick (Baltimore, MD: Johns Hopkins University Press, 2013), pp. 157–71, http://home.uchicago.edu/ludwigj/papers/Impact%20of%20Brady%20Act%20 2013.pdf (accessed December 11, 2015).

37. Out of the twelve gun massacres that occurred while the AWB was in effect, three involved assault weapons and six involved extended-capacity magazines. I have been unable to uncover any evidence that any of these instruments were illegal under the AWB. In fact, most were grandfathered, meaning that they were exempted by the ban because they were legally in circulation prior to the AWB's enactment.

38. When viewed in terms of full calendar years, the massacre-free period ran five consecutive years, from 1994 to 1998, although it must be noted that the AWB was not in effect for most of 1994. There were also no gun massacres in 2001. When 2001 is combined with the four-and-a-half-year period without a high-fatality mass shooting from September 13, 1994, through April 20, 1999, we see that over half of the decade that the AWB was in effect was massacre-free.

39. It's worth noting that, in the years since the expiration of the AWB, there has never again been a year of reprieve from gun massacres. In every single year since 2004, the United States has not only experienced gun massacres every calendar year, but there hasn't been a single year without at least two gun massacres.

40. As shown in chapter 6, it's important to remember that assault weapons are not used frequently in gun massacres. In terms of weaponry regulated by the AWB, extended-capacity magazines are employed much more frequently in gun massacres. An examination of the AWB's impact on these two instruments shows that, during the ten-year period that the AWB was in effect, assault weapons use was cut in half compared to the decade immediately prior to the AWB's adoption. In the decade following the AWB, the use of assault weapons in gun massacres more than doubled, slightly edging out the use of such weapons in the decade prior to the ban. Deaths resulting from massacres involving assault weapons followed a similar pattern, dropping by two-fifths between the decade prior to and the decade of the ban. Deaths resulting from incidents involving assault weapons then tripled in the decade after the ban. Extended-capacity magazines saw a less sizeable decrease of only one-third between the decade prior to and the decade of the ban. This was then followed by a quadrupling in the decade immediately following the expiration of the AWB. Deaths from incidents involving extended-capacity magazines followed a nearly identical pattern, dropping by roughly a third and then roughly quadrupling. In terms of deaths per incident, the average number of deaths in attacks involving assault weapons went from 7.3 in the decade prior to the ban, to 8.7 in the decade of the ban, followed by 11.1 in the decade after the ban. The average number of deaths in attacks involving extended-capacity magazines followed a different trajectory. Deaths per incident went from 9.1 in the decade prior to the ban, to 7.7 in the decade of the ban, followed by 9.2 in the decade after the ban. This last finding suggests that the AWB's impact was most profound in the area of curtailing the carnage that results from employing extended-capacity magazines in mass shootings.

41. Critics might retort that my test is biased in that it only assesses the AWB's impact on gun massacres, which are mass shootings resulting in six or more victims being murdered. It's true that if the fatality threshold is lowered, there wouldn't be a period of five consecutive years without a mass shooting. But this misses the point. Gun massacres are the most troubling mass shootings precisely because they are the deadliest acts of gun violence. While the AWB might not have eliminated all mass shootings, it did drastically reduce the worst ones. And that matters.

42. See, for example, Gregor Aisch and Josh Keller, "How Gun Traffickers Get around State Gun Laws," *New York Times*, November 13, 2015, http://www.nytimes

.com/interactive/2015/11/12/us/gun-traffickers-smuggling-state-gun-laws.html (accessed December 11, 2015).

43. Tom Jackman, "Inside Sharpshooters, the Newington Gun Store Where Aaron Alexis Bought His Shotgun," *Washington Post,* September 18, 2013, https://www.washingtonpost.com/blogs/local/wp/2013/09/18/inside-sharpshooters-the-newington-gun-store-where-aaron-alexis-bought-his-shotgun (accessed August 3, 2015).

44. See, for example, Emma Graham- Harrison, "Paris Attacks Highlight France's Gun Control Problems," *Guardian,* November 15, 2015, http://www.theguardian.com/world/2015/nov/15/paris-attacks-highlight-frances-gun-control-problems (accessed December 11, 2015); and Naina Bajekal and Vivienne Walt, "How Europe's Terrorists Get Their Guns," *Time,* December 7, 2015, http://time.com/how-europes-terrorists-get-their-guns (accessed December 11, 2015). One of the firearms used in the November 2015 Paris terrorist attacks was even traced back to the United States. See Liz Henderson, Meg Wagner, and Denis Slattery, "Florida-Based Gun Dealer Known for Supporting NRA Is Linked to Weapon Used in Paris Terror Attacks," *New York Daily News,* December 12, 2015, http://www.nydailynews.com/news/national/gun-paris-terror-attack-linked-florida-dealer-article-1.2462573 (accessed April 24, 2016).

45. For a detailed analysis of the Hungerford massacre, see the Smith Report, which is reproduced in *Murderpedia,* s.v., "Michael Robert Ryan," n.d., http://murderpedia.org/male.R/r/ryan-michael-robert-report.htm (accessed December 11, 2015).

46. Clare Feikert-Ahalt, "Great Britain," in *Firearms-Control Legislation and Policy,* by Law Library of Congress (Washington, DC: Library of Congress, 2013), pp. 89–107, http://www.loc.gov/law/help/firearms-control/firearms-control.pdf (accessed December 11, 2015).

47. The Honorable Lord W. Douglas Cullen, *The Public Inquiry into the Shootings at Dunblane Primary School on 13 March 1996* (Edinburgh: Scottish Office, 1996), https://www.gov.uk/government/uploads/system/uploads/attachment_data/file/276631/3386.pdf (accessed December 11, 2015). One of the wounded was a staff member who was struck by a bullet that passed into the school's library.

48. Feikert-Ahalt, "Great Britain"; and Michael J. North, "Gun Control in Great Britain after the Dunblane Shootings," in *Reducing Gun Violence in America: Informing Policy with Evidence and Analysis,* ed. Daniel W. Webster and Jon S. Vernick (Baltimore, MD: Johns Hopkins University Press, 2013), pp. 185–93, http://home.uchicago.edu/ludwigj/papers/Impact%20of%20Brady%20Act%202013.pdf (accessed December 11, 2015).

49. James Meikle, "Twelve Killed in Cumbria Shooting Spree," *Guardian,* June

2, 2010, http://www.theguardian.com/uk/2010/jun/02/gunman-sought-person
-shot-dead-whitehaven (accessed December 11, 2015).

50. The following gun massacres occurred in Australia prior to the Port
Arthur rampage: the Milperra Father's Day shootout in New South Wales (1984);
the Hoddle Street shootings in Melbourne, Victoria (1987); the Queen Street
massacre in Melbourne, Victoria (1987); the Strathfield massacre in Sydney,
New South Wales (1991); the Central Coast shooting spree in New South Wales
(1992); and the Hillcrest murders in Queensland (1996). Simon Chapman et
al., "Australia's 1996 Gun Law Reforms: Faster Falls in Firearm Deaths, Firearm
Suicides, and a Decade without Mass Shootings," *Injury Prevention* 12 (December
2006): 365–72, http://injuryprevention.bmj.com/content/12/6/365.full.pdf+html
(accessed December 11, 2015).

51. Kelly Buchanan, "Australia," in *Firearms-Control Legislation and Policy*, by
Law Library of Congress (Washington, DC: Library of Congress, 2013), pp. 16–36,
http://www.loc.gov/law/help/firearms-control/firearms-control.pdf (accessed
December 11, 2015).

52. Philip Alpers, "The Big Melt: How One Democracy Changed after
Scrapping a Third of Its Firearms," in *Reducing Gun Violence in America: Informing
Policy with Evidence and Analysis*, ed. Daniel W. Webster and Jon S. Vernick
(Baltimore, MD: Johns Hopkins University Press, 2013), pp. 205–11, http://
home.uchicago.edu/ludwigj/papers/Impact%20of%20Brady%20Act%202013.
pdf (accessed December 11, 2015). See also "How a Conservative-Led Australia
Ended Mass Killings," *New York Times*, December 4, 2015, http://www.nytimes.
com/2015/12/05/world/australia/australia-gun-ban-shooting.html (accessed
December 11, 2015).

53. Buchanan, "Australia."

54. Ibid.; Alpers, "Big Melt"; and Rebecca Peters, "Rational Firearm
Regulation: Evidence-Based Gun Laws in Australia," in *Reducing Gun Violence in
America: Informing Policy with Evidence and Analysis*, ed. Daniel W. Webster and Jon
S. Vernick (Baltimore, MD: Johns Hopkins University Press, 2013), pp. 195–204,
http://home.uchicago.edu/ludwigj/papers/Impact%20of%20Brady%20Act%20
2013.pdf (accessed December 11, 2015). For an overview of the types of firearms
that remain legal to possess in Australia, see Australian Federal Police, "Firearm
Categories," 2015, http://www.police.act.gov.au/crime-and-safety/firearms/
firearms-categories (accessed April 24, 2016).

55. Laura Smith-Spark, "This Is What Happened When Australia Introduced
Tight Gun Controls," CNN, June 19, 2015, http://www.cnn.com/2015/06/19/
world/us-australia-gun-control (accessed December 11, 2015); and Zack
Beauchamp, "Australia Confiscated 650,000 Guns. Murders and Suicides

Plummeted," *Vox*, December 3, 2015, http://www.vox.com/2015/8/27/9212725/australia-buyback (accessed December 11, 2015).

56. John Howard, "I Went after Guns. Obama Can, Too," *New York Times*, January 16, 2013, http://www.nytimes.com/2013/01/17/opinion/australia-banned-assault-weapons-america-can-too.html (accessed December 11, 2015).

CHAPTER EIGHT: THE BAD MAN'S AWE

1. Monica von Dobeneck, "Lebanon Sheriff Revokes Soccer Mom's Gun Permit," *PennLive*, September 24, 2008, http://www.pennlive.com/midstate/index.ssf/2008/09/lebanon_soccer_mother_loses_gu.html (accessed December 23, 2015).

2. Ibid.

3. One of the strengths of Hain's argument was that she was open-carrying her weapon, meaning it was visibly exposed as opposed to being concealed. Because Pennsylvania is a state that allows lawful gun owners to openly carry their firearms, she believed that her actions were permitted under state law. But the sheriff, instead of invoking a violation of the state's open-carry laws, revoked her concealed-carry permit. Hain felt that this was a punitive action given that the situation in question didn't involve Hain carrying a concealed firearm. See Barbara Miller, "Gun Rights Advocates Might Attend Lebanon Woman's Hearing," *PennLive*, October 13, 2008, http://www.pennlive.com/midstate/index.ssf/2008/10/guns_rights_proponents_may_sho.html (accessed December 23, 2015).

4. Monica von Dobeneck, "Soccer Mom Gets Concealed-Weapon Permit Back," *PennLive*, October 14, 2008, http://www.pennlive.com/midstate/index.ssf/2008/10/soccer_mom_gets_gun_permit_bac.html (accessed December 23, 2015); and Monica von Dobeneck, "Soccer Parents Wince at Prospect of Guns at Games," *PennLive*, October 14, 2008, http://www.pennlive.com/midstate/index.ssf/2008/10/soccer_parents_wince_at_prospe.html (accessed December 23, 2015).

5. Quoted in Monica von Dobeneck, "She's Just 'a Mom Who Happens to Carry a Gun,'" *PennLive*, December 27, 2008, http://www.pennlive.com/midstate/index.ssf/2008/12/jim_zengerle_the_lebanon_daily.html (accessed December 23, 2015).

6. "NRA: Full Statement by Wayne LaPierre in Response to Newtown Shootings," *Guardian*, December 21, 2012, http://www.theguardian.com/world/2012/dec/21/nra-full-statement-lapierre-newtown (accessed December 23, 2015).

7. Ibid.

8. Ibid.

9. Ibid.

10. Ibid.

11. Ibid.

12. Ibid.; emphasis added.

13. Quoted in "Full Transcript of Biden and Obama's Remarks on Gun Laws," *New York Times*, January 16, 2013, http://www.nytimes.com/2013/01/16/us/politics/full-transcript-of-biden-and-obamas-remarks-on-gun-laws.html (accessed December 23, 2015).

14. Ibid. The Obama administration plan has evolved and expanded since it was initially proposed. For a full overview of the Now Is the Time initiative, see White House, "Now Is the Time to Do Something about Gun Violence," n.d., https://www.whitehouse.gov/issues/preventing-gun-violence (accessed December 23, 2015).

15. Quoted in "Full Transcript of Biden and Obama's Remarks on Gun Laws."

16. Jonathan Weisman, "Senate Blocks Drive for Gun Control," *New York Times*, April 17, 2013, http://www.nytimes.com/2013/04/18/us/politics/senate -obama-gun-control.html (accessed December 23, 2015).

17. Quoted in ibid.

18. Frustrated by Congressional inaction, in January 2016 President Obama announced a series of executive actions aimed at further regulating the sale and transfer of firearms. Eric Lichtblau and Michael D. Shear, "Tearful Obama Outlines Steps to Curb Gun Deaths," *New York Times*, January 5, 2016, http://www.nytimes .com/2016/01/06/us/politics/obama-gun-control-executive-action.html (accessed April 24, 2016). It soon became apparent that the president's measures would have a limited impact on curbing gun violence. Eric Lichtblau and Michael D. Shear, "Obama's Lofty Plans on Gun Violence Amount to Little Action," *New York Times*, February 7, 2016, http://www.nytimes.com/2016/02/08/us/politics/obamas-lofty -plans-on-gun-violence-amount-to-little-action.html (accessed April 24, 2016).

19. For public opinion on a variety of gun-control proposals in the immediate aftermath of the Newtown massacre, see Colleen L. Barry et al., "After Newtown— Public Opinion on Gun Policy and Mental Illness," *New England Journal of Medicine* 368 (March 21, 2013): 1077–81, http://www.nejm.org/doi/pdf/10.1056/ NEJMp1300512 (accessed December 23, 2015).

20. The tally and time of the vote is available at "Senate Vote 97 - Defeats Manchin-Toomey Background Checks Proposal," *New York Times*, April 17, 2013, http://politics.nytimes.com/congress/votes/113/senate/1/97 (accessed December 23, 2015).

21. Ralph Nader, *Unsafe at Any Speed: The Designed-In Dangers of the American Automobile* (New York: Grossman Publishers, 1965).

22. Data on automobile fatalities from the 1950s and 1960s can be found in US Bureau of the Census, *Statistical Abstract of the United* States, 1975 (Washington, DC: GPO, 1975), p. 577. See also "Annual US Street & Highway Fatalities from 1957," Public Purpose, n.d., http://www.publicpurpose.com/hwy-fatal57+.htm (accessed December 23, 2015).

23. John Moore Williams, "The Hotly Contested History of the Seat Belt," *Esurance Blog*, May 23, 2011, http://blog.esurance.com/seat-belt-history (accessed December 23, 2015).

24. Nader, *Unsafe at Any Speed.*

25. Paola Antonelli, *Safe: Design Takes on Risk* (New York: Museum of Modern Art, 2005), pp. 33–35.

26. Centers for Disease Control and Prevention, "Policy Impact: Seat Belts," Centers for Disease Control and Prevention, January 21, 2014, http://www.cdc.gov/motorvehiclesafety/seatbeltbrief (accessed December 23, 2015).

27. "Myths and Facts about Seat Belts," Michigan State Police, n.d., http://www.michigan.gov/msp/0,4643,7-123-1878_1711-13689-,00.html (accessed December 23, 2015).

28. Quoted in David Cohen, "Cold Comfort," *Guardian*, January 31, 2005, http://www.theguardian.com/education/2005/jan/31/highereducation.internationaleducationnews (accessed December 23, 2015).

29. National Highway Transportation Safety Administration, "Seat Belt Use in 2014—Overall Results," *Traffic Safety Facts Research Note*, February 2015, http://www-nrd.nhtsa.dot.gov/Pubs/812113.pdf (accessed December 23, 2015).

30. Donna Glassbrenner, "Estimating the Lives Saved by Safety Belts and Air Bags," National Highway Traffic Safety Administration, National Center for Statistics and Analysis Paper No. 500, 2003, http://www-nrd.nhtsa.dot.gov/pdf/esv/esv18/cd/files/18esv-000500.pdf (accessed December 23, 2015).

31. Centers for Disease Control and Prevention, "Policy Impact: Seat Belts."

32. National Highway Transportation Safety Administration, "Overview," *Traffic Safety Facts: 2006 Data*, March 2008, http://www-nrd.nhtsa.dot.gov/Pubs/810809.PDF (accessed December 23, 2015).

33. Franklin E. Zimring, "Firearms and Federal Law: The Gun Control Act of 1968," *Journal of Legal Studies* 4 (January 1975): 133–98, http://scholarship.law.berkeley.edu/facpubs/1114 (accessed December 23, 2015).

34. Richard M. Aborn, "The Battle over the Brady Bill and the Future of Gun Control Advocacy," *Fordham Urban Law Journal* 22 (January 1994): 417–39, http://ir.lawnet.fordham.edu/cgi/viewcontent.cgi?article=1425&context=ulj (accessed December 23, 2015).

35. Joe Johns and Stacey Samuel, "Would Background Checks Have Stopped

Recent Mass Shootings? Probably Not," CNN, April 10, 2013, http://www.cnn.com/2013/04/10/politics/background-checks-mass-shootings (accessed April 24, 2016). For a similar criticism against President Obama's 2016 executive actions, see Michael R. Sisak, "Obama Measures Wouldn't Have Kept Guns from Mass Shooters," Associated Press, January 5, 2016, http://bigstory.ap.org/article/d0a31a86e9a64d78aaf3213b034993fc/obama-measures-wouldnt-have-kept-guns-mass-shooters (accessed April 24, 2016).

36. Glenn Kessler, "The Stale Claim that 40 Percent of Gun Sales Lack Background Checks," *Washington Post*, January 21, 2013, https://www.washingtonpost.com/blogs/fact-checker/post/the-stale-claim-that-40-percent-of-gun-sales-lack-background-checks/2013/01/20/e42ec050-629a-11e2-b05a-605528f6b712_blog.html (accessed December 23, 2015); and Kate Masters, "Just How People Get Their Guns without a Background Check? Fast-Tracked Research Is Set to Provide an Answer," *Trace*, October 21, 2015, http://www.thetrace.org/2015/10/private-sale-loophole-background-check-harvard-research (accessed December 23, 2015).

37. Amanda Paulson, "On Columbine School Shooting Anniversary, Focus on Gun 'Loophole,'" *Christian Science Monitor*, April 20, 2010, http://www.csmonitor.com/USA/2010/0420/On-Columbine-school-shooting-anniversary-focus-on-gun-loophole (accessed December 23, 2015).

38. Christopher Ingraham, "There Are Now More Guns Than People in the United States," *Washington Post*, October 5, 2015, https://www.washingtonpost.com/news/wonk/wp/2015/10/05/guns-in-the-united-states-one-for-every-man-woman-and-child-and-then-some (accessed December 23, 2015).

39. In a federal lawsuit seeking to have Colorado's prohibition of magazines holding more than fifteen bullets declared unconstitutional, the plaintiffs' expert was asked to cite an instance where a civilian armed with a semiautomatic firearm required more than fifteen rounds to successfully defend themselves. The expert was only able to raise three examples, two of which didn't involve semiautomatic weapons. The one instance where the defender was armed with a semiautomatic firearm equipped with an extended-capacity magazine involved someone thought to have fired more than fifteen rounds. But even in this example, which the expert believed might have involved more than fifteen rounds, the plaintiffs failed to establish that the civilian needed to fire more than fifteen rounds to defend himself. See "Findings of Fact, Conclusions of Law, and Order," *Colorado Outfitters Association et al. v. Hickenlooper*, Civil Action No. 13–cv–01300–MSK–MJW, US District Court for the District of Colorado, June 26, 2014, http://michellawyers.com/wp-content/uploads/2013/05/Cooke-v.-Hickenlooper_Findings-of-Fact-Conclusions-of-Law-and-Order.pdf (accessed November 23, 2014), pp. 28–29.

40. On the cost and failure of the US military's counter-ISIS training program

in Syria, see Michael D. Shear, Helene Cooper, and Eric Schmitt, "Obama Administration Ends Effort to Train Syrians to Combat ISIS," *New York Times*, October 9, 2015, http://www.nytimes.com/2015/10/10/world/middleeast/pentagon-program-islamic-state-syria.html (accessed April 24, 2016).

41. There are an estimated forty million extended-capacity magazines in circulation in the United States. While it's hard to estimate the total value of these magazines, many used magazines are worth under $20. See Patrik Jonsson, "Gun Debate 101: Time to Ban High-Capacity Magazines," *Christian Science Monitor*, January 16, 2013, http://www.csmonitor.com/USA/Politics/DC-Decoder/2013/0116/Gun-debate-101-Time-to-ban-high-capacity-magazines (accessed December 23, 2015). Given that over 75 percent of the adult population in the United States contributes less than a quarter of all cumulative revenue generated from income taxes, the contribution of this segment of Americans toward funding a $500 million buy-back program could, on average, amount to as little as $0.15 per person annually. To make up for the shortfall, however, wealthier Americans, who earn over $100,000 per year, might, on average, have to pay as much as $3.50 per person annually. For a breakdown of what percentage each income segment of the population contributes in income taxes, see Drew Desilver, "High-Income Americans Pay Most Income Taxes, But Enough to Be 'Fair'?" Pew Research Center, April 13, 2016, http://www.pewresearch.org/fact-tank/2016/04/13/high-income-americans-pay-most-income-taxes-but-enough-to-be-fair (accessed April 24, 2016).

42. Frank Heinz, "Aaron Alexis' History of Gun Incidents," KXAS, September 16, 2013, http://www.nbcdfw.com/news/local/Aaron-Alexis-Fort-Worth-Arrest-Report-223953911.html (accessed August 3, 2015); John de Leon, "SPD: Navy Yard Shooter Arrested in Seattle in 2004 for Shooting," *Seattle Times*, September 16, 2013, http://blogs.seattletimes.com/today/2013/09/washington-navy-yard-shooter-once-lived-in-seattle (accessed August 3, 2015); and Richard Serrano and David S. Cloud, "Aaron Alexis Had Extensive Disciplinary Problems, Official Says," *Los Angeles Times*, September 17, 2013, http://articles.latimes.com/2013/sep/17/nation/la-na-nn-aaron-alexis-navy-yard-insubordination-20130917 (accessed August 3, 2015).

43. For more on how those with misdemeanor violence convictions go on to commit felonies with guns, see Garen J. Wintemute, "Broadening Denial Criteria for the Purchase and Possession of Firearms: Need, Feasibility, and Effectiveness," in *Reducing Gun Violence in America: Informing Policy with Evidence and Analysis*, ed. Daniel W. Webster and Jon S. Vernick (Baltimore, MD: Johns Hopkins University Press, 2013), pp. 77–93, http://home.uchicago.edu/ludwigj/papers/Impact%20of%20Brady%20Act%202013.pdf (accessed December 11, 2015). See also Garen

J. Wintemute et al., "Prior Misdemeanor Convictions as a Risk Factor for Later Violent and Firearm-Related Criminal Activity among Authorized Purchasers of Handguns," *Journal of the American Medical Association* 280 (December 23, 1998): 2083–87, http://jama.jamanetwork.com/article.aspx?articleid=188297 (accessed December 23, 2015).

44. Christopher Ingraham, "From 2004 to 2014, Over 2,000 Terror Suspects Legally Purchased Guns in the United States," *Washington Post*, November 16, 2015, https://www.washingtonpost.com/news/wonk/wp/2015/11/16/why-the-nra-opposed-laws-to-prevent-suspected-terrorists-from-buying-guns (accessed December 23, 2015). While we can't know for certain if someone on the watch list bought a gun and then went on a rampage, as that information is generally classified and not publicly disclosed, there have definitely been several killers who perpetrated gun massacres in the name of socio-political objectives: Marx Essex, Nidal Hasan, Syed Farook, and Tashfeen Malik, to name a few. For more on closing the terrorism watch list loophole, see Louis Klarevas, "Crack Down on Handguns—They're a Tool of Terror, Too," *New York Daily News*, October 25, 2007, http://www.nydailynews.com/opinion/crack-handguns-tool-terror-article-1.228028 (accessed December 23, 2015); and Louis Klarevas, "Easy Target," *New Republic*, June 14, 2010, https://newrepublic.com/article/75515/easy-target (accessed December 23, 2015).

45. Jennifer Mascia, "Domestic Abusers Frequently Get to Keep Their Guns. Here Are the Big Reasons Why," *Trace*, October 26, 2015, www.thetrace.org/2015/10/domestic-abuse-guns-boyfriend-loophole (accessed December 23, 2015). See also "Domestic Violence & Firearms Policy Summary," Law Center to Prevent Gun Violence, May 11, 2014, http://smartgunlaws.org/domestic-violence-firearms-policy-summary (accessed December 23, 2015).

46. Dan Morain and Mark A. Stein, "Unwanted Suitor's Fixation on Woman Led to Carnage," *Los Angeles Times*, February 18, 1988, http://articles.latimes.com/1988-02-18/news/mn-43514_1_mr-farley-richard-farley-sunnyvale-public-safety-department (accessed December 23, 2015).

47. Louis Klarevas, "Closing the Gap," *New Republic*, January 13, 2011, https://newrepublic.com/article/81410/us-gun-law-reform-tucson (accessed December 23, 2015).

48. James Holmes's psychiatric treatment was well documented during his trial. For more on the testimony pertaining to his care, see the exhaustive blog coverage of the criminal proceedings provided by the *Denver Post*: "Aurora Theater Shooting Trial," *Denver Post*, August 26, 2015, http://theatertrial.denverpost.com (accessed August 29, 2015); and "Live Blog: The Aurora Theater Shooting Trial," *Denver Post*, August 26, 2015, http://live.denverpost.com/Event/LIVE_BLOG_The_Aurora_Theater_Shooting_Trial (accessed August 29, 2015). For a review

of Adam Lanza's mental-health care, see State of Connecticut Office of the Child Advocate, *Shooting at Sandy Hook Elementary School: Report of the Office of the Child Advocate* (Hartford, CT: Office of the Child Advocate, November 21, 2014), http://www.ct.gov/oca/lib/oca/sandyhook11212014.pdf (accessed December 23, 2015).

49. Michael S. Schmidt, "Background Check Flaw Let Dylann Roof Buy Gun, FBI Says," *New York Times*, July 10, 2015, http://www.nytimes.com/2015/07/11/us/background-check-flaw-let-dylann-roof-buy-gun-fbi-says.html (accessed December 23, 2015); Alex Yablon, "The Next Big Question about Dylann Roof's Background Check," *Trace*, July 16, 2015, http://www.thetrace.org/2015/07/dylann-roof-background-check-fbi-nics (accessed December 23, 2015); and Jennifer Mascia, "How Americans Wound up with a Gun Background Check System Built More for Speed Than Certainty," *Trace*, July 21, 2015, http://www.thetrace.org/2015/07/brady-bill-amendment-default-proceed-loophole-amendment-nra (accessed December 23, 2015).

50. For background on gun courts, see Alex Yablon, "The Case for Gun Courts," *Trace*, September 24, 2015, http://www.thetrace.org/2015/09/gun-courts-drug-courts-rochester-shooting (accessed December 23, 2015).

51. For more on GVROs, see Shannon Frattaroli et al., "Gun Violence Restraining Orders: Alternative or Adjunct to Mental Health-Based Restrictions on Firearms?" *Behavioral Sciences & the Law* 33 (June 2015): 290–307.

52. Klarevas, "Closing the Gap."

53. Nakia Cooper, "Violent Past of Alleged Mass Shooting Gunman Ronald Lee Haskell," KPRC, July 11, 2014, http://www.click2houston.com/news/violent-past-of-alleged-mass-shooting-gunman-ronald-lee-haskell (accessed December 23, 2015); Amanda Marcotte, "Ronald Lee Haskell Has a History of Domestic Violence. How Did He Get a Gun?" *Slate*, July 11, 2014, http://www.slate.com/blogs/xx_factor/2014/07/11/ronald_lee_haskell_charged_how_did_a_man_previously_arrested_for_domestic.html (accessed December 23, 2015); and Jeremy Rogalski, "Court Records Reveal Haskell Planned and Plotted Shooting Rampage," KHOU, September 9, 2014, http://www.khou.com/story/news/investigations/2014/09/09/court-records-reveal-haskell-planned-and-plotted-cross-country-trip-shooting-rampage/15359063 (accessed December 23, 2015).

54. Don Thompson, "State Senate OKs Money for Gun Seizure Program," KBAK, March 7, 2013, http://bakersfieldnow.com/news/local/state-senate-oks-money-for-gun-seizure-program (accessed December 23, 2015); Carol Ferguson, "State Takes Man's Guns: 'He Said We Made a Big Mistake,'" KBAK, February 3, 2014, http://bakersfieldnow.com/news/local/state-takes-mans-guns-he-said-we-made-a-big-mistake (accessed December 21, 2015); and Nina Golgowski, "More than 500 Illegal Guns Seized from California Man's Home," *Huffington Post*,

November 23, 2015, http://www.huffingtonpost.com/entry/illegal-guns-seized
-from-california-home_564dfee5e4b08c74b734a7e0 (accessed December 23, 2015).

55. Federal Bureau of Investigation, "Protecting America from Terrorist
Attack: Our Joint Terrorism Task Forces," FBI, n.d., https://www.fbi.gov/about-us/
investigate/terrorism/terrorism_jttfs (accessed December 23, 2015).

56. For a similar suggestion, see Tom Junod, "Why Mass Shootings Keep
Happening," *Esquire*, October 24, 2014, http://www.esquire.com/news-politics/
a30024/mass-shooters-1014 (accessed December 23, 2015).

57. For an example of a successful prosecution of a parent following a mass
shooting by their child, albeit for unlawful possession as opposed to criminal
negligence, see Mike Carter, "Father of Marysville Shooter Convicted of Gun
Charges," *Seattle Times*, October 30, 2015, http://www.seattletimes.com/seattle
-news/crime/father-of-marysville-school-shooter-convicted-of-gun-charges
(accessed December 23, 2015).

58. James Holmes's notebook is available from the *Denver Post*: http://extras
.denverpost.com/trial/docs/notebook.pdf (accessed August 29, 2015).

59. Adam Lanza's comments are from an e-mail he sent dated December 11,
2012, three days before he went on his rampage. The e-mail is reproduced in State
of Connecticut Office of the Child Advocate, *Shooting at Sandy Hook Elementary
School*, p. 105.

60. "Police: Man Who Was Cut off at Bar Went on Rampage with Golf Club,"
KPTV, February 6, 2015, http://www.kptv.com/story/27802772/police-man
-who-was-cut-off-at-bar-went-on-rampage-with-golf-club (accessed December 23,
2015); and Colton Lochhead, "Man Accused in Hammer Attacks Had Been High
on Meth, Report Says," *Las Vegas Review-Journal*, October 28, 2014, http://www
.reviewjournal.com/news/las-vegas/man-accused-hammer-attacks-had-been-high
-meth-report-says (accessed December 23, 2015).

61. Catherine E. Shoichet and Joe Sutton, "Sheriff: Student Plotted TX
College Attack, Fantasized about Stabbings," CNN, April 10, 2013, http://www
.cnn.com/2013/04/09/justice/texas-college-stabbing (accessed December 23,
2015); and Ashlie Hardway, "No Bail for Alex Hribal in Franklin Regional High
School Stabbing Case," WTAE, October 26, 2015, http://www.wtae.com/news/
franklin-regional-hs-stabbings-suspect-wants-bond-to-get-out-of-jail/36049368
(accessed December 23, 2015).

62. Stephen Ceasar, "Venice Boardwalk Driver Sentenced to 42 Years to Life
in State Prison," *Los Angeles Times*, September 25, 2015, http://www.latimes
.com/local/lanow/la-me-ln-venice-boardwalk-20150925-story.html (accessed
December 23, 2015); and "Deadly Las Vegas Crash Suspect Told Police She Was
Tired, Stressed," Fox News, December 22, 2015, http://www.foxnews.com/us/

2015/12/22/deadly-las-vegas-crash-suspect-told-police-was-tired-stressed.html (accessed December 23, 2015).

63. Louis Klarevas, "It's the Guns, Stupid: Why Handguns Remain One of the Biggest Threats to Homeland Security," *Huffington Post*, May 25, 2011, http://www.huffingtonpost.com/louis-klarevas/its-the-guns-stupid-why-h_b_349705.html (accessed December 23, 2015).

64. "NRA: Full Statement by Wayne LaPierre."

65. Butch Mabin, "I-80 Crash Claims UNL Student's Life," *Lincoln Journal Star*, January 3, 2005, http://journalstar.com/news/local/i–crash-claims-unl-student-s -life/article_d61cc109-3492-54ef-849d-0a5d7f48027a.html (accessed December 23, 2015); and Barbara Miller, "Meleanie Hain Shooting Was Witnessed on Web Cam, Police Say," *PennLive*, October 9, 2009, http://www.pennlive.com/midstate/index .ssf/2009/10/meleanie_hain.html (accessed December 23, 2015).

66. Quoted in Tryon Edwards, *A Dictionary of Thoughts* (Detroit, MI: F. B. Dickerson, 1908), p. 292, https://archive.org/stream/dictionaryof thou007549mbp#page/n335/mode/2up (accessed April 24, 2016).

CHAPTER NINE: THE NEW NORMAL

1. For background on the gun massacre perpetrated by George Banks, see David Lohr, "Mass Murder in Eastern Pennsylvania: The True Story of George Emil Banks," reproduced at *Murderpedia*, s.v. "George Banks," n.d., http://murderpedia .org/male.B/b/banks-george.htm (accessed December 28, 2015).

2. Barack Obama, quoted in "Remarks by the President at the Memorial Service for Victims of the Navy Yard Shooting," White House, September 22, 2013, https://www.whitehouse.gov/the-press-office/2013/09/22/remarks-president -memorial-service-victims-navy-yard-shooting (accessed December 28, 2015).

3. Barack Obama, quoted in "Statement by the President on the Shootings at Umpqua Community College, Roseburg, Oregon," White House, October 1, 2015, https://www.whitehouse.gov/the-press-office/2015/10/01/statement-president -shootings-umpqua-community-college-roseburg-oregon (accessed December 28, 2015).

APPENDIX

1. Reprinted from Virginia Tech Review Panel, *Mass Shootings at Virginia Tech, April 16, 2007: Report of the Review Panel* (August 2007), pp. N1–N5, http://www.washington post.com/wp-srv/metro/documents/vatechreport.pdf (accessed May 2, 2015).

INDEX

Pages in *italic* indicate figures and tables.